EXPLORING CHRISTIAN THEOLOGY

Edited by
Ronnie Littlejohn
Belmont College

UNIVERSITY
PRESS OF
AMERICA

D0874767

Copyright © 1985 by

University Press of America,™ Inc.

4720 Boston Way
Lanham, MD 20706

ISBN (Perfect): 0-8191-4460-6
ISBN   (Cloth): 0-8191-4459-2

All University Press of America books are produced on acid-free
paper which exceeds the minimum standards set by the National
Historical Publications and Records Commission.

To

Patty, Jeff, Jeremy

TABLE OF CONTENTS

PREFACE

Prior to the modern era the challenge facing theology students largely consisted of the mastery of a recognized systematic explanation of Christian doctrine. Of course, even this was no simple task. Rigorous study and grueling examination were required. But nevertheless, the principal evidence that one understood the faith was that he could reproduce the system taught to him.

To be sure many students of theology still expect introductory courses to consist of a sort of indoctrination. According to some students the professor's task is to present the correct explication of the faith in order that it might then be learned. The student's responsibility, then, is a narrow one. He has only to memorize what is taught.

This book is based on the assumption that the above approach to theology is fundamentally erroneous. Students have registered surprise, resentment, suspicion and anger when I have refused to tell them which of several theological constructions of a doctrine is the correct one, as though "the" correct theology could be determined. Such an assumption cannot go unchallenged, especially given the fallibility of all theologians and their constructs. The truth is, telling a student which explication is correct is really quite dishonest. What does correct mean? Correctness in theology is itself a theological question: the question of what constitutes heresy and how heresy is determined. I have included an excursus essay on this subject at the beginning of the book. For some, perhaps they should read it first.

What introductory theology students need is not our theology, nor even Tillich's, Warfield's, Strong's,

Barth's or any other's one might name. They need
their own theology, and such a theology should be a
developing and maturing one: students will not have
a complete theological understanding of the faith when
they finish even an extensive course of theological
study. Such an understanding will never come; they
will always grow and the doctrines of our faith will
be continually reappropriated, revealing new vistas
not seen before.

Accordingly, this book is based on the presupposition that a first course in theology must teach a
student to think theologically. Students must know
what questions to ask of human experience, traditional
teachings, and scriptural passages. Students must be
able to function as theologians themselves. The social, ideological and religious pressures of modern
culture require that theologians be able "to think on
their feet." Independence of thought, born out of
critical study and intensive dialogue, is of more
lasting value than dependence on another person or
school of theology whose situation and questions were
different from those faced by the contemporary student.

This understanding of teaching theology gave rise
to the present book of readings. My own students
needed dialogue with important but divergent treatments of a doctrine. And I felt no systematic in
print actually performed this task satisfactorily.

The topics presented represent some of the
recurring themes which the great systematicians of
Christian history address. The objective has been
to identify modern works which have contributed significant constructive formulations of a doctrine; or
in some cases, have cleared the ground for constructive work. I have edited the important passages into
coherent essays. Footnotes contained in the original
are preserved as endnotes with altered numbering.
Professors may assign the topics in the order they
deem most appropriate (which is itself a theological
decision). I believe one of the strengths of the book
to be that it not only tells about theology, but it
also confronts the student with selections of theological writings.

Not all of the essays are easy. Neither have I
been able to avoid completely the use of technical
vocabulary. But I do not consider these two factors
to be weaknesses. Difficulty in an essay frequently

(although not always) reflects the complexity of the issue being examined. Simplicity of expression is a virtue only if it does not sacrifice nuance and depth. In my judgment the complexity of the essays included herein is necessary. As to the use of technical vocabulary, my own opinion is that learning to use the vocabulary of a discipline is part of learning the discipline. Language expresses; indeed, it constitutes reality. Every elementary theology student should buy a theological dictionary and he should learn the language as soon as possible.

In this book I have chosen to continue the traditional use of the masculine gender in exposition and symbolization. However, I do not wish this to be understood as in any way condoning the chauvinism often found in the use of the male gender whether applied to God or humanity. Nor do I wish to neglect or devalue the rich meaning of feminine symbolism in theological construction.

I wish to include in my acknowledgements a special gratitude to Profs. C. W. Christian and Bob Patterson of Baylor University. These mentors taught me how to think theologically. And many of my observations were first theirs. Yet, they should not be held responsible for the weaknesses of this work. To Dr. Christian particularly I wish to offer a direct word of appreciation. He has meant much to me personally as well as professionally. He is indeed a good teacher and friend.

I also wish to express my appreciation to my colleague Steven H. Simpler for his contribution to this work and to my understanding of theology. We have argued theology and celebrated our friendship for fifteen years, and I hope he will continue to force me to grow professionally and personally. Kim Peterson and Linda Cartlidge helped greatly by typing the manuscript. They did a remarkable job. Both of these fine secretaries are associated with Wayland Baptist University, where I was teaching when I began this project. During the summer of 1984 they helped several of those of us who are junior scholars break into publication for the first time. Without them, we really could not have completed our work. I owe them my sincere thanks. Finally, I wish to thank my students at Baylor and at Wayland Baptist University for working through this material with me.

Ronnie Littlejohn
Belmont College
Nashville

xi

PART ONE

THEOLOGICAL METHOD

THEOLOGICAL METHOD

Theological method is concerned with several things. The analysis of these issues is normally called <u>prolegomena</u> because it precedes the theological enterprise itself. However, it will be evident as the essays in this section are read that the issues usually taken up in prolegomena are not independent of the theological task, they are a part of it.

The Geist of Culture

The first issue of method concerns the degree of responsibility the theologian has to consider what the Germans call the <u>Geist</u> of culture. The Spirit of the age, or of his time, has much to do with the theologian's task.

If his culture recognizes no religious text as authoritative over the reason of man, then this fact requires some reassessment of how the Bible is used in theology. The reassessment may mean changing one's theology about the Bible and relying upon it in a different way. Or, as Cornelius Van Til suggests in his essay, culture's attitude toward the Bible may testify only to its sinfulness and alienation. Accordingly, the theologian must not forsake his presuppositions about the Bible's authority but fortify them. If the theologian's culture tolerates religious pluralism and indeed views it as healthy and necessary, then he must do some reassessment of Christianity's exclusivism and particularism.

The essay by Langdon Gilkey explores the Geist of the contemporary era; the era of secularity. Gilkey is convinced that theologians can ignore secular paradigms only if they are willing to sacrifice the cogency of their constructive theologies.

Along these same lines, the essay by Jerry Gill is an attempt to examine ordinary human experience as a basis for doing theology in a secular era. Gill is intent on showing the multidimensional character of experience. He holds that there is a religious dimension which must be expressed in some language form. In this way he seeks to provide a universally acceptable basis for speaking of Christian theological statements as meaningful. Indeed, the interfacing of this dimension with common human experience may be understood as a mediated form of revelation. In this sense, Gill's position is quite close to what has been called a natural theology.

Where to Begin

A second but related issue of theological method is the question of where to begin doing theology. Should a theologian begin with the Bible, the teachings or creeds of the historic church, or with ordinary human experience. Traditionally, this has been the question of whether a natural theology is possible, and if so, how far it can carry the theologian until he must draw on the distinctive sources of revelation. But this dichotomy is too simple, and its simplicity breeds inaccuracy. It implies that natural theology is not based on revelation. Perhaps the terms "general revelation" and "special revelation" are preferable to "natural theology" and "revealed theology" because any appearance of God in natural experience may still be regarded as revelation.

Some notable theologians have held that ordinary human experience poses existentially significant questions to which the Christian faith offers the answers. Such a method of correlation is associated with Paul Tillich, and it is similar to the approaches taken by Gilkey and Gill. All of these thinkers stress that no theology will be meaningful unless it begins on the common ground which all humans acknowledge.

Theologians in the Calvinist tradition, such as Van Til, hold that human sin and alienation are too endemic to allow even an understanding of our own being and experience. Thus, we must presuppose the truth and authority of God's revelation, primarily in scripture. Nothing short of conversion will put one

3

in a position to see the truth of Christianity.

Source-Norms

A third issue under the heading of method concerns the various resources from which the theologian may draw to construct his own understanding of the faith. A survey of the history of Christian thought reveals a dialogue between three primary and closely interdependent source-norms. Theological formulations emerge from the creative tension between (1) what the scriptures say, (2) what the Christian church has believed, and (3) what the theologian's own experience bears witness to.

At first it may be thought that previous generations depended solely on one of these norms. Sometimes Protestants think that Catholic theology was and is merely a matter of repeating the teachings of the Fathers or the magisterium. But the authorities of the church always seek to base their teachings on scripture, and they do not fail to test them against experience.

On the other hand, the Protestant affirmation that theology should be done sola scriptura (scripture only) cannot ever be achieved completely as the essay by C. W. Christian demonstrates. Biblical passages require interpretation. No theologian can construct a systematic theology by simply rearranging biblical affirmations. He would be asked constantly, "But what does that mean?"

The interpreting process is not done in a vacuum. Experience, including reason and personal faith, along with church tradition, even if this only means denominational understanding, must be employed in the hermeneutical task. The essay by Christian is a careful analysis of the relationship between scripture and theological statements, and it underscores the central role of hermeneutics.

The essay by David Tracy is an attempt to summarize the source-norms of Christian faith and to show how they regulate and correct one another.

ON THEOLOGICAL JUDGMENT

There is too easy an identification of theological explication and personal faith in some quarters of the church. If faith and theology were equated, then theologians would be the most faithful. However, I have met many persons whose faith was lively and devout, but whose theology was imprecise and contradictory. On the other hand, I have known articulate and brilliant theologians who claim no personal faith. They are essentially technicians.

When the ancient church grappled with the great Trinitarian and Christological heresies the creeds that were formulated stated the orthodox position without elaboration and there was a close identification between correct theology and saving faith.

These creedal statements we can still affirm. But whenever we step away from the creed in order to exegete a scripture or perform a pastoral care task or explain what the statement means, we invariably deviate somewhat from the creed and become to that extent heretical. The elementary diagram below is an attempt to illustrate my point.

'	'	'
Docetism (Jesus was only divine)	Chalcedonian Formula (Jesus was fully God and fully man)	Ebionism (Jesus was only human)

In interpreting the passage in which Jesus is praying to the Father no theologian will articulate the Chalcedonian formula exactly. Every theologian will proffer an explanation that will put his Christology on one side or another of the orthodox norm. Interestingly, when dealing with another Christological or Trinitarian question the same person may find his response places him on the other side of the continuum. In other words, the same person may at one time over-emphasize the humanity of Jesus, and at another time stress too heavily Jesus' divinity.

Our diagram is helpful in another way too. The figure helps us see how relative are our evaluations of one another. For example, someone maintaining a highly Docetic view of Jesus' temptation, according to which Jesus could not have yielded to the tempter, will view a person near the center of the continuum, who recognizes a real possibility of Jesus' yielding, as an Ebionite. Even though our alleged Ebionite may really be nearer the orthodox position, the Docetist's judgment is based on where he is on the continuum on that particular question.

Even this cursory analysis of theological adjudi-cation shows how dangerous it is to identify faith and theological explication. Our judgments are too rela-tive, and our own theology too subject to heresy, to attack the faith of another merely because he disa-grees theologically with us. It also reveals the extreme naivete and meaninglessness of terms such as "liberal" and "conservative."

But there is another way to illustrate that personal faith and theological construction are not identical. Faith is experiential. Theology is the rational explication and construction of the faith experience. The Biblical figures had experiences which they articulated theologically. We use their theology to reclaim and re-present the experience and encounter. It can become a path to experience for us.

The reason why the question of orthodoxy remains of modern interest is that we continue to recognize that some theological modes of expression open up the experience of faith better than do others. According-ly, we expect converts to use certain expressions, or else we try to lead them to have certain experiences by the language we use.

However, every theologian must deal at some point with the fact that his most important theological formulas might not open experiential faith for another. Or, as Paul Tillich pointed out, the formulas may be-come broken symbols and no longer open the experience of encounter even for him. And then, suppose new theological explications like those of the process theologians, or those of some other religion, do open up the experience of ultimate reality. What has occurred then? Can we say that a theological construction is heretical or idolatrous if it opens up the experience of faith? Are we left with only the vaguest criteria for theological judgment and differentiation or none at all?

Recent attempts to resolve these difficult questions by appealing to ritual and worship as acted expression of faith, vis-a-vis theology as spoken expression, probably will not be successful. The only thing that these attempts accomplish is that the debating ground is changed. Why some rituals are doors to the sacred, as Joseph Martos calls them, and others are not may not be answerable, or at least we may not know how to answer them as yet.

Perhaps one of the most serious obstacles to theological study is that we categorize thinkers and tend to read only those who agree with us. Young theology students are often taught to buy only the books published by certain presses, or whose authors have German names. But this selection process is a form of judgment itself. Its danger is that we will not have the type of dialogue with competing viewpoints which pulls us toward the center of the theological continuum. And this danger is as real for those on one side of the continuum as it is for those on the other. One reason why we need a community of Christians is that we might test one another and balance each other. It is my hope that this book will contribute to that ongoing dialogue.

THE PRESENT SITUATION WITHIN WHICH
THEOLOGY IS DONE

The first reading on theological method is by
Langdon Gilkey. Gilkey made a significant contribution to American theological thought at the end of the
turbulent Death of God years. Indeed, in several
respects Gilkey's landmark work *Naming the Whirlwind:
the Renewal of God-Language* marked the death of the
Death of God movement.

Among the important contributions made by this
work we should number Gilkey's brilliant exposé and
analysis of the fundamental assumptions of secularity
which he considers to be the *Geist* of modernity.
Since the enlightenment period a shift in intellectual
and metaphysical paradigms or assumptions has occurred.
Gilkey holds that the theologian must address his task
in light of these new assumptions, otherwise his work
is remote and stale. Indeed, it may be dishonest,
since the shift toward secularity has occurred not
only outside of the church but within it as well.
And this point is one of the most significant made by
Gilkey. Under attack is not merely conservative orthodoxy, but also liberal sophisticated religion; indeed
religion itself. Furthermore, no doctrine is exempt
from debate. In the past, various doctrines such as
the virgin birth, the resurrection, and the trinity
have been questioned. But there has never been such a
fundamental and sweeping challenge to the essence of
the faith as in modern times. In short, the present
situation is characterized by a radical "shaking of
the foundations" upon which theology has been built.

The four key elements of the secular spirit are
contingency, relativity, temporality and autonomy. By
contingency Gilkey means the modern understanding that

8

the world around us, life's events and even we ourselves are merely the accidental brute facts of all
there is. There is no need to look beyond the given
for a higher purpose or order because there is none
to be found.

Relativity is that general characteristic of
secularity which means that modern persons recognize
no unchanging absolutes. Conversely, it also implies
that every belief held has some relative merit. For
example, in place of the absolute Word of God, modern
secular man speaks of the "Hebrew understanding" or
the "Lukan tradition," or the "apostolic faith."

Temporality is Gilkey's term for the secular
consciousness of our finitude. Everything we are
comes and goes, the becoming and the death of all that
once lived. What we know passes away. It is changed,
corrected, discarded. Eternality is not an available
concept to the secular mind.

To his sense of autonomy modern man owes his
great achievements. His drive to know the truth for
himself, to determine what he shall believe, rather
than to be told what to believe (heteronomy) has
undermined greatly the church's authority. Secular
man is dependent upon himself. He decides what is
true, and he invents right and wrong. Indeed, it is
assumed that he must do these things to be fully
human.

When these four characteristics function in tan-
dem they form a world view which seems substantially,
if not completely, antagonistic to religious faith and
theological explanation. The interesting point to
note is that these same characteristics are directly
responsible for the ideological framework upon which
modern technology is based; that technology which we
enjoy and profit from.

THE PRESENT SITUATION WITHIN WHICH
THEOLOGY IS DONE*

Anyone who is at all aware of the intellectual and spiritual goings-on in our present culture knows that there is abroad a ferment in theology. Through reports and articles in the mass media, through public lectures, and through widely read books, he will have gathered that many prominent religious thinkers have begun in the last few years radically to question the traditional beliefs of our culture's major religious faiths. From the same sources, moreover, he knows that even the most stable and unchanging of our religious institutions has openly admitted that its doctrines, as well as its practical structures and many of its basic policies, must be "brought up to date" to meet the demands of the current crisis. And probably either he himself, his son, or perhaps a close friend has at one time or another said, "I just can't believe any longer what my church (or synagogue) teaches; it seems so anachronistic, so unreal, so unrelated to everything else."[1] Whether, that is, we look outside ourselves at intellectual movements in our cultural environment or inside at current changes in our feelings, attitudes, and convictions, we find religious concepts and certainties in upheaval, criticized not only by those outside the religious establishment, but even more by those within.

While such external and internal criticism of traditional Christian notions was, of course, characteristic of nineteenth- and early twentieth-century liberal religion, by and large it was, in that period, only rigidly orthodox, fundamentalist beliefs that were under vigorous attack. The new in the present situation is that the upheaval inside the religious community has fully as much to do with liberal or sophisticated religion as with orthodoxy; consequently it seems to question the very roots of any form of

*Source: From *Naming the Whirlwind: The Renewal of God-Language,* copyright 1969, by Langdon Gilkey, used with permission of the publisher, The Bobbs-Merrill Co.

religious belief at all. Our task here is to describe the background and present character of this ferment within religion and its most fundamental beliefs, to see what major cultural forces make religious affirmations difficult, and so to explore what possibilities there may be for meaningful theology in our time.

The current ferment spans almost the entire range of religious concepts and concerns. Every familiar Christian doctrine, from those of the authority of scripture, the trinity, or the deity of Christ, to the more fundamental question of the reality of God, has been questioned, in some instances in order to make room for reformulation, in others in order to abandon the conception altogether. Moreover, many nondoctrinal but nevertheless essential issues have been made the center of the debate: for example, such questions as "What does it mean to be a Christian today, what sort of style of life, or action and attitude in and toward the world--in matters of sex, or race, or property, or war--characterize the Christian?" and "How should the Church relate to the world, to its ways, its ideas, its standards and its needs; is it essentially separate and autonomous in relation to the world, drawing its life from elsewhere and leading men to another realm; or is its task to be in the world serving the world?"

The present theological situation, then, is characterized by a radical "shaking of the foundations," and this upheaval has, we believe, been recently experienced by almost all those concerned with Christian belief, with theology, preaching, and religious existence generally. Can we, however, be more precise than this and pinpoint what the foundation is that has been thus shaken, what it is that is now suddenly and in a new way problematic or in doubt? For after all, in the last two centuries almost every fundamental religious belief has at one time or another been regarded as questionable if not downright irrational by the modern secular world, and we are all used to this form of radical doubt about traditional religion.

This upheaval, this radical questioning of the foundations of religious affirmation and so of the theological language reflective of it, is now taking place _within_ and not outside of the Church. Heretofore in this century, the radical questioning of religious beliefs was a characteristic of the secular world outside the Church, and thus rather automatically

11

such doubt signaled the departure of the doubter from the ranks of the faithful, and certainly from the professional enterprises of either the ministry or theology. In the present crisis, however, one finds not only concerned laymen wondering about the usage and meaning of religious language; even more one encounters younger clergy and theologians questioning whether it is any longer possible to speak intelligibly of God. The Church itself, the religious community itself, through the experience and the reflective thought of its official representatives and functionaries, is not so much expounding "faith" to a doubting world as it is itself exploring the depths of its own uncertainty, and itself searching for possible foundations for its language, its worship, and its works. This *is* new, and it is radical.

Not only is the situation radical because the community of Christians itself is experiencing this upheaval; even more is it radical because it is the most fundamental of all our Judeo-Christian religious affirmations that is under searching and critical scrutiny by all, and forthrightly rejected by many. For it is the reality of what our tradition has called "God" that is now the subject of theological debate, and the question of God is, of course, the most fundamental of all theological questions. As we shall argue throughout, all other theological issues are logically secondary to this one. Such issues--as, for example, that of revelation, of faith, of a theological hermeneutics of scripture, of Christology, of law and gospel, of Word and sacrament, of an eschatological view of history, and of eternal life--simply do not exist as *theological* issues if there be no God, if the totality of what is real be devoid of a divine dimension transcendent to the finite, contingent, transient creatures--for then there can be no revelation, no divine word, no incarnation, no revealed gospel, no sacrament, no eschatological "view" in history, and no eternity. The question of the reality of God and so of the possibility, meaningfulness, and validity of any religious faith and of any theological discourse at all, forms the center of our present ferment--which is as fundamental a question as theology can raise. One cannot begin, for example, with the presupposition of the presence of the Word of God, if one is asking the question of God--nor, as we shall argue, can one begin with the assumption of a divine Logos which makes metaphysics possible. If the question of *God* is raised, theology literally must begin from the beginning, it must deal with its own most

12

basic foundations.

At the present, however, the thrust of the question of theological language has significantly shifted. It is not merely the question of what sort religious language should be, but the question whether any talk about God is possible at all; the debate concerns not whether God is known by philosophy or by revelation, but whether he is dead or alive, and so whether any language about him is empty or meaningful.[2] Consequently, the present form of the question of religious language is such that it drives theological inquiry to the new task of justifying religious discourse as a whole. And that task can be accomplished only by seeking to locate within concrete experience some element, aspect, or being which calls for religious symbolization, for which religious or theological language is necessary, and in relation to which it communicates and so has "meaning."

The major historical cause of the current ferment in religious belief lies in the interaction between two important forces in our cultural life, namely the developing "secularity" of our cultural existence on the one hand, and our traditional religious communities, with their convictions, values, shared experiences and loyalties on the other. Thus a large part of the intellectual background of the current situation in theology is the maturation of the secular spirit which almost all present theological commentators, however they may assess that spirit, agree is predominant in our age.

Our thesis in this analysis is that "the secular spirit," or "secularity," represents the cultural *Geist* of our time, and that it is the particular character of this mood or self-understanding as dominant in the minds of all of us that creates most of the important problems for belief and for theological reflection which we will discuss here. By the phrase "the secular spirit," therefore, I do not mean to refer merely to the historical process of secularization, although that is clearly related to the referent of our use of the word. Rather, we wish to point to that fundamental attitude toward the world and toward life, slowly developing into the dominant *Geist* of the West since the Medieval period, and so which has been both the cause and the effect of the cultural and social process of secularization. We wish to delineate this attitude or spirit because it is precisely this mood which raises all our contemporary theological problems, and which makes the meaningfulness alike of the Biblical, the traditional, and the philosophical forms of Christian belief so problematic in our time.

The causes of fundamental cultural change are as baffling as they are complex.

1.   As technology and urbanization have slowly progressed in the West, the setting of man's life has significantly shifted. He is not dependent any longer on the eternal, changeless, given order of nature to which he must accommodate himself; rather, the environment to which he adapts himself is now composed of the ever-changing and relative arrangements of human enterprise. He seems to have moved from God's world to man's, from being the participant in an eternal order to becoming the creator of a relative and fluctuating one.

2.   Concurrently, his view of this human world about him, of the social institutions, traditions, and customs in which he lives his life, has changed. These institutions--state, church, class, and even family--are no longer for him "given" unalterably by a transcendent authority which he must obey; they are no longer temporal expressions of a divine and eternal order, participation in and obedience to which give coherence and meaning to man's fragmentary life on earth--as they were for our Greek and Christian forebears. Rather, man now knows that they are created by historical, geographical, and above all human forces, that they are, indeed, relative, temporal, and so "secular" institutions, and not the sacred orders which God eternally willed for his world. Consequently, the rulers of these institutions--king, ruler, father, Pope, schoolmaster--are no longer sacral, unquestioned authorities and models for all that man is and knows.

3.   Above all, as modern man has learned to know and think about his world, he has not found it peopled with spiritual beings; nor has his present understanding of it seemed to support the traditional assumption that it was, so to speak, engineered by "someone" with human purposes and needs in mind. Rather, insofar as he feels he can know anything with certainty at all, he realizes he knows his natural environment only through scientific inquiry, and the picture he finds implied there is that he and his world are the results of countless, strangely harmonious, but utterly blind causes whose fortuitous inter-

14

action has produced his relatively benevolent environment and even his own admirable powers of life, love, and thought.

The modern spirit is thus radically this-worldly. We tend not to see our life and its meanings as stretching out toward an eternal order beyond this existence, or our fortunes as dependent upon a transcendant ruler of time and history. We view our life as here, and our destiny as beginning with birth and ending with the grave, as confined in space and time to this world in nature and among men. Consequently, whatever knowing we can achieve will deal with this limited environment, and whatever meaning we can find in our short life will, we feel, depend entirely on our own powers of intellect and will and the relative historical and communal values we can create--and not on the grace and mercy of an ultimate heavenly sovereign. Modern man thus feels he has "come of age" in a contingent, faceless world. He can, and should, depend on no one or on no other beyond himself to continue in being, to know and to decide about his life. If anyone is to rule and direct his destiny, it must be man himself alone. Such, we suggest, is the "secular spirit" which dominates our age and which, as a fundamental attitude toward reality, truth, and value, is expressed not only by our own most fundamental reactions to life, but also objectively in the dominant philosophies, the creative arts, and the most profound literature of our day. Needless to say, not every member--even every creative member--of present Western culture understands himself and his world in this way, any more than every man possessed a "Renaissance spirit" during that period. But that this secular mood characterizes the pervasive and fundamental attitudes of those urban and semiurban middle classes who participate in and so are dominantly creative of our cultural existence, there can be little doubt.

There are four general characteristics of this secular spirit, the brief conceptual elaboration of which will help to make its experienced shape more precise. We shall encounter these four elements of the modern *Geist* throughout our study of the contemporary possibilities for religious discourse.

1. *Contingency*. This is the sense that what is--the world around us and we ourselves--is the result of causes that are neither necessary, rational, nor purposive. The flow of events, to be sure, may exhibit a

proximate order sufficient to maintain us and to allow
us to trace out its recurrent habits and so to pre-
dict--sufficient, that is, for practical decisions,
for science, and for technology. But none of these
things that have evolved in time is necessary or
intended; they are accidental, and why things either
are, are thus mysteries which our minds cannot fathom.

This most basic apprehension of the radical
limitation of thought to the contingent given is expressed in the insistence of much of linguistic philosophy that all assertions that have to do with what
there is, all, as they put it, "factual" assertions,
are contingent and therefore empirical or scientific
in form. What is crucial here is the identification,
first, of assertions about what is with "factual" and
contingent statements *alone* (i.e., nonnecessary or
"might not have been" statements); and secondly, of
contingent statements with empirically verifiable or
sensory statements alone. Thus, putting this point in
less logical language, the only way we can talk about
what is real is through statements based upon and
confined to concrete, sensory data: this is our only
cognitive contact with what is, and so the only way
we can speak about it. Only the immediately given is
knowable and intelligible, and nothing else *is* for us;
contingency equals the real and limits the knowable.

Perhaps the strongest assertion of the contingency of whatever is appears in existentialism, for which
contingency practically defines the meaning of the
word "existence." Here one does not observe contingency from the outside as a phenomenon of things; one
grasps it from within as the character of one's own
existence. Our being is, says Heidegger, most fundamentally defined as "being there," and he does not
mean "being there for this or that reason," but *just*
"being there," being posited--for the essence of being
there is the experience of being thrown or cast into
existence. Our existence is thrown, but there is no
thrower and so no reason for the throw.[3] Apparently,
for all its proximate orders traced by science, existence comes at modern man as if out of the dark, from
no further reality, within no ultimate order and for
no ultimate reason. It is brute fact, the absolutely
given, the ultimately arbitrary, the merely posited:
beyond what is thus starkly given, there is merely a
Void. This is what contingency means in our age, and
it is in large part this sense of existence as ultimately arbitrary that makes language which moves beyond
the given, whether in speculative philosophy or in

theology, seem unreal, empty, and irrational to modern man. The antimetaphysical as well as the antitheological bent of the secular spirit finds its deepest roots in this sense of the radical contingency of what we experience, and so of the utter mystery--even the irrationality--in all that lies beyond the immediately given. Our radical empiricism is an outgrowth of the more fundamental ontological vision that all that there is that can be known is exhausted by the proximate patterns of immediate sensory experience. All intelligible language is thus monodimensional, referent to the plane or surface of events in immediate or phenomenal experience. Symbolic language referent to depths beneath the surface reveals for modern man more about our psychological and verbal problems than it does about any transcendent or divine dimension of reality.

2. The second general characteristic or category of contemporary life, central to all we mean by the secular spirit, is that of *relativity*, or, in its other context, *relativism*. This sense of relativity is a product not so much of the cosmology of seventeenth-century science as it is the result of the historical consciousness which developed in the late eighteenth and the early nineteenth centuries, and of the ontologies and then the biology that grew out of this historical consciousness. The resultant sense of the relativity of all things to one another in the passage of time--of the forms of the cosmos itself, of natural life, of our own species, of political and social structures, of the most significant historical events, the noblest of ideas, the most sacred of scriptures, institutions or creeds--practically defines our era.

For this modern view, all that is is pinioned within the flux of passage or of history, determined in large part by all that lies behind it, shaped by all that surrounds it, and to be replaced by what follows. Nothing in nature or history, and so by implication nothing at all that is, is thus "a *se*," an unchanging and self-sufficient substance, capable of existing in and by itself and thus exhibiting an essence underived from and so unrelated to the other things that surround it. Nothing anywhere in experience, space, time, or any mode of being is, in that sense, absolute; all is relative to all else and so essentially conditioned by its relevant environment.

Again the effects on religion, and on theology,

17

of this aspect of relativity have been devastating.
If the ontological relativity of all things has cast
doubt on the possibility of a transcendent and self-
sufficient God, the relativism of all things historical has seemed to make impossible any of those concrete, sacral evidences of his presence to his creatures upon which all religions are founded and on
which depends any intelligible usage of religious
language. Where are the ultimate events of relevation
when all in history swims in the relativity of time;
what is the Word of God amidst the welter and variety
of historical words in scripture; what is the mind of
the Church in this manifold of changing historical
minds, each rooted in and so directly relevant only to
its own epoch? The divine bases for authority in
theology seem to have fled with this historicizing of
everything historical, leaving us with only the tatters
of merely human authorities--a "Hebrew understanding,"
an "apostolic faith," a "patristic mind," "Medieval
viewpoints," a "Reformation attitude," and even
"nineteenth-century cosmologies." And if, correspondingly, all faiths and world views are thus historical,
relative to their stage and place in general history,
how can any one of them claim our ultimate allegiance
or promise an ultimate truth or an ultimate salvation?

    3. Another major theme of the modern conscious-
ness, closely related to the preceding, is that of
temporality or *transience*, the becomingness and so the
mortality of all things there are. All is in time,
and time being in all things, each has its appointed
terminus.[4] The Greeks, of course, realized this transience; but, as with the older view of contingency,
they never thought of asserting it about reality as a
whole. Just as to Aristotle and to Thomas contingency
pointed beyond itself to a level of necessity and utter
rationality, so transience and becoming pointed the
Hellenic mind beyond itself to a ground that was eternal being.[5] As in the case of the concept of contingency, however, the meaning of the modern sense of
temporality or becoming is precisely the opposite, for
here any dependence of that which is temporal on that
which is not transient or in passage is denied. What
is new, therefore, in the modern sense of transience
is its *total* character. For moderns, time is the most
fundamental structure of all experienced being. All
is becoming, all is changing, all is in passage out of
the past and into the future, and so all causes and all
effects come and go--and all is mortal--and nothing
else is real. There is in direct experience nothing
else besides creatures which "never really are"--and

18

death or perishing claims all creatures.

In theology the influence of this "temporalism" has been enormous and, making union with the Biblical emphasis on history, has tended to replace Hellenic categories of eternity with those of historical activity,[6] and to understand Christian hope not in terms of a supratemporal end to time but in the terms of political progress and of eschatological expectation for a "new" in the continuing processes of time. The modern secular spirit is thus "time-bound" in a way that no previous age in our culture has been; our life is bounded by birth and by death, and the relevant environment for our hopes, as for our fears, is confined to the temporal processes of nature and of history.

As a result, of almost all the concepts in the theological tradition that seem meaningless and unreal to the modern mind, the primary one is surely that of a divine eternity that transcends temporal passage, and the correlative concepts of everlasting life, eternal judgment, and eternal salvation. Where on earth, asks the modern empirical man, except in the abstract and therefore unreal realms of mathematics, logic, and fantasy, does a concept such as that of eternity find its base in experience? What lodgment has it in reality when all our experience, external and internal alike, knows only transience, the becoming and the death of all that once had life? Does not all we know come to be and pass away--and how can we know or experience anything more than this? Is not all talk of things transcendent to mortal passage just protective illusion, the product of fears and of hopes--and even harmful besides, since its comforting but illusory fantasy dulls the cold shock of the prospect of our own death, that final term toward which all authentic existence, existence decisively at grips with its own reality, points? Such are the searching questions facing current theology which the fact of universal transience poses for us--questions which in unreflective form each layman's gaze asks of the cleric when the latter tries stumblingly to speak of the Christian answer to the death of some loved one.

4. *Autonomy*. The three faces of the modern secular spirit so far portrayed--contingency, relativism, and temporality--might seem grim indeed were it not for the fourth, which is the source of whatever optimism and courage the modern spirit possesses. Little if any confidence or courage come to modern man from his wider, cosmic environment where, as we have

19

seen, all is blind, relative, and transient. In this sense, he is truly "on his own," an alien set within a context that is indifferent and so irrelevant to his own deepest purposes, and whatever hope and meaning he may have must come to him from himself.

The fourth category of modern secularity is, therefore, the autonomy and freedom of man, his inalienable birthright and, fortunately, his innate capacity to know his own truth, to decide about his own existence, to create his own meaning, and to establish his own values. This view of man as a self-creative being first began to manifest itself, one might say, in the Renaissance and Reformation, but has become stronger, more precise and more inward since then. It increased in the Enlightenment drive for intellectual and political freedom,[7] and in the Romantic movement's emphasis on the uniqueness and inwardness of each individual man's experience and feeling;[8] and it has been made fully explicit in our day in existentialism, psychoanalysis, and democratic theories. This affirmation of freedom, or of self-determination by one's own mind and will, as the essential character of man and so as the necessary condition for human self-realization, is one of the strongest voices of modernity and possibly the most creative.

In any case, this emphasis on freedom and autonomy lies behind those social ideals, essential to modern existence, of the unhampered freedom of scientific and of scholarly inquiry. It forms both the deepest basis and the acknowledged goal of our educational institutions, our creative political structures, our efforts at social reform, our burgeoning psychoanalysis and counseling, and even our endeavors to control our environment and ourselves through scientific knowledge and technology.[9] And it provides the deepest themes for our current literature, existentialist philosophy and theology. If it believes anything at all, the modern spirit holds that a man must, in some essential regard, live his life in autonomy if that life is to be creative and human, and insofar as it is optimistic in mood, this spirit believes that man can increasingly exercise his freedom over the blind forces of destiny and so "be master of his own fate." Thus the modern spirit, at least in the West, is dedicated to the proposition that any external social authority--whether of church, of state, of local community, or of family-- will in the end only crush man's humanity if his own personal being does not participate fully and voluntar-

ily in whatever help that authority represents and in
whatever creative forms his life may take.

Obviously, this assertion of autonomous freedom
and self-direction as the key to human self-fulfilment
is subversive of many of the historic forms of religion, with their traditional authorities of various
sorts stemming from the distant past, their requirements of faith, obedience, submission, and self-
surrender, and their insistence that man is fulfilled
when he patterns himself according to the divine
image. Is not--so the modern spirit declares--
revelation the denial of all autonomy in inquiry and
rationality; is not a divine law the denial of personal autonomy in ethics; above all, is not God, if he be
at all, the final challenge to my creativity as a man?
Religion, said Ludwig Feuerbach, drains away all the
vitality and interest man may summon for autonomous
efforts; it smothers in passivity the infinite possibilities of control over his own destiny which man
might exert; and it makes of him a submissive, weak,
empty creature dependent on unreal forces beyond him.[10]

In the above, we have tried to give a picture of
the main elements of the secular spirit, those fundamental assumptions about reality, truth, and value
which determine our period and in terms of which any
creative cultural expression, literary, artistic,
philosophical, or religious, must express itself if
it is to be relevant and meaningful to us. The main
picture we have gained from our description is that
which shows man as set within a contingent, relative,
and temporal context in which no ultimate order,
coherence, or meaning--either in terms of an eternal
rational structure or a sovereign divine will--appears,
and so in which man is forced (or enabled) to create
by his own powers whatever meaning his life on earth
may achieve. What man can know and speak meaningfully about is only the changing natural and social
world around him which he directly experiences, and
possibly his own inner psyche; what he can do is confined to the world of engineering, economics, politics,
and culture; what he values are his relations to
nature, the products of his industry, the artistic
works he can create or enjoy, the reforms in historical
life he can institute, and the personal contacts with
others he can have. Whatever reality, knowledge, or
value there may be anywhere lies in the immediate, the
here and now, in this world which we can sense and
manipulate. And whatever language is intelligible and
meaningful in such a world is monodimensional language,

referent to the nexus of natural, historical, and psychological causes that surround and create us, but not referent to any dimension or factor beyond that realm of contingency, relativity, and transience. Such a mood knows or needs no other sacred world beyond this and agrees that language referent to another such world, in terms either of philosophical thought or of religious faith, seems unreal and meaningless.

At its worst, this secular spirit is explicitly materialistic, hedonistic, and driven toward worldly success and power. At its best, it has developed a healthy love of the joys of life and, in its developing humanitarianism, a compassionate concern for the neighbor's welfare, seeking to bring well-being into all of life, to increase freedom, to strengthen selfhood and dignity, and to spread the goods brought by technology and industry to all men alike.

As this last comment illustrates, churchmen, laity and theologians alike, are also secular. We not only accept, consciously and unconsciously, most of the attitudes we have here described; what is more, we rejoice in them and would defend them if challenged-- possibly for theological reasons derived from the Bible! We use and enjoy the technology this spirit has produced; we approve its scientific methods and the knowledge derived therefrom; we seek to interpret and to validate our own religious faith as best we can with its categories and its criteria; and we understand whatever blessings religion gives to us largely in its valuational terms. We in the Church have, moreover, learned much from it. Mutual tolerance of differences of viewpoint and a humble spirit about the relative truths we continue to treasure have both come from this secular mood of relativity, historicity, and perpetual change. Above all, its humanitarian spirit has forced us to reaffirm that New Testament ideal of love for the neighbor that the churches had been wont to ignore. Secularism has been a more faithful and helpful critic of the churches than they have been of their society.

It is because of this developing vision that modern man's institutions, standards, and decisions have gradually become secular, based on his own powers of knowledge and of comprehension, and directed by his own pragmatic and immediate needs for this life, rather than on a sacred or ultimate ground given to us from beyond. Moreover, and this is a most relevant point for our purposes, each of these particular

elements of this mood: its this-worldly character,
its sense of contingency, relativism, temporality,
and autonomy, and its confinement of thought and language to the sphere of the immediately given, have been
in increasing tension if not in contradiction with
traditional religious beliefs, ideas, and attitudes.
It is in the light of this tension between the secular
vision so understood and the characteristic emphases
of Christian faith that the recent history of theology,
and especially the present ferment, are to be understood.

Endnotes

[1]See, for example, the very perceptive article
on this experience by Thomas F. O'Dea, "The Crisis of
the Contemporary Religious Consciousness," in *Daedalus*,
96, no. 1 (Winter 1967).

[2]The advent of a new and more ultimate question
in theology is again illustrated by Ogden, in a later
essay (1966): "One of the obvious conclusions to be
drawn from the latest developments in Protestant theology is that the reality of God has now become the
central theological problem. . . . Rightly understood,
the problem of God is not one problem among several
others; it is the only problem there is." Schubert M.
Ogden, *The Reality of God* (New York: Harper and Row,
1966), p. 1.

[3]"As something thrown, Dasein has been thrown *into*
existence. It exists as an entity which has to be as
it is and as it can be. *That* it is factically, may be
obscure and hidden as regards the *'why'* of it; but the
that-it-is has *itself* been disclosed to Dasein. . . .
The caller is Dasein in its uncanniness: primordial,
thrown Being in the world as the 'not-at-home'--the
bare 'that-it-is' in the 'nothing' of the world."
Martin Heidegger, *Being and Time*, trans. J. Macquarrie
and E. Robinson (New York: Harper & Row, 1962),
p. 321.

[4]Nathan A. Scott, Jr., puts this very beautifully
in his essay "Mimesis and Time in Modern Literature":
"Human life is drenched in time . . . for we are but
the merest reeds in nature, feeble at best, and soon
withering away: we are not creatures of permanence;

nothing stays for us, and there is no escaping what Camus called 'the cruel mathematics that command our condition' . . . for the career of anything that grows and develops is bracketed within the consecutive flow of temporality, and death is the form that finality takes for all living things, whether they be vegetable or animal or human." Nathan A. Scott, Jr., *The Broken Center; Studies in the Theological Horizon of Modern Literature* (New Haven: Yale University Press, 1966), p. 25.

[5]Cf. Aristotle, *The Physics*, Book IV, Chapter 12, 221a, 221b; Marcus Aurelius, *Meditations*, Book II, Sections 14, 17; Book VII, Section 19; Book IX, Sections 14, 28. Cf. also Psalms 39 and 90. For the most acute sense in ancient literature of the passage of all things, and of the unreality of the fleeting present, which is all that "is" for us, cf. Augustine, *The Confessions*, Book XI, Chapter 15, Sections 18-20.

[6]Almost all of recent "Biblical theology" has represented this temporalist, dynamic mind-set as opposed to the static categories of changelessness and of eternity of the Hellenic tradition. Most prominent among them, of course, is Oscar Cullman in his *Christ and Time* (Philadelphia: Westminster Press, 1940), and now, in a new "eschatological" vein, the thought of Jürgen Moltmann, *The Theology of Hope* (New York: Harper & Row, 1967), Wolfhart Pannenberg and Johannes B. Metz, S.J.

[7]Cf., as three examples, John Locke, *Concerning Civil Government*, Chapters I and IX; Immanuel Kant, "What Is Enlightenment?"; and John Stuart Mill, *On Liberty*.

[8]Cf., for example, F. Schleiermacher, *On Religion: Speeches to Its Cultured Despisers*, trans. John Oman (New York: Frederick Ungar, 1955), Speeches I and II.

[9]This assertion of freedom and autonomy is, of course, in real tension with that other aspect of the modern spirit which emphasizes that all events, including those which make up the human organism, have determining causes and are therefore amenable to scientific understanding. To unravel this paradox of freedom and determinism within modern scientific thought itself is too big a task for a footnote. Suffice it here to say that, when modern science reviews its conclusions about man as an *object* of its inquiry, it finds man almost totally determined. When, however,

it considers science itself as a human enterprise carried on necessarily by free, inquiring scientists
manipulating their environment and rationally arriving
at their conclusions, that is, when scientific man is
the *subject* and not the *object* of science, the scientific mentality is inclined to emphasize freedom and
not determinism. That is to say, it emphasizes the
necessity for science of a context of freedom, and
the real possibilities of new freedom over human
destiny which scientific knowledge and technology
bring to man.

[10]Cf. Ludwig Feuerbach, *The Essence of Christianity* (New York: Harper Torchbooks, 1957), especially
Chapter 1.

Discussion Questions

1.   What does Gilkey mean when he says that the modern
era is a "shaking of the foundations?"

2.   Do you think Gilkey's description of the modern
mood is accurate? Has the contemporary Spirit changed
since he wrote in the late 1960s?

3.   To what extent is Gilkey correct in stating that
members of the church, and theologians themselves, are
influenced by secularity?

4.   Which of the elements of secularity do you believe
poses the greatest threat to Christian theology? Why?

5.   Gilkey seems to be saying that much about secularity is constructive. Do you agree? Would it be
possible to be non-secular? If so, in what senses?

SCRIPTURAL FOUNDATIONS FOR THEOLOGY

Every Christian community and certainly every theology purporting to be Christian recognizes that the Scriptures hold a special place as source and norm for the theological explication of the faith. To be sure, the exact role and authority of Scripture vary greatly from tradition to tradition and even within a church or denomination.

As C. W. Christian points out, previous centuries probably have allowed the Scripture a broader scope of authority and a more decisive normative role in shaping theology than is the case in the modern period. It is important to remember that the Scriptures not only function as a source norm *for* theology, but also that every Christian theologian must formulate some theology of Scripture. Indeed, many problems in understanding and appropriating the Biblical witness arise not from the Bible itself, but from one's theology of the Bible. If, for example, I hold the Bible in front of me to protect me from harm as though it was a supernatural amulet, and it does not protect me, then it is my thought about the Bible which is to be blamed and not the Bible itself.

In this essay, Christian insists that the task of a theologian is to make the agreement between revelation and theology as consistent as possible. At the same time, however, he argues that theology cannot be simply a synopsis of the contents of Scripture as revelation. Such a view of Scripture as revelation is too narrow. Christian stresses that modern historical study of the Scripture discloses a much greater dogmatic variety than previous eras thought present. Scriptural accounts reflect differences in historical detail, as well as literary and cultural variety. But most important is Scripture's considerable plurality

26

of theological viewpoints which cannot easily be harmonized into an organic unity.

Although Christian cites a few examples of such diversity in this essay, several other illustrations could be given with no difficulty. Source analysis of the Israelite monarchial traditions in Samuel reveals variant perspectives on the question of God's attitude toward the request for a king. Writings which offer prescriptions for the restored nation after the Babylonian exile hold up conflicting models. The vision of Ezekiel and that of the Isaianic suffering servant songs are probably the most divergent. Comparison of the function of Jesus' miracles in the synoptics with the way in which John uses them also indicates a different theological intent.

Once this diversity is made apparent the question of development arises quite naturally. From the earliest centuries of Christianity theologians have given consent to a difference in authority or adequacy between the Testaments. Practically speaking, Christians return to the same passages over and over to receive inspiration and instruction. By so doing, we show that we not only recognize the greater authority of the New Testament over the Old, but also that we regard some passages within the New Testament or the Old Testament to be of greater authority than others. By disregarding passages in our Bibles we effectively establish in some sense a canon within the canon.

Nevertheless, Christian argues that there are several important senses in which theologians are bound by the Scriptural witness. Most notable among these reasons is that the Scriptures force themselves on theologians. They correct and confound us. They call us beyond reason, and convict us of our pettiness.

SCRIPTURAL FOUNDATIONS FOR THEOLOGY*

Every Christian community and every Christian theology recognize that the Scriptures hold a special place as source and norm for faith. But the exact place and authority of Scripture vary widely from church to church and even within a church or denomination. Between the Catholic and non-Catholic churches there has even been a difference of opinion concerning the content of Scriptures. Furthermore, the degree and character of the authority given to Scripture has been affected by changing historical circumstances.

It is probably true that most previous centuries have allowed the Bible a wider range of authority and a more decisive role in shaping, not only theology proper, but their understanding of nature, life and ethics as well, than is the case in the present century. Indeed, it would probably be safe to say that the question of the authority of Scriptures has undergone a rather complete reexamination in the last century and a half. It is also true that faith in the reliability or the adequacy of Scripture is going through a crisis in contemporary life. This is as true for those who still profess a doctrine of infallibility and defend the absolute authority of Scripture as it is for those who do not. This crisis grows out of the fact that the whole understanding of the universe has changed radically in the past three centuries. The world view of the first century A.D., in which the New Testament came to life and which so deeply shaped the language and thought of the biblical writers, is no longer that of modern men. And this is true not only of the religious or theological liberal; it is true of every modern man.

We do not choose our world view; it is not an option but a given fact. Thus one of the critical questions facing the Christian theologian today is that of understanding how the Scriptures, which were con-

*Source: From *Shaping Your Faith: A Guide to a Personal Theology* by C. W. Christian. Copyright 1973 by Word, Inc. Publishers. Used by permission of C. W. Christian.

ceived and written in a different world, can be meaningful and powerful for our own. Are there respects in
which we can and must admit that Scripture is limited
or not authoritative? Are there ways in which it can
be translated or reinterpreted into the vernacular of
our world so that it can speak with power?

It seems doubtful that any modern man can look
upon the Scriptures as a valid and reliable authority
in matters scientific as did medieval Christians.
Beginning with Copernicus, scientific study has created
a view of the world which is both different from the
biblical world view and for us absolutely authoritative.
In place of a relatively small, world-centered universe
created in a moment only a few millennia ago, we now
are confronted by an inconceivably vast universe which
has come into being in an almost equally vast time
span. And although many of us are made most uncomfortable by such a world, and especially by what it implies about man's place and value in that world, we
can't really escape it. Those who continue to carry
on a rear guard action against geology and evolution
can't conceal from us the fact that our children have
no choice about the matter. For them and for all
future generations some form of developmentalism will
be not theory but fact, and not a conclusion but a
starting point.

Furthermore, we all *live* by this new view, whether
we like to admit it or not, as witnessed by the fact
that the most conservative theologian consults a geologist and not the Scriptures when he wants to dig for
oil. At every practical level we accept the sovereignty
of the scientific picture of the world. This is borne
out by the fact that even when we seek to "harmonize"
science and Scripture we usually seek to show that
Scripture really doesn't disagree with science, rather
than the reverse. Nor can we any longer take refuge
in the minor disagreements of scientists or their frequent revisions of their theories, for it is the practical effectiveness of their basic theory which enables
them to broaden and modify the details with confidence.
For example, while biologists may disagree on the details of evolution or the mechanisms at work in it,
there is no disagreement on the principle of biological development. Evolution is not theory to modern
scientists, it is fact. Nor is it less than fact to
a whole generation of school children for whom the
Scopes trial in Tennessee cannot be seen as anything
other than a page from a comic opera. Clarence Darrow
did not need to win his case. Time and the cumulative

effects of research have won it for him. The dis-
parity between Genesis and Darwin, if it comes down to
it, has really been decided for all of us in Darwin's
favor.

If the Scriptures are not then reliable in matters
scientific, how can they be trusted in other matters?
Furthermore, scientific ("critical") study of the
Scriptures has made clear the very human quality of
the Bible itself, and has shown the rather surprising
variety of outlook, witness, opinion and theology to
be found in the Bible. What does this say about its
authority? If indeed this book is shot-through with
humanity, how can it be relied on as a testimony to
faith and a source of doctrine?

These and other related problems have led many
Christians in the last century and a half to reexamine
the nature and character of scriptural authority, or
to develop a new doctrine of Scripture more commen-
surate with the modern world view. Now whether the
reader agrees with the above judgments or himself
feels that the authority of Scripture in these matters
has been called into question, we must insist that
those who felt these problems to be real were not simply weak or malicious men, seeking to destroy faith
by their reexaminations. On the contrary, they sought
to face the problems confronting biblical faith because
they believed in its basic truth and were willing to
seek for answers.

Nevertheless the shock of the nineteenth century
to the collective nervous system of faith was considerable. It did shatter the older and often comfortable
securities of the age of faith. Yet the very crisis
of Scripture has proved to be at least in part a
blessing, for it has driven Christian thinkers to reexamine the Scriptures, and to ask new questions about
the nature and extent of its authority and truth, and
to point us in new and fruitful directions. It is no
accident that the biblical critical movement of the
nineteenth century led to a biblically centered theology in the first half of the twentieth in theologians
such as Karl Barth, Emil Brunner, Reinhold Niebuhr,
and Paul Tillich.

Understanding the Nature and Authority of the Scriptures

Many (though not all) of our problems in hearing
and understanding the Bible arise not from the nature
of the Bible itself, but from our ideas about the

30

Bible--in other words, from our *theology* of the
Bible. If we attribute to the Scriptures a kind of
power or authority which they never claimed or needed
and then they turn out not to possess such a power,
it is not the Scriptures which have proved false but
our theology of Scripture. If, for instance, I make
of the Bible a magic amulet or charm, and it does not
protect me from injury, then the Scripture cannot be
blamed. Yet the authority of Scripture has become
so closely identified for many with the theological
idea of "infallibility" or "factual inerrancy" that
many feel that they must give up the Bible altogether
when they can no longer accept the dogma of inerrancy.

The first step for many in developing a personal
theology is to rethink the nature and character of
biblical authority, asking, "What do honesty and common sense require me to affirm? What actual power
and authority can the Bible have for my life? How
does the Bible as a source of faith relate to the
other source-norms of faith?" Perhaps even more
basically, "What sort of a book is it after all?" The
answers to the questions must finally be your own,
but I can point out for your consideration certain
ways of looking at the Bible which seem to me preliminary to any workable doctrine of Scripture for our time:

*1. We need to understand the Bible as a creation of
faith.*

The Scriptures were born out of the believing
community. The Catholic authorities say that the
church created the Bible, and historically they are
correct. This tells us something about the purposes
behind its creation. It was the product of religious
faith. It was written by a religious community (or
communities) in order to express and communicate their
faith and its meaning to their children and to those
who would listen.

Now while the purpose of the Bible was religious,
it necessarily had to be written in the language and
the thought patterns of its day. What other language
did they have at their disposal? Since its various
writers, Hebrew and Greek, were men living in the
physical world, they could not avoid couching their
thoughts in the world view, even in the primitive
science of their day. Yet it was not their purpose
or their chief concern to comment on cosmology or
physics any more than a poet or a preacher expects
his random or descriptive references to nature to be

31

drawn out of their literary or homiletic context and
set up as criteria of natural truth for all ages. On
such matters they did not (and did not intend to)
speak as authorities but as men who took for granted
the common opinions of their day.

They had a somewhat deeper interest in history
than they had in astronomy or physics because Hebrew
and Christian alike saw history as the arena of God's
redemptive work. But their concern was not in the
disinterested examination of past events. They were
not antiquarians. Their interest in history was a
concern for bearing witness to the acts of God within
it. Thus their history is "prejudiced." Biblical
writers not only write what happened but they interpret
it in the light of faith. In fact, they might even on
occasion rearrange or modify the facts so as to make
clear the religious meaning.

The facts were for them nothing unless they testi-
fied to the gracious, loving and redemptive Lord of
history. Their purpose was not to inform or to report
but to *bear witness*. And one cannot begin to understand the clearly provable inadequacies of Scripture
scientifically and historically, or its peculiar
richness and power to move men to worship and to
repentance unless he takes this purpose seriously. The
Old Testament is not science or history; it is *confession* to the marvelous grace of God who called Israel
forth to be his people. At the heart of the Old Testament is an event which must be confessed ("A wandering
Aramean was my father . . . and the Lord heard our
voice . . . and brought us out of Egypt with a mighty
hand."), and proclaimed ("Hear, O Israel, the Lord is
one!"). So also at the heart of the New Testament is
an event to be confessed ("God . . . who called you
out of darkness into his marvelous light") and witnessed to ("God has made him both Lord and Christ.").

Our first step then in discovering what kind of
authority the Scripture can have for today and in
developing an adequate doctrine of Scripture is to
learn to listen to the Bible for what it is, a book of
witness and of faith, in order that we might hear what
it seeks to say and what it is really *able* to say.
The proper reaction to a word of witness and confession
is not assent but response. Somehow we must find the
real power and value of Scripture in its word of confession and proclamation. It speaks the language of
faith and its real authority is an authority of faith.

2. We need to understand that, like every living thing, the Scripture grew!

That is, it was not given to Israel and the church as a single document perfectly conceived and executed by the hand of God. It grew as the experience of Israel with God grew and matured, and it grew as the early church grew in its experience of God in Christ. There are religions which teach that their sacred documents were handed down intact from heaven untouched, so to speak, by human hands. Christians have sometimes been tempted to understand the Bible this way.

I recall the college friend who one night in the dormitory defended the position that after Paul had written Romans he had to read it to see what it said. I was reminded of the painting which is alleged to have hung in a German monastery. It pictured a bearded scribe at a desk with pen in hand. The writer was clearly unconscious or asleep, while behind him stood an angel who over his shoulder guided the pen. The painting was called "Inspiration." Both illustrations imply the absence of any human experience or personality in Scripture and therefore deny any real human history to it. The Hebrew-Christian tradition as a whole has never sought to make such a claim, because such a view is inappropriate and unworthy of the dynamism of the biblical faith. Thus we are under no obligation, as are those who hold such views, to explain away the obvious evidences of growth through human experience in the Scriptures.

While the Bible is the book of God, it is also the book of Israel and the book of the church. It is a living book of human experience born out of a living community. It is saturated with the personalities not only of the men who wrote the individual works it contains, but with the corporate personality of the community of faith from which it comes. The authors and compilers of the Bible clearly understood this when they affixed the names of its authors to its divisions. The Bible may be a writing through which God speaks, but David also speaks through it as does Paul.

Now such a dynamic view of Scripture is in harmony with our understanding of theology as a living product of Christian life and experience, but more important, it prepares us to recognize without fear two facts about the Bible which more rigid views may obscure or even drive us to deny. First is the rich diversity

of the biblical writings. These texts tell us of God
but they also tell us of the people. Now, we don't
mean merely literary variety (poetry, prophecy, etc.)
or cultural variety (Egyptian customs, Greek customs,
etc.). It is also clear that we have *theological*
variety in the Scriptures, as each prophet or apostolic
writer bears witness to his faith in God and his knowledge of God in terms of his own experience and understanding. In other words, we have the "personal theology" of Amos, Jeremiah, Isaiah, Luke, John and many
others in Scripture. And once we have recognized the
living character of the Bible, we are no longer under
any compulsion to deny this variety. We can accept it
joyfully and see how it enriches our total picture of
Christ and of God as revealed in Scripture.

Now if it is objected that theological variety
destroys the unity of the Scriptures, we must ask,
"Does the variety of personal faith within a church
destroy its unity?" Not so long as there is a common
experience of God and a common sense of forgiveness.
This is the cement of the fellowship which encourages
and makes possible personal uniqueness and honest
expression. There is abundant evidence that in ancient
Israel and in the Apostolic church there were differences and even disagreements, but all such were within
the common life of the Spirit. Why should we not expect the writings which record their experience with
God to reflect this difference in unity which marked
the believing community?

The second fact which we are now ready to recognize is that of development. The Scriptures reflect
the growing experience of men with God. Therefore we
can expect their own slow maturing in faith to be
evidenced. And this is so. The Christian is already
prepared for the fact of development by his belief that
the Old Testament, though truly from God, is neither
so clear, complete or adequate as the New Testament.
Thus we have usually agreed there is growth of understanding from the Old Covenant to New. This is what
we mean when we accept the Old Testament as truly
Scripture but interpret it in the light of the New
Testament and of Christ. Thus we give tacit consent
to a difference in authority or adequacy between the
testaments. We need now to recognize different degrees
of adequacy and fullness of understanding *within* the
testaments. We would have no trouble recognizing
this fact were it not for the idea of "equal inspiration" often associated with some of the more rigid
views of the Scripture. This doctrine maintains that

all parts of Scripture are equally inspired and authoritative for faith. But such views, far from helping
to strengthen the authority of Scripture, have eroded
it away by calling on people to accept as equally binding differing and sometimes deeply troubling passages.

For example, my Christian students who have learned
to see God through the eyes of Isaiah and Jesus Christ
have a great moral difficulty with Joshua's tactics at
Jericho and Ai. How can one who takes Christ seriously
believe that the slaughter of the Jericho children
really pleased God? If Jesus says the Kingdom is of
little children and Joshua has them slain in the name
of God, how can we hold these to be equally authoritative? The subterfuges we create to avoid the problem
(for example, the analogy of "radical surgery") don't
really solve it, but usually leave us with the guilty
feeling that we have evaded the issue. But can we not
agree that Joshua, a most sincere and devout man, led
Israel at a time when she had not yet reached the
mature understanding implied by her calling? Surely
God had made himself known at Sinai as the God of
creation and therefore of all men (even Canaanites),
but it was a long time before the full implications of
his calling and of his character would become clear.
It is a long way from the first Joshua to the last.
(Joshua and Jesus both mean "Savior.") We can recognize that God used Joshua's imperfect leadership to
move Israel toward his future redemptive purpose, but
we need not insist that everything Joshua thought or
did represents the perfect truth or will of God. And
the examples could be multiplied endlessly. Is Abraham's example of faith equally a guide for Christian
conscience when he "believes God" and when he indulges
in multiple wives?

Since the New Testament was written in the full
light of the cross and the resurrection, we will not
find there such great differences of outlook. Nevertheless, the early Christians also had to pioneer in
faith. They had to take the realities of Easter and
Pentecost and work out their meaning for the church.
Again the results show a growing understanding from the
first halting efforts in Acts to the mature theologies
of Paul, Luke, and John. And again this growth points
us to the living nature of the New Testament and of
the community which created it.

3. *We must recognize the Bible to be a human document.*

What we have been saying points inescapably to a

conclusion. The Bible is a *human* book. Now, I am
not saying that it is nothing *more* than a human
book, or that its religious value and authority is no
more for Christians than other books of devotion or
religion. Nor am I saying that it is not the unique
and decisive book of divine revelation. But I am
urging that we cannot understand its divine character
until we accept the very real human element through
which God has chosen to speak. Our proper concern
for the dignity and authority of Scripture has sometimes led us into a position regarding Scripture which
is not only not true to the facts, but comes close to
a kind of biblical docetism.

Docetism was an early doctrine or understanding
of Christ which so emphasized Christ's deity that it
denied his true humanity and so denied the incarnation.
It felt that to admit that Christ was truly human was
to corrupt his purity and lessen his authority. Thus
he was said to be a divine figure, a "theophany" which
didn't really become flesh, hunger, suffer or die, but
only seemed (*doceo*, "to seem") or pretended to do so.
But the church wisely saw that in the interest of
Christ's authority the docetists had deprived man of a
Savior who was really like man and therefore could be
his high priest and representative. They also saw
that such a view made nonsense of the obvious humanity
of Jesus in the New Testament, as manifested, for
example, in the wilderness temptation, in Gethsemane,
and on the cross. Therefore docetism was rejected by
the church as a heresy, although it still persists in
much popular Christology.

Now, much thought about the Scriptures borders on
a kind of biblical docetism because with the good
intention of preserving its dignity and authority it
strips the Bible of the human dimension which is so
necessarily a part of its witness and so obviously a
fact. By denying the real human element of Scripture
we do it no service, and we deny what each of us
knows from his own Christian experience, namely, that
God always works through human agency. Thus to paraphrase Paul Tillich, when one asks of us, "Do you
think the Bible is merely a human book?" we need to
learn to answer, "Not *less* than a human book! Tho'
for those who answer to the name of Christian, it is
immeasurably more!"

What do we mean, "inspired"?

The description of the Bible as a growing, human

creation of the worshiping community raises a series
of important questions, most of which are related to
a doctrine commonly held by Christians and more or less
formally sanctioned by most historical communions.
This is the doctrine of inspiration. Christians are
accustomed to speaking of the Bible as divinely inspired,
and when they do so they are trying to say that it has
final authority or at least special authority for
faith. But if the Scripture is human, what does it
mean to say it is "inspired"?

   To begin with we need to remind ourselves that the
concept of inspiration is only marginally a biblical
concept. This of course does not disqualify it, for
the church has learned to use many nonbiblical terms
to clarify the meaning of its faith. It does, however,
require that we examine its meaning and ask how it came
to be used by the church. The English word *inspiration*
translates the Greek *theopneustos* meaning "God-breathed."
Our word *inspire* and its several cognates carry the
same suggestion. One who inspires breathes in. One
who expires breathes out, for the last time, presumably.
The basic idea then in inspiration is that God has
breathed through or in the Scripture. In both Hebrew
and Greek, the idea of breath was closely associated
with that of life. Thus *pneuma*, "breath," is also
the word used for spirit, the vivifying part of the
body, without which it would be only a corpse. Inspiration was therefore originally a "living" idea,
suggesting that the presence of God as Spirit in
Scripture gave these writings a living vitality.

   Accordingly, whatever meaning we give to inspiration must preserve this understanding. The Scriptures
are inspired insofar as God lives and breathes within
them and through them. On the other hand, the word
becomes of doubtful value when it loses this living
character and is intended to suggest some "quality"
which the books possess quite apart from their power
to communicate the living presence of God. And it is
cheapened almost beyond recall when inspiration becomes
a kind of special ingredient in the Bible which other
books don't possess, something equivalent to "Ingredient X" or "Fluoristan" which gives our book the edge
over others. Such a view puts us in the unenviable
position of having to defend the existence of this
"Ingredient X" without very good evidences. Usually
we fall back on some theory of infallibility and this
leads us into a meaningless series of "games," by
which we seek to "prove" inspiration by appeal to fulfilled prophecies, miracles or the like. But the usual

result is that *no one is convinced by these arguments except those who already believe.*

It is a significant fact that there was almost no interest in a doctrine of inspiration in the Apostolic church. This is because when one is aware of the power of the Spirit he doesn't worry about the authority of the Word. The living presence of God in church and Scripture argued for itself. The idea of inspiration appears to have grown up in the church for two reasons, one healthy and one less so:

1. *It arose an an "explanatory" doctrine.* That is, it was the church's attempt to express and explain the living power of these writings which spoke to them the Word of God and called them to repentance. Notice then that they did not hang the authority of the Scripture on the doctrine of inspiration, as is so often the case today. The argument was not thus, "The Scriptures are inspired; therefore they must have authority for us and we must believe them," but rather, "The Scriptures have authority for us because they speak to us the truth of God! We cannot deny them! They must be inspired!" The order is critical. Inspiration is not the starting point of the Bible's authority. It is a conclusion based on and drawn from that authority. This is the healthy source of the idea of inspiration.

2. *It became a defensive doctrine.* In the centuries following the apostolic age the immediate sense of the power of God in the church began to cool for many reasons. Other interpretations of Christ began to arise to challenge the mainline doctrine of the emerging church. How does one answer or refute such critics? One answer was to develop a "polemic" doctrine of inspiration, the purpose of which was to stop the mouth of dissenters by appeal to an infallible book of doctrine. But whenever it becomes necessary to bulwark the Bible by such a rigid concept of inspiration, we are confessing that the actual power of the Scriptures has subsided and that it cannot convince by its own impact. And when this has become the case, it is doubtful that any efforts of ours to shore it up by inspiration will suffice.

Thus inspiration must remain always an explanatory doctrine, and refer to the fact that God *speaks to us* in living power through this book. It is a way of saying that we confront God in his Spirit in its pages. This means, of course, that we cannot really talk of "God's speaking" if we do not also talk of our hearing and responding. We speak of the Bible as the Word of God, but Word, like inspiration, is a living concept. And there is no Word, no speaking unless there is also hearing.

I am sometimes asked if the Bible is the Word of God for a person if he does not hear, if it does not move him to repentance. Now I suppose there is a manner of speaking in which one can answer, "Yes, it is still the Word of God," but I confess that I cannot see what religious value there is to say so, if it does not communicate to someone his word of acceptance and love. For the Word of God to be the Word of God *for me*, there must be appropriation. This is why the church has usually spoken not only of inspiration but also of illumination. When God speaks (what we might call "giving grace") he also quickens the heart to hear by the Spirit ("receiving grace"). In the final analysis then, the Bible is inspired if it "speaks" to you. If it does not, then its inspiration is an academic matter at best.

What I have said raises another question. Is it proper to call the Bible the "Word of God"? Again, there is a certain sense in which it is correct to speak of it so, as I have done above. But there is a need for caution at this point, because the expression "Word of God" has a more specific and also a wider meaning than the Bible. In the broadest sense, any speaking of God to us (through preaching, through doctrine, or directly to the heart of the believer) can be called the Word of God. Thus we must not be so arbitrary as to demand of God that he *never* speak anywhere except in Scripture, even though our experience is that he does most frequently speak through this medium. So the Word of God can be understood in a wider sense than Scripture. But it also has a narrower meaning than Scripture. Indeed, the expression "the Word of God," *ho logos tou theou*, in the New Testament normally refers not to the Bible at all but to the one who is himself the ultimate revelation and living "Word" of God. "In the beginning was the Word . . . and the Word was God . . . and the Word became flesh and dwelt among us." The Bible can be called God's Word insofar as it bears witness to him who *was* God's Word, God's self-communication, and we must not let ourselves forget this primacy of Jesus Christ himself.

I am afraid that in many evangelical circles the

the Word of God has come to mean exclusively the Bible, and if this is so we are in danger of making an idol of the Scriptures themselves. A few years ago I was directing a choir in the singing of the hymn "Break Thou the Break of Life." I asked the choir what the phrase "bread of life" meant, and a member answered, "The nourishing Word of God." So far so good! So I asked, "What is this Word of God the song speaks of?" She answered, "Why, the Bible, of course." So I read the words of the hymn with proper emphasis, and she could make nothing of them:

> Beyond the sacred page, I seek thee, Lord!
> My spirit pants for thee, O living Word.

Two questions remain to be answered, one briefly, the other demanding a more thorough answer:

Is the Bible Theology?

Insofar as the Bible contains the reflection of believers and of the church on its faith it contains theology and in some degree is theology. Since the theology it contains is that of those who knew the Savior and his redemptive work firsthand and participated in the birth of the community of faith, it remains a uniquely rich and irreplaceable source for our theology. But not even the theology of the Apostolic church can be allowed to take the place of a personal theology.

Are We Bound by the Bible?

We have said that one's own theology is born out of dialogue, and that three members of the dialogue, Bible, church and believer, are central. Therefore to the question, "Are we bound by the authority of the Bible?" we must give a two-fold reply. We must first answer yes. If our theology is to be Christian theology, it cannot escape the Bible. There are at least four reasons why this is so:

(1) It is the only source of information concerning Jesus Christ, who is the focal point of every properly Christian theology. (2) It is the original witness and confession to Christ. We can never come nearer, historically speaking, to the redemptive event than we do in the Apostolic church. The persistent desire of the church to return to the New Testament and to the faith of the Apostolic church is an expression of this conviction. (3) It has continued to

create the church. While it is true that the church
created the Scriptures, it is equally true that the
church through the centuries has found a power for
correction and for renewal in the Scriptures. Scripture re-creates church! The church has returned again
and again to the prophets and apostles for its own
dynamic and life. (4) It has forced itself upon us!
In the final analysis, the only answer the church can
give to the question, "Why this book and not another?"
is Karl Barth's answer. We haven't had a choice!
Other books have been helpful, but this one has *seized*
us, required us to hear, and refused to let us go! It
has been "inspired," breathed with the power and word
of God. Finally no other answer than this can be given
to the question, "Why the Bible?" And the church can
scarcely anticipate a time when it will be otherwise.
We are bound to its word. We cannot do theology without it.

But to the question, "Are we bound by the Bible?"
we must also answer no, for within the dialogue of
faith are other sources of insight which we must hear.
Our theology is not exclusively biblical theology,
even if we formally hold to an exclusive biblical
authority, because we continually measure, test and
select from biblical insights in the light of the
belief of the church and in the light of our own experience. Now once again, I am not saying that we *should*,
but that we *do*. We are continually selecting from the
vast reservoir of religion which is the Bible those
passages which are most able to express our understanding of faith. The process of selection is often subtle, so that we may not even notice that in returning
frequently to a few passages we exclude others, but
the selectivity is no less real. Ministers habitually
preach from texts which speak to them and just as
habitually avoid other passages, because for various
reasons these passages do not say what they wish to
say. What pastor preaches on Obadiah with his little
"hymn of hate" to Edom as often as he does the thir-
teenth chapter of 1 Corinthians? And is this not so
because the history of the church and the experience
of the Christian heart see love as the center of faith
and feel uncomfortable with hate? To select is to
exercise judgment in the name of some critical principle which itself is not properly scriptural.

But not only do we select, we interpret! And
every interpretation of the Bible is in some sense an
attempt to explain difficult and unclear passages on
the basis of some more certain principle, usually

theological. In my own tradition it is often asserted that we do not interpret the Bible by tradition or by personal standards but by the Bible itself. Scripture interprets Scripture. This is a Reformation principle but it is far older than Luther. What this means, though, is that we interpret the uncertain and unclear passages by the clear and explicit ones. But what determines which passages are clear and decisive? Usually our tradition.

For example, on the surface there appears to be a real theological tension between the doctrine of salvation expressed in Ephesians and in James. Paul says, "By grace are ye saved through faith . . . not of works, lest any man should boast." James says, "Faith without works is dead." Interpreters in the Baptist fellowship always opt for Paul, explaining that James really isn't saying what he appears to say, namely, that one's works are a factor in his salvation. But James really seems rather explicit. How can we say he means something else? Why, because the New Testament clearly rejects works salvation! But is this really so? There are numerous passages, including the words of Jesus himself, which could be understood to teach works righteousness. Why not say these are the clear teachings of the New Testament? Isn't the real reason the fact that we are in the tradition of the Reformers whose fundamental principle of justification by faith alone has determined our own understanding of salvation? Thus we choose Paul not because his meaning is clearly the meaning of the New Testament but because his understanding agrees with *our* understanding, and we reject James (or reinterpret him) because he seems to stand in another tradition.

We may also interpret, translate, evaluate the Bible in the light of our Christian conscience. Thus we may reject a seemingly clear intention because it seems unworthy of God or of one of his people. Thus when the Book of Exodus or Paul speaks of God hardening Pharaoh's heart, we may reject this by saying that what they mean is that Pharaoh hardened his own heart. Or when Jesus curses a fig tree, apparently, according to the text, because he was hungry and it had no fruit, we hasten to say that wasn't the *real* reason, and explain that the withering was an acted parable of Israel's rejection. Why so? It nowhere says this. But surely, it must be so, because Jesus wasn't the kind who went around spitefully withering trees! Agreed! But isn't it our conviction of what Christ was like born out of Bible and tradition and personal experience of his

42

love which leads us to reject what *appears* to be unworthy of him?

I have labored this point because it may be a
critical one for those in the most strongly biblical
tradition. For such a person it will be easy to see
and admit that we qualify the other members of the
dialogue by Scripture, but not so easy to see that
every attempt to evaluate or to interpret represents
a qualification of the scriptural witness. No Christian, no matter how literalistic he claims to be, can
avoid doing this. And we must understand that *in so
doing we do not weaken the witness of our theology but
strengthen it*. We are right to determine what Scripture can mean in the light of faith. We are right to
call the withered fig tree an "acted parable," because this makes sense in the light of what we have
come to know of Christ in Scripture, in the church,
and in our personal forgiveness.

Thus we are bound to Scripture as one of the
indispensable members of the dialogue of faith, but it
is also a part of the larger dialogue, which includes
both church and personal experience.

Discussion Questions

1. What doctrinal examples can you give to support
Christian's position that theology cannot be merely a
synopsis of the contents of scripture?

2. What biblical illustrations could you give which
reflect a variety of theological perspectives?

3. Discuss the implications of Christian's position
that the origin of scripture is in the process of
tradition. Or, to put it more clearly, that the
church created the Bible.

4. It is sometimes held that the problem of interpreting the scripture may be resolved by allowing
scripture to interpret scripture. The Reformation
principle was that clearer passages should be used to
illumine the less obvious. But how do we determine
which are the clearer passsges? What role is played
by the theological presuppositions we have derived

from our church or denomination when we approach the text and call certain passages "clear"?

5. Offer well-thought-out responses to the following:

    a.   "If you cannot trust the Bible on everything, you cannot trust it on anything."

    b.   "The Bible is the Word of God whether we believe it or not."

EMPIRICAL FOUNDATIONS FOR THEOLOGY

Much that is said in this essay depends on the acceptability of the model of dimensions as a way of viewing experience. Traditionally, experience was understood as a series of hierarchially arranged isolated realms. The realms were regarded as the physical, emotional and spiritual. Other interpretations were that the realms of experience were simply best understood as the natural and supernatural.

Gill regards realmism as a serious theological and philosophical handicap. Many other theologians agree with him. They hold that the notion of realms makes it possible to separate the sacred and the secular. If evidence for sacred beings or realities is lacking; or, if persons cease having encounters of sacred significance, then perhaps that realm does not exist. Thus one is left only with the secular. Some theologians argue that the Death of God movement followed this line of reasoning.

At the same time, some thinkers retain the notion. In his essay in this collection, C. S. Lewis depends heavily on the notion of realms to explain his understanding of miracles. Different realms may have extremely variant categories of time, location, and causality--if these categories are meaningful at all in some other realm. If they do have such different categories, Lewis holds that their intersection of our realm might produce extraordinary things which we call miracles.

But Gill believes that the dangers in realmism are too great for theologians to accept it as a viable model. He thinks that it is the separation of experience into realms which is partly responsible for the prevalent humanism of contemporary culture. More

importantly, however, Gill simply believes that realmism is inaccurate. It is wrong in its description of
how experience occurs. His recommendation is for a
change in models. Experience is best understood, Gill
holds, as a nexus of interpenetrating dimensions.

One may conceive of a machine which does not become itself except as all of its gears mesh. It is
the symbiosis created by the meshing process that
gives the machine its definition. So it is for experience. Experience is a series of interlocking, interpenetrating, non-isolated dimensions. Or, to use
another example, all of our experienced reality includes smell, hearing, touch, sight, taste. These are
experienced simultaneously. One may not be aware of
these sensations individually, unless he focuses on
them. Nevertheless, they constitute experienced
reality. Experience comes as a whole, not in discrete parts.

The point Gill wishes to make to secular man is
that one dimension of experience is sacred or religious. Secular man's problem, Gill holds, is one of
discernment. The religious dimension is as surely
in his experience as smell is in yours as you read
this line. However, you may not attend to smell
while reading, and thus you may not be aware that it
is part of the whole that you are experiencing.

According to Gill, religious persons are those
who have had disclosure experiences which have caused
them to attend to the religious dimension of reality.
Disclosure experience is a notion Gill borrows from
Ian Ramsey. To illustrate what is meant by this idea
Gill uses Ramsey's example of a figure made of twelve
straight lines which at first sight appears to be
no more than two squares joined at the corners. However, when "depth" is disclosed to the observer he
recognizes the figure as a cube.

The implications that such a perspective can
have for theology are many. Theological language
and symbols may be regarded as a way of adding disclosure to experience. Worship rituals may be regarded as acted behaviors designed to open the worshipper to new dimensions of experience.

Gill believes that this approach can establish
the meaningfulness of theological language. Such
language symbolizes the religious dimension universally present in experience. The religious dimension

universally present in experience. The religious
dimension is known only tacitly until it is brought
into awareness by language (or, I may add, ritual).
Gill suggests how Biblical language reflects the
experience of the writers with disclosure situations
of a special nature such as the Exodus, Jesus' resurrection or Pentecost. The statement "Jesus was the
Son of God" is symbolic because "son" is not being
used in the same way as when I say, "Jeff is the son
of Ronnie." It may also be symbolic because "God" may
not be performing the same task, or standing for a
reality in the same way that "Ronnie" is, but that is
a question reserved for the chapters to follow. For
Gill, "Jesus was the Son of God" is a symbol for the
experienced dimensional reality opened up to those
who witnessed Jesus' words and deeds. Thus, according
to Gill, what theologians call revelation occurs
through the medium of ordinary experience and also
special situations.

Secularity is essentially a truncated view of
experience. It leaves dimensions of experience unex-
plicated, or else uses languages and symbols not
suited to the task. The task of a theologian, according to Gill, is to reveal the dimension of the religious in ordinary experience and to show that it is
best explicated by theological language. Only by
adopting this approach can theological language and
witness be restored to meaning in a secular age.

EMPIRICAL FOUNDATIONS FOR THEOLOGY*

The Religious Dimension

In Chapter Five a case was argued for attempting
to understand experience in terms of the model of

*Source: From *The Possibility of Religious Knowl-
edge*, copyright 1971, by Jerry H. Gill, used by permis-

simultaneously interpenetrating dimensions. This model was offered as a replacement for the traditional model of a hierarchy of isolated realms. The difference between these two ways of viewing experience and reality is especially crucial with respect to the question of revelation. The more traditional realm-model forces one to conceive of revelation as something which comes from a realm which is totally distinct from, and in some sense foreign to, our own world. Thus when the question of identifying revelation arises, the religious person is forced either to maintain the necessity and reality of miraculous events and/or infallible communications (since these alone can serve as marks of the divine realm), or to give up the claim that revelation takes place. In the latter case religion becomes identified with humanism, while in the former it becomes identified with the bizarre. The realm-model offers little if any place to stand between these two alternatives.

The dimension-model, on the other hand, makes it possible to conceive of revelation as the mediation of the religious dimension through the other dimensions of experience. Moreover, this way of viewing experience is more in line with the way the various aspects of reality are, in fact, experienced. The physical, moral, personal, and religious aspects of life are not experienced as separate blocks or compartments, but as vitally interrelated areas of concern and focus. Thus to conceive of experience as dimensional in structure is in harmony both with cognitive experience and with the possibility of a more adequate conception of revelation. This would indicate that the first step toward understanding religion and theology is to think of man as existing within a multi-dimensional universe where knowledge of the various dimensions, especially the religious dimension, is mediated through the others.

To my mind the thinker who has developed this dimensional view of religious experience most fruitfully is John Hick. A presentation of his thought on this subject should clarify my own view. Hick addresses himself to the question of how religious knowledge is possible by maintaining

sion of the publisher, William B. Eerdmans Publishing Company.

. . . that "mediated" knowledge, such as is postulated by this religious claim, is already a common and accepted feature of our cognitive experience. To this end we must study a basic characteristic of human experience, which I shall call
"significance," together with the correlative
mental activity by which it is apprehended, which
I shall call "interpretation." We shall find that
interpretation takes place in relation to each of
the three main types of existence, or orders of
significance, recognized by human thought--the
natural, the human, and the divine; and that in
order to relate ourselves appropriately to each,
a primary and unevidenceable act of interpretation
is required which, when directed toward God, has
traditionally been termed "faith." Thus . . .
while the object of religious knowledge is unique,
its basic epistemological pattern is that of all
our knowing.[1]

Hick uses the term "significance" to refer to
that which gives order, or intelligibility, to the
whole of experience. It involves the ability to differentiate between, and gather together, the various
particulars of experience. Indeed, it might be defined as the very capacity to have what we call human
experience. Hick seems to be saying that this "significance" is objective in that it is "built in" to
the very structure of experience. Another way to
characterize it is to call it that quality which
enables the various aspects of experience to be
brought into focus, reorganized, compared, and contrasted.

The concept of "interpretation" is introduced by
Hick to specify the subjective correlate of significance. It represents the activity, or response, of
the mind in perceiving, or becoming aware of, significance in experience. On the object level, for instance, one becomes aware that the sense datum of his
present experience can be interpreted, or responded
to, in a variety of ways--as, for example, a red patch,
a red thing, and a red book. Interpretations of significance in the various aspects of experience can
occur on increasingly inclusive levels, depending on
the extent and nature of one's past experience. Thus,
to use Hick's example, a piece of paper with writing
on it will be one thing to an illiterate savage, quite
another to a literate person who does not know that
particular language, and still another to someone who
does know the language. In each case the person

involved can be said to perceive both what the previous person does and something more as well.

Hick goes on to suggest that this pattern of significance-interpretation works itself out on three levels of human experience, namely the object level, the personal (or moral) level, and the religious level. The significance of personal experience is mediated through, but is not reducible to, object-significance. In like manner, the significance of religious experience is mediated through, but is not reducible to, object and personal experience.

Even on the physical (object) level of experience an act of interpretation is needed before any significance can be apperceived. Until some active, organizing response is made, one does not have "experience" at all, only a "booming, buzzing confusion." Logically speaking, even a solipsistic interpretation of experience as a dream is a live option, and is by nature an interpretive act. Thus our disposition to interpret the sense-data of our experience in terms of the point of view of realism is pragmatically, but not logically, necessary. In a word, it is part of our form of life.

The apperception of significance on the moral level of experience is very similar to that on the physical level. A sense of moral obligation is the result of an interpretive response to an awareness of the significance of personal experience. It is, of course, possible to be unaware of, or to refuse to respond to, the significance of personal experience, and thereby fail to sense moral obligation. Such a situation is, in reality, simply giving another interpretation to personal experience. The difference between the interpretive apperception of physical and moral significance is this: It is less difficult to refuse to interpret personal experience as having moral significance than it is to refuse to interpret sensory experience as having physical (or real) significance. Nonetheless, for most human beings, moral interpretation is also part of the human form of life.

Hick is especially interested in the relation of mediation existing between the physical and moral levels of significance. He maintains that moral significance is mediated through physical experience in such a way as to be dependent on it, but not reducible to it. Moral obligation is sensed *in* the experience of physical situations, but is clearly more than an objective description of such situations would indicate.

50

It is important to note this, since the same relation
is held to exist between the apprehension of religious
significance and moral and physical experience. Hick
argues:

Has this epistemological paradigm--of one order
of significance superimposed upon and mediated
through another--any further application? The
contention of this essay is that it has. As
ethical significance interpenetrates natural
significance, so religious significance interpenetrates both ethical and natural. The divine
is the highest and ultimate order of significance,
mediating neither of the others and yet being
mediated through both of them.

Thus the primary religious perception, or
basic act of religious interpretation, is not to
be described as either a reasoned conclusion or
an unreasoned hunch that there is a God. It is,
putatively, an apprehension of the divine presence
within the believer's human experience. It is
not an inference to a general truth, but a
"divine-human encounter," a mediated meeting
with the living God.[2]

Such an apprehension of mediated, divine presence
results in a total interpretation of all of human
experience in terms of the religious dimension. This
interpretation is not based on some knowledge of
"outside reality," but is rather a perspective which
a religious person takes toward the totality of his
experience.

To the crucial question "What induces a man to
experience the world religiously?", Hick says:

The general nature of the answer is I think clear
enough. Religious interpretations of human
experience arise from special key points within
that experience which act as focuses of religious
significance. These key-points both set going
the tendency of the mind to interpret religiously
and also act as patterns guiding the forms which
such interpretations take. Among the infinite
variety of life's phenomena some moment or object
or person stands out as uniquely significant and
revealing, providing a clue to the character of
the whole. Some item of experience, or group of
items, impresses the mind so deeply as to operate
as a spiritual catalyst, crystallizing what was

hitherto a cloud of relatively vague, amorphous
feelings and aspirations, and giving a new and
distinctive structure to the "apperceiving mass"
by which we interpret our stream of experience.

In Christianity the catalyst of faith is the
person of Jesus Christ. It is in the historical
figure of Jesus the Christ that, according to the
Christian claim, God has in a unique and final way
disclosed himself to men.[3]

In this way the historical personality of Jesus
Christ serves as the key point in experience for
interpreting religious significance in terms of Christian theism. It is through the personality and activity of Jesus Christ that religious significance is
uniquely mediated to Christians. There are, of course,
other catalysts which serve a similar purpose in other
religious traditions.

Given this understanding of the relationship
between the religious dimension and the other dimensions, it is both possible and helpful to conclude
that revelation is mediated in structure. That is to
say, rather than being a communication from another
realm (as with Barthianism) or an encounter which
transcends the other dimensions of life (as with
Bultmannianism), revelation is best viewed as an
awareness of another dimension of reality being
mediated through the more familiar dimensions. Thus
in and through his everyday experience the religious
person becomes aware of the activity of another, in
many ways more essential, dimension to which he responds with his total being.

Religious Knowledge as Awareness
and Response

With the dimensional and mediational structure of
religious experience firmly established, it is now
necessary to discuss its two-fold contextual nature
in terms of awareness and response. The basic thrust
of the claim to religious knowledge is that the person
involved discerns (by means and in the midst of his
everyday experience in the physical and moral dimensions of life) yet another dimension of reality which
enriches his understanding of the more common dimensions. The discernment which takes place in such a
disclosure especially enhances the person's moral
sensitivity and his own self-understanding. In

response to this disclosure-discernment situation, which corresponds to the "awareness continuum" in connection with Polanyi's thought, the person's life becomes characterized by a profound sense of commitment which penetrates every aspect of his behavioral and conceptual existence.

In his *Religious Language*, Ramsey develops examples of disclosures which take place within perceptual, especially visual, experience. Here he draws heavily upon the work of Gestalt psychology.

> Let us recall how there could be drawn twelve straight lines which at first sight might look no more than two squares with corners joined. But then there dawns on us "depth," and we see the twelve straight lines as a "unity." The lines indeed represent a cube and this cube may, as is well known, seem to enter into or stand out of the surface on which the lines are drawn. Here again is a characteristically different situation which dawns on us at some recognizable point. This is the point where twelve straight lines cease to be merely twelve straight lines, when a characteristically-different situation is evoked which needs odd words like "depth" and "unity," or mathematically the idea of a "new dimension," "volume" besides "area."[4]

In other contexts, Ramsey mentions the recognition of an old friend, the rearrangement of pieces in a puzzle, and the way in which a series of polygons of an increasing number of sides may suggest a circle, as examples of perceptual situations that give rise to a disclosure which involves a dimension other than the sum of the particulars.

Moving on to examples of disclosure which are humanistically more significant, it is important to examine what may be called moral discernment. Ramsey uses such examples because he is convinced that the most significant disclosures religiously are those which center in personal and inter-personal relationships. In a review of a lecture on "Reason and Experience in Ethics," he takes a definite stand against the tendency in contemporary ethics to segregate ethical discourse from other uses of language as *sui generis*. He maintains that moral judgments must be based in, and thus are closely related to, the judgments of psychology and sociology. It is impossible for ethical discourse to take place in a vacuum.

Nevertheless, ethical judgments cannot be reduced to factual judgments. This dilemma, which forms the very heart of contemporary ethical debate, can be overcome only by acknowledging that ethical judgments result from disclosures which go beyond, but are not independent of, the factual elements of a given situation. When a duty is discerned, or an ethical judgment is made, a disclosure has been mediated by the spatio-temporal facts; a disclosure which, although common in everyday experience, is not exhaustible in terms of straightforward, descriptive language.

Ramsey offers as an example of a disclosure situation the sense of moral obligation a bystander experiences when a child is drowning.[5] A purely physical description of the situation does not exhaust the sense of duty. In fact, it would always be possible to say, "Well, there goes another blob of protoplasm." Nevertheless, it is just as true that the sense of duty does not occur apart from a cognition of the facts.

Similarly, our knowledge of other persons, *qua* persons, involves a disclosure which arises out of, but cannot be equated with, our knowledge and talk of their behavior.

Perhaps the most illuminating illustration Ramsey gives of the type of disclosure involved in knowing other persons is an imaginary conversation between Robin Hood and the Tinker who was out to arrest him.

The Tinker unexpectedly meets Robin Hood and the conversation proceeds like this:

Q. Do you know Robin Hood?
A. Oh, very well indeed, I have the closest knowledge of him.
Q. Where is he now, I wonder?
A. I am sure he cannot be very far away.
Q. Is he strong?
A. Fairly so. He had a successful bout with a very skilled wrestler the other day.
Q. How tall is he?
A. Just about my height.
Q. Colour of hair?
A. Brown.
Q. Is he clever?
A. He has misled a lot of folk.

Now supposing Robin Hood had concluded such question-and-answering like this: "And I'm the man." What would be added by this claim that "It is I"? There are two possible answers. Some might say, as I have admitted, that "I" is purely indicative. It just says: What you see now, this body, this chap talking with you, is of a part with all we have been describing. Nor can this be denied. The leading question is: Is that all? For another answer is possible. When Robin makes his confession, there might be a disclosure. The sequence to date, plus the pattern before the Tinker, then becomes part of a disclosure situation where the Tinker discerns around "Robin Hood" an objective challenge.[6]

Here again one can see the basic disclosure-pattern involved in personal knowledge. Clearly, the facts which are freely given by Robin while incognito are of real importance for a knowledge of Robin Hood. Nonetheless, they are given a new "depth" when experientially related to the one additional statement, "It is I!" In Ramsey's oft-used phrase, "the light dawns, the penny drops," and a whole new perspective is revealed. This type of situation takes place quite frequently within the framework of intimate friendships as well. Our knowledge of close friends and loved ones is related to, but is more than the sum of, our observations of their behavior. In fact, it is often the case that our knowledge of them as persons makes it possible for us to observe and understand certain aspects of their behavior more adequately.

Having laid the groundwork for understanding the concept of disclosure by means of the foregoing examples, it is time to consider the concept of religious disclosure proper. Ramsey often uses the term "cosmic disclosure" in his discussion of this sort of experience. It is absolutely essential to be perfectly clear at the outset about the one most important characteristic of religious, or cosmic, disclosure. Even as the disclosures discussed above are always mediated through empirical situations, religious disclosures are always so mediated as well. Moreover, and this is equally as important, one must view religious disclosures as mediated through the above-mentioned disclosures themselves! That is to say, disclosures of what may be called "the divine dimension" do not occur in an experiential vacuum, but rather arise out of perceptual, conceptual, moral, and personal disclosures, which in turn arise out of empirical settings.

It is in this way, then, that one best understands what has been traditionally classified as religious experience. When one speaks of experiencing God, he is calling attention to a discernment in which there has been disclosed to him a cosmic dimension of reality by means of the more common disclosures arising out of experiential situations. A person's awareness of God is similar to his awareness of objects (as opposed to "sense data"), moral obligation, and persons (including himself). All of this, of course, is not to say that the claimed awareness of God is as common as these other awarenesses, nor that it is necessarily a veridical experience.

Although this is not the place to delve into a consideration of theology proper, a word should be said about the distinction most religious people draw between their awareness of the religious dimension and their relation to a divine being. Becoming aware of the religious dimension is not to be equated with becoming aware of God. Perhaps the crux of the distinction is that it is within his awareness of the former that the theist discerns an aspect or focal point to which only the concept of a personal being can come close to doing justice. This is especially true in the case of the Christian theist, who finds a corresponding focal point in the person of Jesus. The focal point occurs within the broader awareness of religious awareness.

With respect to the Christian religion, the historical dimension plays an especially important role. The basic characteristic of the Christian concept of revelation is that God reveals himself in the events in the life of the ancient Hebrews, and most fully in the life of Jesus and his church. Here again the concept of cognitive experience as contextual harmonizes fruitfully with the case for the possibility of revelation by means of historic event. Within the contexts provided by the activities of Jesus, both in their original setting and in the biblical record, the Christian becomes aware of a disclosure of the divine dimension to which he responds with total commitment. Thus it is that the historical facts and records are the necessary mediators of religious knowledge. Revelation cannot be equated with them, but it is impossible apart from them as well. In a way, these factors function as catalysts for focusing religious awareness and response.

Although throughout this and previous chapters it
has been necessary to speak of the two interacting
continua of awareness and response singly, it should
be borne in mind that the relationship between them is
not one of sequence. That is, a person does not
usually become aware of a dimension or context and *then*
respond to it. Although this is a convenient way of
speaking, and harmless if not carried too far, the
whole drive of this book has been to establish the
simultaneous interaction between the two continua
within the various contexts and dimensions of existence.
There is a sense in which one does not become aware of
certain realities until he responds in certain ways.
The dynamic and contextual structure of cognitive
experience cannot be subjected to a more thorough
analysis in terms of "the given" and the response.
Awareness and activity occur simultaneously. Together they give rise to knowledge. The intricacies
of the relation between these two aspects of the knowing situation cannot be made explicit. Nevertheless,
they can be known tacitly since they lie at the base
of the very possibility of all other knowledge.

The Confirmation of Religious Knowledge

The truth of a tacit claim to knowledge can be
adjudicated only by tracing the overall harmony and
fruitfulness of the claim as it is embodied in the
behavior and linguistic posits of the person making
the claim.

It is on this basis, then, that the criteria for
judging claims to religious knowledge must be understood. There are, to be sure, certain standard (although not absolute) criteria for judging certain
explicit claims. Historical, sociological, and psychological statements often form part of one's claim to
religious knowledge, and these are to be treated in
the same way as other such statements and claims.
However, as this explicit talk begins to shade off
into more properly theological discourse, the situation
becomes more tricky. Here the explicit and tacit factors become inextricably mixed and must be dealt with
simultaneously. Finally, when the claims to religious
knowledge operate entirely beneath the threshold of
explicit knowledge, then they can be judged only in
terms of activity and styles of life. Nonetheless, it

is possible to evaluate such claims in terms of their overall consistency and fruitfulness.

The approach to the criteria of religious truth which I am here defending is in large measure based upon the insights of Max Black. Black calls attention to the necessity of viewing the "models" upon which theoretical frameworks are built as cognitive in nature. Although more will be said in the next chapter about the model-nature of theological discourse, something needs to be said at this point in order to adequately explain the nature of religious confirmation.

Following Black and others, it must be realized that high-level models in both physical and social science are "analogue models" and not "picture models." By this I mean that such models do not simply represent the parts of a certain aspect of reality, like a model ship or cell. Rather, they integrate and illuminate the functional and structural relationships between the parts and the whole, and between the particular aspect of reality in question and human experience. Thus they are closer to metaphor in nature than they are to exact pictures. The confirmation of this type of model is not based on a one-to-one correspondence between its elements and those of an external reality. The analogue model is confirmed or disconfirmed in terms of its ability to organize, integrate, and illuminate past and present experience, and to predict and suggest new possibilities in future experience. Such confirmation is pragmatic and experiential, but is also extremely complex and flexible. In addition, there will always remain a certain element of mystery and uncertainty. The purpose of making this point is to underline the fact that the theoretical sciences are not as straightforwardly "empirical" as many empiricists maintain.

Like the high-level models of science, the models of theological discourse are also analogical. Moreover, since they are meant to help us map the complex mysteries of personal and ultimate reality, they will of necessity be even more complex and flexible than those of the theoretical sciences. Nevertheless, they are still based upon, and must be confirmed by, human experience. Every model must be scrutinized not in terms of its ability to make strict, deductive predictions about carefully controlled experiments, but in terms of its broad "empirical fit" with the facts of every area of human experience.

In particular, this contextual epistemology, and especially its concept of tacit knowledge, has provided a way of approaching the possibility of religious knowledge in a more fruitful way. In this chapter I have argued on behalf of this possibility by suggesting the following: 1) that religious experience be understood as a mediated awareness of a religious dimension; 2) that revelation be viewed as mediated by means of the other dimensions of experience; 3) that religious knowledge be interpreted as primarily tacit in structure; 4) that religious truth be ascertained as a function of the relation between the claim and the total context in which it is made. An understanding of knowledge as tacit combines the factual and valuational dimensions in such a way as to make the concept of religious knowledge a viable possibility.

Endnotes

[1] *Faith and Knowledge* (Ithaca: Cornell University Press), p. 110.

[2] *Ibid.*, pp. 127, 129.

[3] *Ibid.*, pp. 196-97.

[4] Ian T. Ramsey, *Religious Language* (New York: Macmillan, 1955), pp. 25-26.

[5] *Ibid.*, pp. 17-18.

[6] "On the Possibility and Purpose of a Metaphysical Theology," *Prospect for Metaphysics* (New York: The Philosophical Library, 1961), pp. 169-170.

Discussion Questions

1. Gill speaks of the religious dimension being mediated through experience. Explain the distinction between a mediated experience and an immediate one. What are the strengths and weaknesses of these two methods?

2. What obstacles are posed to theological systems based on realmism? Are there arguments which can be made to justify the choice between realm models and dimensional models or is the decision made on some other basis?

3. Gill says that the religious dimension is not equated with God, nor is its experience the same as encounter with God. If not, how exactly does the identification of a religious dimension help the theologian in his task?

4. If religious encounters are primarily disclosure experiences in which the awareness continuum is enlarged, then how does one judge the truth or relative value of competing religious experiences? Why are Christian ones better than any others, if they are?

PRESUPPOSITIONAL THEOLOGICAL METHOD

Perhaps no two approaches could be any different than those of Gill and Van Til. Like Gill, who believes that theologians must find some common ground with secular men before their theological constructions can be presented as meaningful, Van Til thinks that there is a point of contact with secular man. However, Van Til's approach is quite different than Gill's. The point of contact between secular man and theology according to Van Til is the fact that man is made in the Image of God. The difference between Gill and Van Til is in the way Van Til discovers this point of contact and in the implications of it which he suggests.

To begin with, Gill uses a method of describing experience in order to reveal its multidimensional character. His method is called phenomenological. He thinks that this method avoids debilitating presuppositions to which modern secularists might object. Van Til, however, presupposes the authority of the scripture. The scripture says all men are created in God's image. No empirical method needs to be employed.

The implications of these different starting points are numerous. Whereas Gill thinks that secularity is the product of a limited awareness of experience itself, Van Til believes it results directly from sin. Because man is created in God's image, he knows God exists, his conscience tells him when he is acting immorally and sinfully, and he knows that the Christian revelation is true. The fact is, modern secular persons deny knowing these things because they are depraved. Van Til agrees with John Calvin's position that no sinner reacts properly to God's revelation.

Van Til argues that contemporary theologians should set aside the traditional method, of which Gill is a sophisticated example. Van Til is critical of both inductivist methods such as Gill's, and *a priori* methods. *A priori* methods are those not derived from experience. As Van Til uses the concept an *a priori* method is one which begins with certain agreed upon assumptions, such as the immortality of the soul, the orderliness of the universe, etc.

In place of these methods Van Til commends a presuppositional method which assumes the authority of the scripture. The task of theology then becomes the proclamation of the scriptural revelation. The claims of God, Van Til says, are made upon men without apology. Only by presenting the claims of scripture and allowing the Spirit of God to work can the sense of deity in all men rise in rebellion against man's sin. No deals are to be made with secularists and all of their assumptions are open to question.

PRESUPPOSITIONAL THEOLOGICAL METHOD*

I am, to be sure, opposed to the traditional method of apologetics as this has found its most fundamental expression in the *Summae* of Thomas Aquinas the Roman Catholic and in Bishop Butler the Arminian. I seek to oppose Roman Catholicism and Arminianism in Apologetics as I seek to oppose it in theology.

To begin with then I take what the Bible says about God and his relation to the universe as unquestionably true on its own authority. The Bible requires men to believe that he exists apart from and

*Source: From *The Defense of the Faith*, copyright by Cornelius Van Til, used by permission of the publisher, Presbyterian and Reformed Publishing Company.

above the world and that he by his plan controls whatever takes place in the world. Everything in the created universe therefore displays the fact that it is
controlled by God, that it is what it is by virtue of
the place that it occupies in the plan of God. The
objective evidence for the existence of God and of the
comprehensive governance of the world by God is therefore so plain that he who runs may read. Men cannot
get away from this evidence. They see it round about
them. They see it within them. Their own constitution so clearly evinces the facts of God's creation of
them and control over them that there is no man who
can possibly escape observing it. If he is self-
conscious at all he is also God-conscious. No matter
how men may try they cannot hide from themselves the
fact of their own createdness. Whether men engage in
inductive study with respect to the facts of nature
about them or engage in analysis of their own self-
consciousness they are always face to face with God
their maker.

If there has been any "obscuration" in the
revelation situation on account of sin this sin is in
any case the fault of man. If in Adam, the first man,
who acted for me representatively, I have scratched
the mirror of God's general revelation round about and
within me, I know at bottom that it is I who have
scratched it.

One thing should be particularly stressed in this
connection. It is the fact that man today is sinful
because of what happened at the beginning of history.
"We are told that man could never have had any frui-
tion of God through the revelation that came to him
through nature as operating by itself. There was
superadded to God's revelation in nature another
revelation, a supernaturally communicated positive
revelation. Natural revelation, we are virtually
told, was from the outset incorporated into the idea
of a covenant relationship of God with man. Thus
every dimension of created existence, even the lowest,
was enveloped in a form of exhaustively personal relationship between God and man. The 'ateleological'
not less than the 'teleological,' the 'mechanical' no
less than the 'spiritual,' was covenantal in character"
(*The Infallible Word*, p. 259). Even in paradise,
therefore, supernatural revelation was immediately
conjoined with natural revelation. Revelation in and
about man was therefore never meant to function by
itself. "It was from the beginning insufficient without its supernatural concomitant. It was inherently a

limiting notion" (*Idem*, p. 267).

Having taken these two, revelation in the created universe, both within and about man, and revelation by way of supernatural positive communication as aspects of revelation as originally given to man, we can see that natural revelation is even after the fall perspicuous in character. "The perspicuity of God's revelation in nature depends for its very meaning upon the fact that it is an aspect of the total and totally voluntary revelation of a God who is self-contained" (*Idem*, p. 269). God has an all comprehensive plan for the universe. "He has planned all the relationships between all the aspects of created being. He has planned the end from the beginning. All created reality therefore actually displays this plan. It is, in consequence, inherently rational" (*Idem*, p. 269).

At this point we may add the fact of Scriptural revelation. God has condescended to reveal himself and his plan in it to sinners. It is the same God who speaks of his grace to such as have broken his covenant, to such as have set aside his original revelation to them. And as the original revelation of God to man was clear so is the revelation of grace in Scripture. "The Scriptures as the finished product of God's supernatural and saving revelation to man have their own evidence in themselves" (*Idem*, p. 271).

In all of this there is one thing that stands out. It is that man has no excuse whatsoever for not accepting the revelation of God whether in nature, including man and his surroundings, or in Scripture. God's revelation is always clear.

The first and most basic point on which my approach differs from the traditional one is therefore that: (a) I start more frankly from the Bible as the source from which as an absolutely authoritative revelation I take my whole interpretation of life. Roman Catholicism also appeals to Scripture but in practice makes its authority void. Its final appeal is to the church and that is, in effect, to human experience. Even Arminianism rejects certain Scripture doctrines (e.g., election) because it cannot logically harmonize them with the general offer of salvation. (b) I stress the *objective clarity* of God's revelation of himself wherever it appears. Both Thomas Aquinas and Butler contend that men have done justice by the evidence if they conclude that God *probably* exists. I consider this a compromise of simple and fundamental

Biblical truth. It is an insult to the living God to
say that his revelation of himself so lacks in clarity
that man, himself through and through revelation of
God, does justice by it when he says that God *probably*
exists. "The argument for the existence of God and
for the truth of Christianity is objectively valid.
We should not tone down the validity of this argument
to the probability level. The argument may be poorly
stated, and may never be adequately stated. But in
itself the argument is absolutely sound. Christianity
is the only reasonable position to hold. It is not
merely as reasonable as other positions, or a bit
more reasonable than other positions; it alone is the
natural and reasonable position for man to take. By
stating the argument as clearly as we can, we may be
the agents of the Holy Spirit in pressing the claims
of God upon men. If we drop to the level of the
merely probable truthfulness of Christian theism, we,
to that extent, lower the claims of God upon men"
(*Common Grace*, p. 62). Accordingly I do not reject
"the theistic proofs" but merely insist on formulating
them in such a way as not to compromise the doctrines
of Scripture. "That is to say, if the theistic proof
is constructed as it ought to be constructed, it is
objectively valid, whatever the attitude of those to
whom it comes may be" (*Idem*, p. 49). (c) With Calvin
I find the point of contact for the presentation of
the gospel to non-Christians in the fact that they are
made in the image of God and as such have the ineradi-
cable sense of deity within them. Their own consciousness is inherently and exclusively revelational of God
to themselves. No man can help knowing God for in
knowing himself he knows God. His self-consciousness
is totally devoid of content unless, as Calvin puts it
at the beginning of his Institutes, man knows himself
as a creature before God. There are "no atheistic men
because no man can deny the revelational activity of
the true God within him" (*Common Grace*, p. 55). Man's
own interpretative activity, whether of the more or
less extended type, whether in ratiocination or intu-
ition, is no doubt the most penetrating means by which
the Holy Spirit presses the claims of God upon man"
(*Idem*, p. 62). Even man's negative ethical reaction
to God's revelation within his own psychological constitution is revelational of God. His conscience
troubles him when he disobeys; he knows deep down in
his heart that he is disobeying his creator. There is
no escape from God for any human being. Every human
being is by virtue of his being made in the image of
God accessible to God. And as such he is accessible
to one who without compromise presses upon him the

65

claims of God. Every man has capacity to reason
logically. He can intellectually understand what the
Christian position claims to be. Conjoined with this
is the moral sense that he knows he is doing wrong
when he interprets human experience without reference
to his creator. I am therefore in the fullest agreement with Professor Murray when he speaks of the
natural man as having an *"apprehension of the truth
of the gospel* that is *prior* to faith and repentance."
But I could not thus speak with assurance that the
natural man could have any such apprehension of the
truth of the gospel if I held with the traditional
view of Apologetics that man's self-consciousness is
something that is intelligible without reference to
God-consciousness. If man's self-consciousness did
not actually depend upon his God-consciousness there
would be no meaning to Romans 1:20. Each man would
live in a world by himself. No man could even have
that intellectual cognition of the gospel which is
the prerequisite of saving faith. In short if the
universe were not what the Calvinist, following Paul,
says it is, it would not be a *universe*. There would
be no system of truth. And if the mind of man were
not what Calvin, following Paul, says it is, it could
not even intellectually follow an argument for the
idea that the universe is a *universe*. All arguments
for such a universe would come to him as outside that
universe.

Yet it is the very essence of the positions of
Aquinas and Butler that human self-consciousness is
intelligible without God-consciousness. Both make it
their point of departure in reasoning with the non-
believers that we must, at least in the area of things
natural, stand on the ground of neutrality with them.
And it is of the essence of all non-believing philosophy that self-consciousness is taken as intelligible
by itself without reference to God. Moreover the very
theology of both Romanism and Arminianism, as already
noted, requires a measure of subtraction of the self-
consciousness of men from its creaturely place. (d)
Implied in the previous points is the fact that I do
not artificially separate induction from deduction, or
reasoning about the facts of nature from reasoning in
a priori analytical fashion about the nature of human-
consciousness. I do not artifically abstract or
separate them from one another. On the contrary I see
induction and analytical reasoning as part of one process of interpretation. I would therefore engage in
historical apologetics. (I do not personally do a
great deal of this because my colleagues in the other

departments of the Seminary in which I teach are doing it better than I could do it.) Every bit of historical investigation, whether it be in the directly Biblical field, archaeology, or in general history, is bound to confirm the truth of the claims of the Christian position. But I would not talk endlessly about facts and more facts without ever challenging the non-believer's philosophy of fact. A really fruitful historical apologetic argues that every fact *is* and *must be* such as proves the truth of the Christian theistic position.

It is only in the light of this positive approach that my statements to the effect that epistemologically believers and non-believers have nothing in common can be seen for what it is. Even in *Common Grace* it is evident that by the sinner's epistemological reaction I mean his reaction as an ethically responsible creature of God. Does the sinner react properly to the revelation of God that surrounds him, that is within him and that comes to him from Scripture? As I have followed Calvin closely in stressing the fact that men *ought* to believe in God inasmuch as the evidence for his existence is abundantly plain, so I have also closely followed Calvin in saying that no sinner reacts properly to God's revelation. Is this too sweeping a statement? It is simply the doctrine of total depravity. All sinners are covenant breakers. They have an axe to grind. They do not want to keep God in remembrance. They keep under the knowledge of God that is within them. That is they try as best they can to keep under this knowledge for fear they should look into the face of their judge. And since God's face appears in every fact of the universe they oppose God's revelation everywhere. They do not want to see the facts of nature for what they are; they do not want to see themselves for what they are. Therefore they assume the non-createdness of themselves and of the facts and the laws of nature round about them. Even though they make great protestations of serving God they yet serve and worship the creature more than the Creator. They try to make themselves believe that God and man are aspects of one universe. They interpret all things immanentistically. Shall we in the interest of a point of contact admit that man can interpret anything correctly if he virtually leaves God out of the picture? Shall we who wish to prove that nothing can be explained without God first admit some things at least can be explained without him? On the contrary we shall show that all explanations without God are futile. Only when we do this do we appeal to that knowledge of God within men which they seek to suppress. This is what I mean by presupposing God for the possibility of intelligent predication.

What then more particularly do I mean by saying that epistemologically the believer and the non-believer have nothing in common? I mean that every sinner looks through colored glasses. And these colored glasses are cemented to his face. He assumes that self-consciousness is intelligible without God-consciousness. He assumes that consciousness of facts is intelligible without consciousness of God. He assumes that consciousness of laws is intelligible without God. And he interprets all the facts and all the laws that are presented to him in terms of these assumptions. This is not to forget that he also, according to the old man within him, knows that God exists. But as a covenant breaker he seeks to suppress this. And I am now speaking of him as the covenant breaker. Neither do I forget that no man is actually fully consistent in working according to these assumptions. The non-believer does not fully live up to the new man within him which in his case is the man who worships the creature above all else, any more than does the Christian fully live up to the new man within him, which in his case is the man who worships the Creator above all else. But as it is my duty as a Christian to ask my fellow Christians as well as myself to suppress the old man within them, so it is my duty to ask non-believers to suppress not the old man but the new man within them.

The necessity for this can be observed every time there is some popular article on religion in one of the magazines. There was a questionnaire sent out recently by one of them asking a certain number of people whether they believed in God. By far the greater number of them said that they did. But from further questions asked it appeared that only a very small number believed in the God of the Bible, the Creator and Judge of men. Yet they said that they believed in God. From such an article it is apparent that every sinner has the sense of deity and therefore knows God as his Creator and Judge. But from such an article it is also apparent that *every* sinner seeks in one way or another to deny this. They are therefore without God in the world. They must, as Charles Hodge so well points out, be renewed *unto* knowledge (Colossians 3:10) as well as unto righteousness and holiness (Ephesians 4:24).

68

Now neither Aquinas nor Butler makes any such
distinctions as I have made. And in that they are
but consistent. They do not make the Creator-creature
distinction absolutely fundamental in their own thinking. How then could they consistently ask others to
do so? It is of the essence of their theology to
maintain that God has made man so that he has such
freedom as to be able to initiate something that is
beyond the counsel of God. For them the human self
therefore is supposed to be able to think of itself as
intelligible and of the facts and laws of the world as
manipulable and therefore intelligible apart from
their relationship to God. I have already pointed
out that for this reason the traditional view of apologetics has no universe and has no real point of contact in the unbeliever. If either Romanism or Arminianism were right in their view of the self-consciousness of man there could be no apologetics for Christianity at all. There would be no all-comprehensive
plan of God. This much being clear it can be seen
that the Romanist and the Arminian will, in consistence with their own theology, not be able to challenge the natural man's false assumptions. The traditional apologist must somehow seek for a point of
contact within the thinking of the natural man as this
thinking has been carried on upon false assumptions.
He cannot seek to stir up the old man in opposition
against the new man in the non-Christian. He makes
no use of such a distinction. He will allow for
gradational differences within the natural man. He
will even make a great deal of these. To him therefore the passages of Paul to the effect that every
man knows God and that man is made in the image of
God are interpreted so as to do injustice to other
equally important teaching of Scripture to the effect
that the natural man knoweth not God. All this is
compromising theology. It is no wonder that the
Romanist and the Arminian will also follow a compromising apologetics.

The basic falseness of this apologetics appears
in the virtual if not actual denial of the fact that
the natural man makes false assumptions. Aquinas and
Butler hold that the natural man, whom the Calvinist
knows to be a covenant breaker and as such one who
interprets God himself in terms of the universe, has
some correct notions about God. I mean correct notions as to content, not merely as to form. Anyone
who says "I believe in God," is formally correct in
his statement, but the question is what does he mean
by the word *God*? The traditional view assumes that

the natural man has a certain measure of correct
thought content when he uses the word God. In reality
the natural man's "God" is always a finite God. It is
his most effective tool for suppressing the sense of
the true God that he cannot fully efface from the
fibres of his heart.

The natural man's god is *always* enveloped within
a Reality that is greater than his god and himself.
He always makes Reality, inclusive of all that exists,
the *All* the final subject of which he speaks. With
Thales he will say *All* is water, with Anaximenes *All*
is air. With others he may be a dualist or a plural-
ist or an atomist, a realist or a pragmatist. From
the Christian point of view he still has a monistic
assumption in that he makes Reality to be inclusive
of God and himself. And there is not much that the
traditional apologist can do about this. He has bound
himself to confusion in apologetics as he has bound
himself to error in theology. He must tie on to some
small area of thought content that the believer and
the unbeliever have in common without qualification
when both are self-conscious with respect to their
principle. This is tantamount to saying that those
who interpret a fact as dependent upon God and those
who interpret that same fact as not dependent upon God
have yet said something identical about that fact.

All this is bound to lead to self-frustration on
the part of the traditional apologist. Let us watch
him for a moment. Think of him first as an inductivist. As such he will engage in "historical apologetics" and in the study of archaeology. In general he
will deal with the "facts" of the universe in order to
prove the existence of God. He cannot on his position
challenge the assumption of the man he is trying to
win. That man is ready for him. Think of the traditional apologist as throwing facts to his non-Christian friend as he might throw a ball. His friend
receives each fact as he might a ball and throws it
behind him in a bottomless pit. The apologist is
exceedingly industrious. He shows the unbelieving
friend all the evidence for theism. He shows all the
evidence for Christianity, for instance, for the
virgin birth and the resurrection of Christ. Let us
think of his friend as absolutely tireless and increasingly polite. He will then receive all these
facts and toss them behind him in a bottomless pit of
pure possibility. "Is it not wonderful," he will say,
"what strange things do happen in Reality. You seem
to be a collector of oddities. As for myself I am

more interested in the things that happen regularly. But I shall certainly try hard to explain the facts you mention in accord with the laws that I have found working so far. Perhaps we should say that laws are merely statistical averages and that nothing can therefore be said about any particular event ahead of its appearance. Perhaps there are very unusual things in reality. But what does this prove for the truth of your view?"

You see that the unbeliever who does not work on the presupposition of creation and providence is perfectly consistent with himself when he sees nothing to challenge his unbelief even in the fact of the resurrection of Christ. He may be surprised for a moment as a child that grows up is surprised at the strange things of life but then when he has grown up he realizes that "such is life." Sad to say the traditional Christian apologist has not even asked his unbelieving friend to see the facts for what they really are. He has not presented the facts at all. That is he has not presented the facts as they are according to the Christian way of looking at them and the Christian way of looking at them is the true way of looking at them. Every fact in the universe is what it is by virtue of the place that it has in the plan of God. Man cannot comprehensively know that plan. But he does know that there is such a plan. He must therefore present the facts of theism and of Christianity, of Christian theism, as proving Christian theism because they are intelligible as facts in terms of it and in terms of it alone.

But this is also in effect to say that the Christian apologist should never seek to be an inductivist only. He should present his philosophy of fact with his facts. He does not need to handle less facts in doing so. He will handle the same facts but he will handle them as they ought to be handled.

Now look at the traditional apologist when he is not an inductivist but an *a priori* reasoner. He will first show his fellow worker, the inductivist, that he defeats his own purposes. He will show that he who does not challenge the assumptions of his non-Christian friends has placed himself on a decline which inevitably leads down from Locke through Berkeley to Hume, the skeptic. Then for his own foundation he will appeal to some internal ineffable principles, to some *a priori* like that of Plato or of Descartes. He will appeal to the law of contradiction either posi-

71

tively or negatively and boldly challenge the facts to meet the requirements of logic. Then he will add that the facts of Christianity pass the examination *summa cum laude*. Well, they do. And in passing the examination they invariably pass out of existence too. He can only prove the immortality of the soul if with Plato he is willing to prove also that man is divine. He can only prove the universe to have order if with the Stoics he is also willing to say that God is merely its principle of order. With the Hegelian idealists such as Bradley and Bosanquet or Royce he will prove all the facts of the Bible to be true by weaving them into aspects of a Universe that allows for them as well as for their opposites.

But usually the traditional apologist is neither a pure inductivist nor a pure *a priorist*. Of necessity he has to be both. When engaged in inductive argument about facts he will therefore talk about these facts as proving the existence of God. If anything exists at all, he will say, something absolute *must* exist. But when he thus talks about what *must* exist and when he refuses even to admit that non-believers have false assumptions about their *musts*, let alone being willing to challenge them on the subject, he has in reality granted that the non-believer's conception about the relation of human logic to facts is correct. It does not occur to him that on any but the Christian theistic basis there is no possible connection of logic with facts at all. When the non-Christian, not working on the foundation of creation and providence, talks about *musts* in relation to *facts* he is beating the air. His logic is merely the exercise of a revolving door in a void, moving nothing from nowhere into the void. But instead of pointing out this fact to the unbeliever the traditional apologist appeals to this non-believer as though by his immanentistic method he could very well interpret many things correctly.

That this traditionalist type of apologetics is particularly impotent in our day I have shown in my review of Dr. Richardson's and Dr. Carnell's books on Apologetics. Dr. Richardson is a modernist. But he says he holds to the uniqueness of the facts of Christianity. At the same time he holds that this holding to the uniqueness of Christianity and its facts is not inconsistent with holding to a form of coherence that is placed upon human experience as its foundation. Dr. Carnell is an orthodox believer. To an extent he has even tried to escape from the weaknesses of the traditional method of apologetic argument. But he merely rejects its inductivist form. By and large he falls back into traditional methodology. And just to that extent he has no valid argument against Richardson. To the extent that he admits the type of coherence which Richardson holds to be valid he has to give up the uniqueness of the events of Christianity as he himself holds them. On the other hand, to the extent that he holds to the uniqueness of events the way Richardson holds to them, to that extent he has to give up the coherence to which he himself as an orthodox Christian should hold. (See *The Westminster Theological Journal*, November, 1948).

The general conclusion then is that on the traditional method it is impossible to set one position clearly over against the other so that the two may be compared for what they are. Certainly there can be no confrontation of two opposing positions if it cannot be pointed out on what they oppose each other. On the traditional basis of reasoning the unbeliever is not so much as given an opportunity of seeing with any adequacy how the position he is asked to accept differs from his own.

But all this comes from following the Roman Catholic, Thomas Aquinas, or the Arminian, Butler. If one follows Calvin there are no such troubles. Then one begins with the fact that the world is what the Bible says it is. One then makes the claims of God upon men without apologies though always *suaviter in modo*. One knows that there is hidden underneath the surface display of every man a sense of deity. One therefore gives that sense of deity an opportunity to rise in rebellion against the oppression under which it suffers by the new man of the covenant breaker. One makes no deal with this new man. One shows that on his assumptions all things are meaningless. Science would be impossible; knowledge of anything in any field would be impossible. No fact could be distinguished from any other fact. No law could be said to be law with respect to facts. The whole manipulation of factual experience would be like the idling of a motor that is not in gear. Thus every fact--not *some* facts--every fact *clearly* and not probably proves the truth of Christian theism. If Christian theism is not true then nothing is true. Is the God of the Bible satisfied if his servants say anything less?

And have I, following such a method, departed radically from the tradition of Kuyper and Bavinck?

On the contrary I have learned all this primarily from them. It is Kuyper's *Encyclopedia* that has, more than any other work in modern times, brought out the fact of the difference between the approach of the believer and of the unbeliever. It is Bavinck's monumental work which set a natural theology frankly oriented to Scripture squarely over against that of Romanism which is based on neutral reason. It is Bavinck who taught me that the proofs for God as usually formulated on the traditional method prove a finite god. I have indeed had the temerity to maintain that these great Reformed theologians have in some points not been quite true to their own principles. But when I have done so I have usually tried to point out that when they did so and to the extent that they did so they had departed from Calvin.

Discussion Questions

1. Discuss several possible responses Van Til might make to Gilkey's position that secularity is as formidable a force within the church as outside of it.

2. Van Til seems uncomfortable with the notion of probability when used in theology. Christianity is not probably correct, it is the only reasonable position to hold. But if this stance of absolutism is taken, what dangers might be on the horizon?

    a. Given our discussion in the essay "On Theological Judgment" what dangers become apparent?

    b. If one perspective is "probably" true, or one interpretation of life is "more adequate" than another, does this mean that relativity prevails and the distinctiveness of Christianity is undermined? Give reasons for your answer.

3. When Van Til says he accepts the scripture as his absolute authority, what questions arise in light of Christian's essay? Would Van Til accept Christian's approach to scripture or does it reveal presuppositions Van Til would reject?

4. Van Til says that he thinks reason and historical investigation are necessary to theology. But he says

that all historical investigation is bound to confirm
the truth of the Christian position.

    a.   How does he know this?

    b.   How can he speak of "confirming" the Christian
position if it is assumed as the absolutely true one?

    c.   How can he be certain what "the" Christian
position is?

REVISIONIST THEOLOGICAL METHOD

Five theses are proposed by David Tracy to explain revisionist theological method. The first thesis is that the two principal sources for theology are Christian texts (and tradition) and common human experience. The second thesis is that theology will consist of a critical correlation of the sources mentioned in the first thesis. Tracy distinguishes his correlative procedure from that recommended by Paul Tillich. Tillich's method is a correlation of the questions posed by existence and the answers given by Christianity. Tracy believes Tillich's method is a juxtaposition of questions from one source and answers from another. Tracy, in contrast, holds that the answers given by ordinary human experience, and not just its questions, must be critically correlated into the theological enterprise.

Tracy's third thesis is that the principal method for investigating common human experience is a phenomenology of the religious dimension of existence. In this sense his method is similar to that of Gill. The task is to find an adequate expression of the religious dimension of common experience.

The fourth thesis is that the principal method of investigating the Christian texts is a critical historical one. In this sense, Tracy's method is similar to that of Christian. The fifth thesis represents Tracy's advance of theological method past the point of dialectical affirmation. Tracy maintains that theology must press beyond this point if it is to make any intelligible truth-status claims. If a religious dimension to everyday experience can be identified, one may then ask what the relation of the theological symbol "God" is to this dimension. To make any statement about this relation, according to

Tracy, requires explicit philosophical and metaphysical language. Conceptual language, not just symbolic language, is required.

Tracy suggests some criteria for theological judgment. Among these he proposes that there must be a necessary and sufficient ground in common experience for any theological claim. He also holds that theological assertions must have internal coherence (that is they cannot be contradictory). Finally, theological statements must be consistent with other essential categories of our knowledge and belief. By this latter criteria, Tracy means that theological statements cannot contradict established ways of knowing.

REVISIONIST THEOLOGICAL METHOD*

In its briefest expression, the revisionist model holds that a contemporary fundamental Christian theology can best be described as philosophical reflection upon the meanings present in common human experience and language, and upon the meanings present in the Christian fact.[1] To explain and to defend this model for the task of theology, five theses will be proposed which are intended to explicate the principal meanings involved in this model for the task of theology. The structure of the present argument is best grasped by an understanding of the interrelationships of the theses themselves. The first thesis defends the proposition that there are two sources for theology, common human experience and language, and Christian texts. The second thesis argues for the necessity

*Source: From *Blessed Rage for Order: The New Pluralism in Theology* by David Tracy. Copyright 1975 Winston/Seabury. Published by Winston Press, 430 Oak Grove, Minneapolis, MN 55403 (formerly published by The Seabury Press). All rights reserved. Used with permission.

of correlating the results of the investigations of
these two sources. The third and fourth theses attempt to specify the most helpful methods of investigation employed for studying these two sources. The
fifth and final thesis further specifies the final
mode of critical correlation of these investigations
as an explicitly metaphysical or transcendental one.
At the time of the discussion of this final thesis,
one should be able to provide a summary of the meaning
and truth-value of the present model proposed for
theology, viz., philosophical reflection upon common
human experience and language, and upon Christian
texts.

First Thesis: *The Two Principal Sources for Theology
Are Christian Texts and Common Human Experience and
Language.*

This thesis seems the least problematic of the
five proposed. For it seems obvious that any enterprise called Christian theology will attempt to show
the appropriateness of its chosen categories to the
meanings of the major expressions and texts of the
Christian tradition.[2] Hence a principal task of the
theologian will be to find appropriate interpretations of the major motifs[3] of the scriptures and of
the relationship of those interpretations to the con-
fessional, doctrinal, symbolic, theological, and
praxis expressions of the various Christian traditions.
Except for those few theologians who would maintain
that theology is without remainder a philosophical
reflection upon our contemporary experience and language, this commitment to determining the ability of
contemporary formulations to state the meanings of
Christian texts remains an obvious, albeit difficult
task.

Even from the limited perspective of this understanding of the nature of a theologian's responsibility
to the tradition, it would also seem that the task of
theology involves an attempt to show the adequacy of
the major Christian theological categories for all
human experience. In fact, insofar as the scriptures
claim that the Christian self-understanding does, in
fact, express an understanding of authentic human
existence as such, the Christian theologian is impelled
to test precisely that universalist claim. He will
ordinarily do so by developing criteria that generical-
ly can be labelled "criteria of adequacy" to common
human experience. However, this demand is not forced

upon the Christian theologian only by his commitment to the authentic aspects of modernity, much less by a search for contemporary relevance. Rather that task is primarily demanded for inner theological reasons. Rudolf Bultmann, for one, clarifies these reasons by his firm insistence that demythologizing is demanded not only by the contemporary world-view but also by the universalist, existential assumptions of the New Testament self-understanding itself.[4]

This commitment to determine methods and criteria which can show the adequacy of Christian self-understanding for all human experience is a task demanded by the very logic of the Christian affirmations; more precisely, by the Christian claim to provide the authentic way to understand our common human existence. This insight *theologically* disallows any attempt to force a strictly traditional inner-theological understanding of the sources of theological reflection. Whether that inner theological self-understanding be explicated through any of the forms of theological orthodoxy or through the kind of neo-orthodoxy represented by Karl Barth in the *Church Dogmatics* is a relatively minor matter. The major insight remains the insistence present in theological reflection at least since Schleiermacher: the task of a Christian theology intrinsically involves a commitment to investigate critically both the Christian faith in its several expressions and contemporary experience in its several cultural expressions.

Second Thesis: *The Theological Task Will Involve a Critical Correlation of the Results of the Investigations of the Two Sources of Theology.*

Given the fact of two sources needing investigation, some way of correlating the results of these investigations must be developed. The full dimensions of this task of correlation cannot, of course, be developed until the methods of investigation analyzed in the next two theses are clarified. For the moment, however, it is sufficient to clarify the need for some method of correlation. Perhaps the clearest way to clarify the meaning of this thesis will be to compare the method of correlation proposed here with the best known method of correlation in contemporary theology, Paul Tillich's. This "clarification through contrast" procedure[5] is here a useful one since so many contemporary theologians are justly indebted to Tillich for formulating the task of theology in terms of the general model of a method of correlation.

However, many critics find Tillich's own formulation of how the method of correlation actually functions neither intrinsically convincing nor consistent
with the task of theology which he himself articulates.
The fact is that Tillich's method does not call for a
critical correlation of the results of one's investigations of the "situation" and the "message."[6] Rather,
his method affirms the need for a correlation of the
"questions" expressed in the "situation" with the
"answers" provided by the Christian "message." Such a
correlation, in fact, is one between "questions" from
one source and "answers" from the other. Even on the
limited basis of the position defended in the first
thesis, one cannot but find unacceptable this formulation of the theological task of correlation. For if
the "situation" is to be taken with full seriousness,
then its answers to its own questions must also be
investigated critically. Tillich's method cannot
really allow this. A classic example of this difficulty can be found in Tillich's famous dictum, "Existentialism is the good luck of Christian theology."[7]
We are all indebted to Tillich's brilliant reinterpretation pointing out the heavy debt which existentialist
analyses of man's estranged situation owe to classical
Christian anthropology. Yet no one (not even a Christian theologian!) can decide that only *the questions*
articulated by a particular form of contemporary
thought are of real theological interest.[8]

Correlatively, from the viewpoint of the Christian message itself, the very claim to have an answer
applicable to any human situation demands logically
that a critical comparison of the Christian "answer"
with all other "answers" be initiated. To return to
the existentialist example, why do we not find in
Tillich a critical investigation of the claims that
either Jean Paul Sartre's or Karl Jaspers' philosophies of existence provide a better "answer" to the
question of human estrangement than the Christian
"answer" does?

In summary, a commitment to two sources for
theology does imply the need to formulate a method
capable of correlating the principal questions and
answers of each source. Yet Tillich's method of correlation is crucially inadequate. Tillich's method
does not actually correlate; it juxtaposes questions
from the "situation" with answers from the "message."
Insofar as this critique is true, the contemporary

theologian can accept Tillich's articulation of the
need for a method of correlation, but he cannot accept
Tillich's own model for theology as one which actually
correlates.

Third Thesis: *The Principal Method of Investigation
of the Source "Common Human Experience and Language"
Can Be Described as a Phenomenology of the "Religious
Dimension" Present in Everyday and Scientific Experience and Language.*

The principal intention of this thesis is to
clarify the method needed to investigate the first
source of theology. It should be emphasized at once,
however, that the present thesis does not involve a
determination of the truth-value of the meanings
uncovered. Rather this thesis merely attempts to
analyze what method will best allow those meanings to
be explicated as accurately as possible.[9]

A widely accepted dictum of contemporary theological thought holds that all theological statements
involve an existential dimension, indeed a dimension
which includes a claim to universal existential relevance.[10] That task is the need to explicate a pre-
conceptual dimension to our common shared experience
that can legitimately be described as religious.
Historically, that task is best represented by the
liberal theological tradition's search for a method
capable of explicating an ultimate or final horizon
of meaning to our common everyday life and language,
and to our scientific and ethical reflection which can
properly be described as both ultimate and religious.[11]

One way of formulating this task is to suggest
that contemporary phenomenological method is the
method best suited for it. The reasons for the choice
of the title "phenomenology" at this point are basically twofold. First, several major figures in the phenomenological tradition from Max Scheler through the
recent work of Langdon Gilkey have demonstrated the
effectiveness of phenomenological reflection in explicating that final or ultimate horizon precisely *as a
religious one.*[12] Second, the history of phenomenological reflection on the nature of the method itself has
developed ever more sophisticated ways to formulate
the full dimensions of any phenomenological investigation. If the most recent formulations of phenomenology's task (the hermeneutic) be sound, then it seems
reasonable to suggest that theologians might employ

such a method to analyze those symbols and gestures present to our everyday life and language that may legitimately manifest a religious dimension to our lives.

To be sure, the present position does not argue that only phenomenological method can succeed in this analysis. It does argue that a recognition of the real possibilities of that method promises a new surety to the several attempts to explicate the religious dimension of our common experience and language.

Thus far in this third thesis the emphasis has been upon the kind of method needed for this common theological task. Hopefully, such an emphasis does not obscure the nature of the task itself: the continued search in most contemporary theology for an adequate expression of the religious dimension of our common experience and language.[13] To repeat, that task seems demanded both by the universalist claim of Christian self-understanding and by the otherwise inexplicable character of our shared experience itself.

Fourth Thesis: *The Principal Method of Investigation of the Source "The Christian Tradition" Can Be Described as an Historical and Hermeneutical Investigation of Classical Christian Texts.*

The theological *need* for history and hermeneutics concerns us first. If the phenomenon labelled the "Christian fact" includes the significant gestures, symbols, and actions of the various Christian traditions, then the theologian must learn those historical methods capable of determining exactly what facts can be affirmed as probable. For the present investigation of texts, he must also learn historical methods in order to allow for the historical reconstruction of the basic texts of Christian self-understanding. On that historical basis of reconstruction, the theologian must then find a hermeneutic method capable of discerning *at least* the central meanings of the principal textual expressions of Christianity (viz., the scriptural). The general need for historical method articulated here is a modest one. It does not imply that the theologian employ a specific category like "salvation-history" as a useful theological one. The call for historical method does imply that the theologian as historian pay heed to those historical reconstructions of Christian events and texts which modern historical scholarship has made available. The

argument for historical method implied by the first
three theses, then, is a limited but important aspect
of the theologian's larger task. If one were to define Christian theology as simply a philosophy of religion, then historical method need not be employed.[14]
But if Christian theology is adequately defined only as
a philosophical reflection upon both common human experience and language and upon Christian texts, then a
historical reconstruction of the central texts of that
tradition is imperative.

Perhaps the exact nature of the historical task of
the theologian might best be understood by recalling a
familiar instance of its exercise. That instance is
the common Christian affirmation "Jesus of Nazareth is
the Christ." That exercise is the attempt to determine
what historical and hermeneutical methods can best aid
the contemporary theologian to understand what Christians have actually meant by this familiar affirmation.[15]

The first questions to be addressed to the affirmation that "Jesus is the Christ" are ordinarily historical ones. The historian does want to know what
conclusions historical inquiry can reach about the person Jesus of Nazareth and about the belief of the
Christian community that Jesus was the Christ. On
these historical questions it seems fair to state that,
short of a position like J. M. Allegro's at least,[16]
the accumulation of historical evidence on the existence of Jesus of Nazareth seems secure, even if the
range of interpretations of his significance is wide
indeed. Yet whatever interpretation of the "historical
Jesus" is accepted as most probable by various historians through old and new "quests,"[17] the principal factor demanding *theological* clarification is the religious existential meanings expressed in the New Testament christological texts as those texts are reconstructed by contemporary historical scholarship.

If the historian can reconstruct the texts in
question,[18] then the next problem becomes the need to
discover what discipline will allow one to determine
the meanings of those metaphors, symbols, and "images"
used in the New Testament texts to express the religious significance of the proclamation that Jesus of
Nazareth is the Christ.[19] Much of the language of the
New Testament texts is metaphorical, symbolic, and
parabolic as distinct from conceptual; the principal
meaning expressed by the texts is one which manifests
or represents what can be properly labelled a religious meaning, a religious way of being-in-the-world.

These two factors can be discerned by various combinations of historical and linguistic methods.[20]

First, the historian, by a full application of his methods of historical inquiry, can reconstruct the christological texts, i.e., both those texts of Jesus and about Jesus. Semantics can then help the interpreter to determine the linguistic structure of the images and symbols involved in the text; with literary-critical methods, the interpreter can determine the particular character of the literary genres by means of which the images, metaphors, and symbols are structured, codified, and transformed.[21] Still the meaning of major import *to the theologian*[22] reamins a concern that can be formulated by a question like the following: what is the mode-of-being-in-the-world *referred to* by the text?[23] That question is not really answered until an explicitly hermeneutic enterprise is advanced. On this understanding, hermeneutics is the discipline capable of explicating *the referent* as distinct from either the sense of the text or the historical reconstruction of the text.

To continue this reflection upon the christological example, let us suppose that a prospective interpreter of the New Testament christological texts found a degree of high probability in Herbert Braun's dictum that in the New Testament the christologies are the variable while a theological anthropology (the understanding of humanity as existing in the presence of a gracious God) is the constant.[24] In one's search for the theological anthropology referred to by the christological texts, one would be engaged in the explicitly hermeneutical (as distinct from historical, semantic, or literary-critical) task of explicating that mode-of-being-in-the-world, that way of looking at reality which the texts express (a religious, Christian way of being-in-the-world). It seems fair to state that this understanding of hermeneutics could then show that the referent of the christological texts is properly described as a theological anthropology. In short, that referent is the specifically religious mode of being-in-the-world characterized by Braun in the statement that the existential meaning of the christological texts is that one can now live as though in the presence of a gracious God.[25]

Such a determination of a religious referent would, in fact, complete the explicitly hermeneutic task of the theologian.[26] The further question of the truth-status of the referent explicated by hermeneutics remains. For that question, a distinct mode of reflection is needed. Even if his hermeneutic enterprise were successful, the theologian must still face the further task of correlating the results of his hermenutic reflections with the results of his reflections upon contemporary experience and language. To achieve this correlation he must ask what further reflective discipline will allow him to determine whether his earlier conclusions can legitimately be described not only as accurate meanings but also as true. It will be the purpose of the fifth and final thesis to articulate one understanding of what discipline can undertake this.

Fifth Thesis: *To Determine the Truth-Status of the Results of One's Investigations into the Meaning of Both Common Human Experience and Christian Texts the Theologian Should Employ an Explicitly Transcendental or Metaphysical Mode of Reflection.*

This final thesis on the task of fundamental theology is probably the least commonly accepted position of those argued for thus far. For that reason, I will concern myself here with the attempt to show only the need for and the basic nature of the metaphysical reflection involved in the task of theology.

The word "need" is used advisedly since the proposed argument for metaphysical inquiry is not posed as one alternative way of doing theology.[27] Rather the present claim is that, if the argument of the first four theses is sound, then one cannot but recognize an exigence for metaphysical or transcendental reflection. Indeed, by recalling the conclusions of these earlier theses we should also be able to show the need for the metaphysical reflection suggested here. Summarily stated, the argument has had the following structure: there are two sources for theology (common human experience and language, and Christian texts); those two sources are to be investigated by a hermeneutic phenomenology of the religious dimension in common human experience and language and by historical and hermeneutical investigations of the meanings referred to by Christian texts; the results of these investigations should be correlated to determine their significant similarities and differences and their truth-value.[28] The kind of correlation needed depends, of course, primarily upon the nature of the phenomena manifested in the prior investigation of the two sources. Thus far, the argument has been principally for the formal

85

methods of investigation needed as distinct from the material conclusions reached by such methods. Yet in order to show the need for metaphysical inquiry it will be necessary to advance the earlier discussion by suggesting what conclusions may be reached by contemporary investigations of the type outlined above.

In an intellectual context where a religious dimension to everyday experience and language has been rendered intelligible, the question of God can be formulated anew as the question of the necessary referent (or object) of such a religious or "basic faith" dimension.[29] This theistic question, to be sure, involves further and extensive reflection insofar as it is the case that even some explicitly religious persons (e.g., some Buddhist and lately some Christian theologians) are also non-theistic. However, the theistic question itself seems both logically unavoidable and, as chapter eight will argue, capable of receiving a positive answer once an authentically religious dimension is admitted and explicated.

Correlatively, if one accepts the notion of "referent" articulated in the previous thesis, then religious and theistic meanings can also emerge from properly hermeneutical investigations of Christian texts. From the viewpoint of historical investigation, a secure conclusion would seem to be that whatever else Christianity has been it has also been (and ordinarily understood itself to be) a theistic religion.[30] From the viewpoint of the kind of hermeneutic enterprise suggested above, *the* referent of the classical texts of the Christian tradition can be described as a religious way of being-in-the-world which understands itself in explicitly theistic terms.

If the interpretation of both contemporary experience and language and of Christian texts could legitimately reach such similar conclusions, then the first moment of critical correlation--the comparative moment --would be accomplished. For the results of one's investigations into both major sources of theology would conclude to an identical insight: the fundamentally religious and theistic self-understanding presupposed by common human experience and language and explicitly referred to in representative Christian texts. But even this moment of correlation does not complete the theological task. Such analysis does not of and by itself resolve the question of the truth-status of such meanings.

For that we must ask what reflective discipline can adequately investigate the truth-claims of the religious and theistic meanings manifested by the prior investigations. The exact nature of that discipline is admittedly difficult to determine.[31] However, certain characteristics of the discipline needed seem clear. First, the discipline will have to be a reflective one capable of articulating *conceptual* and not merely *symbolic* categories. Otherwise, the theologian can never be sure that he has avoided either incoherence or vagueness in determining the cognitive character of religious and theistic claims. Second, the discipline must be able to explicate its criteria for precisely those cognitive claims. It seems fair to affirm that such criteria will involve at least such widely accepted criteria as the following: there must be a necessary and a sufficient ground in our common experience for such claims; any such claims must have a coherence both internally and with other essential categories of our knowledge and belief.[32]

If such criteria are in fact the criteria widely accepted for any cognitive claims, it becomes imperative for the theologian to specify how such criteria might function in theology since theology too makes cognitive claims about the nature of experience. Yet the dimension of meaning in question for theology (the religious) is not simply a meaning coordinate with other meanings like the scientific, the aesthetic, or the ethical. Rather the religious dimension precisely as such can be phenomenologically described as an ultimate or grounding dimension or horizon to all meaningful human activities.[33] The reflective discipline needed to decide upon the cognitive claims of religion and theism will itself have to be able to account not merely for some particular dimension of experience but for *all experience* as such.[34] Indeed, precisely this latter insight is required to show why the theologian cannot resolve the religious and theistic cognitive claims of theology by any ordinary criteria of verification or falsification. Rather the very nature of the cognitive claim involved in religious and theistic statements demands a metaphysical or transcendental mediation. As Antony Flew quite properly insists, an investigation of the cognitive claims of religion and theism demands that one seek to answer two fundamental questions: (1) the ground in our common experience for having any notions of religion and God at all; (2) how these notions may may be conceptually explicated to avoid both vagueness and incoherence.[35] But as it has been argued that Antony Flew fails to see, only a reflective discipline capable of explicating criteria for the "conditions of the possibility" of all experience could really resolve the question of the meaning and truth of authentically religious and theistic claims.

In outline form, I have tried to present the principal elements in the revisionist model of a contemporary fundamental theology. Whether that model can be successfully employed is, of course, another and more difficult question. However, one may continue to take heart from the fact that others who have a similar understanding of the basic elements involved in the task of theology will continue to advance these collaborative efforts which may lead to its resolution.

Notes

(1) The task outlined here is a fundamental theology insofar as it attempts to articulate the criteria and evidence for theological argument. It is a task that can be distinguished from dogmatic theology proper, historical theology, and practical theology. For distinct though related articulations of this enterprise, recall Karl Rahner's notion of a "formal-fundamental theology" and Bernard Lonergan's notion of a "foundational" theology. It should be noted that this chapter is a revised version of my essay in the *Journal of Religion* 54 (1974), 13-34.

(2) The concept "tradition" in Catholic theology since the work of Newman and of Maurice Blondel is one that can no longer be interpreted in the narrow and relatively static categories of neo-Scholasticism. Note also that the present analysis is limited to texts; cf. chapter one, n. 5, on the reasons for this present self-limitation.

(3) For the concept "motif-research," see Anders Nygren, *Meaning and Method in Philosophy and Theology: Prolegomena to a Scientific Study of Religion*, trans. P.S. Watson (Philadelphia: Fortress Press, 1972), pp. 351-78.

(4) Inter alia, see Rudolf Bultmann, "New Testament and Mythology" in *Kerygma and Myth: A Theological Debate*, ed. Hans Werner Bartsch, trans. Reginald H. Fuller (New York: Harper & Row, 1953), esp. pp. 10-16.

(5) The phrase is Bernard Lonergan's. Examples of Lonergan's own practice of this procedure may be found in his book *Insight: A Study of Human Understanding* (London: Longmans, Green, 1958), pp. 401-31.

(6) I admit the possibility that, if Tillich had argued that the "questions" of both the "situation" and the "message" are of the logical type of fundamental philosophical questions whose very explication is a "self-answering" one, he would not be open to this charge. Yet Tillich, in his articulation of the relationships between philosophy and theology (ST,I,18-28), does not argue in that manner. Nor does his actual use of the method of correlation throughout the *Systematics* suggest that such a "critical" reformulation is what he actually meant.

(7) Tillich, ST,II,27.

(8) Again, such an argument would be convincing only if it were also argued that the "questions" under study were the "self-answering" questions involved in fundamental philosophical reflection. For an example of such an argument, see Schubert M. Ogden, "The Task of Philosophical Theology," in *The Future of Philosophical Theology*, ed. Robert A. Evans (Philadelphia: Westminster Press, 1971), pp. 59-65.

(9) This implies, of course, a legitimacy to the frequent analytic distinction between "meaning" and "truth": see Raeburne S. Heimbeck, *Theology and Meaning* (Stanford: Stanford University Press, 1969), esp. pp. 15-46; and James A. Martin, Jr., *The New Dialogue between Philosophy and Theology* (New York: Seabury Press, 1966). Whether this distinction can hold for the properly metaphysical questions of religion and theism will be one of the concerns of the fifth thesis in the text and of chapter seven.

(10) This does not necessarily imply that theological statements have *only* an existential referent. Indeed, they also refer to God and they *may* also refer to the nonhuman world. In all cases, however, they continue to refer to the *self*.

(11) I refer, of course, to the tradition of theological reflection since Schleiermacher's originating attempt to fulfill this goal. Insofar as any theological position makes the same attempt it may legitimately be considered as possessing a "liberal" emphasis. For a contemporary example, see Richard R. Niebuhr, *Experi-*

ential Religion: A Theology of Power and Suffering (New York: Harper & Row, 1972).

(12) For example: Max Scheler, *The Eternal in Man* (New York: Harper, 1960); Louis Dupré, *The Other Dimension: A Search for the Meaning of Religious Attitudes* (New York: Doubleday, 1972); Langdon Gilkey, *Naming the Whirlwind: The Renewal of God-Language* (Indianapolis: Bobbs-Merrill, 1969).

(13) The phrase "religious dimension" or "horizon" is used throughout this text in preference to the concept "religious experience" in order to indicate that "religion" is not another human activity coordinate with such activities as art, morality, and science, but is rather a dimension of or horizon to *all* human activities. Chapters five and six will study the concepts "religious dimension of our common experience" and "explicit religious experience" in terms of the notion of "limit."

(14) There would, of course, remain a historical dimension to philosophy of religion but it would not involve determining the meanings and truth-status of the historical components of the "Christian fact."

(15) Insofar as this aspect of the task of "fundamental theology" successfully completes this task, it is coterminous with the primary role of "historical theology."

(16) See J. M. Allegro, *The Sacred Mushroom and the Cross* (New York: Doubleday, 1970).

(17) For this discussion, see James M. Robinson, *A New Quest of the Historical Jesus* (Naperville, Ill.: Alec R. Allenson, 1959).

(18) For example, in the manner that Joachim Jeremias employs historical method to reconstruct the texts of the parables: cf. Joachim Jeremias, *The Parables of Jesus* (New York: Scribner, 1962). It should be noted again that the interest here is confined to the question of interpreting written texts. The category the "Christian fact" encompasses not only texts but events, symbols, witnesses, images, rituals, etc. In more traditional theological language, the "Christian fact" includes not only the Protestant emphasis on scripture but also the Catholic insistence upon tradition. As mentioned in chapter one, I hope in a future work to address these further aspects of the question. The

present enterprise, if successful, can at least initiate that process of interpretation by providing an account of the interpretation rules for the written texts which all Christians recognize as their charter document.

(19) A clarification of these terms may be found in chapter six. For the moment, the following observations may suffice: metaphors refer to linguistic phenomena; images to non-linguistic; symbols to certain permanent and prevailing metaphors and images; myths to the narrative extension of symbols. The usage here reflects that of Paul Ricoeur outlined in chapter six.

(20) As in Van Harvey's own concluding chapter in *The Historian and the Believer*, pp. 246-93.

(21) For an explicit example, see inter alia, Dan O. Via, *The Parables: Their Literary and Existential Dimension* (Philadelphia: Fortress Press, 1967). Cf. discussion of "parables" in chapter six.

(22) The assumption here remains the one articulated earlier, viz., that the theologian *qua* theologian is committed to explicating the meaning and truth of the answers provided by the text to the "fundamental questions" of human existence.

(23) For a defense of the position that the question formulated in the text is not merely a result of this theory of hermeneutics but is implied by the more general position that all theological statements are existential, see the earlier discussion on thesis three of this chapter.

(24) See Herbert Braun, "Der Sinn der neutestamentlichen Christologie," *Gesammelte Studien zum Neuen Testament und seiner Umwelt* (Tubingen: J. C. B. Mohr, 1962), pp. 243-82.

(25) This rephrasing of the religious referent is dependent on the work of Herbert Braun referred to above.

(26) More exactly, such an understanding of hermeneutics would not complete the task of "appropriation" as Ricoeur defines that need in "Interpretation Theory," pp. 22-23. That task, in my judgment, demands further extra-hermeneutical criteria--as I argue in the fifth thesis of this text, and as I suggest in relationship to Ricoeur's own position in my "Paul Ricoeur's Ontology," pp. 7-18.

(27) It might be noted that, insofar as the "meanings" uncovered by the earlier investigations are authentically religious and theistic ones, then their phenomenological and hermeneutic manifestation is also a manifestation of their truth-status. Yet, this insight is clearly affirmed, I believe, only when the metaphysical character of these phenomena as manifesting "self-answering fundamental questions" is explicitly (i.e., transcendentally) formulated. Hence, the reason for the fifth thesis is actually more one of making explicit what is already present than it is a really new concern. But such is the character of all metaphysical and transcendental reflection: metaphysics mediates the most basic and, hence, most obvious presuppositions of all our thinking and living. Some of the objections against the use of metaphysics in theology can be seen by reading several of the comments recorded in the summary of the discussion in Donald M. Mathers, "Dialogue on the Future of Philosophical Theology: A Report," in *The Future of Philosophical Theology*, pp. 169-89. For a fuller discussion, cf. chapter seven.

(28) It might be noted that, as chapters five and six will argue, an interpretation of the limit-language present in the limit-situations of our everyday experience implies a need for the limit-language of explicit religious experience. Alternatively, the latter needs the locus of limit-situations and limit-questions for its existential meaning. The whole forms a hermeneutical circle informed by the self-answering fundamental questions of theology whose formulation and whose answers take on a properly religious-as-limit character: cf. the fuller discussions in chapters five and six.

(29) A similar judgment is advanced by Smith, *Experience and God*, pp. 46-68. An important constructive summary on the problem of God may be found in Gordon D. Kaufman, *God the Problem* (Cambridge: Harvard University Press, 1972).

(30) This is intended as a purely historical observation. In principle, the theistic self-understanding of Christianity may be as time-bound and indeed erroneous as other of its once-cherished beliefs.

(31) This is factually true at least insofar as "metaphysics," until fairly recently, has been a highly suspect source for contemporary thought. See the history outlined in James Richmond, *Theology and Metaphysics* (New York: Schocken Books, 1971), esp. pp. 1-

49.

(32) For an example of a recent exchange on these is-
sues, cf. Antony Flew, "Theology and Falsification in
Retrospect," and Schubert M. Ogden, "Reply," both to be
published in *Theology and Verification*, ed. Malcolm L.
Diamond and Thomas Litzenburg, Jr. (Indianapolis:
Bobbs-Merrill, 1975).

(33) The analyses of Paul Tillich, the process philso-
phers, or Bernard Lonergan referred to in the text may
be employed as familiar examples of this kind of argument for the ontological character of religious meaning
as ultimate. For an "ontic" analysis of the same, see
Gilkey, *Naming the Whirlwind*.

(34) This insight can be formulated in more explicitly
transcendental terms as follows: if transcendental reflection does mediate the conditions of the possibility
of experience as such, there is no "special" particular
experience or set of experiences that one can appeal to
for "verifying" or "falsifying" that mediation.

(35) I take these general criteria as well-nigh universally acceptable. The basic formulation itself may be
found in Antony Flew, *God and Philosophy* (New York:
Harcourt, Brace and World, 1966), pp. 27-29.

Discussion Questions

1.   What objections would Van Til have to Tracy's method?

2.   What controls, if any, are built into Tracy's method which control the impact of secularity on theology
and preserve the integrity of Christian theological
formulations?

3.   How would a Christian theology based on Tracy's
method differ from a philosophy of religion?

4.   In a critical correlation is something always
gained and something always lost?

     a.   If so, are you in agreement that some content
from the Christian texts or tradition may be lost to
knowledge or truth gained from ordinary experience?

93

b. If something is gained and something lost, is it important what is gained or lost?

c. Is it possible in a correlation of the type suggested by Tracy that a higher truth emerges in the correlation such that nothing of enduring value and significance is lost?

RETROSPECTIVE

No contemporary theologian can avoid asking whether the Spirit of the modern age has changed since Gilkey wrote. After all, we have observed a steady growth in the most conservative churches. The Moral Majority has exerted considerable influence on our society from an extremely traditional basis. And religious broadcasting is at an all time high. What do these phenomena mean? Is our world less secular now than a few decades ago? Or, is secularity still as powerful a force as ever? Some sociological studies show that the various religious broadcasts are watched by essentially a relatively small-sized audience of the same persons. And perhaps the Moral Majority is made up of those who have taken refuge in some kind of ideological ghetto in order to escape the challenge posed by secular assumptions.

What is interesting is that both Gill and Van Til agree that the age is a secular one. But for Gill this means that theologians must examine common experience in order to disclose the dimension of the sacred which is present in all experience. Only when this common ground is intelligibly established can the theologian build an explanation of life consistent with the Christian faith, but also convincing to secular man.

Van Til, on the other hand, agrees that modernity is secular. Indeed, he contends that secularity is a creation of man's will. It is his affront to God; his attempt to avoid, escape, and oppose God. Van Til also argues that secular man cannot be led by reason to deny or change his assumptions, nor will he admit that life is deeper and more sacral than he imagines. Accordingly, there can be no point of contact with secular man apart from God's prevenient convicting grace. Van Til's point that secular presuppositions rule out the methods of Gill and Tracy is to be reckoned with. His position is that Christian theologians should assume the authority of the scriptures without apology.

Nevertheless, Van Til's position means that nothing short of conversion will make Christian theology intelligible. And his view is challenged formidably by Christian's essay on the connection between scripture and theology. It is doubtful that even Van Til can formulate a theology which does no more or less than re-present the Scripture. And how can persons be converted without some intelligible theological witness?

It seems likely that some correlative method such as Tracy suggests will yield not only a richer theology but also a more cogent witness.

As to where one begins doing theology, this issue may now be seen as lesser significance than we thought in the beginning. If the source norms for theology regulate and control each other, then it is not essential that theology always begin with any one source. What is essential is that all the source norms be used in every theological construction, and that they exercise mutual control.

Every time we interpret scripture we do so from experience and tradition. We cannot escape this dynamism by taking the position that scripture interprets scripture. Such a position assumes that some passages are clearer than others—at least to the extent that they can aid in the interpreting process. But what makes a passage clearer? Perhaps it is our experienced faith, or the teachings of our tradition or denomination which make a passage clear.

The long and short of theological method is that theology is similar to an artistic skill. It must be practiced and refined. Doing theology is complex and it requires a sensitivity to each of the source forms of the faith.

PART TWO

THE DOCTRINE OF GOD

THE DOCTRINE OF GOD

While men in previous centuries have debated the questions of sin, forgiveness, Christology, the authority of church and Scripture, the debate usually proceeded from the basis of a common assumption of the reality of God. It was not God who was in question, but some particular understanding of his self-revelation and how it could best be expressed. But this is no longer the case.

Almost every movement in contemporary culture has progressively challenged the concept of God--its significance and certainty. For the first time in Christian history a culture has emerged in the last two hundred years which feels competent to deal with life without reference to eternal realities, particularly to the notion of God. Indeed, secularism has given birth in the mid-decades of this century to a movement variously called Christian Atheism, Radical Theology or the Death of God Theology. This movement was committed to being Christian without God. During the last few years the Radical Theology movement has waned, perhaps it has even died. But it remains a poignant symbol of the seriousness of the God problem for modern men.

The challenge posed to theology has expressed itself on two fronts. The first of these concerns the very possibility of God, his knowability and meaning. To many modern men God is an impossible reality, because they do not experience him, cannot establish his existence as they can other realities, cannot observe the evidence of his action in the world or human life, and because belief in his existence may actually threaten human development and creativity.

The challenge to those who believe in God's existence is not merely intellectual. In past centuries the helplessness of man in a cosmos which overwhelmed him prepared him psychologically for belief in God. Christian preaching proclaimed that man could not endure existence without God. But modern men do not feel helpless. They have made staggering progress in controlling the heretofore mysterious and terrifying forces of nature and life. This is not to suggest that man has risen above his problems, it is only to say that contemporary men no longer feel that they need God to solve their problems or help them cope with life. Indeed, many secular men are persuaded that they can cope with their problems as well as any religious man. It is true, of course, that many religious persons continue to find gaps in man's ability and knowledge and into these open spaces they plug God. But the gaps get smaller, or less significant, and where is God then? Theologians such as Dietrich Bonhoeffer see this new sufficiency of man as his "coming of age." Bonhoeffer holds that God himself is behind modern man's new-found independence. He likens God to a loving father whose goal is to lead his children to the point that they no longer need him. But both of these approaches, the God of the gaps, and that taken by Bonhoeffer, banish God functionally from common human experience.

There is also a formidable intellectual challenge to the possibility of belief in God's existence. Intellectually speaking, God is often an additional explanatory hypothesis which is not needed. If viruses cause plagues, can we say that the origin and abatement of a plague is the judgment of God? How can we justify saying that it is? If air masses determine the rain, then can we say that a rainstorm refreshing the land is God's bountiful provision? Why? Since God began to disappear from nature, believers have sought to validate his existence by an appeal to some sort of inner religious experience or encounter. Both Nineteenth Century Liberalism and Neo-Orthodoxy turned to such internal evidence, and the approach taken to theological prolegomena by Jerry Gill, Langdon Gilkey and David Tracy may be understood along these lines as well. According to this approach, we know God not by proofs based on nature, but by the witness of our hearts.

But, of course, the most formidable enemy of this model for approaching the God problem is the nineteenth century philosopher Ludwig Feuerbach.

Feuerbach contended, long before Sigmund Freud, that the deep stirrings in our soul were only products of our psychological dynamics. God is a projection of our mind. Belief in his existence is our way of coping with life's problems. We pray asking for miracles because we cannot accept the events life seems to be handing us. We believe he will save us from death because we cannot accept our finitude. We hope that he will judge those who do evil because there seems to be so much of it, and justice seems too often neglected. How can we distinguish a psychological projection from a real entity if there is no contemporary evidence to use? And how can we trust historical evidences, such as in the Scriptures, if we find their authority to be limited?

This first challenge to the very possibility of belief in God has raised anew the question of how a theologian may establish the existence of God. While previous eras relied on proofs for God's existence, since the Enlightenment period the traditional proofs have been under sustained attack. The essay by John Hick in this chapter is a careful analysis of the entire issue of proving God's existence, and what senses of "prove" are meaningful to this question and which are not. Hick deals thoroughly with the question whether God's existence may be established by rational inquiry. Karl Barth's essay is a strongly stated case for the position that man cannot know God unless God reveals himself. And if God discloses his existence and nature, then reason may find these things inscrutible or incredible. It is not in man's capacity to understand God, or even to know his existence, unless God chooses for this to be so, Barth holds. At the other extreme from Barth is the position held by Gordon Kaufman. Kaufman argues that "God" is a human construction. "God" is an inclusive notion under which man can live, and by which he can organize his life's experiences. Thus the proper task of theology is to examine the notion of "God" which is constructed with a view toward a notion that can provide an organizing concept for life that brings fulness and meaningfulness.

The second front on which the problem of God has expressed itself concerns the content of the traditional concept of God inherited from the premodern cultures of medieval, Renaissance, and Reformation Europe. In this sense, many theologians have held that the main problem in understanding God for modern secular man is not really the question of God's

100

reality, that can perhaps be accepted on faith, or perhaps modern man can relate to the argument that there is a religious dimension to life which leads at some point to the use of God language. Instead, the main problem for modern man, it can be said, is the inadequacy of traditional descriptions of God. It is not God that modern men have quit believing in, but the God of traditional theology.

One aspect of traditional theology which is undergoing examination today is the concept of the absoluteness of God. Traditional theology drew heavily on Greek philosophy in its formulation of the doctrine of God. Theologians of earlier centuries held that since the Bible says God created time then the Greeks must be right in saying that God is not in time. Since God is the source of all finite realities, they concluded that God must be totally independent from his creation. God cannot really be effected by other things, this they called the *aseity* of God. Since God does not experience time, then he did not change; especially since God was perfect and any change would have to move him toward imperfection.

To be sure, Biblical support may be garnered for all of these ideas. But modern men see readily the contradiction which emerges when theologians speak of an unchangeable God and of the living God in the same breath. What can it mean to say that God cannot be related to me because of his *aseity*, and that time is not real for him, when love, understanding and historical activity are inseparably bound up with the real stuff of interrelationships and time. If God has acted in history, then time must be real for him. If God cares for me, then what I do must effect him in some way.

In response to the inadequacy of the traditional formulation of the doctrine of God, many theologians have turned both to the Scriptures and to new philo-sophical models. The use of a philosophical model in theology must always follow what has been said about theological method in Chapter One. Philosophical models should not determine theological formulation. However, neither should theologians hesitate to in-clude philosophical understanding in the dynamic process of theological explication which includes Scripture and Tradition. The essay by Eugene Peters is included in this collection as a proposal for some reformulation of the Doctrine of God.

ON PROVING GOD'S EXISTENCE

In the following essay John Hick addresses the two most important questions related to offering proofs for God's existence. These questions are whether the arguments succeed or not, and whether, if they do succeed, they are of any positive religious value. The essay is not an easy one and it presupposes some knowledge of philosophical terminology.

Hick first deals with the locution "God exists." A locution is a linguistic utterance. In his treatment of this subject he follows philosophy since the time of Immanuel Kant in taking the position that existence is not a property that things possess. He simply wishes to clarify the philosophical meaning of the locution "God exists" by establishing that the assertion is meant to say that the definition of "God" has an instance in reality. But more important to theological interest is Hick's point that some theologians, notably Paul Tillich, have objected to the question of God's existence on theological grounds. Tillich holds that the question assumes that God is a being alongside other beings. And he argues that such an assumption turns God into an object and circumscribes him in ways that lead inevitably to distortion of his true reality. Hick rejects Tillich's objection on the grounds that there is still a need to distinguish between there being and there not being an ultimate reality to which we may properly direct our "ultimate concern"; and the question of God's existence is our way of making this distinction.

The analysis of theistic arguments for God's existence pursued by Hick categorizes the arguments as either *a priori* or *a posteriori*. The former type, of which there is only one strict example, that being the Ontological Argument of Anselm of Canterbury and those who reworked it, is an *a priori* argument. This argument claims that on the basis of the concept of God

102

alone, without any appeal to experience, God's existence may be established. Since God is greater and more perfect than any being, and since it is greater to exist in reality than to exist merely in the mind of man, then God must necessarily exist. Hick quickly dismisses this argument on two grounds. One is that it is philosophically erroneous to make inferences from the thought of a given kind of being to the conclusion that there is in fact a being of this kind. His second objection is that existence is not a property to be added to a thing, thereby making it greater, and he appeals to Immanuel Kant's sustained argument on this issue for support. Students may agree with Hick's point, but some philosophers have suggested that the Ontological Argument cannot be easily dismissed. Among those who think that it has real philosophical merit are Norman Malcom and Charles Hartshorne.

The *a posteriori* arguments rely on premises derived from experience, and Hick divides them into two categories: those which claim to establish their conclusions with certainty and those which claim that theism is a probable conclusion. It is in this section of the essay that Hick discusses several senses of the word "prove" and these passages should be read carefully. Hick is critical of *a priori* arguments that purport to establish theism with certainty because they all make presuppositions which are not granted by those to whom the argument is primarily directed. Of those which claim to establish God's existence as probable, Hick says that none of these may be regarded as employing the notion of mathematical probability. To do so, he points out, would mean that one would be able to specify the number of determinate occurrences, or number of determinate universes; and we should also have to be able to specify which of these is God-produced and which are non-God-produced. Only then could we say strictly that it was mathematically more probable that ours was a God-produced universe, and thus God exists; than that ours is a non-God-produced universe, and thus God probably does not exist.

The notion of probability that operates in the theistic arguments is nonmathematical. Instead, it is a matter of more reasonable and less reasonable acts of assent. The claim is that it is more reasonable or rational to interpret the universe theistically than to interpret it naturalistically. But Hick holds that even this understanding of probability is open to criticism. Hick says that every factor suggested as capable of being fitted into a religious or theistic context, may also fit into a naturalistic one. The question then becomes whether one way of interpreting events in nature or life is more probable than another. The choice is never between explanation and absence of explanation, but always between alternative explanations made from radically different contexts. Hick concludes that it is at this point that the theistic proofs loose their cogency. How, after all, does one go about showing that one comprehensive world-view has superior probability to another?

Hick considers also several theological objections to offering proofs for God's existence. The first objection is that faith does not need proof because faith knows God directly, not by inference. Yet, even if faith does know God directly, that does not necessarily mean that a valid argument for God's existence could not be given. And, what does one do in a secular age when the encounter with God seems to be fading? Hick seems more inclined to accept the theological criticism that proofs for theism only establish a God who is abstract; a pale reflection of the living God of Biblical faith.

The conclusion to the essay is that the question whether God exists is a significant one, but that it is incapable of resolution by philosophical argumentation alone. What is more important, says Hick, is whether the faith awareness of God is a mode of cognition which can properly be trusted. Hick does not offer an answer in this essay. However, he gives some definite suggestions for the resolution of this question in the essay in this collection on "Eschatology and Verification". Also not to be neglected by the student is a more careful analysis of Gill's use of tacit knowledge, because this approach suggests that the dichotomy between factual knowledge and faith may not be as simple as once thought. Indeed, faith may have epistemological status if properly reunderstood.

ON PROVING GOD'S EXISTENCE*

The subject of the existence of God, as a problem in philosophy, revolves around the "theistic proofs"

which have been a center of debate since the time of
Plato. Whether or not these arguments succeed in establishing their conclusion and whether or not, supposing that they do succeed, they are of any positive
religious value, are disputed questions.

Something should perhaps be said at the outset
about the phrase "God exists," the propriety of which
has been challenged on both philosophical and theological grounds. We are not at the moment concerned with
the question *whether* God exists, but with the suitabil-
ity of the locution "God exists" used either in affirmation or denial. The philosophical objection that
"x exists" is a logically misleading way of saying
something else, namely that the description or definition indicated by the term x applies to some reality.
Thus the correct question is not whether a being called
God does or does not have the property of existence,
but whether the definition of "God" has or lacks an instance. This well-known Russellian analysis of "exists"[1] entails that "God exists" and "the existence (or
the reality) of God" are solecisms. They remain however very convenient solecisms, and they can be rendered harmless by stipulating that "God exists" is to
be construed as shorthand for "There is an individual,
and only one, who is omniscient, omnipotent, etc."
With this understanding it is perhaps permissible to
retain the traditional phrase even whilst acknowledging
its logical impropriety.

The religious objection to speaking of the existence of God is of a quite different kind and is formulated as follows by Paul Tillich: "Thus the question
of the existence of God can be neither asked nor answered. If asked, it is a question about that which
by its very nature is above existence, and therefore
the answer--whether negative or affirmative--implicitly
denies the nature of God. It is as atheistic to affirm
the existence of God as it is to deny it. God is
being-itself, not *a* being."[2] This is in effect a
theological-semantic recommendation that the term
"existence" be applied only to entities within the
created realm, with the result that it becomes improper
to assert of a postulated creator of this realm that he

*Source: Excerpted with permission of Macmillan
Publishing Co., Inc. from *The Existence of God*, edited
by John Hick. Copyright 1964 Macmillan Publishing
Co., Inc.

exists. The recommendation operates as an emphatic rejection of any notion of God as a finite object along-side others in the universe. But we still want to be able to distinguish between there being and there not being an ultimate reality which is not a part of the universe and to which we may properly direct our "ulti-mate concern"; and the term "the existence of God" ena-bles us to do this. Once again, then, it seems on the whole preferable to retain the traditional phrase than to risk concealing important issues by rejecting it.

The theistic arguments are commonly distinguished as being either *a priori* or *a posteriori*. An *a poste-riori* argument is one which relies on a premise derived from (hence after, or posterior to) experience. Ac-cordingly *a posteriori* arguments for the existence of God infer a deity from evidences within our human ex-perience. An *a priori* argument on the other hand oper-ates from a basis which is logically prior to and in-dependent of experience. It rests upon purely logical considerations and (if it succeeds) achieves the kind of certainty exhibited by mathematical truths.

In point of fact only one strictly *a priori* theis-tic proof has been offered--the ontological argument of Anselm, Descartes, and others. This claims on *a priori* grounds that the idea of "the most perfect and real conceivable being" is the idea of a being which must and therefore does exist; for a Nonexistent could never be the most perfect and real conceivable being.

The basic philosophical objection to this reason-ing is well-developed and widely agreed. The objection is that one is never entitled to deduce from a concept that anything exists which corresponds to that concept. The nature of thought on the one hand and of extra-men-tal reality on the other, and of the distinction be-tween them, is such that there can be no valid infer-ence from the thought of a given kind of being to the conclusion that there is in fact a being of this kind. The mind is free to form concepts of various species of beings which do not exist, and it is impossible to tell from inspection of a concept alone whether or not there is an extra-mental entity answering to it. Only experience can determine this. This objection is most powerfully stated by Kant.

Turning now to the *a posteriori* theistic proofs, it is necessary to distinguish between, on the one hand, those which profess to constitute strict apodic-tic demonstrations or "knockdown arguments" and those on the other hand, which are of the nature of probability arguments, seeking to persuade us that theism is the most reasonable of the available alternatives.

In the following two sections I shall discuss each of these two kinds of *a posteriori* argument and shall argue in each case that a philosophical proof of God's existence is impossible. I shall argue not only that no successful argument of this kind has yet been produced, but that it is in principle impossible that such ever should be produced--and equally impossible irrespective of whether or not God does in fact exist.

Consider first the attempt to demonstrate the reality of God in strict logical fashion from *a posteriori* premises.

In order to define the question at issue it is necessary to distinguish several different senses of "prove." For there are two senses in which we may speak of something being proved in which it is a non-controversial statement that the existence of God can be proved, and these need to be mentioned and set aside in order to isolate our central problem, which concerns a third sense of "prove."

The existence of God can undoubtedly be proved if a proof is equated with a formally valid argument. For it is a familiar logical truism that a valid argument can be constructed with *any* proposition as its conclu-sion. Given any proposition, q, it is possible to supply other propositions such that it would be inconsistent to affirm these and to deny q. The propositions thus supplied constitute premises from which q follows as a conclusion. One can easily construct a proof in this sense for the existence of God. For example: If Princeton exists, God exists; Princeton exists; therefore God exists. The argument is formally impeccable-- one cannot rationally affirm the premises and deny the conclusion.

This first sense of "prove" is referred to here only to be dismissed as an inconvenient and confusing usage. It is much better to follow the more normal practice and to distinguish between an argument being valid and its conclusion being true. The validity of an argument is a purely formal characteristic of the relation between its constituent propositions, and does not guarantee the truth of any of them. It guarantees that *if* the premises are true the conclusion is true also; but it cannot guarantee that the premises, and

107

therefore the conclusion, *are* true.

A second sense of "prove" is that in which a conclusion is said to be proved, not merely if it follows
from premises, but only if it follows from *true* premises. We may consider this second sense in relation
to and in distinction from a third in which these logical conditions are supplemented by the yet further requirement that the premises are *known* or acknowledged
to be true. There might, in sense number two, be all
manner of valid arguments in which true premises lead
to true conclusions but which do not prove anything to
anyone because no one acknowledges their premises as
being true. In this sense, all that can be said is
that there is a proof of God's existence *if* God exists
but not if he does not! But this is so neutral and
noncommittal a point that the atheist will not be concerned to dispute it. It is surely the third sense, in
which to prove something means to prove it *to* someone,
that is really in question when we ask whether the existence of God can be proved.

The sense of "prove" then which most concerns us
is that in which we speak of proving a certain conclusion to an individual or a group. Here it is required
not only that the conclusion follows from the premises,
and not only that the premises from which it follows
are true, but also that they are acknowledged to be
true by those to whom we are seeking to prove the conclusion. It is at this point that a basic philosophical objection emerges to all strict theistic proofs of
the *a posteriori* type--namely that they necessarily beg
the question, in that a person who accepts their premises already acknowledges the reality of God. For
theistic arguments of this type rely upon some connection between God and the world. In order to provide
a basis for a strict proof of God's existence--and we
are at the moment discussing strict proofs--the connection must be such as to warrant the proposition, "If
the world (or some particular aspect of it) exists, God
exists." But clearly anyone who accepts this premise
already either acknowledges the existence of God or
else is unable to reason at all. And it is idle to offer a demonstration to one who does not need it or is
incapable of using it.

Might not someone however who had not previously
accepted a premise of this kind be brought by a process
of philosophical reasoning to accept it? This is of
course possible, and does in fact happen. Indeed many
presentations of the cosmological type of theistic

proof include such a prolegomenon as their first stage; and the additional premise which they use is that the world is ultimately explicable by reference to some reality beyond itself and is not a sheer inexplicable "brute fact" which can only be accepted as such. The first cause argument and the argument from contingency both employ this principle either explicitly or implicitly. Their logical form is that of a dilemma: either there is a God or the world is ultimately unintelligible. The one argument urges that either there is an endless and therefore meaningless regress of causes or else the causal series must finally be anchored in an uncaused first cause which is God. The other argument claims that each item in nature points beyond itself for its sufficient explanation, and urges that either the regress of explanations runs out to infinity, with the result that nothing is ever finally explained, or else that it must terminate in a self-existent being which neither needs nor is capable of further explanation, and which is God. Clearly the force of these arguments depends upon the decisive ruling out of one alternative, namely the conclusion that the world is ultimately inexplicable, so that we may be driven by force of logic to the other conclusion, that God exists. But it is precisely this excluding of the nontheistic alternative that is not and cannot be accomplished by logical considerations alone. For it rests upon a fundamental act of faith, faith in the ultimate "rationality" of existence; and this is part of the larger faith which the atheist refuses. He believes on the contrary that the universe is devoid of ultimate purpose and that the question as to why there is anything at all has no meaning and therefore no answer. Faced with this absence of metaphysical faith the theistic arguer is disarmed.

Since the cosmological argument thus requires a premise which is not granted by those to whom the argument is primarily directed, it follows that from their point of view it begs the question. And this, I suggest, is the basic philosophical objection to this group of arguments. They can only be probative to those who need no proof.

Whilst the first cause argument and the argument from the contingency of the world profess to be strictly demonstrative, the other arguments of the cosmological type—the design and moral arguments, and those based upon religious experience, miracles, and universal consent—attempt to establish a high probability rather than a logical certainty. They direct attention to some aspect of the world or of human experience—for example, the order and beauty of nature and its apparently purposive character, or man's religious experience and appreciation of values—and conclude that this is most adequately explained by postulating a divine creator, an object of religious experience, or a transcendent ground of value. It is not claimed that the intellectual move from these starting points to God proceeds on the ironclad rails of logical entailment. There can be no strict deduction of an infinite deity from the character of finite things. Rather these function as significant signs and clues, pointing with varying degrees of particularity and force to the reality of God. Formulated as arguments directed to the nonbeliever such inferences accordingly center upon the notion of probability. Their general form is: in view of this or that characteristic of the world it is more probable that there is a God than that there is not. Correlatively, it is more rational in the light of these same considerations to believe in God than to disbelieve in him or to remain agnostic.

It is clear that the "probability" invoked here is not the strict mathematical concept employed in the physical and behavioral sciences. To claim that the probability of the universe being God-produced is represented by some particular mathematical ratio, $1/n$, would (according to the widely used frequency theory) presuppose it to be known (a) that there is a certain determinate number of universes and (b) that a certain definite proportion of these, namely $1/n$, are God-produced.

The concept of probability that operates in the theistic arguments must clearly be nonmathematical. Stated in terms of the operations of the judging mind it must be a matter of more reasonable and less reasonable acts of assent; or in terms of the subject matter itself, of the relative antecedent or intrinsic probabilities of different types of hypothesis. It must, in other words, be claimed that it is more reasonable or rational to interpret the universe theistically than to interpret it naturalistically; or formulating the same claim from the other end, that a theistic interpretation of nature is intrinsically more probable than a naturalistic one.

But the question still has to be raised whether even this nonmathematical or "alogical" concept of probability is applicable to the theistic problem. It is of course a fact that as men have looked at the world and have been especially struck by this or that aspect of it they have concluded that there is (or that there is not) a God, or have found in the world confirmation of an already formed conviction as to the existence (or nonexistence) of God in terms varying in degree from "it seems on the whole more likely than not" to "it is overwhelmingly more probable." But the question remains whether the notion of probability or likelihood is being used in such judgments to express more than a purely personal and imponderable "hunch" or feeling.

The situation seems to be this. Of the immense number and variety of apparently relevant considerations some, taken by themselves, seem to point in one direction and some in the other. One group can fairly be said to count as at least prima facie evidence for the existence of God. For not only do believers urge these particular considerations as supporting their own position, but disbelievers concurringly treat them as points requiring special explanation. And likewise there are other considerations which taken by themselves constitute at least prima facie antitheistic evidences. These are matters which nonbelievers emphasize but in which the believer on the other hand sees a challenge to his faith which he must try to meet.

As examples of prima facie theistic evidence, man's distinctively religious experience and the reports of miracles would never be pointed out by an atheist as tending positively to support his own position; they are items for which he feels obliged to seek an explanation other than the one which the facts themselves, when taken at their face value, suggest. It is agreed for example that there is such a thing as "religious experience" and this very name embodies a religious interpretation of the experiences in question as being in some way cognitive of the divine. Accordingly it is incumbent upon the disbeliever to respond by offering a naturalistic interpretation of these same experiences.

On the other side, as examples of prima facie antitheistic evidence, human wickedness and the suffering of all sentient creatures including man are not facts which would be selected by the theist as favorable premises from which to launch his own argument; they are rather difficulties which he must endeavor to meet from the wider resources of theism, as has been done by a succession of thinkers from Augustine to

Austin Farrer.

Now none of these factors, or of the indefinitely many others that could be added to them, points so unequivocally in one particular direction as to admit of only one possible explanation. Although in isolation they each suggest a conclusion, nevertheless each is capable of being fitted into either a religious or a naturalistic context. There is no item offered as either theistic or antitheistic evidence which cannot be absorbed by a mind operating with different presuppositions into the contrary view. The question then is whether one *way* of interpreting them can be said to be more probable than the other or (putting the same query in another way) whether acceptance of one interpretation can be said to be more reasonable or rational than acceptance of the other. For the choice is never between explanation and blank absence of explanation, but always between alternative explanations which employ radically different categories.

In what sense however, or on what basis, can it be claimed to be established that one such total interpretation is more probable than another? Can we, for example, simply count points for and against? Can we say that there are say ten items of prima facie evidence in favor of theism and eight against; and coversely eight items in favor of atheism and ten against it--so that theism wins by two points? Clearly, no such mechanical procedure will do, for the conflicting considerations do not constitute units of equal weight. Can we perhaps however place each item in its position on an evidential scale in which, without being assigned any numerical value, they are listed in order of importance? To some extent this is feasible as a separate operation on each side of the debate. In may instances we can accord a greater weight to one item of theistic (or of antitheistic) evidence than to another, and can thus begin at least to construct two parallel lists. But we still have no agreed way of weighing an item on one list against its opposite number on the other list nor, therefore, of evaluating one list as a whole in relation to the other. There are no common scales in which to weigh, for example, human wickedness and folly against the fact of man's moral experience, or the phenomenon of Christ against the problem of human and animal suffering. Judgments on such matters are intuitive and personal, and the category of probability, if it is applied, no longer has any objective meaning.

What is sought to be done here is something which

no one has ever yet succeeded in doing, namely to show
by arguments acceptable to all parties that one comprehensive world-view has superior probability to another.

We turn now from philosophical to theological considerations. A philosopher unacquainted with modern
developments in theology might well assume that theologians would, *ex officio*, be supporters of the theistic
proofs and would regard as a fatal blow the conclusion
that there can be neither a strict demonstration of
God's existence nor a valid probability argument for
it. In fact however such an assumption would be true
only of certain theological schools. It is true of Roman Catholic theology,[3] of sections of conservative
Protestantism,[4] and of most of those Protestant apolo-
gists who continue to work within the tradition of
nineteenth century idealism. It has never been true,
on the other hand, of Jewish religious thought,[5] and it
is not true of that central stream of contemporary
Protestant theology which has been influenced by the
"neo-orthodox" movement, the revival of Reformation
studies, and the "existentialism" of Kierkegaard and
his successors. Accordingly we have now to take note
of this latter reaction to the theistic proofs, ranging
from a complete lack of concern for them to a positive
rejection of them as being religiously irrelevant or
even harmful. There are several different considerations to be noticed and evaluated.

(1) It has often been pointed out that for the man
of faith, as he is depicted in the Bible, no theistic
proofs are necessary. Instead of professing to establish the reality of God by philosophical reasoning the
Bible throughout takes his reality for granted. Indeed
to the Biblical writers it would have seemed absurd to
try to establish by logical argumentation that God
exists. For they were convinced that they were already
having to do with him and he with them in all the affairs of their lives. God was known to them as a dynamic will interacting with their own wills, a sheer
given reality, as inescapably to be reckoned with as
destructive storm and life-giving sunshine, or the hatred of their enemies and the friendship of their
neighbors. They did not think of God as an inferred
entity but as an experienced reality.

Given the standpoint of religious conviction, this
seems undeniable. The man of faith has no need of
theistic proofs; for he has something which is for him
much better. However it does not follow from this that
there may not be others who *do* need a theistic proof,

113

nor does it follow that there are in fact no such proofs. All that has been said about the irrelevance of proofs to the life of faith may well be true, and yet it might still be the case that there are valid arguments capable of establishing the existence of God to those who stand outside the life of faith.

(2) It has also often been pointed out that the God whose existence each of the traditional theistic proofs professes to establish is only an abstraction from and a pale shadow of the living God who is the putative object of Biblical faith. A First Cause of the Universe might or might not be a deity to whom an unqualified devotion, love, and trust would be appropriate. A divine Designer of the world whose nature is read off from the appearances of nature, might, as Hume showed, be finite or infinite, perfect or imperfect, omniscient or fallible, and might indeed be not one being but a veritable pantheon. It is only by going beyond what is proved, or claimed to have been proved, and identifying the First Cause, Necessary Being, or Mind behind Nature, with the God of Biblical faith that these proofs could ever properly impel to worship. By themselves, and without supplementation of content and infusion of emotional life from religious traditions and experiences far transcending the boundaries of the proofs themselves, they would never lead to the life.

The ontological argument on the other hand is in this respect in a different category. If it succeeds it establishes the reality of a being so perfect in every respect that no more perfect can be conceived. Clearly if such a being is not worthy of worship none ever could be. It would therefore seem that, unlike the other proofs, the ontological argument, if it were logically sound, would present the relatively few persons who are capable of appreciating such abstract reasoning with a rational ground for worship. On the other hand, however, whilst this is the argument that would accomplish most if it succeeded it is also the argument which is most absolutely incapable of succeeding. For it is inextricably involved in the fallacy of professing to deduce existence from a concept.

We conclude then that the theological reasons which have been offered for rejecting the theistic proofs are considerably less strong than the philosophical reasons. Theologians who reject natural theology would therefore do well to do so primarily on philosophical rather than on theological grounds. For the situation would seem to be that it is impossible to demonstrate the reality of God by *a priori* reasoning, since this is confined to the realm of concepts; and impossible to demonstrate it by *a posteriori* reasoning, because this would have to include a premise which begs the question; and impossible to establish it as in a greater or less degree probable, since the notion of probability has no clear meaning in this context. These considerations are of course all entirely independent of the question *whether* God exists. They merely show why it is logically inappropriate to seek to settle the question by means of proofs. If there is a God, this is a fact which must be known in some other way than by means of philosophical argumentation.

We have already noted that the Biblical writings express a consciousness of God at work in and through the events of human history and that this consciousness is not the end product of any process of philosophical reasoning. For those religious thinkers--including today probably the majority of Protestant theologians-- who stand on the same ground as the Biblical writers and in a continuous community of faith with them, the important question is not whether the existence of God can be demonstrated but whether this faith-awareness of God is a mode of cognition which can properly be trusted and in terms of which it is rational to live. The central issue thus concerns the epistemological status of the claimed awareness of God as acting within the borders of human experience.

Endnotes

[1]*See* Bertrand Russell, "Logical Atomism" (1918) in *Logic and Language*, London: Allen & Unwin, Ltd., 1956, pp. 228f and *Introduction to Mathematical Philosophy*, London: Allen & Unwin, Ltd., 1919, ch. 16.

[2]*Systematic Theology*, I (Chicago: University of Chicago Press, 1951), p. 237.

[3]For a recent papal reaffirmation of the position that "human reason can, without the help of divine revelation and grace, prove the existence of a personal God by arguments drawn from created things," *see* Pope Pius XII's Encyclical *Humani Generis*, 1940, especially paras. 2,3,25,29.

[4]*See* e.g. J. Oliver Buswell, *What is God?* (1937); Robert E.D. Clark, *The Universe: Plan or Accident?* (1961).

[5]*See* Abraham J. Heschel, *God in Search of Man: A Philosophy of Judaism* (New York: The Jewish Publication Society of America, 1955), pp. 246f. Cf. Martin Buber, *Eclipse of God* (New York: Harper and Row, 1952), ch. 8.

Discussion Questions

1.   Do you believe that it is necessary to offer some theological justification for belief in God's existence? Why or why not?

2.   The first cause and contingency arguments are usually tied to God as the cause of the universe. Do you think that these are "God of the Gaps" arguments? Could one show that God is a better cause of the universe than matter or energy? How? What is entailed in saying "better" cause?

3.   What significance is there to the fact that the Bible offers no proof for God's existence? Or, does the Bible offer "proofs"? If so, of what kind are they?

4.   Hick argues that no factor, whether natural occurence or religious experience, admits of only one interpretation. Any factor is capable of being fitted into either a theistic or naturalistic model. Do you agree? Try to think of factors incapable of naturalistic explanation, yet avoid the "God of the Gaps."

a.   Is it necessary that theologians be able to isolate factors incapable of natural explanation?

b.   Is it sufficient to say simply that "I choose to view my life's experiences in a theistic framework because it is more meaningful for me."

5.   Read Hick's essay on "Eschatology and Verification." Do you think that the approach taken in that essay is helpful when dealing with the God problem?

6.   Do you agree with Hick that the philosophical

objections to the proofs for God's existence are more
determinative than the theological ones?

OUR KNOWLEDGE OF GOD

This essay by Karl Barth represents a clear statement of the transcendence of God. Between men and God there is a great gulf. God is foreign to man and any fellowship man enjoys with God is completely a result of God's good-pleasure and action. In this sense, Barth is concerned to establish that knowledge of God is not a result of human work or effort.

Barth does not intend to argue an entire theory of knowledge. But he holds that God is not like the other objects of our experience which we can view, analyze, and control. This explains, in part, why we cannot know him apart from his action. However, there is a second implication of this position. Any being apprehended in thought and word, which we call God is not God; at least not as God is in himself. The failing of our language about God is entirely owing to man's limitation and finitude. It is not in our capacity to appropriate, or express, what God is.

But we must not conclude that theology is to be silent. Nor should we infer that there is no true knowledge of God. The revelation of God puts our thought and language to a use for which they have no fitness by themselves alone. The focus of this revelation is in Jesus Christ. Jesus is a sign of God.

Just what sense Barth is giving to "sign" when he says "Jesus is a sign of God" may be debated. Sign and symbol are confusing terms. It is agreed that language is symbolic. Symbols are used when one thing stands for another. If I say, "The elephant is a symbol of the Republican party," then you understand what I mean. But the elephant is such a symbol simply because convention has made it so. Some theologians speak of symbols which "participate" in the reality they stand for. That is, they are not conventional, and certainly never arbitrary. But what is a "sign." This question is not resolved by language philosophers, and perhaps no comprehensive theory of sign-functioning is possible. To say the least, Barth means Jesus stands for God, and participates in God. He may mean more. By using the word "sign" he may mean Jesus is God.

Jesus is God's self-disclosure. In Jesus, God chose and created witnesses; the apostles and the church. Here then is a word that man cannot speak himself. Here is a truth he cannot know by his own understanding or capacity.

What guarantees the truth of what the witnesses report of Jesus? If our language and thought is narrow, finite and fallible how can we know that what is said of Jesus as God's self-revelation is accurate? For Barth, the answer is again found in God's power not man's. God's will to reveal himself corresponds to his power to do so. If God will have it that he be desribed in our language, but truly so, then it shall be so. God can fill the void of our impotence. The focus, then, is not on man's inability, but on God's ability. The result is a strong doctrine of revelation.

The substantiation that God is, and that what is said of him by the witnesses to Jesus Christ is true, must come to us from outside of us. To participate in the comfort of substantiated knowledge claims, requires faith. Faith which does not appeal to any other thing.

OUR KNOWLEDGE OF GOD*

In the act of the knowledge of God, as in any other cognitive act, we are definitely active as the receivers of images and creators of counter-images. Yet while this is true, it must definitely be contested

*Source: From *Church Dogmatics*, Vol. 2, Part 1, by Karl Barth, copyright 1957, T. and T. Clark, Ltd. publishers. Used by permission of T. and T. Clark, Ltd.

that our receiving and creating owes its truth to any
capacity of our own to be truly recipients and creators
in relation to God. It is indeed our own viewing and
conceiving. But we ourselves have no capacity for fellowship with God. Between God and us there stands the
hiddenness of God, in which He is far from us and foreign to us except as He has of Himself ordained and
created fellowship between Himself and us--and this
does not happen in the actualising of our capacity, but
in the miracle of His good-pleasure. Our viewing as
such is certainly capable of receiving images of the
divine. And our conceiving as such is certainly capable of creating idolatrous pictures. And both are
projections of our own glory. But our viewing and conceiving are not at all capable of grasping God. That
is to say, what they grasp as such--as our own viewing
and conceiving, as the work of our nature--is as such
not God but a reality distinct from God. This is not
only so when we are not concerned with God's revelation
and our undertaking to view and conceive God is an
arbitrary undertaking foreign to faith in God's revelation. We are not simply repeating what had to be said
against the undertaking of natural theology. We are
now taking a further step in the same direction; or
rather, we have now reached the place from which the
rejection of natural theology receives its final necessity and strength. For even when we are occupied with
God's revelation, when therefore we are concerned with
giving an answer in faith to God's revelation, we are
still not capable of ourselves of having fellowship
with God, and therefore viewing and conceiving Him, and
therefore realising our knowledge of God. At this very
point it emerges that although the knowledge of God
certainly does not come about without our work, it also
does not come about through our work, or as the fruit
of our work. At this very point the truth breaks im-
periously and decisively before us: God is known only
by God; God can be known only by God. At this very
point, in faith itself, we know God in utter dependence, in pure discipleship and gratitude. At this very
point we are finally dissuaded from trusting and con-
fiding in our own capacity and strength. At this very
point we can see that our attempt to answer God's revelation with our views and concepts is an attempt un-
dertaken with insufficient means, the work of unprofitable servants, so that we cannot possibly ascribe
the success of this attempt and therefore the truth of
our knowledge of God to ourselves, i.e., to the capacity of our views and concepts. In faith itself we are
forced to say that our knowledge of God begins in all
seriousness with the knowledge of the hiddenness of God

The hiddenness of God is the content of a statement of faith. We have already said that it is in faith itself that we are forced to dispossess ourselves of any capacity for viewing and conceiving God. It is in faith, and therefore in the fulfilment of the knowledge of God, and therefore in the real viewing and real conceiving of God, that we can understand the fact that we know, view and conceive God, not as a work of our nature, not as a performance on the basis of our own capacity, but only as a miraculous work of the divine good-pleasure, so that, knowing God, we necessarily know His hiddenness. But we must now continue that it is only in faith, only in the fulfilment of the knowledge of God which is real because it is grounded in God's revelation, that we conceive God's hiddenness. The *terminus a quo* of the knowledge of God is not, therefore, identical with the *terminus ad quem* which we can reach when we discern the inability--i.e., the limitation--of our perception and discursive thinking. When we reach this insight, which perhaps forms the end of self-knowledge, we have not even begun to know God. This is just as true when we remain satisfied with the negation as when we think we need to complete it with the corresponding "position," namely, the affirmation of the possibility of an intuitive cognition, of an immediate sight of the reality intended in our perceiving and thinking. God's hiddenness is the hiddenness of God. It is one of His properties. It is indeed that property of God with which His knowledge as such undoubtedly has its formal beginning. It is not reflections about space and time and about the categories of our thought, nor the *aporia* in which we can entangle ourselves with these reflections, thus setting ourselves a more negative or perhaps a very positive limit, but simply the great positions of the biblical attestation and of the Church's confession of the being and activity of God, which move us to assert God's hiddenness. With this assertion we confess that, knowing God, we do not comprehend how we come to know Him, that we do not ascribe to our cognition as such the capacity for this knowledge, but that we can only trace it back to God. It is God alone, and God's revelation and faith in it, which will drive and compel us to this avowal. Without faith we will definitely remain satisfied with the delimitation which we allotted to ourselves. And the lack of seriousness in this delimitation will probably be betrayed in two ways. We shall ascribe to ourselves a capacity for the knowledge of God in opposition to the revelation of God. And we shall, therefore, treat God's revelation as something which stands at our own disposal, instead of perceiving that the capacity to know God is taken away from us by revelation and can be ascribed to us again only by revelation.

When in Ps. 139[6] it says of God's action: "It is too wonderful for me; it is high, I cannot attain unto it"; or in Job 36[26]: "Behold, God is great, and we know him not"; and when Paul calls God invisible (Rom. 1[20], Col. 1[15], I Tim. 1[17]), we can ascertain from the more immediate and more general contexts of the passages that there is definitely no question here of the *terminus ad quem* set up by man himself, but of the *terminus a quo* set up by God in His revelation.

But this very negation now needs detailed material explanation. The assertion of God's hiddenness (which includes God's invisibility, incomprehensibility and ineffability) tells us that God does not belong to the objects which we can always subjugate to the process of our viewing, conceiving and expressing and therefore our spiritual oversight and control. In contrast to that of all other objects, His nature is not one which in this sense lies in the sphere of our power. God is inapprehensible.

In other words, the lines which we can draw to describe formally and conceptually what we mean when we say "God" cannot be extended so that what is meant is really described and defined; but they continually break apart so that it is not actually described and therefore not defined. In relation to God the means of definition at our disposal are not sufficient to reassure us, when we have applied them to Him, that we have thought what must be thought and said here. The being apprehended by us in thoughts and words is always either not yet or else no longer the being of God. How, then, did we come even to "mean" what is "meant," to "intend" what has to be "intended"? How did we come even to affirm the existence of the being which is here to be perceived and conceived and named?

If we now ask why this is so, we must be careful not to be tempted by the older theology on to the paths of general considerations, which will help us to understand the incomprehensibility of the supreme being in the sense of Plato and Plotinus or even Kant, but not the incomprehensibility of God. Or rather, we shall have to divest of their original character the perhaps inevitable elements of a generally "metaphysical" language structure, giving them a clear theological sense by placing them in the theological context. We must not, therefore, base the hiddenness of God on the inapprehensibility of the infinite, the absolute, that which exists in and of itself, etc. For all this in itself and as such (whether it is or not, and whatever it may be) is the product of human reason in spite of and in its supposed inapprehensibility. It is not, therefore, identical with God is in no way a constituent part of the divine hiddenness. What we shall have to say is that God is not a being whom we can spiritually appropriate. The pictures in which we view God, the thoughts in which we think Him, the words with which we can define Him, are in themselves unfitted to this object and thus inappropriate to express and affirm the knowledge of Him. For God--the living God who encounters us in Jesus Christ--is not such a one as can be appropriated by us in our own capacity. He is the One who will appropriate us, and in so doing permit and command and therefore adapt us to appropriate Him as well. It is because the fellowship between God and us is established and continues by God's grace that God is hidden from us. All our efforts to apprehend Him by ourselves shipwreck on this. He is always the One who will first and foremost apprehend and possess us. It is only on the basis of this, and in the area marked out by it, that there can and should be our own apprehension of God.

The beginning of our knowledge of God--of this God --is not a beginning which we can make with Him. It can be only the beginning which He has made with us. The sufficiency of our thought-form, and of the perception presupposed in it, and of the word-form based on it, collapses altogether in relation to this God. Of ourselves we do not resemble God. We are not master of God. We are not one with God. We are not capable of conceiving Him. But this means, with a backward reference so to speak, in respect of the views to which our concepts must be related, that no man has ever seen God. What "any man" has seen of himself has always been something other than God. God is invisible. He is invisible to the physical eye of man; He is also invisible to the so-called spiritual. He is not identical with any of the objects which can become the content of the images of our external or inner perception. But it also has a forward reference, in respect of the words which express our concepts, enabling us to impact knowledge to others. No one has ever said, or can say, of himself, in virtue of the dynamic of his words, what God is; God is inexpressible, *ineffabilis*. But he is not *invisibilis* and *ineffabilis* in the same way as the infinite, the absolute, the indeterminate, the spirit in the world, can also be described as invisible and

123

inexpressible. For then indeed, as all philosophies and outlooks shew, there is no lack of images of concept, perception or expression as there would have to be if man really knew he had no power to apprehend these quantities. But God is invisible and inexpressible because He is not present as the physical and spiritual world created by Him is present, but is present in this world created by Him in His revelation, in Jesus Christ, in the proclamation of His name, in His witnesses and sacraments. He is, therefore, visible only to faith and can be attested only by faith. But this means that He is to be seen only as the invisible and expressed only as the inexpressible, not as the substance of the goal or origin of our seeing and speaking, but because He Himself has given us permission and command to see and speak, and therefore by His Word, and in His free and gracious decision, has given us the capacity to see and speak.

We thus understand the assertion of the hiddenness of God as the confession of the truth and effectiveness of the sentence of judgment which in the revelation of God in Jesus Christ is pronounced upon man and therefore also upon his viewing and conceiving, dispossessing him of his own possibility of realising the knowledge of the God who encounters him, and leaving him only the knowledge of faith granted to him and demanded of him by the grace of God and therefore only the viewing and conceiving of faith.

But by this same fact we are already impelled to the positive meaning of the statement. Where we really confess God's judgment, we also confess God's grace. The assertion of the hiddenness of God is not, therefore, to be understood as one of despairing resignation, but actually as the *terminus a quo* of our real knowledge of God, as the fundamental and decisive determination, not of our ignorance, but of our cognisance of God. It affirms that our cognisance of God does not begin in ourselves, since it has already begun in God; namely, in God's revelation and in faith to Him. The confession of God's hiddenness is the confession of God's revelation as the beginning of our cognisance of God. Only in a secondary and derived sense is it also a confession of our own incapacity. The emphasis in the confession of God's hiddenness is not primarily that of humility but first and decisively that of gratitude. Because God forgives us our sins we know that we need forgiveness, and that we are sinners. And because God views and conceives Himself in His Word we know that He is not viewable and conceivable in any

124

other way, and that therefore we are incapable of viewing and conceiving Him of ourselves. The negation is only to be understood from this "position." The moment the confession of the negation becomes indispensable to us, we are separated by an abyss from all resignation and scepticism. The moment we have unreservedly to confess God's hiddenness, we have begun really and certainly to know God. As an assertion of revelation and therefore of faith, as a confession of our grateful responsibility to the God present to us, the insight that God is hidden from us is the infallible indication of the fact that it is by God Himself--namely, by His revelation--that we are led to the knowledge of Him, that we and our knowledge do not stand outside and afar off but in the very presence of God Himself. It is in the real knowledge of God that it is a question of apprehending God in His hiddenness, of *comprehendere incomprehensibile*. Only in the real knowledge of God can this be the case. If we apprehend, view and conceive God in His hiddenness, we stand already in the real knowledge of God.

Since this is so, we must not on any account draw from this statement the conclusion that there is no true knowledge of God, and that we are forced to renounce the undertaking to view and conceive God and therefore to speak of Him.

But it is also not true that there is a "simple" thinking and speaking, which, in its "child-likeness," does not stand under the crisis of the hiddenness of God. Even the language of ecclesiastical dogma and that of the Bible is not exempt from this crisis. It is not the case, then, that we have only, say, to rediscover the world of the biblical view and concept or to adopt the biblical language, in order to make the viewing and conceiving and language of truth our own.

If this is established, and if, therefore, it may be regarded as certain that the capacity to know and therefore to view and conceive God cannot be reinterpreted as a capacity of man but only understood as a divine gift, then we can take a second step and say that the God who quickens us to faith in Him by His revelation can and may and must be spoken about, so that He can and may and must be viewed and conceived by us. The limit within which this takes place must be remembered. But we are not now concerned only with the limit, but also with the matter itself. It is no *sophisma*, but clear and true, if we say of the revelation of God that the statement *Deus definiri nequit* is itself annulled if in spite of its predicate (yet also as the possibility of its predicate) its subject cannot be regarded as knowable, i.e., as viewable and conceivable. Even with the *definiri nequit* we define, conceive and indeed apprehend, and therefore we apprehend something which is apprehensible. God is actually apprehensible in His revelation. He is so in such a way that He makes Himself apprehensible to those who cannot apprehend Him of themselves. But He is still apprehensible. Man is not left alone in himself as the final presupposition of all mystical theology would make out. In the miracle of revelation and faith he stands before God, God stands before him, and he knows God and conceives Him therefore in His inconceivability.

In His revelation, in Jesus Christ, the hidden God has indeed made Himself apprehensible. Not directly, but indirectly. Not to sight, but to faith. Not in His being, but in sign. Not, then, by the dissolution of His hiddenness--but apprehensibly. The revelation of God is that God has given to the creature whom He has chosen and determined for this end the commission and the power to take his place and represent Him, to bear witness to Him. The Word was made flesh: this is the first, original and controlling sign of all signs. In relation to this sign, as the sign of this sign, there is also creaturely testimony to His eternal Word, not everywhere, but where His eternal Word has chosen, called and created for Himself witnesses: a testimony by the word of the prophets and apostles of this Word; by the visible existence of His people, His Church; by the Gospel which is delivered and to be heard in it; by the sacraments in which this Gospel has also a physically visible and apprehensible form; and finally, by the existence of us who believe this testimony. Jesus Christ and His visible kingdom on earth: this is the great possibility, created by God Himself, of viewing and conceiving Him, and therefore of speaking about Him. For as we men view and conceive Him, so we can speak of Him. We cannot do so without the veil, and therefore without the reservation of His hiddenness, or apart from the miracle of His grace. It is not true that the grace of His revelation ever or in any relationship ceases to be grace and miracle. Nor is it true that God Himself and His free action ever become superfluous because, instead of Him, we have the creature chosen and determined by him. But it is also not true that we men are now left to ourselves, to our ignorance or to the inventions of our own hearts. On the contrary, what is true is that as men, and in the sphere of our human views and concepts, we have a

direction which derives from God Himself and corresponds to His will and is furnished with His promise.
On the basis of this direction and in accordance with
its guidance, we can and ought to view and conceive
Him, and therefore to speak of the hidden God in human
words. It is not the case, then, that God enters again
the sphere of our own survey and control. This can
happen only as His revelation is misused or sacrificed.
But in the revelation of God, without and against our
capacity, in the form of a taking into service of our
incapable capacity, we are permitted and commanded to
do something which if it came from our own free choice
would be madness, but which in the freedom and obedience of revelation is the good sense of God Himself.
That is to say, we are to view, conceive and follow the
creaturely witnesses willed and ordered by Himself, to
receive them as His witnesses, to repeat and render
them again as His witnesses. God's revelation is God's
condescension to the creature. This condescension is
actualised in His Word by His Holy Spirit. When this
takes place we are authorised and commanded continually
to undertake in faith--not looking back to our own incapacity but trusting only in God's own capacity--the
attempt to respond to His revelation with human views
and concepts and therefore with human words.

We must go further. The veracity of the revelation of God verifies itself by verily laying claim to
the thinking and speaking of man. Our thinking, which
is executed in views and concepts, is our responsibility to ourselves. Our speech is our responsibility to
others. In this twofold responsibility--and this is
how the veracity of the revelation of God verifies it-
self--we are verily claimed by it. That is to say, we
cannot be responsible to ourselves and others without
at the same time being responsible to God's revelation,
as those whom this revelation concerns. By the Word
and Spirit of God we are told that God is and who He
is, what He wills and does and will do, and what this
means for us. We have now to tell ourselves what is
told us, and we have also to tell it to others. This
claim cannot stand, or it cannot stand unconditionally,
if in God's revelation we are not really dealing with
God Himself, or with His true revelation. In that case
we can be responsible to ourselves and others without
thinking of God or speaking of God. But the veracity
of God in His revelation, and the veracity of His revelation, establishes the veracity of the claim laid
upon us to think of Him and speak of Him. This claim
does not annul our human situation. Nor does it ignore
and eliminate the fact that apart from God many other

127

things, conditioned by ourselves and by the world-reality around us, are the content of our twofold responsibility and therefore of our thinking and speaking. But it does not constitute any protection against the fact that God too becomes the content of this twofold responsibility. It confirms our human situation as well to the extent that afterwards as well as before we are still powerless to make God the content of our twofold responsibility and therefore of our speaking and thinking about Him. On the contrary, it is the veracity of the revelation of God which brings our importence home to us, and which therefore puts this judgment on ourselves into our mouth. But the claim is issued--and in this it shews itself to be a true claim--in spite of our powerlessness. It is disclosed to us that we do not view and think of God, that we cannot speak of Him; and because this is disclosed to us, it is brought home to us that the very thing which has to happen, no matter what the circumstances, is that we must not fail to do it. It is the one characteristic of the revelation of God attested in the Bible that when it is issued it is impossible for man not to proceed to think of God, or to be silent about God. When it is issued, man is convicted of his inability to think of God and to speak of God. And when it is issued, it is required of man that in spite of inability, and even in his inability, he should still do both. On the ground of this requirement, thanks to the truth of God in it, there is a true knowledge of God on the part of man. The human knowledge of God is true in so far as it does not evade this requirement, but fulfils it in obedience.

The substantiation of our faith and therefore the necessary confirmation of our systematic deliberations and affirmations in respect of the knowledge of God must also come to us from without. If they are genuine they cannot come from ourselves as a grasping with which we try to save ourselves. They must be the grasping by which they are grasped. Otherwise they will not be genuine confirmations and substantiation. We cannot grasp at the Holy Spirit, or the Church, or Christian experience, or the Trinity, or Christ--not to speak of other supports--in order to try to create certainty for ourselves. The confirmation which our systematic needs cannot itself be systematic under any name, and least of all under the name which tells us that we are helped in our helplessness, which is itself the answer coming to us from without. Most definitely not, then, under the name of Jesus Christ. And therefore not under the name of the Holy Spirit or the Church or whatever else we may name with perhaps a right intention in the light of God's revelation. To adopt this answer and confirmation we are utterly in need of faith. We need faith to become partakers of the comfort, the substantiation, that we have faith and in faith true knowledge of God. And faith does not have recourse to anything. Faith does not assert and boast. Faith refuses to grasp after any axioms and guarantees. Faith knows that man cannot comfort himself; that comfort, like temptation, is the work of God. It is only when we do not believe, only when we consent to this intermitting of faith, that we can come to think of trying in some way to comfort ourselves. Faith has as little time and desire for this as for doubt. He who believes is saved. Faith lives by this comfort. Its comfort, therefore, stands in direct connexion with temptation. It begins at the very point where temptation is at its height, where faith is taken from us, where it is annulled and killed, so that it may really be given to us, so that in this very way it may be surely grounded and alive. This comfort upholds and substantiates faith from it goal and end. It comforts it by directing it to look beyond itself, by instructing it to point above itself. It comforts it with the truth which is outside and above it in the height as God's truth and therefore as its own, faith's truth. It comforts it with hope. In this way it is the real and divine comfort which is as different from all self-comfort as heaven from earth, as temptation from doubt. Therefore the positive conclusion of our doctrine of the knowledge of God and our answer to the open question of the *circulus veritatis Dei* must have nothing whatever to do with an act of synthesis executed by ourselves. It is an answer only when it is not our answer, or when, as our answer, it is only the witness to God's answer. Only then is it indeed the answer in which faith gives the legitimate answer to the question of its being by acting as faith and thus giving factual proof of the truth of our knowledge of God.

In this sense, it is Jesus Christ to whom we must again refer in conclusion. This does not mean that we are speaking our last word. In respect of the *circulus veritatis Dei* we have no last word to speak. We can only repeat ourselves. We can, therefore, only describe Him again, and often, and in the last resort infinitely often. If we try to speak conclusively of the limits of our knowledge of God and of the knowledge of God generally, we can come to no conclusion. We can only speak of it again and again in different variations as God in His true revelation gives us part in

the truth of His knowing, and therefore gives our knowing similarity with His own, and therefore truth. And
the question always remains whether we stand in faith
so that this can be said of us, and therefore whether
we are actually partakers of true knowledge of God. In
this matter we have definitely no last word to speak.
If we think we have, we have already pronounced our own
judgment, because we have denied faith. For this very
reason, the reference to Jesus Christ cannot and must
not on any account try to have on our side the character of a conclusive word. Jesus Christ is really too
good to let Himself be introduced and used as the last
word of our self-substantiation. For this very reason
we have expressly affirmed that, with regard to this
question, it cannot possibly be a matter of self-ques-
tioning and, with regard to its answering one way or
another, it cannot possibly be a matter of self-judgment. With regard to both the question and the answer
it is a matter of Jesus Christ and therefore not of
ourselves; of ourselves only on the basis of the fact
that it is a matter disinterestedly of Jesus Christ.
We certainly cannot refer to Jesus Christ without making use of various articles of Christology. The mention of the name of Jesus Christ is already a christological statement. But we are not referring to the
articles of Christology. If we have these in mind, we
are again caught up in the attempt (the attempt of unbelief) to anchor in a safe harbour, whereas in faith
it is a question of putting out to sea at Christ's command. We are not referring to Christology. We are referring, christologically speaking, to Jesus Christ
Himself. We have already referred to Him by speaking
of God's temptation and of God's comfort as the divine
reality by which the *circulus veritatis Dei* in which we
move is encompassed. This divine reality is Jesus
Christ Himself.

Where is it true that in His true revelation God
gives us a part in the veracity of His knowledge, and
therefore the similarity of our knowing with His own,
and in that way veracity? In our whole line of thought
we have presupposed that this may become and be true in
us. We have also tried to realise, as we must, the
limits and therefore the veracity of *our* knowing of
God. The restraint with which we have made this presupposition lies in the matter itself, because the central concept of our line of thought has to be that of
revelation and therefore of the grace of God, which we
cannot take of ourselves. Yet even with this restraint, which as such could also act as a last powerful assurance, we have actually presupposed that the

content of our line of thought could become and be true in ourselves. That we do this is quite in order. But the very appeal to God's grace under which we do it—whether it means restraint or assurance—means in any case that we put ourselves in the sphere in which we do not withdraw from the temptation of faith, in which we can be comforted only with the comfort of faith. But this sphere is the sphere of Jesus Christ. Grace is not a general possibility, to which as such we can systematically recur and from which we can withdraw, no matter whether we have in mind restraint or assurance in regard to our action. Grace is the "grace of our Lord Jesus Christ" (2 Cor. 13^{14}). If we appeal to it, we not only acknowledge that we are in need of restraint or of assurance in regard to our own action, but we have confessed that our action (in our case, a line of thought) reveals a vacuum within us which is decisive for the whole, shewing it to be either correct or utterly futile. We have confessed that we cannot fill up this vacuum, not even with a central concept, either by restraint or by assurance. We have confessed that there, in this vacuum of our action and line of thought, stands Jesus Christ: not a christological article which we can now utilise as a key to turn this last lock, and therefore not as a last word in our mouth; but Jesus Christ Himself as the pre-eminent Judge and Saviour of our action. We have confessed that our action and line of thought can only be originally and properly true in Jesus Christ and can only become and be true in Him in consequence of the fact that Jesus Christ is also really our Judge and Saviour. We have given ourselves into His hand so that according to His own good-pleasure He may be this Judge and Saviour and as such may act towards us from the place where He must establish His own vacuum. This means the appeal to the grace which has accompanied us on our whole line of thought. It means—if it is not the bad information of an all too crafty philosophy—the renunciation both of placing ourselves under the restraint, and also of creating the assurance for ourselves. If it is genuine, it definitely does not mean anchoring but putting out to sea. It means that in regard to our knowledge of God and its veracity we let the temptation of faith befall us, and that we look for nothing but the comfort of faith.

Discussion Questions

1. Barth holds that fellowship between God and man is established and continued by God's grace. What, then, are we to make of the vast numbers of persons who do not experience this fellowship? Indeed, what about those in the secular age who express a definite experience of the absence of God? What does this say about God's grace? How do you feel about the implications of this position?

2. Barth's emphasis on faith is sometimes called "fideism." Do you think that we can disregard the giving of reasons for our faith? In what way could we justify saying that we had faith that "Jesus is a sign of God" instead of "Gautama (Buddha) is a sign of God" on Barth's terms? Would it matter which we said?

3. If God takes responsibility for insuring that his witnesses proclaim the truth about him, how do we account for the variety of affirmations made about Jesus in the Gospels? Do the titles given to Christ (Messiah, Son of Man, Son of God) conflict or supplement each other?

4. What similarities do you note between the approach taken by Barth and that of Van Til?

5. Barth and one of his colleagues Emil Brunner had a great debate over natural theology. Barth said there could be no natural theology if that meant knowledge of God outside of God's revelation in Jesus as the result of some independent union with God. Do you agree or not?

CONSTRUCTING THE CONCEPT OF GOD

Generally speaking, when dealing with the theological problem of the reality of God we assume that
the task is one of analyzing and theorizing about an
object or being independent of the theologian himself.
Gordon Kaufman argues that this is both a misleading
and erroneous conception. And he thinks that the
concept of the world, by which he means more than the
earth, is also not to be conceived as an object
independent of the theologian.

Kaufman holds that as long as God was regarded
as over against us, then the problem was how we
could know him since he was not perceivable like trees
or other objects of ordinary perception. Revelation
served as the theological answer to this question,
and Kaufman outlines the answer in ways similar to
that proffered by Barth. But Kaufman thinks that
revelational claims are under assault. These claims
are questioned by historical research, science, and
studies in the history of religions. Kaufman does
not believe that it is enough for the theologian to
make an appeal to faith as Barth suggests.

If the concept of God cannot be said properly to
have been constructed on the basis of revelation, then
how do we account for it? Kaufman considers several
examples: that God is an innate idea; that God is an
explanatory hypothesis formulated after observing the
order of the universe (some form of the cosmological
argument); that "God" is our way of understanding the
reality we encounter in certain special kinds of
religious experiences.

Kaufman rejects all of the above approaches.
He has various reasons for doing so, but the one mentioned in this essay is that each of the above

suggestions fails to recognize the logical status and function of the concept of God. Following Immanuel Kant, Kaufman argues that "God" is a regulative idea. "God" is a concept created by the mind, by which we bring unity and significance into life.

To regard "God" as a kind of object over against us, about which we could ask, "When did God begin?" or "Where does God live?" is to make a serious category error. Some concepts like "tree" or "man" are of a category or group of ideas such that we could ask these type of questions. However, "God" and "world" are not of such a category. So, to apply questions appropriate to one category of concepts to another type of concept can only lead to error.

Kaufman does not discuss the difference between "God" and "World" and other Kantian categories such as "Time," "Space," and "Causality." And this issue is really too technical for us to pursue here. However, it is an important one. The reason it is important is that the Kantian categories of the mind (Time, Space, Causality, et al.) are not creations of the mind, they are constitutive patterns by which it must act. But if "God" is a category in this sense, it may still be meaningful to ask why our minds have the categories they do and whether some inferences of theological significance cannot be made simply from the way in which our minds are constructed.

How do we account for the concept of God? Kaufman holds that it is a construction of our minds by which we bring order and personal meaning into experience. As such the concept is of great *practical* importance. Like the concept of "the world," Kaufman seems to think that God is a necessary idea. Accordingly, the task of theology is not to explicate God's revelation in some expository fashion. On the contrary, theology must construct concepts, stories, pictures, explanations which make possible adequate orientation in life. Theologians are engaged in an artistic task controlled to some extent by aesthetic considerations of harmony and balance, consistency and contrast.

It is important to note the absence of fact and reality from the above considerations. Students should not conclude that Kaufman ignores the question of truth. He does not ignore truth. But he recognizes that there is more than one theory of what truth is. Truth may be judged merely by its correspondence to observed fact. But the "facts" we observe may be determined by what we are looking for, or even by our own definition of "fact." Kaufman's theory of truth is more implied than stated. Truth is what we construct. We agree on this construction socially and culturally. To be sure, we do not tolerate "truths" which contradict "corresponding facts." This is what Kaufman means when he says the truth picture we construct must not be highly idiosyncratic or subjective. Yet, we may change our notion of correspondence or of fact if a truth is essential to us. Or, we may modify our belief about what is true. But whatever is the case, truth still remains a constructive enterprise.

It may be asked how Kaufman's approach differs from Feuerbach's theory of projection discussed in the Introduction to Part Two. One difference may be noted immediately. For Feuerbach, God was the projection of an idealized man. But Feuerbach's theory never seems to do justice to the content of the God concept that is prophetic and even contrary to man's expected projections. Would we expect man to construct a God who is a Suffering Servant, or would we expect him to construct a tribal god, the aggressive destroyer of his enemies? In fact, many religious traditions reflect the latter notion and tend to confirm Feuerbach's theory. But Christianity has a different kind of God. Kaufman recognizes this. He knows that man is responsible for his choice of symbols; for his construction of God--and that this is very important. We are not free to construct any God-concept we wish. But the reason is that there are important functions the concept performs, and values it is to preserve. It is not as though God was over against us, checking our conceptualization by his revelation.

CONSTRUCTING THE CONCEPT OF GOD*

> ". . . *it is your phantasy that creates the world for you, and* . . . *you can have no God without a world.*"
> Friedrich Schleiermacher[1]

It may be supposed that theology should be conceived on analogy with modes of study such as psychology or biology: just as these latter seek to investigate the *logos* or structure of the soul or life, so theology seeks to clarify our talking and thinking about God. Each of these sciences has its own object, a reality existing over against and independently of the investigator, a reality to be perceived, studied, analyzed, theorized about, understood. The student of life has many examples--trees, dogs, birds, human beings--which can be examined; the student of the psyche has not only his or her own experience as object for reflection but also observations of the other persons round about. Likewise the theologian: though the object of inquiry here is not so directly evident and available, it too may be thought of as in some sense *there*, over against the theologian as an object of knowledge, as real as--actually, much more real than--any of the objects open to direct perception.

God, of course, is not directly perceivable: he cannot be "pointed out" as can ordinary objects of experience or easily evoked, like feelings or other inner states. Nevertheless, the concept of God has usually been treated as though it referred to a structure or reality that was definitely *there* and *given* (as objects of experience are there and given); God exists independently of the perceiver or knower and has a definite character which can be in some measure described. In short, God is (despite all careful qualifications and disclaimers) conceived on the model of a perceivable object; more specifically, on the

*Source: From Gordon D. Kaufman, *An Essay on Theological Method*, revised edition, pp. 21-41. Copyright 1979 by the American Academy of Religion. Reprinted by permission of Scholars Press on behalf of AAR.

model of a person who can speak and act. (This is
not difficult to understand when one remembers that
theological reflection had its origins in myths in
which God and the gods were pictured as perceivable
beings that walked and talked with men and women,
spoke in human tongues, performed various particular
actions.) Of course no sophisticated theologian has
regarded God as simply a very large and powerful person, living in and ruling from some heaven above;
nevertheless, the model which has determined the
logical character of the concept of God was that of
an object over against us (substance with attributes,
subject to which predicates could be assigned), the
sort of reality that ordinarily comes to be known in
some relatively direct quasi-experiential way.[2]

The concept of the world, God's creation, usually
has had a similar logical standing. Though much more
complex and full than any ordinary object of perception, it was still essentially a kind of *thing* that
was what it was, a very large and complicated object,
containing within itself all the other objects of
experience, and men and women as well. No one has
ever been in a position directly to perceive the world
as such; but this is simply because we are within it:
if it were possible to get outside the world and have
a look at it--as on a space ship one can see the earth
floating in the distance--then the world too would
become an object for direct perception. (The fact
that "world" can denote *earth*--a definitely perceivable object--as well as universe, doubtless contributes
to this sense of its being the name of some kind of
definite object.) Though no thoughtful writer believed that the world was literally simply a very
large thing, the grammatical and logical forms in
which the concept was handled were those derived from
and created for our speaking about and reflection
upon objects of perception. Thus, the model on the
basis of which the concepts of both God and world
were constructed and employed was that of the perceivable, independently existing person or object.

It is not difficult to understand the task of
theology on this presupposition. It is to make as
clear as possible (as a biologist might seek to make
clear what a tree is, or an astronomer what the sun
is) just what kind of realities God and the world are,
showing, of course, how they are interrelated and
interconnected with each other. Doctrines of God's
aseity and creative activity, his work sustaining
the world in being and his providential guidance of

history, were all developed to this end; conversely,
conceptions of the world's creatureliness and contingency, of human sin and the need for redemption,
explored these same relations from the other side.
Despite all claims that we human beings can never
come to know God in his essence, what was in fact
presented by theologians was an elaborate scheme of
interpretation which set out what it was believed
God actually was, and what humanity and the world
were, and how they were related to each other.

An important feature of this scheme was the belief that God was a quasi-personal being, and in
particular that he possessed knowledge (or truth)--
perfect knowledge--of all things in all respects.
This was in sharp contrast with men and women who
frequently fell into error and whose sin, many
thought, imprisoned them in falsehood and untruth.
It was not really possible, therefore, for humans on
their own to come to an adequate understanding of
themselves, the world, or of God. Such understanding
was the possession of God alone and could be had by
them only if God chose to communicate it. Since God
was thought of anthropomorphically as a "speaking
being," such divine revelation was possible and had,
it was believed, in fact occurred. Hence, whatever
true knowledge men and women have--at least with
regard to the ultimate questions about God, themselves and the world--will be what they have received
from God. In any case, the standard for all questions
of truth is the objective reality of God's own knowledge, not anything directly within the grasp of finite
human beings. Truth, therefore, was also conceived
as having a kind of objectivity, or overagainstness;
it was a quality or attribute or possession of (the
objectively existing) God. The human mind had to
conform itself to this objective reality of God's
truth if it was to avoid falling into error.

I have suggested that the presupposition of this
approach to theology has been the acceptance of a
model for conceiving God and God's Truth which is
based on the objectivity and overagainstness of the
object of perception. Sophisticated writers, of
course, have not held that God could be directly "seen"
like yonder tree; nonetheless, his objectivity was
often conceived on that model. This raised--and
raises--some difficult problems. With a perceivable
object, we put together our concept on the basis of
abstraction and generalization from percepts; but if
there are no direct percepts of God how--and out of

138

what--is this concept constructed? As long as the basic schema is unquestioned, this problem remains concealed by belief in revelation; God has *revealed* himself and the truth about (concept of) himself to humankind, so our knowledge of God has a firmer foundation, if anything, than ordinary experiential knowledge. It does not depend upon the vagaries and errors of ordinary perception and cognition but comes right from God himself. However, when the validity or truth of the claims about revelation begin to be doubted, the entire schema starts to break down. It becomes necessary to develop other ways of understanding how the concept of God is constructed in human consciousness.

Several alternatives have presented themselves. Some have held that the concept of God is a part of the basic equipment of the human mind, an "innate idea" which the mind always has available to itself and with which it naturally works in developing its conceptions of the world and the human. Others have contended that the idea of God is developed as a kind of explanatory hypothesis to account for the existence and character of the world (or of some feature[s] of the world) as we grasp it in our experience. Some, working out the implications of the model drawn from ordinary perception, have been prepared to argue that it is developed on the basis of a peculiar or special "religious experience" in which God is somehow directly encountered or known. There are problems peculiar to each of these positions which I cannot go into here; a major difficulty common to them all, however, and characteristic also of the more traditional position, was the failure to recognize certain peculiarities of the logical status and function of the concept of God. It was Kant who first pointed out the root difficulties, but his revolutionary insights remain unappropriated in much theological work.

Kant saw that ideas like "God" and "world" performed a different kind of function in our thinking than concepts like "tree" or "man." While the latter are used to organize and classify elements of experience directly, thus helping to make possible experience itself and serving as the vehicles through which experience is cognized, the former "regulative ideas" function at a remove from direct perception or experience: they are used for ordering and organizing our conceptions or knowledge. The "world," for example, is never an object of direct perception; it is, rather, a concept with which we hold together in a unified totality all our experience and knowledge of objects--everything having its own proper place "within" the world. Kant showed that insoluble antinomies arise when the world is treated as itself an object, like the objects of experience: Did the world have a beginning in time? or has it existed for all eternity? Is it infinite in extent, or finite? Is it infinitely divisible, or made up of ultimate indivisible elements? These questions, which are simply unanswerable when the world is treated as an objective reality, are dissolved when we recognize that the concept of world is a construct of the mind, a heuristic device by means of which the mind orders its own contents but the objective referent for which we have no way of discovering.

For Kant the concept of God, also a construct, has even wider application than the concept of world. It functions, on the one hand, as the ultimate unifier of all experience and concepts both subjective and objective ("world" unifies only the concepts of "objects"), and, on the other, as the most fundamental postulate of the moral life, that which makes moral experience intelligible by rendering the world in which we act a moral universe. Even less than "world," then, could "God" be an object of experience, or a reality conceivable on the model of a perceivable object. It is the mind's most profound and highest creation, that by means of which it brings unity and significance into all dimensions of its life. To regard God as some kind of describable or knowable object over against us (as in the schema on which most theology has been based) is at once a degradation of God and a serious category error.

The treatment of the concept of God as though it referred to some sort of object or entity was characteristic of much traditional theology. It was assumed that God or the divine exists or has reality "out there," i.e., as distinct from and independent of human beings and human thinking about God; it was taken for granted that the name "God" refers to a "real being."[3] The problem of salvation was how the divine--the only truly Real reality--could be appropriated by the human, how our mortality could put on immortality. And so various schemes of salvation-- through attitudes of faith and trust in God--in Christ's victory over the devil, through attitudes of faith and trust in God--were developed. It is God, the divine, the Other over against us, who in his

140

grace is the source or giver of salvation; we are simply its humble recipients. This whole mode of thought takes the objectivity of God for granted.[4]

As long as theologians suppose they are engaged in a kind of "science" which is concerned basically with attempting to describe its "object" in straightforward terms, much as physicists and biologists describe theirs, the issues will tend to be formulated so as to focus attention on just what the object of theology might be. Here everyone and anyone can come forth with his or her own claims, and there is no court in which they can be adjudicated: we simply do not have access to a theological "object" in this sense at all, making it possible to distinguish the invalid and unreliable from the significant and true. This way lies both obscurantism and chaos--precisely the situation we find in the contemporary scene.

If this condition is to be overcome, it is essential for us to recognize that the peculiar logical status of the central concepts with which theology deals demands radical reconception of both the task of theology and the way in which that task is carried out. Theology can no longer conceive of itself as presenting straightforwardly a kind of picture or map of *how things are*--the old schema of God, humankind and the world in their structural relations with each other. Rather, theology must conceive its work as more like building a house: using materials given in experience it is in fact *constructing a world* the fundamental design of which is not found in the materials themselves but is employed to give them a significant order and meaning.

To regard God and the world as constructs with which we bring order and personal meaning into experience does not involve down-grading them in comparison with directly perceivable objects. On the contrary. As defining the context within which the objects of experience are given us, they provide both the basis for our fundamental orientation in life and the chief source of those principles of interpretation by means of which we discern what is of significance or meaning among all the stimuli impinging upon us. They thus have great *practical* import for us; indeed, we could not live and act and think at all without some such ordering principles or images; and we would certainly have no way to deal with crisis or catastrophe. The constructive work of the mind through which humans have produced world-pictures and mythologies is no

141

optional or dispensable speculative activity: it
brings about the ordering of experience in such a way
as to make it possible to see meaning in it, to see
what place human life has within the whole of reality,
and thus to see what we can do, how we should act.
Without the development of overarching concepts and
comprehensive images and stories, we would have no
basis for selecting, from among all the potential
objects of attention impinging upon us, those which
can be ordered and combined into a pattern of sufficient structure and meaning to make possible conscious,
coherent, human life. The concepts or images of God
and world perform ordering and meaning-bestowing functions of this sort in Western culture. In the position
I am sketching here they remain, thus, absolutely
central—that toward which, and in terms of which, all
life and thinking is to be oriented—but now they are
understood not as realities that are simply *there,*
like ordinary perceivable objects, but rather as
essential constructs without which we could not live
or act.
. . . .

Once these facts are recognized, theology must
work along different lines than in the past. It will
no longer be engaged in searching out the channels of
our "knowledge of God" (on analogy with other "knowledge"), then setting out a description of what is
given through those channels; theological construction
is of a different sort, and requires quite different
criteria, from the construction of concepts of ordinary
objects, where we are concerned whether our concepts
do justice to what is actually perceived under certain
appropriate conditions. The purpose of theological
construction is to produce concepts (and world-pictures
and stories) which make possible adequate orientation
in life and the world. Of proposed concepts of God
and world, therefore, one must ask such questions as
these: What forms of human life do these conceptions
of its context facilitate? which forms inhibit?
What possibilities do they open up for men and women?
which do they close off? Like a map guiding the
traveler through unfamiliar territories—or better:
like a compass which faithfully points a direction of
orientation in the uncharted regions where the traveler
through life must move—the concepts of God and world
must be assessed and reconstructed in consideration of
the kinds of activity and forms of experience they
make possible, rather than with reference to some
objects to which they are supposed to "correspond."

The theologian's task is to construct a conception

or picture of the world--the whole that contains all
that is and all that can be conceived--as pervaded by
and purveying a particular kind of (humane) meaning
and significance because of its grounding in an ultimately humane reality. In this respect the theologian
is essentially an artist; and the activity of imaginative unifying and ordering in which he or she is
engaged is to some extent controlled by aesthetic
considerations of harmony and balance, consistency
and contrast. However, unlike much art, theology
does not confine itself to this or that segment or
fragment of experience, attempting to set it forth
clearly and distinctly, but rather addresses itself
to the *whole* within which all experience falls. In
painting his or her picture of the whole, the theological artist must draw on wide ranges and types of
experience, showing how each is grasped in the integrating vision and what each means, for the "whole"
is nothing, an empty abstraction, apart from the parts
that make it up. Moreover, the picture which results
dare not be highly idiosyncratic or "subjective"; it
must be recognizably of *our* world, our life, our
experience. It will have to find place for the terrors and joys, the triumphs and failures, the striving
and the repose, the loves and hatreds of actual human
life. It will have to do justice to the complexity
of political and economic institutional structures in
an industrial society, as well as to the intimacy of
personal communion; it will have to deal with and be
relevant to problems of conservation of the environment
on this planet as well as personal crises of despair
and meaninglessness. No important dimension of experience can be omitted from the theologian's concern and
interest and interpretation, and he or she must exert
every effort to root out one-sidedness, prejudice and
bias. In these respects theological work attempts to
be descriptive and scientific and "objective," and it
is dependent on the natural and social sciences, and
history, for knowledge of the facts. . . . .
. . . .

Even granting this importance of theological
criticism and construction, however, questions about
hubris and idolatry might still be raised in face of
the bald claim that the concept of God is entirely
our construct. Such a claim seems to suggest that it
is merely our arbitrary contrivance, invented by us
for our purposes and to be used by us in any way that
seems convenient.

The problem here arises from supposing that theological conceptual construction is a completely free

and arbitrary activity, that we can make our words
and ideas do whatever we please. But that is obviously
false. Words and concepts have meanings and uses in
the language we have inherited which we ignore at our
peril. They each have an integrity of their own, which
we cannot violate without destroying the possibility of
communication and even of our own clear thinking.
Though they are all human "constructs," they may not
be used arbitrarily but only in accordance with certain
rules (grammatical, syntactical, logical, semantic), if
they are to do their proper work for us. The rules
also, of course, are human creations, but they admit
even less of arbitrary disregard in fruitful and significant work. The concept of God, above all others,
indicating as it does reality with radical independence
and aseity, the ultimate point of reference for all life
and thinking, is simply not at our disposal to construct
any way we please. Serious theology will seek to un-
cover the constituents that give this notion its special meaning and the criteria which govern its use.
If and as that is done, it may be possible to construct
--or better, to reconstruct--that concept with greater
precision and adequacy.
. . . .

Endnotes

[1]*Reden uber die Religion*. Kritische Ausgabe
(Braunschweig: Schwetschke u. Sohn, 1879), p. 128.
(A slightly different English translation will be
found in John Oman, *On Religion* [New York: Harper
Torchbooks, 1958], p. 283.)

[2]An especially clear example of this is to be
found in the theology of Karl Barth. Here we are
told that "God comes into the picture, the sphere, the
field of man's consideration and conception in exactly
the same way that objects do. . . . He is an object
on the human plane just like other objects. . . ."
(*Church Dogmatics* [Edinburgh: T. & T. Clark, 1936-
1962], II, I, pp. 13-14). It is true of course that
Barth recognizes that "although God has genuine objectivity just like all other objects, His objectivity is
different from theirs" (Ibid.), and he devotes considerable effort to working out the distinctions in a
subtle and sophisticated way. But the model for thinking about God, with which he is working and which

remains despite all qualifications, is clearly that of
the perceptual object. In a similar way the philosopher of religion, John Hick, argues that "We become
conscious of the existence of other objects in the
universe, whether things or persons, either by experiencing them for ourselves or by inferring their existence from evidences within our experience. The awareness of God . . . is of the former kind . . . while the
object of religious knowledge is unique, its basic
epistemological pattern is that of all our knowing"
(Faith and Knowledge, Second Edition [Ithaca, N.Y.:
Cornell University Press, 1966], pp. 95,97). It should
not be supposed that thinking about God on the model
of the perceptual object is peculiar to writers with a
special "objectivist" emphasis. The same model will
be found, despite every attempt to avoid it, in Schleiermacher, a man supposedly at Barth's antipodes on
this issue. Schleiermacher is unequivocal that "any
possibility of God being in any way given is entirely
excluded, because anything that is outwardly given
must be given as an object exposed to our counterin-
fluence, however slight this may be. The transference
of the idea of God to any perceptible object, unless
one is all the time conscious that it is a piece of
purely arbitrary symbolism, is always a corruption. .
. ." (The Christian Faith [Edinburgh: T. & T. Clark,
1928], p. 18. Nevertheless, when Schleiermacher attempts to explicate the meaning of the term "God," he
does so by describing God as the correlative or object
of our sense of "absolute dependence," "the Whence of
our receptive and active existence, as implied in this
self-consciousness. . . ." (Ibid., p. 16). Clearly,
the model once again is the perceivable object, in this
case that over against us on which we depend or "hang"
(cf. German Abhangigkeit). The most recent, and by
far the most sophisticated, attempt to found theological work on the "apprehension" of reality which has
quasi-perceptual objectivity will be found in Edward
Farley, Ecclesial Man (Philadelphia: Fortress Press,
1975). Farley works out a Husserlian doctrine of
"appresentation" or indirect apprehension of God
through, or along with, direct apprehension of other
realities (see esp. pp. 194-231). In many respects
his position provides a bridge from the out-and-out
objectivist positions of persons like Barth and Hick
to that taken in this essay, for Farley clearly recognizes that appresentation has a large component of
what I shall call "imaginative construction." However,
Farley still attempts to legitimize the theological
enterprise by (objectivist) claims about "apprehension" of God, and it is just that vestige of objectivist

thinking, I argue here, which theology must once and for all give up.

[3]This straightforward referential talk may have derived in part from the presupposition that language consists essentially in "naming," and that behind every noun or concept there must be some "thing" or "object." The tendency to reify concepts has been fairly common in the theological tradition and many of the paradoxes of traditional theology exemplify it. Thus, human nature was often believed to be composed of two (or three) distinguishable "things"--body, soul (and spirit)--and the problem was to understand how these several things could get unified into a single person. Similarly, christological reflection focused on the question of how the "divine nature" and the "human nature" of Christ--seemingly two distinguishable and almost separable things--could be conceived as unified in one person. And the problem of the Trinity was the issue of how three things--Father, Son and Holy Spirit--were to be thought as one. In these and other theological controversies it seems to be taken for granted that when we have distinct names there must be distinct or separable entities. A great deal of recent philosophical work, particularly associated with the name of Wittgenstein, has shown this sort of move to rest on very gross errors to which we are often brought by the "bewitchment of language." Wittgenstein's basic discussions of these problems are in the *Philosophical Investigations* (Oxford: Blackwell, 1958) and in *The Blue and Brown Books* (Oxford: Blackwell, 1960). In the former there are explicit reflections on Augustine's discussion of the learning of language as typically the learning of names (see pp. 2ff.).

[4]It must be acknowledged that uneasiness about such an undialectical view of the objectivity of God found some expression in Christian thought from the very beginning. Particularly in the so-called negative or apophatic theology it was held that God may not be regarded as any kind of thing or object or essence; indeed, *what* God is is unknowable by us. Here, then, appears to be a complete rejection of objectifying language. However, the matter is not quite that simple. It was not really possible for the negative theology to get away from objectifying talk about God as its actual point of departure: on the one hand, the way of negation gained its meaning by contrast with, or in negation of, the affirmations of the way of eminence; on the other hand, to avoid saying

God is unqualifiedly *nothing*, it was still necessary
to make some positive statements about God, at least
analogically. Obviously there is considerable uneasiness about the use of objectifying models here, but
since no other way of understanding language about
God was available, those models in fact remained
determinative both of affirmations and negations.

Discussion Questions

1. To some extent Kaufman's case for theology as
construction hinges on his doubts about the validity
and truth of the claims of revelation. Do you think
revelational claims have been seriously undermined?
How do you decide between competing revelational
claims?

2. If you do not follow Kaufman's approach to understanding how the concept of God comes into being,
which of the other suggested options would you choose?
What are the weaknesses of your choice? What strengths?

3. If the concept of God is needed for order and
meaning, how do you account for the radical questioning of God's existence in contemporary culture? Are
there God-concepts "in disguise" such as materialism,
nationalism or ethnocentrism?

4. Given Kaufman's position that we cannot simply
construct any God-concept we wish, suggest some reasons why the Christian concept should be regarded as
preferable.

5. If a theological appeal could be made to secular
man on the basis of Kaufman's understanding of God,
what meaning would worship have? Would the function
or role of churches be changed?

6. Suppose we held that Jesus of Nazareth would be
regarded as the pattern for the construction of our
concept of God. Would this change your opinion of
Kaufman's thesis? Would the resultant theological
position be different from Barth's in any practically
significant way--in other words is Jesus the content
of our God-concept or not?

ON GOD'S ATTRIBUTES

The second of the two issues facing contemporary theologians after the question of God's existence is the formulation of an understanding of God's nature. Among the difficulties encountered when forming a modern understanding of God's nature we must surely include the doctrine of the Trinity; the affirmation that God is personal; and the attributes of God, traditionally his perfection, omnipotence, omniscience, and his love. Naturally, all three of these categories cannot be covered in a collection of this nature. Just as surely all the above need explication in order for a <u>Christian</u> theology to emerge.

The doctrine of the Trinity is not, strictly speaking, a biblical doctrine. But then again we have noted that no doctrine of systematic theology is exclusively biblical. The Trinitarian doctrine guards against both polytheism and monism. The living God is neither a bare unitary abstraction, nor a chaotic play of cosmic powers. The heart of the doctrine is that God is a unity in diversity.

God is Father; he creates, orders, and sustains existence. He holds back the powers of chaos and nothingness, and lures universal history toward meaningful ends. But to be told that God is creative power, and even that he is good, would terrify us unless we were also able to affirm that God is the Son. He is redemptive love. God is also the Spirit. He is present in the lives of his people.

Yet, there remain real difficulties for modern man in affirming that God is personal. We have become aware of the distortions which can be created by an uncritical description of God as a perfect human (anthropomorphism). In some sense to be a person is

148

to be limited in ways we would not wish to attribute
to God. Many of the problems connected with the
notion that God is personal stem from inaccurate and
sloppy formulations of God's attributes.

In the essay to follow Eugene Peters suggests a
reconstruction of our theology about God's attributes.
In so doing he relies heavily on philosophical insights formulated by Alfred North Whitehead and
Charles Hartshorne. Their philosophy is called
Process Philosophy because of the extreme emphasis it
places on dynamism, creativity and development.
Peters certainly does not agree with everything
Process thinkers suggest, even less does he believe
that Christian theology must accommodate itself to
Process thought. His position is that in the task of
formulating a doctrine of God Process Philosophy may
provide categories and ways of conceiving which
enable the theologian to be truer to his source-norms
(including the Bible) than older models. The long
history of various attempts to harmonize the Greek
and the biblical concept of God is documented in the
disputes and councils of the Church. The complications resulting from these attempts is what Peters
seeks to avoid. While doing so he wishes to show that
Process metaphysics makes possible a more intelligible
explication of the biblical revelation than the
traditional metaphysic allows.

Peters first deals with the notion that God is
unchangeable. He exposes the extreme difficulty
posed to a doctrine of the living God of the scripture
if one takes seriously the position that God does not
change. While it is true that the scriptures say
Jesus is the same yesterday, today and forever, we
may properly ask whether this is meant to be a doctrinal underpinning, and if so, in what sense? The
scriptures also bear ample evidence of God "repenting
himself" in cases of judgment. Hezekiah's prayers to
God influenced the Lord and he added years to the
king's life.

Part of Peters' objection to the idea that God
is unchangeable is that he does not believe such a
doctrine does justice to the living God of the scriptures. It may also be the case that he thinks the
ways of harmonizing God's unchangeable perfection with
man's prayers and petitions are simply unacceptable.
This a student must decide for himself, and it merits
much more study than can be done here.

The suggestion made in Peters' essay is that God is both changeable and unchangeable. Using Process Philosophy's understanding of God as di-polar, Peters argues that one part of God (his primordial nature) does not change. This is the part of God that makes him God, his essence as it were. Yet, another part of God (his consequent nature) does change. This is God's experience. God can have new experiences, he can be influenced by these experiences and he can enjoy them.

That position leads naturally to another attribute Peters discusses: God's omniscience. Traditional doctrine affirmed that God knew everything. The endless debates about whether God's knowledge of what I will choose tomorrow destroys my freedom to choose what I wish rooted in the doctrine of God's omniscience. Augustine's solution, followed by many since then, was to say that God knows what we in our freedom will choose. Peters' solution is different. He holds that God's knowledge is absolute for everything that has actually happened. Further, God knows with an unqualified accuracy. The difference comes in when Peters speaks of God knowing the possible as possible or the potential as potential.

God does not know what I will choose tomorrow-- at least not with certainty. He does know all the possible choices I can make. He knows the order of their likelihood of realization because he knows the actual me so well.

The main difference in these two approaches is in the place they give to time in relation to God. The traditional view does not consider God to be in time since to be in time would imply change. His eternality is defined as timelessness. He has no past or future, only an abiding present.

The view of the Process Philosophers, and of Peters, is that God experiences time. He has a past, present, and future. His experience increases. His eternality is not timelessness but infinite duration. Peters believes this view to be more in accord with the biblical witness, and he thinks that it restores more practical meaning to the life of faith. He thinks his view resolves the predestination/free-will problem. But does it? Since predestination is in the New Testament teaching, what can it mean?

We are led naturally now to a third attribute

150

Peters discusses: God's omnipotence. Traditionally, theologians argued that God was all powerful. Peters shows the logical mistake that such an understanding makes. He does not deal with the immense problem the traditional doctrine of omnipotence poses when dealing with the problem of evil, but students should read the essay on this issue in Part Three.

For Peters, to affirm God's omnipotence does not mean that he is a cosmic dictator who has decided all things; still less does it mean that God can do absolutely anything. It means that God is the power to which there can not be an equal nor a superior. But this does not mean that whatever happens is to be explained by saying God caused it.

God has chosen to interact with other powers; human and natural. According to Peters, God acts by influence and persuasion. Nothing escapes God's influence, nor can his influence be destroyed. But other powers may act contrary to God's persuasion. Still, God is involved incessantly luring, drawing, and persuading toward his desired ends. But he does not coerce.

God's love is the final attribute Peters discusses. God's love, he says, is forever changeless in its character. Yet, its expression and concrete manifestation differ from person to person. God participates in our joys and sorrows; he is affected by us. Although God sympathetically identifies with us, he does not necessarily endorse our actions or desires. But Peters holds that God actively draws every event toward the greatest possible good.

ON GOD'S ATTRIBUTES*

We find in the first two lines of a famous hymn a full expression of the union of the two notions (permanence and flux) in one integral experience:

> *Abide with me;*
> *Fast falls the eventide.*

Here the first line expresses the permanences, 'abide,' 'me' and the 'Being' addressed; and the second line sets these permanences amid the inescapable flux. Here at length we find formulated the complete problem of metaphysics.
Alfred North Whitehead[1]

The more full-bodied a doctrine of God, the more it will be relevant to actual religious experience and practice, and hence the more it will be able to illumine actual expressions of religion. Such expressions may very well involve questions of metaphysics. As Whitehead points out in the epigraph above, a famous hymn states in its first two lines the complete problem of metaphysics. In its theological form this problem can be found in many hymns--as well as in prayers, scripture, or creeds.

For example, consider the words of the following hymn, which many of us sing from time to time in services of worship:

> "Great is Thy faithfulness," O God my Father,
>   There is no shadow of turning with Thee;
> Thou changest not, Thy compassions, they fail
>   not;
>   As Thou hast been Thou forever wilt be.

> "Great is Thy faithfulness! Great is Thy
>   faithfulness!"
> Morning by morning new mercies I see;
> All I have needed Thy hand hath provided--
>   "Great is Thy faithfulness," Lord, unto me![2]

*Source: From *The Creative Advance*, pp. 92-104, by Eugene H. Peters, copyright 1966, used with permission of the publisher, Bethany Press.

If we examine these words from the point of view of their logic, we become aware that they contain a puzzle. On the one hand, God is regarded as changeless: "There is no shadow of turning with Thee; Thou changest not . . . As Thou hast been Thou forever wilt be." On the other hand, he is regarded as changing: he is fatherly and compassionate, exhibits new mercies morning by morning, and provides for personal need.

How can one who changes not also be compassionate? Can an unmoved being be moved to love and mercy? What father do you know who will forever be as he has been? How can one in whom there is no shadow of turning provide for one's needs, which change throughout his life?

Face to face with the problem of God's immutability, it appears that we must make a choice. (1) We may hold--with the mainstream of classical Christian theology--that God is changeless and complete in all respects. If so, he could in no way grow or increase in value, and service to him would be impossible, since he could receive nothing.[3] (2) We may hold--in opposition to the mainstream of classical Christian theology--that God is in no respect changeless and complete. This implies, however, that he changes (or is capable of change) in every way, is therefore unreliable, and might even cease to be recognizable at all. If we must choose between these alternatives, the choice is hardly a pleasant one.

Hartshorne has shown that the problem is not as simple as this,[4] for it may be wrong to assert that God is changeless and complete in all respects, and it may *also* be wrong to assert that he is in no respect changeless and complete. The truth, as Hartshorne says, may lie in a neglected alternative: that God is changeless and complete in *some* respects, but not in all. In short, we may find the truth not by taking one pole to the exclusion of the other but rather by taking both poles in combination. There is no stupefying paradox in this. Indeed, we meet dipolarity on every hand. A boy may spin a top so expertly that for the moment its axis remains steady and fixed. Yet the top rotates about its axis. Hence, it is changeless in one respect, changing in another. To take another example, "ol' man river" as it rolls along is certainly changing. Still, the *fact* that the river flows is itself unchanging (so long as the river continues to flow and is not dammed, frozen, or dried up). Still another example of dipolarity is furnished by our very experience. A man who was sick last week may now be fully recovered. If so, he is not *precisely* the same person he was, for he is no longer ill. Nonetheless, in reporting his experience, he suggests that the change has not canceled his identity: "I was sick," he tells us. "I am now well." Both permanence and change are present--as in all human experience. Man is dipolar.

The principle of dipolarity sheds light on the problem of God's immutability. Let us consider the problem from the point of view of three of his attributes, namely, power, wisdom, and love.

It is perhaps unfortunate that we call God omnipotent. For the term literally means "all-powerful," which suggests that he wields all the power there is or could be. If so, then only God has power and only he could have power. But, as Hartshorne points out,[5] religion has always distinguished between God's power and the power or powers that enact evil. If God possesses all actual and possible power, it follows that he alone is responsible for the evil which has been done and in addition that he alone will be responsible for all future evil. Furthermore, if God has an absolute monopoly on power, over whom can he exercise it? Over you and me? On this theory, you and I are supposed to possess no power whatsoever. Indeed, there is absolutely nothing over which God--as the sole power in the universe--could exercise his power. If, as Hartshorne holds, power is a meaningful concept only if it entails the notion of opposing power--if, that is, power is *in principle* shared--the doctrine that God has limitless power simply does not make sense.[6]

These considerations prompt us to redefine divine omnipotence. We may say that God is omnipotent, not in the sense that he is the cosmic dictator of all things, but in the sense that no other power is or could be as great as his. Reality is a society of greater and lesser powers in interaction with one another, God being the cosmic power to which there could be neither an equal nor a superior. He influences the actions of all beings in the universe but does not coerce or fully determine them. This conception of God's omnipotence seems to be what men of religion have ordinarily intended when they spoke of divine power. It allows one to affirm that God's power is unalterable and yet forever at work in the world. It is thus a doctrine of the dipolarity of divine power.

In this new conception, God's power in an important sense is changeless and perfect, but this does not mean that whatever happens is God's doing. Rather, it means that in all circumstances God exercises a cosmic influence which no other could equal or surpass. No being can escape the divine influence, nor could anything destroy it. To speak of the providence of God is to refer to this indestructible greatest possible power among all powers, which sways the others according to its undeviating beneficence. In short, God's power is changeless *in character or quality* though changing in its concrete manifestations.

To the question: "But how can you claim that God is omnipotent when there is so much evil in the world?" the reply is that the questioner has failed to grasp the new definition of God's omnipotence. Though God in principle has supreme power, his is not the only power in the universe. Therefore, things can (and do) occur contrary to his will. In fact, if each of the multiplicity of beings enjoys some power, it is highly unlikely that evil and discord among them can be avoided. As Hartshorne remarks, the fact that God possesses the best possible power does not guarantee the best possible world.[7]

We have discussed God's power mainly in terms of his influence upon the beings in the world. It is natural enough when we think of power to think of the capacity to act. But if God is the supreme power *among others*, what the others do will doubtless have an effect on him. Indeed, the perfection of God's power will involve his capacity to *receive the influence of the world* in the most excellent way. This is certainly no news to men of religious faith. Many philosophers and theologians have insisted that God is impassive, independent of all influences, and therefore really indifferent toward the creatures. Men of religious faith, however, have always believed--in the words of another famous hymn--that God is "only wise" (meaning all wise), that his knowledge is both clear and complete. What, after all, is such knowledge except unqualified *sensitivity* to the influences of the world's beings?

The all-wisdom of God, another of his attributes, is called his omniscience. Divine omniscience implies that for every change in the world there is a corresponding change in God. Accordingly, God's knowledge

155

is relative to (dependent on) the feelings and actions of the beings that compose the world. His knowledge, therefore, cannot be regarded as a changeless, inert totality. It grows in content, adding new items of knowledge in accordance with every change in the world. But, as stated above, God's reception of influences is an aspect of his omnipotence, not a weakness or defect.

Hartshorne illustrates this point as follows.[8] He asks us to imagine an eloquent poem read in the presence of: (1) a glass of water, (2) an ant, (3) a dog, (4) a person unfamiliar with the language in which the poem is written, (5) a person who knows the language but is insensitive to poetry, and (6) a person who knows the language and is sensitive to poetry as well. The glass of water will scarcely be affected by the reading. The ant may vaguely experience sound waves from the reader. The dog will perhaps sense some of the emotional tones in the reader's voice. The person unfamiliar with the language of the poem will likely be aware of the moods and verbal music of the poem. The one who knows the language but is insensitive to poetry will perhaps grasp ideas and images, but lack aesthetic enjoyment. Finally, he who listens knowingly and appreciatively will experience an adventure in thought and feeling. The series moves from less to more understanding and *at the same time* from less to more dependence on the poem. The power to know is the power to depend on the objects of knowledge.

If in one sense divine knowledge is dependent and changing, in another it is independent and changeless, for our conception of God is dipolar throughout. In the light of what has been said, it is not difficult to see how God's omniscience is independent and changeless, for it always corresponds to its objects. It *always* does so. God's knowledge is constant--unfailing--in its adequacy to its objects. Hence, his knowledge is absolute, complete, changeless in its infallibility.

Thus, we may say that God's knowledge is changeless, not in its content, but in its type or character. If God knows all things with unqualified adequacy, he knows them just as they are--the actual as actual, the possible as possible. One reason for making this point is that it bears on the age-old problem of divine foreknowledge. It is sometimes claimed that God, being omniscient, knows all those events which for us are future. Such a theory assumes that the future is composed of events as real, definite, and detailed as those which compose the past. But the future is future precisely because it is *not yet* real, definite, and detailed. If this were not the case, then you and I, and all our descendants would already be dead and buried. The function of time, as Hartshorne remarks, is to settle issues in sequence one by one.[9] If the future is as yet unsettled, that is exactly the way God knows it--as unsettled. If God "knew" it in any other way, he would "know" falsely, for, as we have said, God's knowledge is perfectly adequate to its objects: he knows things as they truly are. The upshot is that God knows the past as finished--settled --in every detail, the present as in process of actualization, and the future as indefinite and yet to be settled.

Since God's knowledge of events is infallible, we may suppose that no event ever slips from the divine memory. Events which we remember vaguely and partially are remembered by God clearly and comprehensively. One way of stating this is to say that each event in the world is destined for immortality in God's memory. Such a doctrine clarifies one of our common-sense notions, namely, that once an event occurs, it will forever after be true that it occurred precisely as it did, for God's memory is the perfectly sensitive receptable of all occurrences.

God's knowledge of the world is not remote and indirect. He is no spectator of events external to himself; he does not stare at an alien world. Rather, he takes the life of the world into his own life and "'shares with each creature its actual world.'"[10] Hence, God's knowledge is direct, immediate. If this were not so, it would be subject to such imperfections as inhere in meditated knowing. Were there objects "outside" God, his knowledge of them would be partly inferential (since indirect) and thus inadequate.[11]

Those who insist on the absolute changelessness of God will have particular difficulty with our third topic, the doctrine of divine love, for how can we conceive a being in all respects complete and immutable, a being without need, desire, or feeling, who at the same time loves the creatures? Such a conception involves poor logic and is bound to lead to distortions in religion. Love is nothing less than desire for the good of others, as Hartshorne says.[12]

It is a matter of willing their well-being and happiness. But, as before, our conception is dipolar.
There is a changeless aspect to the divine love, for its *character* is constant. Charles Wesley wrote:

> Jesus, Thou art all compassion,
> Pure, unbounded love Thou art.

The love of God is like that--all compassion, pure and unbounded. His love is pure: it is not mixed with indifference or hardness of heart. His love is unbounded: none can "drift beyond His love and care." The outstretched arms of the crucified Man of Nazareth are an apt symbol for the all-inclusiveness of the divine love. It is the character of God's love, so conceived, that is immutable.

Our love for one another is neither pure nor unbounded. Self-interest always inhibits our wishes for others, and ignorance radically limits our awareness of them. God, being omniscient, knows all actual beings as parts of his own life. It follows that God, in willing your good or mine or any creature's, *also wills his own*. Thus, in God, there is an absolute coincidence of self-interest and other-interest.

When we do good for others, we are always partly ignorant of the good we accomplish. Indeed, a man may be long dead before good he was instrumental in bringing about is realized. But God is deathless, and every beauty and joy he enables us to have becomes an element in his own experience. Hence, there is for God no question of seeking the good of the creatures to the exclusion of his own good. Nor, on the other hand, is there for God any question of seeking his own good in disregard of the creatures' good.[13] Both statements are true for the same reason: the good God intends for the creature is at the same time his very own good.

It is *because* God's love is forever changeless in character that its concrete content and expression differ from person to person, and from situation to situation. We find illustration of this point in human love. A parent's love for his children is constant only if his thoughts, feelings, and actions are tailored to each child at each stage of that child's life. We may assume that the father in Jesus' parable of the prodigal did not love the one son more than the other. Yet in order for his love to remain true and constant, it had to correspond in its concrete content

158

and expression to the differences between the two sons.

God loves the neighbor (that is, the creature) with the same intimacy with which he (God) loves himself, for in God self-interest and other-interest are absolutely coincident. Since God loves us and desires our good, he experiences sorrow when conflict and suffering befall us. Hence, God's love by no means guarantees his unqualified happiness. The good man, as Hartshorne reminds us, suffers more intensely than the bad at the spectacle of suffering and evil in others.[14] The defeat of our interests is the defeat of God's *own* interests[15] and constitutes an element of tragedy within the divine life.

The doctrine that God joys in our joys and sorrows in our sorrows has important ethical implications. For example, there are in our day thousands of people who desperately need education, housing, job opportunities, etc. If our doctrine of God's love tells us anything at all, it tells us that when we deny these people, we deny God; that when we treat them with fairness and concern, we serve God, for what we do "to one of the least of these"[16] we do to God himself. We have all been reared on the idea that God is father and all men brothers. This concept is pale and abstract beside the truth that my fellow man is "a very fragment of the life of God."[17] We are members one of another because we are members of the living whole, which is unified by divine love.

God, on this interpretation, does not stand off and merely wish us well, nor is his love merely eagerness to do things for us. Divine love is instead sympathetic identification with us in our sufferings as well as in our joys. It is important to note that sympathetic identification does not mean endorsement of all our purposes and desires. In the nature of the case, God could not endorse those which are evil. But even among those purposes and desires that are not evil, he must choose some and reject others, for his sway upon the world must take some direction or other--not all directions at once. Doubtless he chooses in such a way that the greatest possible good is realized. In any event, our interests are never discarded as irrelevant or impertinent. Indeed, God passively wishes, that is, he feels with and for all creatures, what they wish for themselves,[18] but he must resolve the conflict of interests which he thus takes upon himself. He will not resolve it in such a way as to rob us of all freedom. Consequently, he

suffers a double tragedy: he is unable to realize the
multifarious interests which he endorses, and he must
endure cruel and insensitive feelings, thoughts, and
acts, which he does not endorse.

Hartshorne's doctrine of God represents a clear
and cogent statement of the religious man's understanding of God. Christian theology, where it has
been under the influence of Greek metaphysics, has
always leaned toward a conception of God which subordinates and even disregards certain fundamental religious insights, a conception in which God is viewed
as utterly changeless and complete in all respects.
What Hartshorne shows (indirectly) is that the biblical picture of God is far more respectable philosophically than theologies which, though wrought by the
wisest of men, are in the grip of the conception of
God as static completion. Conceiving God as a dipolarity of permanence and flux, he provides a rational
interpretation of the God of Abraham, Isaac, and
Jacob--and of Jesus--a rational interpretation of the
God whose power, while unsurpassable, is social;
whose wisdom, while perfect, is ever changing; and
whose love, while constant, is pure sensitivity to
creaturely joy and sorrow.

Endnotes

[1]From *Process and Reality*, p. 318. Used by
permission.

[2]Thomas O. Chisholm, author. Copyright by Hope
Publishing Co. Used by permission.

[3]What is absolutely fixed simply cannot change,
whether for better or worse. And what cannot change
cannot receive anything, since such reception would
constitute a change.

[4]See, for example, Hartshorne, *Reality as Social
Process*, pp. 155-162.

[5]See, for example, Hartshorne, "Omnipotence," *An
Encyclopedia of Religion*, ed. Vergilius Ferm (1945),
p. 545.

6The popular doctrine that God "limits himself," lending some fraction of his power to creatures, involves the supposition that it is theoretically possible for him to possess all power. However, if in the nature of the case power must be shared, this supposition is false and the popular doctrine therefore ill-founded.

7See Hartshorne, *An Encyclopedia of Religion*, p. 546.

8See Hartshorne, *The Divine Relativity*, p. 49.

9See Hartshorne, *Reality as Social Process*, p. 201.

10*Ibid.*, p. 202. See Whitehead, *Process and Reality*, p. 523.

11"The external, it appears, is known by signs which are internal (to the knower), that is, it is known imperfectly, abstractly, partially." Charles Hartshorne, *Man's Vision of God* (Chicago: Willett, Clark & Company, 1941), p. 289.

12See *ibid.*, p. 14.

13Of course, the good that God seeks and realizes may fail to include the good (the genuine good) a creature wishes for itself, not because God is indifferent to its good—indeed, he suffers the sorrow and loss involved—but because he cannot avoid selection among conflicting and incompatible forms of good.

14See Hartshorne, *Man's Vision of God*, p. 14.

15This does not mean that God shares the morally evil "interests" of creatures and is therefore himself wicked. Hartshorne regards moral evil as privative: it is not interest; it is *lack* of interest.

16Matt. 25:40b.

17Hartshorne, *Reality as Social Process*, pp. 151-152.

18See Hartshorne, *Man's Vision of God*, p. 293.

Discussion Questions

1. Do you agree that some aspects of the traditional understanding of God's attributes need revision in order to be more meaningful? More biblical? Which attributes?

2. Recent discussion has emphasized the motherhood of God, and God's femininity. In the source-norms of Christian tradition what factors support this emphasis? Which detract from it? Are there important insights into God's nature which require such reformulation? If so, have these been ignored by the historic church or have they been expressed in other doctrines and ways?

3. Do you think that practical religious life is better served by Peters' reinterpretation or by the traditional conception of God's attributes?

4. How would one go about deciding whether his theology was more shaped by a philosophical model than by the scripture?

5. Given our discussion of the source-norms for theological formulation, is the question above an accurate picture of the issue of interpretation?

RETROSPECTIVE

Hick has demonstrated amply the philosophical difficulties with "proving" God's existence. Do we, then, as theologians, begin with Barth's resolution of the God-question? Is his interpretation not only the most intelligible of the options but also the most accurate one?

It may very well be that Hick's case is so clearly established, and Barth's so manifestly presuppositional, that secular persons feel driven to conclude that Feuerbach's explanation of theism as a psychological projection of idealized humanity is determinative. Even the approach advocated by Gill (Tillich and Gilkey) must show at some point why theistic symbols are more acceptable explications of the religious dimension than are Buddhist symbols or secular ones. If Feuerbach's conclusions are to be avoided on Gill's terms, this transition to explicit theistic explication must be made intelligible. I think Gill has prepared the way for this in his book entitled *On Knowing God*. Barth thinks that such a view is a natural theology, and it does not think the transition can be made explicit because the gulf cannot be bridged by man. Do you agree?

Kaufman's approach is complementary to Gill's in some respects. Like Gill, Kaufman recognizes the active role of the subject in every act of knowing. But unlike Gill, Kaufman is still perhaps too much indebted to Kant's subject-object distinction. He speaks of the concepts of God and the world as human constructs. If we take him seriously, then it seems that he plays directly into Feuerbach's hand. But such a judgment is not entirely fair. After all, he does say that the question whether a reality corresponds to our constructed God-concept is an open one.

Probably Kaufman should be more critical of Feuerbach's projection theory. Again, Gill and others (e.g., Michael Polanyi, J. L. Austin, Maurice Merleau-Ponty, and even Kant) are helpful here. It is the case that the subject-object distinction cannot be maintained rigidly. Every act of knowing is a projected act. We meet, shape, and constitute everything we experience. The force of this observation is that Feuerbach's theory that God is a projection, while other data are directly given, is seen to be totally erroneous. Our God-concept is a human construction, a projection; but then again all our concepts of literally every object are constructions and projections.

This means that Kaufman may be wrong when he says God is not an object among objects, but he may be correct in observing that our constructing activity is too little acknowledged. As to whether Peters' attempt at reconstructing the God-concept of traditional theology is viable, one must adjudicate for himself relying on the source-norms earlier described. How one conceptualizes God's attributes will have much bearing on his understanding of God's relation to the world.

PART THREE

CREATION AND PROVIDENCE

CREATION AND PROVIDENCE

For many centuries traditional Christian beliefs about the divine origin and governance of the world were essential foundational components of the Western world view. The traditional doctrine of creation affirmed that the world had an absolute beginning. God created it. Before creation only God existed. And the scriptures were understood to indicate that the creative activity of God was well defined. It was marked by remarkable *de novum* occurrences. Accordingly, a brief period of seven days was sufficient for creation.

Virtually every element of traditional creation doctrine has been challenged, if not overthrown, by views inspired by modern science. Modern persons accept the sovereignty of the scientific picture of the world at every practical level. Geologists, not the scriptures, are consulted when searching for oil. While biologists and paleontologists may disagree on the details of evolution or the dynamics at work in developmentalism, there is no disagreement on the principle of biological and geologic evolution. Accordingly, the life and earth sciences offer explanations of the origin and development of the world and of humanity which are incompatible with the traditional doctrine of creation.

In the essays which follow, Carl F. H. Henry offers a careful analysis and defense of the traditional doctrine. He is careful to point out that the truth of this doctrine does not depend upon a scientific demonstration that evolution is wrong. Instead, he holds that it depends on the trustworthiness of the scriptural revelation. Nevertheless, Henry is critical of exegesis based on what he calls scientifico-concept presuppositions.

Langdon Gilkey's essay also focuses on the
distinction between the contention that evolution has
in fact happened, and the altogether different thesis
that the process of evolution is to be explained by
random variations and natural selection. Gilkey holds
that certain of the traditional elements of creation
doctrine, such as the short time-span of creation and
the once-for-all creation of species, are not essential
to the theological meaning of the doctrine. He
believes these notions must be abandoned because of
what we know scientifically. Yet, he thinks this is
a challenge to Christian faith only if one insists on
the scientific infallibility of the scriptures.

Gilkey's position implies that a theological
source-norm need not be inerrant in order to contain
truth. And I suspect that he would affirm this of
every source-norm, not just the scriptures. Furthermore, he suggests that a source-norm need not contain
truth about everything (e.g. the scientific explanation of origins) in order to be true in a religious
sense.

The more dangerous threat to Christian faith,
according to Gilkey, is that evolution operates
solely by naturalistic and random influences. He
believes it is at this level that the doctrine of
creation is to be formulated.

Concomitant with the Christian doctrine of creation tradition has affirmed the providence of God.
What this means theologically is that events occur
to serve a divine purpose. Both nature and history
operate to serve the higher purposes of God. To be
sure, of course, there have been varying colorations
to this theme. But there remained until the enlightenment period a persistent belief that humans were
special projects of God's activity, that God provides
food for beast and bird, he takes note of the death of
a sparrow, he controls the forces of nature and decrees
the rise and fall of nations.

Science challenged this view as surely as it did
the doctrine of origins. The increasing comprehensive-
ness of scientific explanation left little room for
the hand of God. Tenaciously, however, theologians
continue to wrestle with this issue; probably because
they recognize its fundamental importance. No doctrine
of God remotely resembling that affirmed by historic
Christianity can be preserved apart from an intelligible theology of providence.

The essay by C. S. Lewis deals with the activity of God identified by a theology of miracles. A more recent work by Colin Brown (*Miracles and the Critical Mind*) is indicative of the sustained interest in a meaningful understanding of God's pronounced activity in nature and history.

Lewis uses a realmistic model to develop an argument for the intelligibility of miracles. He clarifies what is meant by the notion of Laws of Nature and suggests that these Laws hold "all things being equal." In a miraculous occurrence, things are not equal. Another agent, not bound by our categories of existence, is active. To be sure, Lewis leaves many questions unanswered. But his essay is an attempt to set the stage for a more developed under- standing; it is not meant to be definitive.

Although science posed a challenge to a Christian theology of providence, a far more formidable problem is the presence of evil. In the modern world aware- ness of evil, tragedy, and suffering has become the greatest enemy to faith. The legacy of Hiroshima and Auschwitz has been for many the end of any meaningful doctrine of providence.

The effort to interpret and understand evil in the light of the faith is called *theodicy*, which means "the justification of God." The problem of evil asks how a good God, who is sovereign, could allow the agony of Biafra, the floods, the wars, or the whole- sale slaughter of humanity in the holocaust. If God is in control, how can he be good? If he is good, how can he be in control?

One of the most persuasive contemporary theodicies is that given by John Hick. Hick deals primarily with moral evil, the evil produced by intelligent and will- ful beings, rather than natural evil, that produced by impersonal forces (e.g. storms, floods, tornadoes, earthquakes, drought). One should not conclude that the latter of these problems is easily resolved. For a thorough discussion of this issue one may consult David Griffin's work, *God, Power and Evil: A Process Theodicy*.

Hick contends that God's creative intention is to bring forth a creature who can have fellowship with him based on willing cooperation. Such a process requires a free being, and this is of necessity an adventure fraught with potential for evil and sorrow.

A world with potential for evil is the only one in which moral beings may be fashioned. Thus evil is not in itself evidence that God is not providentially in control.

In response to Hick, J. L. Mackie has written a devastating critique of all free-will defenses of God. Mackie holds that there is no contradiction in saying that God could have created beings who freely chose to do good. That is, on the premise that God is omnipotent--a term the meaning of which we have seen is open to debate.

That all things work for the good may be at least as much an eschatological vision as it is a descriptive observation or principle. However, one must wonder with Dostoevsky whether a higher harmony is worth the suffering of innocents. How can a hell for oppressors atone for those who have already suffered?

Creation and providence are intricately interwoven. And no adequate theology can fully separate these doctrines. Somehow one must try to do justice both to God's originating role and to his sustaining role in such a way as to preserve his sovereignty and goodness.

THE DOCTRINE OF CREATION

The question whether the earth is a result of creation is a religious question, not a scientific one. Carl F. H. Henry makes this plain in the essay to follow. To say, "I believe in God, the Maker of heaven and earth" is to make a faith statement not an empirical deduction.

But we should clearly understand what it is that Henry means for us to accept by faith. It is the veracity of the scriptures which must be accepted. Henry holds that the biblical writers accepted the Genesis record as factual, and he concludes, then, that if we believe the scriptures, we should accept it so also. To fail to affirm the doctrine of creation eventuates in a metaphysical and moral outlook which is detrimental to the dignity and worth of humanity.

Henry's main concern is that the scientific theory of evolution has defined the way Genesis is understood. What emerged, he says, is the view that God originated the evolutionary process and he achieves his ends by means of it.

Henry discusses the various models available to theologians who reject the practice of allowing scientific theory to determine how Genesis is understood. He holds that there are creation scientists of various sorts who can account for the scientific data normally interpreted along evolutionary lines, and yet also preserve the six day creation period.

What one must decide as he reads Henry's essay is whether the differences between what he calls "the Biblical view" and "Evolutionary theory" are as clearcut as Henry suggests. Is it the case that evolutionary theory necessarily disavows the theologically significant points in the Biblical view?

Also important for the theologian is the question whether scientific creationism is really a viable science. Is there a comprehensive theory of creation science or is it primarily a reactionary philosophy, intent only on explaining data differently than evolutionary theory? Can it lead to new knowledge? Could we make predictions based on scientific creationism, or is it strictly a hindsight model of explanation?

THE DOCTRINE OF CREATION*

The Bible begins with God the Creator. The initial statement of the Apostles' Creed affirms "God the Father almighty, maker of heaven and earth." Calvin assigns the first book of the *The Institutes* to "the knowledge of God the Creator." Karl Barth devotes some 400 pages to "The Work of Creation" (*Church Dogmatics*, III/1) and in two additional volumes expounds its significance and implications.

The question of the ultimate source of the universe brings human experience and reasoning to a standstill that only revelation from without or above can overcome. As James M. Houston rightly observes, creation "has to be a statement of faith, not an empirical deduction" (*I Believe in the Creator*, p. 72).

Is this faith in a divine Creator credible? Is the humanistic evolutionary alternative rationally preferable? Or is evolutionary dogma itself burdened by immense and insuperable difficulties? The issues are debated today no less vigorously than a century ago.

"Creation cannot be tested by the scientific method," notes Warren H. Johns, "because the scientific

*Source: From *God, Revelation and Authority*, Volume 6, *Part Two* by Carl F. H. Henry, copyright (c) 1983; used by permission of Word Books, Publisher, Waco, Texas 76796.

method can deal only with repeatable events. No scientific experiment can be constructed to test the probability or even the possibility of Creation" ("The Doctrine of beginnings," p. 20). Science can have no theory of an *origin*; it must cope with a given cosmos, and therefore tends to assume an everlasting universe, past and future.

What then can or should be said for the historic Judeo-Christian view, namely, that divine revelation answers the question unresolved by empirical inquiry and does so, moreover, in an intelligible and reasonable way? "Through faith," Scripture declares (Heb. 11:3), "we *understand* that *the worlds* were *framed by the word of God,* so that *things which are seen* were *not made of things which do appear*" (KJV, italics mine).

By focusing attention on natural development, chance variation, and contemporary observational data both modern scientific empiricism and evolutionary theory deflected interest from the transcendent Creator and his dependent creation. Widespread academic endorsement of this evolutionary explanation of the universe and of all forms of life by immanent development factors shunted discussion of supernatural creation out of the public arena and into the religious colleges and churches; but even here the issues are less than fully faced and debated.

In some circles today anyone who mentions divine creation is likely to be reminded of Archbishop Ussher's projected creation date of 4004 B.C., a date once incorporated into the margin of the King James Version and preserved by the first edition of the *Scofield Reference Bible*. There will be scornful reminders, too, of a "young earth" created in six literal twenty-four-hour days, and of identifying the divinely established "kinds" of life in the Genesis account as the modern "species" and insisting on their absolute fixity.

The fact is, and it is often forgotten, that scarcely a century ago almost everyone--scientists and other scholars as fully as the rank and file of people, nonchristians no less than Christians--held such "traditional" views. On the matter of species, moreover, it was actually scientists and not theologians who in the nineteenth century first encouraged the understanding of the created kinds or families of life in the narrow sense of species. When theologians then espoused this view they were challenged by scientists who had moved on to argue for the fluidity of species.

If high penalities attach to saying that the Genesis account teaches more than it actually does, no less severely do they attach to diluting or misrepresenting what the creation narrative affirms. The present confused situation calls for assessing and exhibiting in a balanced way the cognitive claims of both creationist doctrine and evolutionary theory.

What Genesis teaches about man and the world as a divine creation differs remarkably from the other ancient views of orgins. The tendency of *Religionsges-chichte* scholars to minimize the differences between Genesis and so-called nonbiblical "creation" accounts found in other religions of the Near East must not be allowed to obscure certain very real and important dissimilarities. Over against the comparative religions approach Gerhard F. Hasel argues that "the Genesis cosmology represents not only a 'complete break' with the ancient Near Eastern mythological cosmologies but represents a parting of the spiritual ways brought about by a conscious and deliberate antimythical polemic which meant an undermining of the prevailing mythological cosmologies" ("The Polemic Nature of the Genesis Cosmology," pp. 81-102). Even if the creation story may have been first revealed to Adam and antedated pagan cosmologies its implicit indictment of the later religious myths would be no less striking. Sumerian and Egyptian creation stories are not only polytheistic but they also incorporate capricious and immoral elements, are quasi-pantheistic, and at times are exasperatingly ambiguous and in some respects superstitious and even magical. The *Enuma elish*, or Babylonian account, for example, reads: "On the day (when) above not named were heavens, below earth a name was not called"; the contrast here with the straightforward Genesis affirmation that "In the beginning Elohim created the heavens and the earth" is obvious. In the Babylonian account gods and goddesses personify diverse aspects of nature, and the universe results or emerges from a conflict between the gods.

In a world given to worshiping the sun, moon or stars, or to referring the fortunes and misfortunes of life to astral determinism or to cosmic forces, the Genesis writer dares to emphasize that God created the heavenly bodies and that Elohim and Elohim alone is worthy of worship. "Even the polemical avoidance of naming the luminaries is deliberate," comments Houston; "they are just 'great lights,' candelabra set in the

173

sky, without the terrifying powers of fate men ascribed to them. The biblical writer adds laconically and almost parenthetically that God made 'the stars also,' as if to deny any primary potency in astrology" (*I Believe in the Creator*, p. 65).

The Bible sweeps aside strange misconceptions of an original nonbeing, of primal darkness or chaos or undifferentiated matter; it denies notions of a world sprung from an original seed or hatched from a cosmic egg; it routs myths about polytheistic gods that cooperate with fate or destiny, yet also strive against it; it puts to flight philosophical speculations about eternal processes and impersonal forces or about a demiurge contending against recalcitrant matter. The Genesis creation account confronts and challenges these and many other conjectures.

At the center of the scriptural creation narrative, as at the center of the entire Bible, stands the living God. If we turn to Genesis 1 for information first and foremost about the cosmos and man we miss the center of its focus. The subject of Genesis is not quarks or quasars, but God. The biblical subject of the Hebrew term *bara* (to create) is invariably God whose transcendent sovereign will is presupposed by all existence. "In the beginning God. . . ." Elohim is *there* before the universe existed, he is *there* as the sovereign source of all contingent possibilities. More than 40 times between the initial declaration that "God created" (1:1) and the statement that he "rested" (2:2) Genesis names God as the subject of decision and deeds: Elohim "created," his Spirit "hovers" over the waters, he "says," "calls," "sees," "makes," "blesses," "gives," and much else; not least of all he declares his creation to be good.

The sustained impression given by the account is that the living God creates voluntarily according to his sovereign pleasure--that is, he creates first and foremost for his own glory. This fact is attested by later writers as well. The Psalmist for example affirms (19:1; cf. Isa. 43:7, Rom. 1:19f.) that "the heavens declare the glory of God; and the firmament showeth his handiwork" (KJV). Nowhere does the creation account suggest that God was externally motivated or prompted to create, or that he was internally required to do so. The universe is a wholly contingent reality, not a product of divine necessity. Divine creation is not motivated by some inner divine need or lack. The Creator's own transcendent majesty, divinity and eter-

174

nity are attested by the created universe; so also are his wisdom and omniscience (Ps. 104:24; Job 28:24 ff.; Prov. 3:19, 8:27; Jer. 10:12).

The God of the Bible is declared to be the everlasting inexhaustible God (Isa. 40:28-31), the sovereign lord of all creation and of universal history (Isa. 40-55). His covenant embraces the behavior of nature and the direction of history and overrules all chaos and calamity. Whether in Genesis or in the Psalms or Isaiah or elsewhere, *bara* designates God's incomparable creative activity not only in the cosmos but also in history and in the redemptive renewal of sinners (cf. Ps. 51:10, "Create in me a clean heart, O God"). One and the same term is used for God's originating activity in fashioning man and fashioning the world (Gen. 1:1, 21, 27, 2:3 f., 5:1 f., 6:7; Deut. 4:3; and often in the Psalms and in Isaiah) as well as for God's shaping of history (Ex. 34:10; Nu. 16:30; Jer. 31:32; Isa. 45:7, 48:7, 65:18). The New Testament continues this emphasis.

Nothing in the Genesis creation account encouraged subsequent biblical writers to accept it as other than a factual record of God's creation of the universe (cf. Ex. 20:11; Ps. 33:6-9; 2 Cor. 11:3; 1 Tim. 2:13 f.; 2 Pet. 3:5). Jesus as well treats it in this manner (Matt. 19:4 f.). Every New Testament writer refers to the creation narrative, and every such reference proceeds on the clear assumption that the account is to be understood factually, not mythically or symbolically. Although some of the Bible's most lofty teaching is cast in poetic form, the Genesis account is straightforward prose.

This is not to say, however, that if any facets of the biblical account of the creation and of man's fall are to be retained as literal, it follows that all elements must be interpreted literally, if proper principles of hermeneutics are observed, there is no reason why a distinction between literal and figurative sense cannot be made within the creation account. God's "speaking" or "saying" does not involve laryngeal utterance, for example, and in any event man was not present before the sixth day to "hear" the voice and Word of God in creation. That God creates by his Word is expounded by the Johannine prologue to mean that God sovereignly and intelligibly created through the instrumentality of the eternal Logos (Word). A sovereign immaterial Spirit, though lacking a creaturely larynx, can moreover make himself "heard" not only by Adam in the garden but also "overheard" by the inspired writer to whom he subsequently discloses the sacred account of creation, fall and redemption. God does not speak literally as humans speak, yet he nonetheless literally spoke and speaks; his divine speaking and speech cannot be dismissed merely in terms of poetic representation or myth. The reality of divine revelation is related in the Bible to the fact that God truly speaks his word and that the representations of the scriptural writers are not their own but rather a divine word that they report.

The recent tendency to contrast scientific fact with religious myth is currently yielding, and remarkably so, to an age in which science now more candidly considers its own projections as tentative models and creative myths. Some of this change of perspective stems from the fact that earlier scientific dogmatisms have fallen upon hard times. Past claims to scientific finality frequently have had to be revised. There is no good reason to think that the claims presently in vogue are exempt from similar alternation or reversal. Interestingly enough, the Bible mentions not a single scientific law, yet scientists who long spoke dogmatically of a uniform causal network of nature, have had to forsake their insistence on fixed eternal causality.

Despite its computerized knowledge of changing empirical realities, modern science still does not know how life originated. Limitations of the scientific method preclude it from providing the theory of evolutionary beginnings. Its formula of present observational verification of hypotheses, requiring as it does repeatable processes, disqualifies empirical science doubly from ever giving a sure verdict about once-for-all events in the remote past. Since origins are not empirically accessible, the naturalistic scientist cannot by empirical evidence prove the correctness of his theory that life evolved from nonliving matter. Richard Spilsbury calls attention to the obvious limitations confronting scientific method, that is, its inability to reproduce past evolutionary sequences at will under controlled conditions. These limitations, he says, make the testing of an evolutionary theory much less exacting and conclusive than the testing of a nonhistorical or metaphysical theory. This uncertainty and indecision in turn allow greater scope for the prevailing scientific mood to influence a verdict on the significance of evidence (*Providence Lost*. A Critique of Darwinism, p. 21). The evolutionist makes "a leap of faith"--not faith in the Christian sense of belief

grounded upon authoritative divine revelation, but
rather faith venture in the absence of observable primal data. Evolution remains an unproved and unprovable
faith. Scientific experimentation cannot demonstrate
either that primal origins did or did not occur as the
Bible says or as science claims. Neither evolution nor
creation is a matter of pure science; belief in creation or in evolution reflects a struggle between good
faith and bad faith; both views have religious over-
tones. Yet it will not do simply to declare that creation and evolution are divergent faiths about empirical
observational data. The data of science are not the
only data relevant to the discussion. The biblical
data, presenting as Scripture does a special view of
God and of man and of God's purpose in creation, also
exert a relevant faith-claim.

The truth of Christianity, moreover, does not depend upon a scientific demonstration that Darwinism is
wrong; it depends rather on the trustworthiness of the
scriptural revelation. Biological evolution, a revis-
able theory that has already undergone much revision,
is in some respects a useful theory even if it should
be untrue. Gainful predictive premises have in fact
not infrequently been a byproduct of theories that have
later had to be abandoned. The assumption of man's
emergence from an animal ancestry has led to medical
experiments of immense benefit to humanity. To be
sure, morphological and to some extent even psychic
parallels could provide a basis for medical experimentation even if similarities were postulated on the basis of the divine creation of all creaturely life rather than of evolutionary development. But ingenious
scientific visions about the external world need not be
deplored as vicious. Loren C. Eiseley speaks of science as projecting "fairy stories" upon nature, ". . .
stories to which nature seems to conform." Science can
be wrong and yet be scientific in the sense of facili-
tating the predictability of future events.

The Christian challenge to current evolutionary
theory therefore need not imply a repudiation of empirical science per se. Science has openly unmasked numerous superstitions for what they are, namely, a mis-
reading of reality in terms of credulity. Much scientific research has bettered physical health and living
conditions and has facilitated human comfort and con-
venience. Science has important but limited justification. Its limits are such that it can never traffic in
absolutes. Only when scientists trespass the boundaries of empirical observation and lay claim to finali-

ties; when they venture to speak definitively of what cannot be decided by their methodology; when they assume the objective truth of their inferences concerning external reality; when they channel the whole meaning of rationality into scientism; and when they profess to identify the good on the basis of observation or utility, then and then alone must Christians dissent, and must do so, moreover, in view of the Word of God itself which is able to spur science to rise above its prejudices.

What is crucially at stake in the creation account is a distinctive world-life view. It openly repudiates the metaphysical and moral outlook of a world that worships the physical forces of the universe and in so doing loses the sovereign Creator of the world, and man as God's special image. The issues of astrology and naturalism and the dignity and worth of man are no less critically in debate today than in ancient times; the Genesis creation account remains as relevant now as it was then.

When historico-grammatical exegesis of the Genesis record was accommodated to scientific perspectives a significant and ominous turn took place in fixing the meaning of the biblical text; what may be called scientifico-concept exegesis gradually replaced historico-grammatical interpretation. The literal meaning that later biblical writers attached to the Genesis account was dismissed as a matter of culture accommodation, while allegory and metaphor gained a larger role in expounding the creation narrative. Reluctant on the one hand to break completely with the biblical importance of cosmic and human beginnings, and equally reluctant, on the other, to dispute the scientific view of the origins of the earth and man, more and more clergymen professed to discern an evolutionary hypothesis in the scriptural record.

When scientific theory was allowed to define the way in which the Genesis creation account is to be understood, the revelational significance of Genesis came to mean simply that the sovereign living God originated the evolutionary process detailed by empirical science, and that he achieves his ends by means of that process.

Neal C. Gillespie notes that Darwin neither ceased to be a theist, nor did he reject divine creation (*Charles Darwin and the Problem of Creation*). Darwin did, however, reject teleological creation, that is, the idea of God's control of the natural laws that supposedly govern all processes and events. Gillespie's review surveys the scientific transition that took place between nineteenth-century theological creationism and materialistic positivism with its concentration on secondary causes, and therefore on transformational process and not on origins. For Darwin miracles were totally irrelevant and in no way constituted a providential means of divine action. Darwin's emphasis on the development of species by chance variation and natural selection set biology in a context that eliminated purpose and rationality, two essentials in any discussion of a personal creator. The end of the nineteenth century saw the rejection of theological providence and the victory of positivistic scientism. Although Darwin himself had clung to an attenuated theism, his successors completed the total disjunction of scientific concerns from theological and religious referents.

What followed in reaction to the naturalistic view of origins was a variety of theological correlations of science and religion: deistic evolution placed God transcendently at the beginning of the developmental process but excluded all miraculous divine activity; pantheistic evolution viewed the evolution of nature and man as an aspect of the divine life; theistic evolution distinguished God from nature and emphasized both transcendence and immanence but minimized the miraculous in deference to continuity and process. These theories, in turn, subdivided into still other philosophic forms; reflecting personalism, panpsychism, process metaphysics, and other perspectives, each sought to vindicate a role that connects divine creativity with scientific explanation of the universe, so that evolutionary process in time overshadowed confidence in an original or intermediate creation. As the transcendent miracle-working God was made to retreat, the various correlations of evolution with theism tended to give way to naturalistic evolution, since deity's function in the ongoing process was little more than semantic or simply lent a mystical aura of benevolence and fortuity.

In secular circles where scientists have tended to promote evolutionary theory without theological referents the big-bang theory has revitalized interest in theistic evolution. Big-bang cosmology does not require either divine origin of the so-called fireball or divine governance of the cosmic explosion it supposedly precipitated. But to correlate big-bang cosmology with Genesis 1 implies theistic evolution as an explanation of the orderly expansion of the universe.

There is a second evangelical response to Darwinian evolution, however, one that denies to empirical science the right to elucidate the content of the Genesis account of creation; it insists, rather, that the sense of the narrative is properly derived from historico-grammatical exegesis alone and independently of scientific consensus or philosophical conjecture. Unlike many of the members of the American Scientific Affiliation, and alternative group of evangelical scientists in Creation Research Society, some seven hundred of whose members hold postgraduate degrees, contends that theistic evolution is scientifically unjustifiable and involves needless compromise of premises integral to the Genesis creation account. Creation Research Society rejects also the big-bang theory because it implies theistic evolution rather than flat creation.

The main point of difference in theistic theories of origin concerns the recency or antiquity of the earth's beginnings. Proponents of "scientific creationism" insist that the earth and all living things were created during the six successive twenty-four-hour days at the commencement of a timespan that goes back no more than 10,000 to 15,000 years. The entire work of creation, they insist, was finished in a single week of seven standard solar days, each day marked by one complete rotation of the earth.

We tend to speak of things millions and billions of years ago, say creationists, as if we were all but there, and as if no colossal assumptions are involved, assumptions that are quite capable of being wrong or even inverted. Scientists are continually changing their views of both the age and size of the universe. Across a span of twenty years astronomers have doubled the size of the observed universe from five to ten billion light-year; 25 percent of the increase occurred in the short six-year period from 1964 to 1971 through revision of an earlier estimate of about eight billion light-years. Some astronomers still place the big bang eighteen million years ago; the most recently identified galaxies--whose light is estimated to take six billion years to reach the earth--are said to reach back halfway. Adding to the confusion is the fact that a supposed miscalculation has led some astronomers to cut in half the age of the universe from eighteen billion to nine billion years.

Six-day creationists point also to revisions in dating techniques not to mention the limitations of such methods. In corrections of the first edition

(1955) of his *Radiocarbon Dating*, Willard F. Libby notes unresolved difficulties. Although the present method is held to be reliable for computing from a few hundred to more than 30,000 years, the previously used black carbon method is now considered obsolete. Libby contends that the weight of confirmatory evidence makes erroneous computation a low possibility (*ibid*, p. 147); contamination of curatorial samples remains a problem (*Ibid*, p. 44).

But evolutionists maintin that dating procedures for the universe establish beyond any doubt that the cosmic processes now in operation go back billions of years. A gross error, even of a few billion years, or even of the magnitude indicated by Hubble, they say, does not change the basic requirement of an earth vastly older than that indicated by six-day creationists. The quantitative discrepancies over datings projected by evolutionists run twofold or less; those required by "creation science" involve differences varying up to 100,000-fold.

It should be pointed out that the doctrine of the recency of the universe, in contrast to modern scientific views of its staggering antiquity, was the view not only of Christians generally but of most people, including scientists, before the nineteenth century. Augustine's view, that Genesis is compatible with a theory of successive chronological ages, is very much the exception. It is fair to say that six-day creationists, and not theistic evolutionists, reflect what may be taken as the Christian tradition before the rise of modern science, and that theistic evolution represents an adaptation of the traditional view.

Creation doctrine has taken several forms. Some expositors eager for harmony with contemporary science differ little if at all from versions of theistic evolution that give full scope to the miraculous in expounding the creation-days or ages of Genesis. Progressive creationism, a view popular among many evangelical scientists, can therefore also be considered a variety of theistic evolution, yet one which holds that major steps in developmental advance have resulted from flat creation that sporadically penetrated long ages of comparatively gradual change.

So-called scientific creationists insist that a literal twenty-four-hour day interpretation of the Genesis creation account is fully compatible with the assured results of modern science (cf. Henry M. Morris, et al., A *Symposium on Creation*). Henry M. Morris, a founder of the Creation Research Society, contends in *The Genesis Record* that many of the generally accepted views of science are too ill-founded to warrant our disavowing the Genesis account.

This controversy has led to an emphasis now sometimes called "apparent age" creationism, since creationists contend that organic life and even inorganic minerals were divinely created with an apparent, or appearance of, age (cf. of John C. Whitcomb, Jr. and Henry M. Morris, *The Genesis Flood*, p. 233). As Frank L. Marsh tells us, Adam presumably was created "a mature man at least in his twenties, a man of marriageable age. Fruit bearing trees appeared . . . several years old. The great aquatic animals . . . appeared to be sixty to one hundred years old. And the . . . landscape . . . appeared to be millions of years old" (*Life, Man and Time*, p. 69).

The argument that God created Adam with a navel, so that Adam though miraculously made, gave the appearance of physical birth, dates back to Philip Henry Gosse (*Ompholos: An Attempt to Untie the Geological Knot*). This approach was extended and applied to the origin of trees that from the first moment of creation would exhibit apparent annual growth rings; indeed bark and green leaves, ordinarily dependent on chlorophyll, would be an aspect of created tree life. After all, say more serious champions of the view, rings are an integral aspect of trees; to associate tree rings only with an aging process is a purely human decision; what's more the modern correlation of datings with periods of billions of years in the past is also simply a human determination.

Though at first glance such projections may seem ludicrous, the question whether the first trees had rings, or whether Adam and Eve were created with a navel, is not at all in a class with the question, "how many angels can dance on the head of a pin?" Navel or no navel, Adam was a man, not a baby, and even if created a baby, the baby would look as if he had been born. Even Bertrand Russell acknowledged that nobody can "prove to me that the universe wasn't created a second ago with its built-in narrative memories."

"What kind of a Creator," asks Isaac Asimov, in referring to the apparent age theory, "would produce a universe containing so intricate an illusion? . . . It would mean that the Creator . . . supplied human beings

182

with an enormous amount of subtle and cleverly consistent evidence designed to mislead them and cause them to be convinced that the universe was created 20 billions of years ago and developed by evolutionary processes. . . . Can it be that the Creator is a cruel and malicious prankster, with a vicious and adolescent sense of humor?" ("The 'Threat' of Creationism," p. 96). To this line of argument six-day creationists reply that God is not a prankster but the Creator of humans who in their rebellious condition reason illogically, refuse to take seriously the doctrine of creation, and impute their own stupidity of God.

Some creationists who insist on origin of the universe in six successive twenty-four-hour days make a major concession to the scientific demand for the earth's antiquity by inserting geological history between the opening verses of Genesis, that is, between Genesis 1:1 and Genesis 1:3. Unless one dismisses scientific datings as wrong and opts instead for the divinely given "appearance of age" in a 6000-year-old earth, it becomes necessary to invoke catastrophe to compress the geological record. Supporters of the so-called gap theory argue that Genesis 1:2 refers to a destruction of the primal creation; the subsequent six-day activity of Genesis 1, they say, involves a relatively recent recreation of the original universe that existed billions of years ago. To support their view the "catastrophists," as they are sometimes called, invoke the fact that Genesis begins with a statement about a transition from an undifferentiated state ("the earth was formless and empty," 1:2, NIV) to a comprehensively ordered universe. Genesis 1:1-2, they contend, depicts a primal creation engulfed by a prehistoric fall; the remainder of that chapter portrays God's recreation of the despoiled earth and of man.

But if this interpretation is correct, then Genesis records two beginnings but no significant account of creation. The catastrophe theory has many difficulties, moreover, on scientific no less than on theological grounds. The attempt to connect the fall of Lucifer and of rebellious angels (Isa. 14:12) with a prehistorical, pre-Adamic fall and with judgment upon a primal creation had some support among nineteenth-century Christians through the influence of G.H. Pember (*Earth's Earliest Ages*); in the twentieth century it was popularized by the *Scofield Reference Bible* and by Harry Rimmer (*Modern Science and the Genesis Record*) but today it has no following except in a few Bible schools and churches. It rests upon contrived Bible exegesis and interpretation (cf. Ramm, *The Christian View of Science and Scripture*, pp. 199 ff.)

Besides the gap theory there have been several other proposals that correlate the six literal creation days with evidences for the apparent antiquity of the universe. One such theory projects numerous creations, each one followed by a catastrophe; the latest of these creations is identified with the most recent recreation of the universe, that recorded in Genesis 1. George Cuvier, the noted paleontologist, and the naturalist Louis Agassiz, who projected the theory of ice ages, were the first ones to consider earth history as a succession of catastrophes involving massive destruction of plant and animal life, each catastrophe being followed in turn by a new creation. Noah's flood, considered to be the last of the global catastrophes, was not however, followed by a new act of cosmic creation.

An alternative theory, sometimes called the "multiple-gap theory," regards the creation days as twenty-four-hour days in which each new stage in the origin of the world and of man results from the transcendent activity of God; every creation day is separated from the next by whatever time-periods may prove to have been the case. In short, while the Genesis account leaves room, it is said, for whatever process and development actually occurred during whatever timespans may have been required, the creation acts themselves depicted by Genesis are the miraculous activity of the Creator; he is the sovereign source of the pattern of creation, of its distinctive levels of being, and of its qualitatively different "kinds" or orders of life (cf. "Science and Religion," pp. 278 ff.). The difficulties of the multiple-gap theory are that Genesis does not distinguish the antiquity of the world from the creation days nor does it locate geological periods between the days. Furthermore, the same difficulties confront this view as well as the geological-age theory in regard to the chronological sequence of creation events; there is the problem, too, that the multiple-gap theory requires the simultaneous fashioning of man and all animal forms.

Warren H. Johns has helpfully compared and contrasted various creationist and evolutionary theories as to how they deal with the theme of transcendent divine activity and what scope they give to a literal understanding of the Genesis account ("Strategies for Origins," pp. 26-28). Deistic and theistic evolutionists, for example, subscribe to the Bible's insistence that God is Creator, but leave to science the description of how God created, that is, they both espouse an evolutionary process of natural selection and chance variation, although theists adjust evolution in various ways to divine intervention. Creationist theories accept as literally true both the days of creation and the transcendent activity of the Creator that attaches to each species a unique character. Followers of so-called progressive creationism and concordism, on the other hand, view the six days of Genesis symbolically, as representing lengthy geological ages. An essential turning point, observes Johns, is that while creationists insist that the Bible is not a textbook on science, they nonetheless maintain that it implies a philosophy of science and that it includes, even if in nontechnical terms, doctrinal teaching of scientific relevance and importance (*ibid.*, p. 27).

Richard Niessen, a spokesman for scientific creationists, lists twenty-nine divergences between evolutionary theory and theistic creationism ("Significant Discrepancies Between Theistic Evolution and the Bible," *Christian Research Society Quarterly*, pp. 220 ff.):

Evolutionary Theory

1. Space, time and matter are eternal.
2. Primal atmosphere gradually changed from reducing to oxidizing type.
3. Plant life produced the atmosphere.
4. Life initially evolved in the sea, then moved to land.
5. There is continuity between all plant life.
6. Plant evolved gradually.
7. Simple creature emerged into complex animals.
8. Reptiles evolved into birds.
9. All animal development shows continuity.
10. Ape-like animals and man are similar.
11. Fossil records show that death prevailed naturally from the outset of life.
12. Man developed in the image of the apes.
13. Evolutionary process covers billions of years.
14. Evolution is a continuing present-day process.
15. The present is the key to the past (uniformitarianism).
16. Early animals were carnivorous.
17. Rain has always been a cosmic phenomenon.
18. Man emerged from a lower animal.
19. Man is a living animal that acquired a complex psyche.

20. No primal individual can be singled out as Adam.

21. Agriculture is a late development in human history.

22. Language was a gradual development.

23. Adam's psyche was essentially like that of higher animals.

24. Woman, like man, evolved from an animal ancestry.

25. Marriage is a culturally-developed institution.

26. Man has existed only during the last 1/200th of the timespan of animal existence.

27. The Garden of Eden is a myth.

28. Cain and Abel were mythical persons.

29. Early man was quite primitive and technologically immature.

Biblical View

1. The space-time universe is not eternal (Gen. 1:1-3; Heb. 1:2).

2. Atmosphere was created quickly and is always essential the same (Gen. 1:6 ff).

3. The atmosphere preceded plant life (Gen. 1: 6-12).

4. Life was created on land before sea life (Gen. 1:11-13, 20-23).

5. Plants were created as distinct "kinds" (Gen. 1:11 f.).

6. Plants were originally created bearing seed and fruit (Gen. 1:11 f.).

7. Highly developed mammals preceded so-called lower forms (Gen. 1:21).

8. Creation of birds antedated creeping things.

9. Species and kinds of animals are distinct creations (Gen. 1:21).

10. Man is a uniquely created kind (Gen. 1:24-27).

11. Death is a consequence of the Fall.

12. Man was created in God's image (Gen. 1:26 f.).

13. Creation occurred in six literal 24-hour days.

14. God has rested from his work of creation (Gen. 2:1-3).

15. God's activity is repetitive but also miraculous (Gen. 1,2, 6-8).

16. Early animals were herbivorous (Gen. 1:29 f.).

17. There was no rain prior to the Noahic Flood (Gen. 2:5 f.; Heb. 11:7).

18. Man was divinely formed from dust (Gen. 2:7).

19. The first man was a nonliving entity into which God breathed life (Gen. 2:7).

20. Adam was a specific individual from whom man-kind derives (1 Chron. 1:1; Luke 3:38).

21. Adam tended the Garden (Gen. 2:9 ff.) and Cain was a farmer (Gen. 4:2).

22. Man was endowed with language as a divine gift (Gen. 2:18-24).

23. Man is physically and emotionally incompatible with animals (Gen. 2:20).

24. Eve was made by a direct divine act of special creation (Gen. 2:21 ff.).

25. Monogamous marriage was divinely instituted (Gen. 2:24).

26. Man has existed almost from the beginning of organic life on earth (Matt. 19:4; Rom. 1:20).

27. The Garden of Eden was a literal place.

28. Cain and Abel were historical persons.

29. Early civilizations arose within a few centuries of Adamic creation by means of relatively advanced technology (Gen. 4:21 ff.).

But during the past generation scientists representing different disciplines have increasingly questioned and criticized Darwinian theory until now a spirited challenge has emerged to its almost half-century dominance of evolutionary biology. The present-day revolt repudiates the so-called modern synthesis-- a descriptive term used by Julian Huxley in 1942-- which affirms that all species originate by a slow process contingent upon gradual genetic changes; natural selection, moreover, or the survival of variants best adapted to their environments, assertedly determines the direction of such change. The "modern synthesis," John Davey notes, is "for a growing group of critics on both sides of the Atlantic . . . becoming an emperor who is actually wearing very few clothes" ("What If Darwin Were Wrong?," p. C-3). Stephen Jay Gould, the Harvard fossil expert, has declared the synthesis "effectively dead."

In what *Science* magazine calls "one of the most important conferences on evolutionary biology for more than 30 years," held in Chicago in 1980, geologists, paleontologists, embryologists, molecular biologists, ecologists and population geneticists debated anew the mechanisms that underlie the origin of species and their supposed evolutionary relationships. Some observers declared the 1980 meeting "a turning point in the history of evolutionary theory."

The Chicago conference refused to explain the origin of new species and higher taxonomic patterns--that is, macroevolution--by the principle of slow, gradual and almost imperceptible change long dominant in micro-evolution. More than a century after Darwin the sharp-ly conflicting views now extend to the tempo of evolu-tion, to the mode of change, and to limits on the phyi-cal form of new organisms.

Paleontologists now routinely concede that the fossil record fails to confirm an array of life forms constantly changing across million of years, but has a character of stasis more than of change. Gould con-tends that "for millions of years species remained un-changed in the fossil record and they then abruptly disappear, to be replaced by something that is sub-stantially different but clearly related" (cf. Roger Lewin, "Evolutionary Theory Under Fire," pp. 883-887). In short, individual species remain virtually constant for long periods that are interrupted by the sudden ap-pearance of new species whose physical and other fea-tures are but secondary qualifications of a fixed spe-cies. Species stasis, according to Gabriel Dover of Cambridge University, is "the single most important feature of macroevolution." The generations-long ef-fort initiated by Darwin himself to fault the fossil record in order to explain the lack of transition forms between known species has worn thin. As Gould empha-sizes, the "jerkiness" of the fossil record "is not the result of gaps, it is the consequence of the jerky mode of evolutionary change."

While Gould concedes that "much of what passes for evolutionary theory" is "vacuous" and is surrounded by "hogwash" (*Ever Since Darwin*, p. 40), he nonetheless seeks to minimize the defection from Darwin's theory of natural selection and chance variation; the theory's failure to emphasize genetic factors he considers sim-ply "a logical error" in an otherwise "great and in-fluential theory" (*Ibid.*, p. 39).

G.A. Kerkut emphasizes that all seven basic as-sumptions on which evolutionary theory rests are "by their nature . . . not capable of experimental verifi-cation" (*Implications of Evolution*, p. 7). The assump-tion that "non-living things gave rise to living mate-rial . . . is still just an assumption" (*ibid.*, p. 150). The assumption that "biogenesis occurred only once . . . is a matter of belief rather than proof" (*op. cit.*). The assumption that "Viruses, Bacteria, Protozoa and the higher animals were all interrelated" biologically as an evolutionary phenomenon lacks defi-nite evidence (*ibid.*, p. 151). The assumption that

"the various invertebrate phyla are interrelated" depends on "tenuous and circumstantial" evidence and not
on evidence that allows "a verdict of definite relationships" (*ibid.*, pp. 152 f.). The assumption that
"the invertebrates gave rise to the vertebrates" turns
on evidence gained by prior belief (*ibid.*, p. 153).
Although he finds "somewhat stronger ground" for assum-
ing that "fish, amphibia, reptiles, birds and mammals
are interrelated," Kerkut concedes that many key fossil
transitions are "not well documented and we have as yet
to obtain a satisfactory objective method of dating the
fossils" (*ibid.*, p. 153). "In effect, much of the
evolution of the major groups of animals has to be
taken on trust" (*ibid.*, p. 154); "there are many discrete groups of animals and . . . we do not know how
they have evolved nor how they are interrelated"
(*ibid.*, p. vii). In short, the theory that "all the
living forms in the world have arisen from a single
source which itself came from an inorganic form," says
Kerkut, has insufficiently strong evidential supports
"to consider it as anything more than a working hypothesis" (*ibid.*, p. 157). He thinks "premature and not
satisfactorily supported by present-day evidence,"
therefore, "the attempt to explain all living forms in
terms of an evolution *from a unique source*," that is,
from a common ancestor (*ibid.*, pp. vii f.).

Hard-core evolutionists notwithstanding, humani-
ties professor William Irwin Thompson suggests that
pressures on the evolutionary worldview are now so intense that the contemporary outlook may be on the brink
of a major perspectival shift. Thompson writes: "The
Darwinian theory of human evolution by natural selection, which triumphed in the nineteenth and early
twentieth centuries, may fall apart into newly structured pieces in the twentieth and early twenty-first
centuries" (*At the Edge of History*. Speculations on
the Transformation of Culture, p. 135). "All in all,"
Thompson adds, "when one takes into account the problems
that are not honestly faced and questioned in our notions of evolution, primitive culture, and archaeology,
he can see that the specialists are retreating from the
problems and burrowing more deeply into the security of
minutiae. If one lifts his gaze to take in the whole
historical horizon of man, he can see that our present
world view is being put under a strain" (*ibid.*, p.
151).

Creation as an alternative was considered unten-
able, notes Himmelfarb, because it was "obviously not
bound by the usual canons of scientific proof" and

lacked the geologic, especially paleontological, evidences to which evolutionists appealed (*Darwin and the Darwinian Revolution*, pp. 350 f.). Today such judgment falls rather on naturalistic theory, not only in the matter of scientific evidences and rational credibility, but of its consequences for personality and culture as well.

While Christians differ in their views of flat creation and progressive creation, they do agree against naturalists who would make the universe and life simply matters of chance, Christians insist that the biblical account of origins and science's assured results are wholly compatible, that God created graded orders of being and life, that the human race derives its being from a primal Adam and Eve divinely endowed with the forms of rationality and morality, that the fall of the original pair involves the whole human race in sin and guilt. While differences occur among evangelicals within these mainline agreements, they concern mostly the nature and timing of the continuities by which the Creator achieved and continues to achieve his cosmic goals. The debate focuses primarily on the age of the earth and on the time and nature of the creation of man.

If biblical theists were asked to reconcile their views with evolutionary science, they would face the problem of identifying incontrovertible scientific conclusions. The flux of evolutionary theory, and the disposition of many advocates to insist on the evolutionary fact even while supportive data remain in dispute together with the readiness of others to accept evolution simply in lieu of what they would welcome as a viable alternative, prompts A. E. Wilder-Smith to ask: why are so many evangelical Christians so eager to harmonize their beliefs with a "working hypothesis" that is so deficient in scientific evidence of an experimental nature? (*Man's Origin, Man's Destiny*. A Critical Survey of the Principles of Evolution and Christianity, p. 307).

In the present metaphysical debate the burden of proof should not be thrust upon the creationists. Today as in the Scopes trial a century ago, secular educators and the media spend more effort in caricaturing fundamentalist beliefs than in providing conclusive scientific data for naturalistic evolution. If the evangelical dialogue with evolutionists is to be conducted not on Darwinian grounds but on alternative premises, then both neo-Darwinian and post-Darwinian sci-

entists must clearly delineate their positions. If a
non-Darwinian model of evolution now displaces the Darwinian model, if the theory that all earth's life forms
are naturalistically related by a common ancestry and
by genetic continuity is to be more than a cultic
faith, then we need to be told the factual basis of
that faith. If, as Laurie R. Godfrey indicates, we
must "not rule out the logical possibility that life
could have arisen independently on more than one occasion on the earth and in the universe" ("The Flood of
Antievolution," p. 6), then it would be exceedingly
helpful to intelligible discourse if logical supports
were adduced for at least the one occasion when such
life is believed to have arisen on earth.

If orthodoxy appears synonymous with heresy because it refuses to identify itself with prevalent scientific beliefs, then contemporaries should be reminded
that to identify with such beliefs runs the high risk
of historicizing and temporizing orthodoxy. To consider biblical creationism only as one scientific theory
among others demeans it to the level of probabilistic
empiricism. To represent the Genesis account simply as
a "scientific model" overlooks its revelational source
and its absolutistic claim.

On the purely theoretical level of postulating
conflicting explanatory principles it is wholly legitimate to probe which alternative most consistently explains the available data. The comprehensive premise
of universal evolution is not derived from empirical
science but is postulated by faith; Christians are
wholly free to invoke a different governing principle,
even if naturalists dogmatically exclude a revelation-
ally based alternative. As C. Leon Harris observes:
"If the neo-Darwinian theory is axiomatic, it is not
valid for creationists to demand proof of the axioms,
and it is not valid for evolutionists to dismiss special revelation as unproved so long as it is stated as
an axiom" ("An Axiomatic Interpretation of the Neo-Darwinian Theory of Evolution," p. 179).

We are not therefore abandoned to a choice between
myths, however. An intelligible and intelligent faith
asks which postulate most comprehensively fits the data
and bequeaths the fewest problems. Both creationists
and evolutionists must state the nature of their claims
precisely and indicate logical supports for those
claims. Christian theists can hardly be expected to
harmonize the Genesis account with modern scientific
theory at points of possible conflict unless they are

told exactly what evolutionary premises its advocates consider beyond revision. If the fossil record gives no evidence of an upward evolution of all life during prehistory, and if no current illustrations of present evolution are or can be adduced, then on what factual basis are we to believe in evolution?

Discussion Questions

1. If you were a farmer and you wanted a scientist to estimate the probability of finding oil on your land, do you think a creation scientist could perform the task? Is your answer based on your lack of knowledge about creation science, or is it based on the nature of that discipline?

2. Does Henry correctly interpret the scriptures he cites when he says that later biblical writers accept Genesis as a factual record of creation? How crucial is this point to Henry's case? To your theology?

3. Do you think Henry believes all of the creation science models to be equally valuable? How would you decide which would be preferable?

4. Read over Richard Niessen's summary of the discrepancies between evolution and the biblical view. Study first those under "Evolution Theory." Are Niessen's observations necessary implications of evolution? Are others possible which are more compatible with the Christian faith?

EVOLUTION AND THE DOCTRINE OF
CREATION

Langdon Gilkey holds that the distinction between the fact of evolutionary development and the understanding of its causes is crucial for the relation of the theory to theology. Unlike Henry, Gilkey believes that the important religious values of the Christian doctrine of creation may be preserved even though the Genesis description of origins is understood as scientifically erroneous.

Like Henry, Gilkey maintains that science cannot deal with the question whether God has created the world. Science is fitted for dealing with empirical phenomena, events and causation. But the question of what began all things is a question of final or ultimate causes. Science is unable to understand an event caused by non-finite agency.

The position that secondary or finite causality is sufficient to explain the origins of the world is a naturalistic extension of scientific understanding beyond the range of science. Gilkey's point is that any scientific theory expanded into a philosophical world view poses a threat to theology. Accordingly, it is not the theory of evolution itself which Gilkey considers a threat to theology. It is the extension of the theory into the status of a religious or philosophical world view.

At the same time, Gilkey cautions us against accommodating our theology to evolutionary frameworks simply because developmentalism seems to be the most accurate description of biological and geological phenomena.

Aside from the points above, the most important
feature of this essay is Gilkey's call for theology
to develop some understanding of the relation between
God's causality and the secondary causality of nature
and history. This is to raise the issue of providence,
and even miracles. Gilkey suggests that God's activity
does not push aside the force of finite agents--as if
God would cause a storm without the concomitant
meteorological factors. But if the finite factors are
present, how can we distinguish God's involvement?

For example, if Aunt Jane is in the hospital and
we pray for her return to health, while our secular
cousin hires the best doctors, what shall we say if
Aunt Jane improves? If we say, "God has heard us and
healed you," our secular cousin may say, "God, nothing,
we had the best surgeon available." Is the issue
merely a matter of perspective? If not, how can we
identify God's action vis-a-vis the activity of medicine and physician? Gilkey leaves the resolution to
"the eye of faith," but is this adequate?

EVOLUTION AND THE DOCTRINE OF
CREATION*

During the past year the intellectual world of
the West has been celebrating the centenary of the
publication of Charles Darwin's *Origin of Species* and
seeking once again to estimate its significance for
our cultural life. It is appropriate that the church
attempt to make an evaluation of her own in relation
to Darwin's influence. The church must continually
rethink her relation to culture, or which relation the
impact of Darwinism remains a potent symbol.

*Source: "Darwin and Christian Thought," by
Langdon Gilkey, copyright 1984, Christian Century
Foundation. Reprinted by permission from the January
6, 1960 issue of *The Christian Century*.

The relations between Christian faith and the Darwinian theory of evolution have been complex. The simple picture, dear to the secular mind, of a head-on clash between prejudiced religionists and open-minded scientists is about as inaccurate historically as is the fundamentalist's view of the clash as one more joust between God and Satan. Actually, the Christian religion in significant ways prepared the ground for the theory of evolution.

The Christian concept of creation provided one of the necessary foundations for the development of Western empirical science, of which Darwinism is certainly an important result. The biblical view that time is both linear and irreversible, and therefore capable of cumulative development, is perhaps the most crucial of all the distant progenitors of the concept of evolution. It is no accident that evolutionary theories of origins appeared within a culture saturated with biblical concepts of creation and of providence.

It is true however that three notions, derived from and supported by biblical ideas, had to be dislodged if evolution was to be intelligle to Western minds. First, the limited time-span of the biblical view needed extension if natural scientists were to think of a gradual development of the forms of life. Largely on biblical grounds, most intelligent men before the end of the 18th century assumed that the world was only about 6,000 years old; Thomas Browne, for example, asserted in 1635, "Time we may comprehend; 'tis but five days elder than ourselves." Clearly, if there had been so little time since the beginning, no slow development of the forms of life by gradual changes was possible or even conceivable.

The second biblical notion in conflict with evolutionary concepts was that the present forms of life had come into being all at once at the beginning through a single act of divine creation. Western thought had always assumed that whatever we see around us had been put there once and for all by God. Thus John Ray was in 1695 able to affirm that the "universal opinion of divines and philosophers" is "that since ye first Creation there have been no species of animals or vegetables lost, no new ones produced."

Closely associated with this notion of a single initial creation was the concept of fixed, unchanging

species or forms of life. The assumption that there
are certain immutable "kinds of things" is as old as
Greek philosophy, but for Western minds it received
its most fundamental sanction from the biblical account of creation. At his initial act of creation God,
in the biblical view, made all the present species of
plants and animals, and since then they have not sub-
stantially changed. Each species represents an essential and eternal structure in the nature of things,
purposed from the beginning, and while there may be
variety here and there in details these essential
natures remain immutable. This general concept of
certain fixed forms of life, certified by revelation
and confirmed by early biological studies, was the
common assumption of most scientists, philosophers
and theologians until the latter part of the 18th
century.

II

In estimating our attitude to Darwin it is important to recall that the orthodox religious and
scientific picture of the origins of species had undergone steady attack from the newer sciences of geology
and historical biology long before Darwin appeared.
The development of geological inquiry and speculation
at the turn of the 19th century had generally established the immense age of the earth--an intellectual
change almost as significant as the advent of Darwinism. Instead of the traditional estimate of a 6,000-
year span, scientists now offered the awesome picture
of time stretching backward almost to infinity: "We
find no vestige of a beginning," said James Hutton in
1795. By the 1820s the simple, homely biblical time-
span had been rigorously challenged; the Flood was
consequently removed as a significant event in geological history. Scientists, intellectuals and clerics
alike accepted the new "unbiblical" age of the earth.
As Lyell, the real founder of geology, showed in the
1830s, the earth was given its present form neither by
recent divine acts of creation nor by the simple
miraculous cataclysm of the Flood, but rather by the
gradual working of natural forces controlled by immutable laws over ages of time. With the rise of the
science of geology, the biblical view of creation suffered its first real defeat, for now for the first
time the endless world of uniform natural law really
impressed itself on the Western mind--a fact to be
remembered by fundamentalists who castigate Darwin and
yet hire geologists to find oil, coal or water.

196

The concept of the fixity of species, moreover, was shaken if not yet dislodged by the new understanding of fossilized bones which, when reconstructed, revealed species long since extinct. Geological discovery had shown that even the firm earth was subject to change; now, with horrendous skeletons of long-vanished reptiles rising in every museum, men became aware that the forms of life also could change, realizing that behind our brief age there lay mysterious reaches of time in which species had appeared and then died, to be replaced by other species which eventually would also disappear. And cats, dogs and cows and all the Ark's medley of animals were nowhere to be found in the distant past; their day was yet to come.

Thus by 1850 the "biblical" account of creation, and with it the three concepts we have noted, was already radically questioned in countless Christian minds. A new view of nature and her early processes had been in slow formation in the early 19th century, a view which contradicted at almost every point the concrete picture of origins in Genesis. The result was that long before 1859 there was widespread doubt about the inerrant validity of Scripture, accompanied by an anxious search for some new basis of faith. Before 1850 such literary figures as Alfred Tennyson, Thomas Arnold and George Eliot both reflected the doubt and carried on the search, and the great theologian Schleiermacher formulated a new interpretation of religion to resolve the problem. Thus the *Origin of Species* does not represent an initial or isolated challenge to the biblical view of origins, and no disproving of Darwin's theory of evolution could lead to re-establishment of the biblical world view as literally infallible. In order to re-establish that early view of the world, one would have to reject almost every major scientific hypothesis on which our present culture has been nourished.

III

If the literal biblical history had already been widely questioned by 1859, why was it that Darwin's theory raised such a storm among scientists, philosophers and churchmen? The answer lies not so much in the particular scientific theories of Darwin, although they were certainly unacceptable to the older patterns of thought, as in the deeper philosophical and religious assumptions that the new understanding of origins seemed to imply. First, Darwin's theory completed, confirmed and radically symbolized the new scientific

197

world view. As astronomy and physics had explained
the origins of the solar system by uniform and mechanical law, and as geology had explained the formation of
mountains and valleys by a similar set of uniform laws,
so Darwin explained the one seemingly unexplainable
mystery, the origins of living species, by the same
sort of uniformity of mechanical law. Men can with
some aplomb regard stars and rocks as merely "caused,"
as products of purposeless change. But Darwin's
explanation not only completed the system of natural
explanation, it brought man's own existence under
such laws of change. And the inclusion of man was a
step having not merely quantitative but qualitative
significance; now even man had become engulfed within
the blind flux. With the inclusion of himself in the
reign of endless and purposeless law, man found himself a citizen of an entirely new and alien world.

Darwinism implied that just as rocks, mountains
and even stars are caught in endless change, so is life
itself; species come and go, dinosaurs rise and fall--
and so does man. In a world of endless change, man's
existence itself suddenly became but a moment within
that change. Also, in Darwin's theory man is regarded
as the temporary product not of the providential activity of God but of random factors and causal sequences
in the shifting realm of nature. According to Darwin
the sources of man's life are twofold: chance variations within the passage of countless generations and
selection of the most favorable of these variations by
the requirements of survival within the universal
struggle for existence. Random variations plus natural
selection of the fittest mold the fluid forms of life
into types more and more adaptable to their environment.

Man, then, was seen as arising not from the purposive providence of God but out of the conflux of the
random novelty of variation and the ineluctable law of
survival--strictly and solely the child of chance and
determinism. The dinosaurs rose and passed away for
no reason at all except the whim of chance and the
laws of survival; so it will be with the whole human
enterprise, which has arisen and will disappear at the
dictation of the same two blind goddesses.

Unlimited change and unqualified purposelessness
were thus the twin philosophical implications of Darwinism that sent shudders through the 19th-century
soul. These philosophical concepts had been equally
implicit in every scientific advance since Galileo,

198

but Darwin brought them into the open when he applied them to the hitherto sacrosanct topic of the origin and destiny of man. With Darwin's book the meaningless sea of endless, mindless nature seemed to close forever over man's existence. Philosophical naturalists often say that the 19th century was not immediately attracted to Darwin's thought because he "made man an animal" and thus compromised man's presumptuous sense of superiority. This is to miss the real issue: it was because Darwinism seemed to make man a child of blind Fate, rather than of God, that it became the center of heated if short-lived controversy.

IV

What rescued the 19th century from the despair implicit in Darwinism? It was the fact that quite quickly in scientific and philosophical minds blind Fate was transformed into a benevolent cosmic Progress. The new secular religion of progressive evolutionism made it possible for Victorian culture, both religious and irreligious, to absorb evolution with truly astounding serenity and speed; believing firmly in inevitable Progress they were able to forget the deeper implications of Darwinism. In our own day, when the faith in inevitable progress has almost completely disappeared, those implications have finally come home to roost. It is our age, not the 19th century, which has had aching acquaintance with the void of meaninglessness.

From the foregoing we can see that in the Darwinian controversy, ideas clashed on two levels: the level of specific scientific theories about origins and the level of fundamental philosophical comprehension of the ultimate character of existence. On the first level such ideas as the limited age of the world, the fixity of species, and specific divine acts of creation confronted the Darwinian view of an unlimited past in which random variations and natural selection transformed the mutable forms of life into their present species. On the second level philosophical and theological ideas affirming that existence is created and guided by the divine Providence clashed with an implicit philosophical affirmation that only chance and determinism rule in the universe as a whole. It was the conjunction of the scientific with the philosophical-religious level that made the controversy so significant. The difficulty was that to both sides of the argument controversy over the first level really involved at each point controversy on the second level,

199

and leading scientists as well as bishops took issue
with the Darwinian theory both because of its particular scientific hypotheses and its philosophical implications.

V

In seeking to understand the controversy it is
necessary to remember that Darwin's theory actually
contains two closely associated but distinct elements.
The first element is the hypothesis that evolution has
in fact happened, that species have developed by evolving from other, now extinct, forms of life. An affirmation of evolution in this general sense clearly con-
tradicts the earlier biblical and scientific concepts
of an original divine creation of species each of which
is independent of other species and fixed in its nature. The second element in Darwin's theory is the
hypothesis that the process of evolution is to be explained by random variations and natural selection.
In Darwin's own work these two elements are so inter-
twined as to be almost inseparable--for good historical
reasons. Many theories of evolution had appeared in
the 100 years before 1859, but Darwin's was the first
which purported to give a natural and scientific cause
for evolution. It was the theory of the cause of
evolution that made the theory as a whole scientific,
hence Darwin kept the two elements together in the
closest possible relation. But in the development of
the theory since Darwin's time a tacit separation has
taken place; while the fact of evolution has been
generally accepted and is the foundation for all
present sciences of life from biology to medicine to
agronomy, the understanding of its causes has been
continuously subject to scientific debate, criticism
and transformation.

The distinction between the fact of evolutionary
development and the understanding of its causes is
important for the relation of the theory to religion.
The fact of evolution certainly challenged certain
views defended by orthodoxy: the short time-span of
the earth, the once-for-all creation of species and
the fixity of species. But as most theologians now
agree, these views are "religious" only in the limited
sense that they are the theories of the origins of
species implied in Genesis. This aspect of Darwin's
theory is a challenge to Christian faith only if one
insists on the verbal infallibility of Scripture and
the literal truth of all of its statements, "scientific" and historical as well as religious. As we have

200

shown, such a view of religious truth had been under scientific attack well before Darwin. Anyone who uses the science of geology to find oil or coal has already implicitly abandoned the literalist view of Scripture. In any case it is not at all certain that belief in God as the Creator and Providential Ruler of all of life necessarily involves a belief that the world is only 6,000 years old and that all present species were named by Adam in the first days.

The issue of the causes of evolution, however, is more complex. Here the two levels of the controversy --the level of particular scientific hypotheses and the level of philosophical implications--meet in the most subtle manner. On the one hand science can deal only with what have generally been called "secondary causes": explanations of phenomena and events in terms of other finite causes interpreted according to the known relations of natural experience. Scientific inquiry can investigate only the interrelations between finite events. Divine power cannot be brought into the laboratory to be tested; by definition the "causes" of a miracle are beyond human investigation. Science as a mode of inquiry is not equipped to understand an event in theological or religious terms as the work of God; it must understand an event as the work of finite and hence nondivine causes. This is just what Darwin sought to do; by explaining the evolution of species solely in terms of natural, finite causes, his theory is a prime example of scientific method.

VI

If scientific understanding is thus incurably *un*theological, is it then also *anti*theological? This question raises the most fundamental issue in the controversy over Darwinism. To many moderns a scientific explanation does preclude the activity, the "causality" of God. To them an adequate explanation of the origins of life in terms of secondary causation seems to make both irrelevant and unintelligible an additional "higher" explanation. If all the causes of a thing have been assembled, there can be no other causes. For example, if the science of meteorology can specify in scientific terms all the relevant causes of a thunderstorm, does this not preclude the simple biblical causality which holds that God willed and brought forth the storm? Similarly is not the assertion that random variations (or mutations, as geneticists now call them) plus natural selection "caused" the rise of man another way of saying that God did not create man? Especially does this implication appear valid when the two types of causality seem to be directly opposed. Darwin's essential emphasis on *random* variations denies effective purpose in the variations and the natural selection that mold life. The essence of God's activity is, of course, its purposive character. Thus the explanation in terms of secondary causes seems not only to make unnecessary and irrelevant further theological understanding, but actively to exclude it as contradictory to science.

The implication that secondary causality excludes the primary causality of God is at the center of the position known as philosophical naturalism; the real debate raised by Darwin revolves about this philosophy. Two things should be noted about this implication of Darwinism. First, both the naturalistic opponents of religion and the religious opponents of evolution should recognize that to rule out God's activity because it cannot become a part of a scientific explanation of events is to draw a philosophical conclusion which is not itself a part of the scientific hypothesis. The naturalistic world view is an extension of scientific understanding beyond the range of science. It is an extension into metaphysics, into a general description of the ultimate nature of the universe. Though naturalistic philosophy has been a clear implication of Darwin's theory to many of his followers, it is not part of this theory as that theory appears in the field of biological science--which can no more establish the absence of God from the universe than it can certify his presence in the biology laboratory.

Religious antievolutionists, furthermore, should note that the scientific method itself--and thus every particular hypothesis--*if* expanded into a philosophical viewpoint, carries the same threat as does Darwin. If scientific explanation excludes divine activity--and this seems to be the terror which Darwinism held for those Christians who feared it--then no hypothesis of physics, chemistry, geology or meteorology is acceptable to Christian minds, and no faithful Christian can plan his morrow on the basis of a scientific weather forecast. Again we see that Darwin is not alone in supplying problems for religious thought. His theory is merely the most powerful and poignant symbol of the challenge which all of modern science raises for Christian faith when scientific understanding is made into an all-embracing world view. It is not the specific theory, which challenges the truth of faith;

what is at issue is the philosophical conclusion
which contends that scientific hypotheses provide an
all-sufficient understanding that excludes Providence.

VII

What then does the Christian say about Darwinian
thought? He will neither reject it nor give it unqualified endorsement. The theory of evolution can in
itself be accepted by any Christian willing to question
the verbal infallibility of Scripture and the specific
theories of time and of species contained in it. In
fact on these terms it is possible for evolution and
Christian thought to cohere with surprising and even
dangerous ease. Liberal theology effected such an
amalgamation, interpreting the theological concepts of
revelation, creation and redemption in accordance with
the fundamental idea of the evolutionary development
of the cosmos, of life, of culture and of religion.
In the late 19th century, far from being antithetical
to all religion, evolution became the bulwark of liberal religious thought. As Lyman Abbott said: "The
history of the world, whether it be the history of
creation, or providence, or of redemption, whether the
history of redemption in the race or of redemption in
the individual soul, is the history of a growth in
accordance with the great law interpreted and uttered
in that one word evolution."

Contemporary theology has had a more ambiguous
relation than did liberalism to scientific and philosophical notions such as evolution. Unlike liberalism
it has carefully tried to construct its theological
concepts on the basis of revelation rather than on
that of either science or philosophy; it does not use
the concept of evolution as a means of interpreting
the religious ideas of creation, providence or revelation. On the other hand, unlike the older orthodoxy
it has sought to interpret the realities of Christian
faith without denying any specific theories of the
various sciences. Most contemporary theologians
accept the theory of evolution as a probably accurate
biological description of the way in which life has
developed, just as they accept the hypotheses of
physics, chemistry or geology. But they maintain that
this biological understanding of man, while providing
illumination of man as "creature," does not produce a
total understanding of man in all the dimensions of
his existence. Thus modern theology affirms that man
is not only a creature evolved from nature but also a
child of God made in his image and destined through

faith for eternal life with him. Evolution is accepted as a scientific concept, but like all such it is regarded as neither in conflict with nor determinative of theological concepts.

If Christian thought accepts evolution as the most probable description of the natural origins of man's life, how are Christians then to understand the causes of evolution? Specifically, how are we to think about God's creation of man in God's image if we also recognize the biologist's explanation of human origins in terms of random mutations and natural selection? What is the relation of God's primary causality to the secondary causality of natural and historical life? Modern theology by and large has side-stepped this difficult question, partly out of concern for the issues of revelation and redemption and partly out of fear of domination by science and philosophy. But it cannot be permanently avoided, for on a sound answer depends the intelligibility of the central Christian affirmation that God is the Lord of nature and the Sovereign of history.

If Christians are to accept the modern world of scientific inquiry and technology, they must learn to think of God's providence as working through and within the finite relations of things to one another and not, so to speak, alongside of and separate from those relations. Divine causality, whether it concern the movements of natural forces in climate and weather or of historical forces in the doings of men, does not push aside the activity of finite agents--as if God would cause a storm without the contributing meteorological factors or bring about an historical event without the action of men or effect our salvation without the activity of our wills. Rather, divine causality works through the finite; in regard to origins, God works through all the secondary causes that have played their part in the development of life on earth. Science studies by its empirical methods these finite causes--in the case of evolution, genetic mutations and natural selection--in the workings of which religious faith discerns, however dimly, the mysterious activity of God's providence. And just as the events of history or of an individual's life seem from the outside to be "random," yet in them the eye of faith can discover the workings of God, so the processes of natural development seem to the inquiries of science to be entirely random, yet to the mind of faith they manifest the mystery of God's creative and providential will.

204

For the Christian, then, the inquiries of science --and with them the theory of evolution--do not conflict with his faith. The scientist is studying the finite causes through which God's providence is acting on the world; Christians should not be surprised when the scientist, who by his method can find only those finite causes, does not discover God's activity therein. But the Christian does not concur with his inquiring friend if he abandons his scientific role and extrapolates from the explanations of scientific inquiry the philosophical doctrine which maintains that only finite causes are at work, that nature is self-sufficient and provides the sole source and environment of man. The naturalism that denies the category of the divine is, however, not a part of science, but a philosophical extension of it. Let us recall that such a naturalistic view of reality, far from being a new product of modern science, is as old as philosophy itself and that the controversy of religious faith with this ancient view is as old as human culture.

In summation evolution as a scientific hypothesis presents no new or fundamental challenge to Christian faith. In its biological aspect it illuminates extensively the creatureliness which is a God-given aspect of our being. And in its deeper implications the theory of evolution embodies for us a reminder of two of the perennial tasks of the church: the task of rethinking our faith in God and his works in the light of all we know and the task of carrying on in as intelligible terms as we can the continual debate with a cultural wisdom that knows nothing of God.

Discussion Questions

1. Is the distinction between the fact of evolution and the philosophical interpretation of evolution a valid one? Does this distinction alter your doctrine of creation?

2. Do you agree with Gilkey that divine power cannot be tested? If so, can it ever be distinguished from finite powers? If not, to what events would you point as evidence of God's activity?

3. Aside from their different theologies of scripture, are there significant differences between Gilkey and Henry on the essence of the doctrine of Creation?

4. How would you resolve the problem of distinguishing divine causality and natural causality?

PROVIDENCE, MIRACLES, AND THE LAWS
OF NATURE

We have all heard it said, "God used to work miracles back in biblical times, but he does not work that way anymore." Whether such an assertion intends to or not it certainly serves as an excellent explanation for why it is difficult to distinguish God's activity from natural and human causation. However, though it may serve well for the believer, it may not convince anyone else that providence is a meaningful idea. Furthermore, even for a great many believers such a position effectively removes God; he becomes rather inconsequential.

Scholars remind us that the biblical writers lived in a period when there was no hard and fast distinction between nature and supernature. God was active in literally every event. Some occurrences were more transparent than others, revealing his presence to those of faith. But even these events might be interpreted without reference to God, or they might be attributed to the causal activity of some other non-human power, either divine or demonic.

The nature/supernature distinction is largely a modern one. Scientific development occurred under the theory that causal explanations along natural lines were not only necessary but also sufficient. Causality became closely associated with natural law. And in the essay to follow C. S. Lewis discusses three meanings given to the idea of natural law in the Western history of science.

Lewis' intention is to demonstrate that none of the prevailing notions of natural law require a view of Nature such that intervention with the natural system is an impossibility. To be sure, the guiding notions of order and "lawfulness" are necessary to scientific inquiry and advancement. We would not even initiate experimental inquiry if we did not believe there was some discoverable rhyme and reason to things. And if we did not assume lawfulness, we would not necessarily heat our eggs each morning to boil them.

Nevertheless, Lewis argues that even the strongest conception of natural law, defining it as a necessary truth of reality, does not exclude the possibility of miracles. We cannot say, "event X cannot occur because nature just does not operate that way." We cannot say this because natural laws hold only if all other things are equal; that is, if the situation has not been tampered with. Lewis' point is that in a miracle God tampers with the situation. The situation is different than that for which the natural laws were prescriptive.

Lewis reminds us that Laws do not make things happen or prevent them from happening. They state the pattern to which an event will conform, if only it is induced by something else. Accordingly, Lewis says miracles do not break the laws of nature. If a miraculous act is induced, then immediately the laws of nature take over. Virgins who conceive must nevertheless carry the child through the months of pregnancy and then give birth.

It is important that one understand the extent of Lewis' contribution in this brief essay. He has not proven that miracles occur. To attempt such a proof would require considerable investigation: historical and scientific. Even then, one must deal with the problem of whether a miracle is revealed only to the eye of faith, or whether it is discernible by any objective observer. Is the judgment, "this is a miracle, a work of God," a descriptive one or is it a gift of God's grace? What Lewis has done is to try to show that miracles are not necessarily ruled out by any prevailing understanding of natural law.

PROVIDENCE, MIRACLES, AND THE LAWS
OF NATURE*

The question is whether Nature can be known to be
of such a kind that supernatural interferences with
her are impossible. She is already known to be, in
general, regular: she behaves according to fixed
laws, many of which have been discovered, and which
interlock with one another. There is, in this discussion, no question of mere failure or inaccuracy to
keep these laws on the part of Nature, no question of
chancey or spontaneous variation. The only question
is whether, granting the existence of a Power outside
Nature, there is any intrinsic absurdity in the idea
of its intervening to produce within Nature events
which the regular "going on" of the whole natural
system would never have produced.

Three conceptions of the "Laws" of Nature have
been held. (1) That they are mere brute facts, known
only by observation, with no discoverable rhyme or
reason about them. We know *that* Nature behaves thus
and thus; we do not know why she does and can see no
reason why she should not do the opposite. (2) That
they are applications of the law of averages. The
foundations of Nature are in the random and lawless.
But the numbers of units we are dealing with are so
enormous that the behaviour of these crowds (like the
behaviour of very large masses of men) can be calcu-
lated with practical accuracy. What we call "impossible events" are events so overwhelmingly improbable--
by actuarial standards--that we do not need to take
them into account. (3) That the fundamental laws of
Physics are really what we call "necessary truths"
like the truths of mathematics--in other words, that
if we clearly understand what we are saying we shall
see that the opposite would be meaningless nonsense.
Thus it is a "law" that when one billiard ball shoves
another the amount of momentum lost by the first ball
must exactly equal the amount gained by the second.

*Source: From *Miracles: A Preliminary Study* by
C. S. Lewis, copyright 1947, published by William Col-
lins and Sons, Ltd. Used by permission of William
Collins and Sons, Ltd.

It will at once be clear that the first of these
three theories gives no assurance against Miracles--
indeed no assurance that, even apart from Miracles,
the "laws" which we have hitherto observed will be
obeyed to-morrow. If we have no notion why a thing
happens, then of course we know no reason why it
should not be otherwise, and therefore have no certainty that it might not some day be otherwise. The
second theory, which depends on the law of averages,
is in the same position. The assurance it gives us
is of the same general kind as our assurance that a
coin tossed a thousand times will not give the same
result, say, nine hundred times: and that the longer
you toss it the more nearly the numbers of Heads and
Tails will come to being equal. But this is so only
provided the coin is an honest coin. If it is a
loaded coin our expectations may be disappointed. But
the people who believe in miracles are maintaining
precisely that the coin *is* loaded. The expectations
based on the law of averages will work only for
undoctored Nature. And the question whether miracles
occur is just the question whether Nature is ever
doctored.

The third view (that Laws of Nature are necessary
truths) seems at first sight to present an insur-
mountable obstacle to miracle. The breaking of them
would, in that case, be a self-contradiction and not
even Omnipotence can do what is self-contradictory.
Therefore the Laws cannot be broken. And therefore,
shall we conclude, no miracle can ever occur?

We have gone too quickly.

If the laws of Nature are necessary truths, no
miracle can break them: but then no miracle needs to
break them. It is with them as with the laws of arithmetic. If I put six pennies into a drawer on Monday
and six more on Tuesday, the laws decree that--*other
things being equal*--I shall find twelve pennies there
on Wednesday. But if the drawer has been robbed I
may in fact find only two. Something will have been
broken (the lock of the drawer or the laws of England)
but the laws of arithmetic will not have been broken.
The new situation created by the thief will illustrate
the laws of arithmetic just as well as the original
situation. But if God comes to work miracles, He
comes "like a thief in the night." Miracle is, from
the point of view of the scientist, a form of doctor-
ing, tampering, (if you like) cheating. It introduces
a new factor into the situation, namely supernatural

force, which the scientist had not reckoned on. He calculates what will happen, or what must have happened on a past occasion, in the belief that the situation, at that point of space and time, is or was A. But if supernatural force has been added, then the situation really is or was AB. And no one knows better than the scientist that AB *cannot* yield the same results as A. The necessary truth of the laws, far from making it impossible that miracles should occur makes it certain that if the Supernatural is operating they must occur. For if the natural situation by itself, and the natural situation *plus* something else, yielded only the same result, it would be then that we should be faced with a lawless and unsystematic universe. The better you know that two and two make four, the better you know that two and three don't.

This perhaps helps to make a little clearer what the laws of Nature really are. We are in the habit of talking as if they caused events to happen; but they have never caused any event at all. The laws of motion do not set billiard balls moving: they analyse the motion after something else (say, a man with a cue, or a lurch of the liner, or, perhaps, supernatural power) has provided it. They produce no events: they state the pattern to which every event--if only it can be induced to happen--must conform, just as the rules of arithmetic state the pattern to which all trans- actions with money must conform--if only you can get hold of any money. Thus in one sense the laws of Nature cover the whole field of space and time; in another, what they leave out is precisely the whole real universe--the incessant torrent of actual events which makes up true history. That must come from somewhere else. To think the laws can produce it is like thinking that you can create real money by simply doing sums. For every law, in the last resort, says "If you have A, then you will get B." But first catch your A: the laws won't do it for you.

It is therefore inaccurate to definite a miracle as something that breaks the laws of Nature. It doesn't. If I knock out my pipe I alter the position of a great many atoms: in the long run, and to an infinitesimal degree, of all the atoms there are. Nature digests or assimilates this event with perfect ease and harmonises it in a twinkling with all other events. It is one more bit of raw material for the laws to apply to, and they apply. I have simply thrown one event into the general cataract of events and it finds itself at home there and comforms to all

to all other events. If God annihilates or creates
or deflects a unit of matter He has created a new
situation at that point. Immediately all Nature
domiciles this new situation, makes it at home in her
realm, adapts all other events to it. It finds itself
conforming to all the laws. If God creates a miraculous spermatozoon in the body of a virgin, it does not
proceed to break any laws. The laws at once take it
over. Nature is ready. Pregnancy follows, according
to all the normal laws, and nine months later a child
is born. Miraculous wine will intoxicate, miraculous
conception will lead to pregnancy, inspired books will
suffer all the ordinary processes of textual corruption,
miraculous bread will be digested. The divine art of
miracle is not an art of suspending the pattern to
which events conform but of feeding new events into
that pattern. It does not violate the law's proviso,
"If A, then B": it says, "But this time instead of A,
A2," and Nature, speaking through all her laws,
replies, "Then B2" and naturalises the immigrant, as
she well knows how. She is an accomplished hostess.

A miracle is emphatically not an event without
cause or without results. Its cause is the activity
of God: its results follow according to Natural law.
In the forward direction (i.e. during the time which
follows its occurrence) it is interlocked with all
Nature just like any other event. Its peculiarity is
that it is not in that way interlocked backwards,
interlocked with the previous history of Nature. And
this is just what some people find intolerable. The
reason they find it intolerable is that they start by
taking Nature to be the whole of reality. And they
are sure that all reality must be interrelated and
consistent. I agree with them. But I think they
have mistaken a partial system within reality, namely
Nature, for the whole. That being so, the miracle
and the previous history of Nature may be interlocked
after all but not in the way the Naturalist expected:
rather in a much more roundabout fashion. The great
complex event called Nature, and the new particular
event introduced into it by the miracle, are related
by their common origin in God, and doubtless, if we
knew enough, most intricately related in His purpose
and design, so that a Nature which had had a different
history, and therefore been a different Nature, would
have been invaded by different miracles or by none at
all. In that way the miracle and the previous course
of Nature are as well interlocked as any other two
realities, but you must go back as far as their common
Creator to find the interlocking. You will not find

it *within* Nature. The same sort of thing happens with
any partial system. The behaviour of fishes which are
being studied in a tank makes a relatively closed
system. Now suppose that the tank is shaken by a bomb
in the neighbourhood of the laboratory. The behaviour
of the fishes will now be no longer fully explicable
by what was going on in the tank before the bomb fell:
there will be a failure of backward interlocking.
This does not mean that the bomb and the previous
history of events within the tank are totally and
finally unrelated. It does mean that to find their
relation you must go back to the much larger reality
which includes both the tank and the bomb--the reality
of war-time England in which bombs are falling but
some laboratories are still at work. You would never
find it within the history of the tank. In the same
way, the miracle is not *naturally* interlocked in the
backward direction. To find how it is interlocked
with the previous history of Nature you must replace
both Nature and the miracle in a larger context.
Everything *is* connected with everything else: but
not all things are connected by the short and straight
roads we expected.

The rightful demand that all reality should be
consistent and systematic does not therefore exclude
miracles: but it has a very valuable contribution to
make to our conception of them. It reminds us that
miracles, if they occur, must, like all events, be
revelations of the total harmony of all that exists.
Nothing arbitrary, nothing simply "stuck on" and left
unreconciled with the texture of total reality, can be
admitted. By definition, miracles must of course
interrupt the usual course of Nature; but if they are
real they must, in the very act of so doing, assert
all the more the unity and self-consistency of total
reality at some deeper level. They will not be like
unmetrical lumps of prose breaking the unity of a
poem; they will be like that crowning metrical audacity
which, though it may be paralleled nowhere else in the
poem, yet, coming just where it does, and effecting
just what it effects, is (to those who understand)
the supreme revelation of the unity in the poet's
conception. If what we call Nature is modified by
supernatural power, then we may be sure that the
capability of being so modified is of the essence of
nature--that the total event, if we could grasp it,
would turn out to involve, by its very character, the
possibility of such modifications. If Nature brings
forth miracles then doubtless it is as "natural" for
her to do so when impregnated by the masculine force

beyond her as it is for a woman to bear children to a man. In calling them miracles we do not mean that they are contradictions or outrages; we mean that, left to her own resources, she could never produce them.

DISCUSSION QUESTIONS

1. To what extent would the work of a scientist or a physician be altered if Lewis' theory were taken seriously? If there were always the possibility that God would intervene and alter a situation, would this be detrimental to scientific advance? Would one's theology of the character of God guard against undesirable conclusions about this issue?

2. Is there another understanding of natural law which Lewis overlooks? Does such an understanding exclude the possibility of miracles, or is it covered by Lewis' argument?

3. What do you think is the relationship of faith to miracle?

4. Do Christian believers tend to accept the miracles reported in their tradition but reject those reported by other faiths? If so, why?

GROUND RULES FOR FORMING A THEODICY

In this essay J. L. Mackie clarifies the way in which the problem of evil arises. He holds that three propositions must be affirmed as true if evil is to be a theological problem. These are: God is omnipotent, God is wholly good; and yet evil exists. Mackie argues that the simplest way out of the problem of evil is to deny one of the above propositions. But the thrust of Mackie's essay is to demonstrate how theologians tend to reject explicitly one of the propositions (e.g., by saying God is not omnipotent since man is free), but covertly reassert it.

Mackie discusses four attempted solutions to the problem of evil. The first of these is that good cannot exist without evil as its counterpart. In ordinary language we express this solution when we say something like "I would never have known joy unless I had cried." Although he has several reservations about this solution, I think the most important point he makes is that this solution rests on an assumption that a quality (good) must have an opposite (evil). Unless this assumption is understood as a principle of reality which limits God's power, then God could have created everything good, and this solution to the problem of evil fails. A corollary of this important point is that those who hold this solution must be prepared to say that there is only enough evil to serve as the counterpart of good. But this would be a difficult position to maintain.

The second of Mackie's inadequate solutions to the problem of evil is that one which holds that evil is necessary as a means to good. This solution differs from the first because it is based on the notion that

215

God must use evil as a means to create higher goods. The first solution said evil was a counterpart to good, but it did not emphasize any causal relation.

The essay which follows Mackie's was written by John Hick. Hick's solution to the problem of evil is related to this second approach which Mackie calls fallacious. To be brief, the reason Mackie rejects this model is that it severely limits God's power. This approach maintains that God is subject to the causal law that some evil is necessary to produce good. Such subjection means that God must use contrivances such as evil in order to accomplish his desired ends. If I must use a jack to change a flat tire on my automobile, then the jack is an evidence of some weakness on my part. Mackie argues that if God is omnipotent then he can create good without using evil as a means.

It is easy to see why we cannot avoid this difficulty by saying that God does not use contrivances because he must do so, but because he chooses to do so. To hold this position would mean that God chooses to use evil and this would tend to undermine our belief in his goodness.

The third fallacious solution to the problem of evil which Mackie discusses is that the universe is actually better with some evil in it than it would be if there were no evil. This is a kind of aesthetic theodicy. Just as dark hues and shadows are needed to enhance the beauty of some paintings, so evil is necessary to add to the richness of the good. Mackie believes that this solution fails because the evils most prevalent are those God should be most desirous of eliminating: malevolence, cruelty, callousness, et al.

For theologians, the most important proposed solution to the problem of evil is the fourth one Mackie mentions. This solution says evil is due to human free will. Mackie rejects this solution largely because it turns upon a notion of freedom that is incoherent, if not equivocal. To say that theologians use a term equivocally means that they use the term in two different senses.

Mackie believes that those who depend on the free will defense to solve the problem of evil are really using "freedom" in two senses. In one sense freedom means "choosing what I want;" in the other sense it means complete randomness.

If freedom is understood in the first sense, then Mackie holds that the free will defense fails as a solution to the problem of evil. It fails because God might have created beings who always wanted to do good, and thus freely choose it. Since we do not always choose good, then God did not create us to choose good freely. Either he is not omnipotent, or he is not good.

Mackie's point is that God was not faced with a choice between making robots and making beings who, in acting freely would sometimes choose evil. He contends there was a third possibility: making beings who would act freely (in the first sense of acting freely), but always choose good.

One cannot escape the dilemma Mackie poses for us by taking refuge in the second definition of freedom as randomness or complete indeterminacy. The reason one cannot entertain seriously this response is that it would mean that free actions were not determined by the nature of the agent at all, and that would mean there was no virtue in being free.

One final criticism must be made of the free will defense. If God's gift of freedom to man means that God cannot control our wills then his power is limited and we may wonder whether his ultimate ends can ever be achieved. On the other hand, if he refrains from controlling our wills, even though he is able to do so, then either God is not wholly good or freedom is itself a higher good than any evil we might inflict.

GROUND RULES FOR FORMING A THEODICY*

The problem of evil, in the sense in which I shall be using the phrase, is a problem only for someone who believes that there is a God who is both omnipotent and wholly good. And it is a logical problem, the problem of clarifying and reconciling a number of beliefs: it is not a scientific problem that might be solved by

217

further observations, or a practical problem that might be solved by a decision or an action. These points are obvious; I mention them only because they are sometimes ignored by theologians, who sometimes parry a statement of the problem with such remarks as "Well, can you solve the problem yourself?" or "This is a mystery which may be revealed to us later" or "Evil is something to be faced and overcome, not to be merely discussed."

In its simplest form the problem is this: God is omnipotent; God is wholly good; and yet evil exists. There seems to be some contradiction between these three propositions, so that if any two of them were true the third would be false. But at the same time all three are essential parts of most theological positions: the theologian, it seems, at once *must* adhere and *cannot consistently* adhere to all three. (The problem does not arise only for theists, but I shall discuss it in the form in which it presents itself for ordinary theism.)

However, the contradiction does not arise immediately; to show it we need some additional premises, or perhaps some quasi-logical rules connecting the terms "good," "evil," and "omnipotent." These additional principles are that good is opposed to evil, in such a way that a good thing always eliminates evil as far as it can, and that there are no limits to what an omnipotent thing can do. From these it follows that a good omnipotent thing eliminates evil completely, and then the proposition that a good omnipotent thing exists, and that evil exists, are incompatible.

A. Adequate Solutions

Now once the problem is fully stated it is clear that it can be solved, in the sense that the problem will not arise if one gives up at least one of the propositions that constitute it. If you are prepared to say that God is not wholly good, or not quite omnipotent, or that evil does not exist, or that good is not opposed to the kind of evil that exists, or that there are limits to what an omnipotent thing can do, then the problem of evil will not arise for you.

*Source: From *Mind*, Vol. 64 (1955), pp. 200-212. Reprinted by permission of *Mind*.

There are, then, quite a number of adequate solutions of the problem of evil, and some of these have been adopted, or almost adopted by various thinkers. For example, a few have been prepared to deny God's omnipotence, and rather more have been prepared to keep the term "omnipotence" but severely to restrict its meaning, recording quite a number of things that an omnipotent being cannot do. Some have said that evil is an illusion, perhaps because they held that the whole world of temporal, changing things is an illusion, and that what we call evil belongs only to this world, or perhaps because they held that although temporal things *are* much as we see them, those that we call evil are not really evil. Some have said that what we call evil is merely the privation of good, that evil in a positive sense, evil that would really be opposed to good, does not exist. Many have agreed with Pope that disorder is harmony not understood and that partial evil is universal good. Whether any of these views is *true* is, of course, another question. But each of them gives an adequate solution of the problem of evil in the sense that if you accept it this problem does not arise for you, though you may, of course have *other* problems to face.

But often enough these adequate solutions are only *almost* adopted. The thinkers who restrict God's power, but keep the term "omnipotence," may reasonably be suspected of thinking, in other contexts, that his power is really unlimited. Those who say that evil is an illusion may also be thinking, inconsistently, that this illusion is itself an evil. Those who say that "evil" is merely privation of good may also be thinking, inconsistently, that privation of good is an evil. (The fallacy here is akin to some forms of the "naturalistic fallacy" in ethics, where some think, for example, that "good" is just what contributes to evolutionary progress, and that evolutionary progress is itself good.) If Pope meant what he said in the first line of his couplet, that "disorder" is only harmony not understood, the "partial evil" of the second line must, for consistency, mean "that which, taken in isolation, falsely appears to be evil," but it would more naturally mean "that which, in isolation, really is evil." The second line, in fact, hesitates between two views, that "partial evil" isn't really evil, since only the universal quality is real, and that "partial evil" is really an evil, but only a little one.

In addition, therefore, to adequate solutions, we must recognise unsatisfactory inconsistent solutions, in which there is only a halfhearted or temporary rejection of one of the propositions which together constitute the problem. In these, one of the constitutent propositions is explicitly rejected, but it is covertly reasserted or assumed elsewhere in the system.

B. Fallacious Solutions

Besides these half-hearted solutions, which explicitly reject but implicitly assert one of the constituent propositions, there are definitely fallacious solutions which explicitly maintain all the constituent propositions, but implicitly reject at least one of them in the course of the argument that explains away the problem of evil.

There are, in fact, many so-called solutions which purport to remove the contradiction without abandoning any of its constituent propositions. These must be fallacious, as we can see from the very statement of the problem, but it is not so easy to see in each case precisely where the fallacy lies. I suggest that in all cases the fallacy has the general form suggested above: in order to solve the problem one (or perhaps more) of its constituent propositions is given up, but in such a way that it appears to have been retained, and can therefore be asserted without qualification in other contexts. Sometimes there is a further complication: the supposed solution moves to and fro between, say, two of the constituent propositions, at one point asserting the first of these but covertly abandoning the second, at another point asserting the second but covertly abandoning the first. These fallacious solutions often turn upon some equivocation with the words "good" and "evil," or upon some vagueness about the way in which good and evil are opposed to one another, or about how much is meant by "omnipotence." I propose to examine some of these so-called solutions, and to exhibit their fallacies in detail. Incidentally, I shall also be considering whether an adequate solution could be reached by a minor modification of one or more of the constituent propositions, which would, however, still satisfy all the essential requirements of ordinary theism.

1. "Good cannot exist without evil" or "Evil is necessary as a counterpart to good."

It is sometimes suggested that evil is necessary as a counterpart to good, that if there were no evil there could be no good either, and that this solves the prob-

lem of evil. It is true that it points to an answer to
the question "Why should there be evil?" But it does
so only by qualifying some of the propositions that
constitute the problem.

First, it sets a limit to what God can do, saying
that God *cannot* create good without simultaneously
creating evil, and this means either that God is not
omnipotent or that there are *some* limits to what an omnipotent thing can do. It may be replied that these
limits are always presupposed, that omnipotence has
never meant the power to do what is logically impossible, and on the present view the existence of good
without evil would be a logical impossibility. This
interpretation of omnipotence may, indeed, be accepted
as a modification of our original account which does
not reject anything that is essential to thesim, and I
shall in general assume it in the subsequent discussion.

But, secondly, this solution denies that evil is
opposed to good in our original sense. If good and
evil are counterparts, a good thing will not "eliminate
evil as far as it can." Indeed this view suggests that
good and evil are not strictly qualities of things at
all. Perhaps the suggestion is that good and evil are
related in much the same way as great and small. Certainly, when the term "great" is used relatively as a
condensation of "greater than so-and-so," and "small"
is used correspondingly, greatness and smallness are
counterparts and cannot exist without each other. But
in this sense greatness is not a quality, not an intrinsic feature of anything; and it would be absurd to
think of a movement in favour of greatness and against
smallness in this sense. Such a movement would be
self-defeating, since relative greatness can be pro-
moted only by a simultaneous promotion of relative
smallness. I feel sure that no theists would be content
to regard God's goodness as analogous to this--as if
what he supports were not the *good* but the *better*, and
as if he had the paradoxical aim that all things should
be better than other things.

This point is obscured by the fact that "great"
and "small" seem to have an absolute as well as a relative sense. I cannot discuss here whether there is
absolute magnitude or not, but if there is, there could
be an absolute sense for "great," it could mean of at
least a certain size, and it would make sense to speak
of all things getting bigger, of a universe that was
expanding all over, and therefore it would make sense

221

to speak of promoting greatness. But in *this* sense
great and small are not logically necessary counterparts: either quality could exist without the other.
There would be no logical impossibility in everything's
being small or in everything's being great.

Neither in the absolute nor in the relative sense,
then, of "great" and "small" do these terms provide an
analogy of the sort that would be needed to support
this solution of the problem of evil. In neither case
are greatness and smallness *both* necessary counterparts
and mutually opposed forces or possible objects for
support and attack.

It may be replied that good and evil are necessary
counterparts in the same way as any quality and its
logical opposite: redness can occur, it is suggested,
only if non-redness also occurs. But unless evil is
merely the privation of good, they are not logical opposites, and some further argument would be needed to
show that they are counterparts in the same way as
genuine logical opposites. Let us assume that this
could be given. There is still doubt of the correctness of the metaphysical principle that a quality must
have real opposite: I suggest that it is not really impossible that everything should be, say, red, that the
truth is merely that if everthing were red we should
not notice redness, and so we should have no word
"red," we observe and give names to qualities only if
they have real opposites. If so, the principle that a
term must have an opposite would belong only to our
language or to our thought, and would not be an ontological principle, and correspondingly, the rule that
good cannot exist without evil would not state a logical necessity of a sort that God would just have to put
up with. God might have made everthing good, though *we*
should not have noticed it if he had.

But, finally, even if we concede that this *is* an
ontological principle, it will provide a solution for
the problem of evil only if one is prepared to say,
Evil exists, but only just enough evil to serve as the
counterpart of good." I doubt whether any theist will
accept this. After all, the *ontological* requirement
that non-redness should occur would be satisfied even
if all the universe, except for a minute speck, were
red, and if there were a corresponding requirement for
evil as a counterpart to good, a minute dose of evil
would presumably do. But theists are not usually willing to say, in all contexts, that all the evil that occurs is a minute and necessary dose.

2. "Evil is necessary as a means to good."

It is sometimes suggested that evil is necessary for good not as a counterpart but as a means. In its simple form this has little plausibility as a solution of the problem of evil, since it obviously implies a severe restriction of God's power. It would be a *causal* law that you cannot have a certain end without a certain means, so that if God has to introduce evil as a means to good, he must be subject to at least some causal laws. This certainly conflicts with what a theist normally means by omnipotence. This view of God as limited by causal laws also conflicts with the view that causal laws are themselves made by God, which is more widely held than the corresponding view about the laws of logic. This conflict would, indeed, be resolved if it were possible for an omnipotent being to bind himself, and this possibility has still to be considered. Unless a favourable answer can be given to this question, the suggestion that evil is necessary as a means to good solves the problem of evil only by denying one of its constituent propositions, either that God is omnipotent or that "omnipotent" means what it says.

3. "The universe is better with some evil in it than it could be if there were no evil."

Much more important is a solution which at first seems to be a mere variant of the previous one, that evil may contribute to the goodness of a whole in which it is found, so that the universe as a whole is better as it is, with some evil in it, than it would be if there were no evil. This solution may be developed in either of two ways. It may be supported by an aesthetic analogy, by the fact that contrasts heighten beauty, that in a musical work, for example, there may occur discords which somehow add to the beauty of the work as a whole. Alternatively, it may be worked out in connexion with the notion of progress, that the best possible organisation of the universe will not be static, but progressive, that the gradual overcoming of evil by good is really a finer thing than would be the eternal unchallenged supremacy of good.

In either case, this solution usually starts from the assumption that the evil whose existence gives rise to the problem of evil is primarily what is called physical evil, that is to say, pain. In Hume's rather half-hearted presentation of the problem of evil, the evils that he stresses are pain and disease, and those

223

who reply to him argue that the existence of pain and disease makes possible the existence of sympathy, benevolence, heroism, and the gradually successful struggle of doctors and reformer to overcome these evils. In fact, theists often seize the opportunity to accuse those who stress the problem of evil of taking a low, materialistic view of good and evil, equating these with pleasure and pain, and of ignoring the more spiritual goods which can arise in the struggle against evils.

But let us see exactly what is being done here. Let us call pain and misery "first order evil" or "evil (1)." What contrasts with this, namely, pleasure and happiness, will be called "first order good" or "good (1)." Distinct from this is "second order good" or "good (2)" which somehow emerges in a complex situation in which evil (1) is a necessary component--logically, not merely causally, necessary. (Exactly *how* it emerges does not matter: in the crudest version of this solution good (2) is simply the heightening of happiness by the contrast with misery, in other versions it includes sympathy with suffering heroism in facing danger, and the gradual decrease of first order evil and increase of first order good.) It is also being assumed that second order good is more important than first order good or evil, in particular that it more than outweighs the first order evil it involves.

Now this is a particularly subtle attempt to solve the problem of evil. It defends God's goodness and omnipotence on the ground that (on a sufficiently long view) this is the best of all logically possible worlds, because it includes the important second order goods, and yet it admits that real evils, namely first order evils, exist. But does it still hold that good and evil are opposed? Not, clearly, in the sense that we set out originally: good does not tend to eliminate evil in general. Instead, we have a modified, a more complex pattern. First order good (e.g., happiness) *contrast with* first order evil (e.g., misery): these two are opposed in a fairly mechanical way; some second order goods (e.g., benevolence) try to maximise first order good and minimise first order evil; but God's goodness is not this, it is rather the will to maximise *second* order good. We might, therefore, call God's goodness an example of a third order goodness, or good (3). While this account is different from our original one, it might well be able to be an improvement on it, to give a more accurate description of the way in which good is opposed to evil, and to be consistent with the essential theist position.

There might, however, be several objections to this solution.

First, some might argue that such qualities as benevolence--and a *fortiori* the third order goodness which promotes benevolence--have a merely derivative value, that they are not higher sorts of good, but merely means to good (1), that is, to happiness, so that it would be absurd for God to keep misery in existence in order to make possible the virtues of benevolence, heroism, etc. The theist who adopts the pressent solution must, of course, deny this, but he can do so with some plausibility, so I should not press this objection.

Secondly, it follows from this solution that God is not in our sense benevolent or sympathetic: he is not concerned to minimise evil (1), but only to promote good (2); and this might be a disturbing conclusion for some theists.

But, thirdly, the fatal objection is this. Our analysis shows clearly the possibility of the existence of a *second* order evil, an evil (2) contrasting with good (2) as evil (1) contrasts with good (1). This would include malevolence, cruelty, callousness, cowardice, and states in which good (1) is decreasing and evil (1) increasing. And just as good (2) is held to be the important kind of good, the kind that God is concerned to promote, so evil (2) will, by analogy, be the important kind of evil, the kind which God, if he were wholly good and omnipotent, would eliminate. And yet evil (2) plainly exists, and indeed most theists (in other contexts) stress its existence more than that of evil (1). We should, therefore, state the problem of evil in terms of second order evil, and against this form of the problem the present solution is useless.

An attempt might be made to use this solution again, at a higher level, to explain the occurrence of evil (2); indeed the next main solution that we shall examine does just this, with the help of some new notions. Without any fresh notions, such a solution would have little plausibility: for example, we could hardly say that the really important good was a good (3), such as the increase of benevolence in proportion to cruelty, which logically required for its occurrence the occurrence of some second order evil. But even if evil (2) could be explained in this way, it is fairly

clear that there would be third order evils contrasting
with this third order good: and we should be well on
the way to an infinite regress, where the solution of a
problem of evil, stated in terms of evil (n), indicated
the existence of an evil (n+1), and a further problem
to be solved.

4. "Evil is due to human freewill."

Perhaps the most important proposed solution of the
problem of evil is that evil is not to be ascribed to
God at all, but to the independent actions of human
beings, supposed to have been endowed by God with freedom of the will. This solution may be combined with the
preceding one: first order evil (e.g., pain) may be
justified as a logically necessary component in second
order good (e.g., sympathy) while second order evil
(e.g., cruelty) is not *justified*, but is so ascribed to
human beings that God cannot be held responsible for
it. This combination evades my third criticism of the
preceding solution.

The freewill solution also involves the preceding
solution at a higher level. To explain why a wholly
good God gave men freewill although it would lead to
some important evils, it must be argued that it is better on the whole that men should act freely, and sometimes err, than that they should be innocent automata,
acting rightly in a wholly determined way. Freedom,
that is to say, is now treated as a third order good,
and as being more valuable than second order goods
(such as sympathy and heroism) would be if they were
deterministically produced, and it is being assumed
that second order evils, such as cruelty, are logically
necessary accompaniments of freedom, just as pain is a
logically necessary pre-condition of sympathy.

I think that this solution is unsatisfactory primarily because of the incoherence of the notion of
freedom of the will: but I cannot discuss this topic
adequately here, although some of my criticisms will
touch upon it.

First I should query the assumption that second
order evils are logically necessary accompaniments of
freedom. I should ask this: if God has made men such
that in their free choices they sometimes prefer what
is good and sometimes what is evil, why could he not
have made men such that they always freely choose the
good? If there is no logical impossibility in a man's
freely choosing the good on one, or on several, occa-

226

sions, there cannot be a logical impossibility in his freely choosing the good on every occasion. God was not, then, faced with a choice between making innocent automata and making beings who, in acting freely, would sometimes go wrong: there was open to him the obviously better possibility of making beings who would act freely but always go right. Clearly, his failure to avail himself of this possibility is inconsistent with his being both omnipotent and wholly good.

If it is replied that this objection is absurd, that the making of some wrong choices is logically necessary for freedom, it would seem that "freedom" must here mean complete randomness or indeterminacy, including randomness with regard to the alternatives good and evil, in other words that men's choices and consequent actions can be "free" only if they are not determined by their characters. Only on this assumption can God escape the responsibility for men's actions; for if he made them as they are, but did not determine their wrong choices, this can only be because the wrong choices are not determined by men as they are. But then if freedom is randomness, how can it be a characteristic of *will*? And, still more, how can it be the most important good? What value or merit would there be in free choices if these were random actions which were not determined by the nature of the agent?

I conclude that to make this solution plausible two different senses of "freedom" must be confused, one sense which will justify the view that freedom is a third order good, more valuable than other goods would be without it, and another sense, sheer randomness, to prevent us from ascribing to God a decision to make men such that they sometimes go wrong when he might have made them such that they would always freely go right.

This criticism is sufficient to dispose of this solution. But besides this there is a fundamental difficulty in the notion of an omnipotent God creating men with free will, for if men's wills are really free this must mean that even God cannot control them, that is, that God is no longer omnipotent. It may be objected that God's gift of freedom to men does not mean that he *cannot* control their wills, but that he always *refrains* from controlling their wills. But why we may ask, should God refrain from controlling evil wills? Why should he not leave men free to will rightly, but intervene when he sees them beginning to will wrongly? If God could do this but does not and if he is wholly good, the only explanation could be that even a wrong

227

free act of will is not really evil, that its freedom is a value which outweighs it wrongness, so that there would be a loss of value if God took away the wrongness and the freedom together. But this is utterly opposed to what theists say about sin in other contexts. The present solution of the problem of evil, then, can be maintained only in the form that God has made men so free that he *cannot* control their wills.

Conclusion

Of the proposed solutions of the problem of evil which we have examined, none has stood up to criticism. There may be other solutions which require examination, but this study strongly suggests that there is no valid solution of the problem which does not modify at least one of the constituent propositions in a way which would seriously affect the essential core of the theistic position.

Quite apart from the problem of evil, the paradox of omnipotence has shown that God's omnipotence must in any case be restricted in one way or another, that unqualified omnipotence cannot be ascribed to any being that continues through time. And if God and his actions are not in time, can omnipotence, or power of any sort, be meaningfully ascribed to him?

Discussion Questions

1. Which of the three propositions would you alter in order to affect a solution to the problem of evil?

2. Do you think that Mackie's analysis of the problem of evil is too much dependent upon our perspective as human beings? Would it be legitimate to say that evil is a mystery of God's providence? Why or Why not?

3. Is there any evil which you think would be so abominable that it would cause you to question God's existence?

4. If God is limited in power, does that mean that he may be caught up in the same mess we are? Can a limited God be assured that his purposes will triumph?

THE VALE OF SOUL-MAKING THEODICY

The effort to understand and interpret the fact of evil in the light of faith is called theodicy. At the heart of the problem are the two central affirmations every Christian theology must preserve: God's sovereignty and his love. The task of theodicy is to make intelligible how both of these affirmations can be true in the face of evil and suffering.

Various theodicies have been attempted in Christian history. Augustine argued that evil was not real in itself. Evil was merely a privation of good. To be sure, evil is not an illusion, but neither is it an independent reality. But one must wonder why a sovereign God (i.e., omnipotent) would create a deficient order which distracts from that which is good if he is loving. Thus the problem is not assuaged.

Several theodicies are dependent on some understanding of God by which his power is sufficiently limited as to allow evil, both natural and moral. David Griffin's use of process theology leads him to develop a theodicy in which God's power is limited by other agents and forces, human and natural.

Every form of the free-will theodicy, by which evil is attributed to the malevolence and sin of man, is a version of a limited-God theodicy. The version offered in the following essay by John Hick depends on a view held by one of the early church fathers, Irenaeus of Lyons. According to Hick's interpretation of Irenaeus, man as a personal being is only the raw material for a further work of God, the creation of a being which finitely reflects the divine life.

Experience is the stage for a transition from one level of existence (animal) to another (spiritual).

229

Such a transition cannot occur in any authentic sense if done by divine fiat. Instead, man must meet and master temptation and suffering. The long and painful trail of the soul-making process is justified, according to Hick, by the good which God has for his creatures.

Hick is careful to stress that the transition of being into the likeness of God is neither automatic, nor natural, nor inevitable. It is a result of free choice. Accordingly, God does not treat man as though he were a pet. God's relation to the world is not such that he will always insure the happiness and comfort of man, as we would do with a pet. Rather, he must fashion an environment suited for the purpose of fashioning moral beings through their own insights and responses. Thus the absence of all pain and suffering may not serve the higher end God has for man. The justification of evil lies in the magnitude and type of good to which it leads.

As one studies Hick's essay several considerations should inform the reader. Many of these are made clear in the essay by J. L. Mackie but deserve to be mentioned here. Hick holds that God wishes to move man toward a transition from mere biological life to spiritual life and he says this cannot be accomplished by a divine creative act, but why not? Where is the contradiction in saying that God might have made everything good, and made us finite reflections of the divine life? Well, Hick says that the quality of life God wishes to produce must come from trial and testing. This seems to imply that evil is necessary to God, and such a view may undermine God's sovereignty, but only on certain definitions of omnipotence. The question is whether omnipotence may be understood in such a way as to allow God to create beings who always freely choose the good. If freedom means doing what I want to do, when I want to do it, then perhaps an omnipotent God could have created humans in such a way that they would have always wanted to choose the good, and thus they would have been free in every meaningful sense, but also good. If these observations stand, then Hick's case is severely compromised and the problem of evil in Christian theology is not yet intelligibly surmounted.

THE 'VALE OF SOUL-MAKING' THEODICY*

As well as the 'majority report' of the Augustinian tradition, which has dominated Western Christendom,
both Catholic and Protestant, since the time of
Augustine himself, there is the 'minority report' of
the Irenaean tradition. This latter is both older
and newer than the other, for it goes back to St.
Irenaeus and others of the early Hellenistic Fathers
of the Church in the two centuries prior to St.
Augustine, and it has flourished again in more developed forms during the last hundred years.

Instead of regarding man as having been created
by God in a finished state, as a finitely perfect
being fulfilling the divine intention for our human
level of existence, and then falling disastrously
away from this, the minority report sees man as still
in the process of creation. Irenaeus himself expressed the point in terms of the (exegetically dubious) distinction between the 'image' and the 'likeness' of God referred to in Genesis i. 26: 'Then God
said, Let us make man in our image, after our likeness.'[1] His view was that man as a personal and moral
being already exists in the image, but has not yet
been formed into the finite likeness of God. By this
'likeness' Irenaeus means something more than personal
existence as such; he means a certain valuable quality
of personal life which reflects finitely the divine
life. This represents the perfecting of man, the fulfilment of God's purpose for humanity, the 'bringing
of many sons to glory,'[2] the creating of 'children of
God' who are 'fellow heirs with Christ' of his glory.[3]

And so man, created as a personal being in the
image of God, is only the raw material for a further
and more difficult stage of God's creative work. This
is the leading of men as relatively free and autonomous persons, through their own dealings with life in
the world in which He has placed them, toward that

*Source: Specified selection from *Evil and the
God of Love*, Revised edition, by John Hick. Copyright
(c) 1966, 1977 by John Hick. Reprinted by permission
of Harper and Row Publishers, Inc.

quality of personal existence that is the finite
likeness of God. The features of this likeness are
revealed in the person of Christ, and the process of
man's creation into it is the work of the Holy Spirit.
In St. Paul's words, 'And we all, with unveiled faces,
beholding the glory of the Lord, are being changed
into his likeness (εἰκών) from one degree of glory to
another; for this comes from the Lord who is the
Spirit';[4] or again, 'For God knew his own before ever
they were, and also ordained that they should be
shaped to the likeness (εἰκών) of his Son.'[5] In
Johannine terms, the movement from the image to the
likeness is a transition from one level of existence,
that of animal life (Βίος), to another and higher
level, that of eternal life (Ζοε), which includes but
transcends the first. And the fall of man was seen by
Irenaeus as a failure within the second phase of this
creative process, a failure that has multiplied the
perils and complicated the route of the journey in
which God is seeking to lead mankind.

     In the light of modern anthropological knowledge
some form of two-stage conception of the creation of
man has become an almost unavoidable Christian tenet.
At the very least we must acknowledge as two distinguishable stages the fashioning of *homo sapiens* as a
product of the long evolutionary process, and his
sudden or gradual spiritualization as a child of God.
But we may well extend the first stage to include the
development of man as a rational and responsible
person capable of personal relationship with the
personal Infinite who has created him. This first
stage of the creative process was, to our anthropomorphic imaginations, easy for divine omnipotence. By an
exercise of creative power God caused the physical
universe to exist, and in the course of countless
ages to bring forth within it organic life, and finally
to produce out of organic life personal life; and when
man had thus emerged out of the evolution of the forms
of organic life, a creature had been made who has the
possibility of existing in conscious fellowship with
God. But the second stage of the creative process is
of a different kind altogether. It cannot be performed by omnipotent power as such. For personal life
is essentially free and self-directing. It cannot be
perfected by divine fiat, but only through the uncompelled responses and willing co-operation of human
individuals in their actions and reactions in the world
in which God has placed them. Men may eventually become the perfected persons whom the New Testament calls
'children of God,' but they cannot be created ready-

232

made as this.

The value-judgment that is implicitly being invoked here is that one who has attained to goodness by meeting and eventually mastering temptations, and thus by rightly making responsible choices in concrete situations, is good in a richer and more valuable sense than would be one created *ab initio* in a state either of innocence or of virtue. In the former case, which is that of the actual moral achievements of mankind, the individual's goodness has within it the strength of temptations overcome, a stability based upon an accumulation of right choices, and a positive and responsible character that comes from the investment of costly personal effort. I suggest, then, that it is an ethically reasonable judgment, even though in the nature of the case not one that is capable of demonstrative proof, that human goodness slowly built up through personal histories of moral effort has a value in the eyes of the Creator which justifies even the long travail of the soul-making process.

The picture with which we are working is thus developmental and teleological. Man is in process of becoming the perfected being whom God is seeking to create. However, this is not taking place--it is important to add--by a natural and inevitable evolution, but through a hazardous adventure in individual freedom. Because this is a pilgrimage within the life of each individual, rather than a racial evolution, the progressive fulfilment of God's purpose does not entail any corresponding progressive improvement in the moral state of the world. There is no doubt a development in man's ethical situation from generation to generation through the building of individual choices into public institutions, but this involves an accumulation of evil as well as of good.[6] It is thus probable that human life was lived on much the same moral plane two thousand years ago or four thousand years ago as it is today. But nevertheless during this period uncounted millions of souls have been through the experience of earthly life, and God's purpose has gradually moved towards its fulfilment within each one of them, rather than within a human aggregate composed of different units in different generations.

If, then, God's aim in making the world is 'the bringing of many sons to glory,'[7] that aim will naturally determine the kind of world that He has created. Antitheistic writers almost invariably assume a conception of the divine purpose which is contrary to the

Christian conception. They assume that the purpose of
a loving God must be to create a hedonistic paradise;
and therefore to the extent that the world is other
than this, it proves to them that God is either not
loving enough or not powerful enough to create such a
world. They think of God's relation to the earth on
the model of a human being building a cage for a pet
animal to dwell in. If he is humane he will naturally
make his pet's quarters as pleasant and healthful as
he can. Any respect in which the cage falls short of
the veterinarian's ideal, and contains possibilities
of accident or disease, is evidence of either limited
benevolence or limited means, or both. Those who use
the problem of evil as an argument against belief in
God almost invariably think of the world in this kind
of way. David Hume, for example, speaks of an architect who is trying to plan a house that is to be as
comfortable and convenient as possible. If we find
that 'the windows, doors, fires, passages, stairs,
and the whole economy of the building were the source
of noise, confusion, fatigue, darkness, and the ex-
tremes of heat and cold' we should have no hesitation
in blaming the architect. It would be in vain for him
to prove that if this or that defect were corrected
greater ills would result: 'still you would assert in
general, that, if the architect had had skill and good
intentions, he might have formed such a plan of the
whole, and might have adjusted the parts in such a
manner, as would have remedied all or most of these
inconveniences.'[8]

But if we are right in supposing that God's purpose for man is to lead him from human *Bios*, or the
biological life of man, to that quality of *Zoe*, or the
personal life of eternal worth, which we see in Christ,
then the question that we have to ask is not, Is this
the kind of world that an all-powerful and infinitely
loving being would create as an environment for his
human pets? or, Is the architecture of the world the
most pleasant and convenient possible? The question
that we have to ask is rather, Is this the kind of
world that God might make as an environment in which
moral beings may be fashioned, through their own free
insights and responses, into 'children of God?'

Such critics as Hume are confusing what heaven
ought to be, as an environment for perfected finite
beings, with what this world ought to be, as an environment for beings who are in process of becoming
perfected. For if our general conception of God's
purpose is correct the world is not intended to be a

be a paradise, but rather the scene of a history in which human personality may be formed towards the pattern of Christ. Men are not to be thought of on the analogy of animal pets, whose life is to be made as agreeable as possible, but rather on the analogy of human children, who are to grow to adulthood in an environment whose primary and overriding purpose is not immediate pleasure but the realizing of the most valuable potentialities of human personality.

Needless to say, this characterization of God as the heavenly Father is not a merely random illustration but an analogy that lies at the heart of the Christian faith. Jesus treated the likeness between the attitude of God to man, and the attitude of human parents at their best towards their children, as providing the most adequate way for us to think about God. And so it is altogether relevant to a Christian understanding of this world to ask, How does the best parental love express itself in its influence upon the environment in which children are to grow up? I think it is clear that a parent who loves his children, and wants them to become the best human beings that they are capable of becoming, does not treat pleasure as the sole and supreme value. Certainly we seek pleasure for our children, and take great delight in obtaining it for them; but we do not desire for them unalloyed pleasure at the expense of their growth in such even greater values as moral integrity, unselfishness, compassion, courage, humour, reverence for the truth, and perhaps above all the capacity for love. We do not act on the premise that pleasure is the supreme end of life; and if the development of these other values sometimes clashes with the provision of pleasure, then we are willing to have our children miss a certain amount of this, rather than fail to come to possess and to be possessed by the finer and more precious qualities that are possible to the human personality. A child brought up on the principle that the only or the supreme value is pleasure would not be likely to become an ethically mature adult or an attractive or happy personality. And to most parents it seems more important to try to foster quality and strength of character in their children than to fill their lives at all times with the utmost possible degree of pleasure. If, then, there is any true analogy between God's purpose for his human creatures, and the purpose of loving and wise parents for their children, we have to recognize that the presence of pleasure and the absence of pain cannot be the supreme and overriding end for which the world exists. Rather, this world

must be a place of soul-making. And its value is to
be judged, not primarily by the quantity of pleasure
and pain occurring in it at any particular moment, but
by its fitness for its primary purpose, the purpose
of soul-making.[9]

In all this we have been speaking about the
nature of the world considered simply as the God-given
environment of man's life. For it is mainly in this
connection that the world has been regarded in Irenaean and in Protestant thought.[10] But such a way of
thinking involves a danger of anthropocentrism from
which the Augustinian and Catholic tradition has
generally been protected by its sense of the relative
insignificance of man within the totality of the
created universe. Man was dwarfed within the medieval
world-view by the innumerable hosts of angels and
archangels above him--unfallen rational natures which
rejoice in the immediate presence of God, reflecting
His glory in the untarnished mirror of their worship.
However, this higher creation has in our modern world
lost its hold upon the imagination. Its place has
been taken, as the minimizer of men, by the immensi-
ties of outer space and by the material universe's
unlimited complexity transcending our present knowledge. As the spiritual environment envisaged by Western man has shrunk, his physical horizons have correspondingly expanded. Where the human creature was
formerly seen as an insignificant appendage to the
angelic world, he is now seen as an equally insignificant organic excrescence, enjoying a fleeting moment
of consciousness on the surface of one of the planets
of a minor star. Thus the truth that was symbolized
for former ages by the existence of the angelic hosts
is today impressed upon us by the vastness of the
physical universe, countering the egoism of our
species by making us feel that this immense prodiga-
lity of existence can hardly all exist for the sake
of man--though, on the other hand, the very realization that it is not all for the sake of man may itself
be salutary and beneficial to man!

However, instead of opposing man and nature as
rival objects of God's interest, we should perhaps
rather stress man's solidarity as an embodied being
with the whole natural order in which he is embedded.
For man is organic to the world; all his acts and
thoughts and imaginations are conditioned by space and
time; and in abstraction from nature he would cease to
be human. We may, then, say that the beauties and
sublimities and powers, the microscopic intricacies

and macroscopic vastnesses, the wonders and the terrors of the natural world and of the life that pulses through it, are willed and valued by their Maker in a creative act that embraces man together with nature. By means of matter and living flesh God both builds a path and weaves a veil between Himself and the creature made in His image. Nature thus has permanent significance; for God has set man in a creaturely environment, and the final fulfilment of our nature in relation to God will accordingly take the form of an embodied life within 'a new heaven and a new earth.'[11] And as in the present age man moves slowly towards that fulfilment through the pilgrimage of his earthly life, so also 'the whole creation' is 'groaning in travail,' waiting for the time when it will be 'set free from its bondage to decay.'[12]

And yet however fully we thus acknowledge the permanent significance and value of the natural order, we must still insist upon man's special character as a personal creature made in the image of God; and our theodicy must still centre upon the soul-making process that we believe to be taking place within human life.

This, then, is the starting-point from which we propose to try to relate the realities of sin and suffering to the perfect love of an omnipotent Creator. And as will become increasingly apparent, a theodicy that starts in this way must be eschatological in its ultimate bearings. That is to say, instead of looking to the past for its clue to the mystery of evil, it looks to the future, and indeed to that ultimate future to which only faith can look. Given the conception of a divine intention working in and through human time towards a fulfilment that lies in its completeness beyond human time, our theodicy must find the meaning of evil in the part that it is made to play in the eventual outworking of that purpose; and must find the justification of the whole process in the magnitude of the good to which it leads. The good that outshines all ill is not a paradise long since lost but a kingdom which is yet to come in its full glory and permanence.

[1]A.H. v. vi. I. Cf. pp. 211 f. above.

[2]Hebrews ii. 10.

[3]Romans viii. 17.

[4]II Corinthians iii. 18.

[5]Romans viii. 29. Other New Testament passages expressing a view of man as undergoing a process of spiritual growth within God's purpose, are: Ephesians ii. 21; iii. 16; Colossians ii. 19; I John iii. 2; II Corinthians iv. 16.

[6]This fact is symbolized in early Christian literature both by the figure of the Antichrist, who continually opposes God's purposes in history, and by the expectation of cataclysmic calamity and strife in the last days before the end of the present world order.

[7]Hebrews ii. 10.

[8]*Dialogues Concerning Natural Religion*, pt. xi. Kemp-Smith's ed. (Oxford: Clarendon Press, 1935), p. 251.

[9]The phrase 'the vale of Soul-making' was coined by the poet John Keats in a letter written to his brother and sister in April 1819. He says, 'The common cognomen of this world among the misguided and superstitious is "a vale of tears" from which we are to be redeemed by a certain arbitrary interposition of God and taken to Heaven--What a little circumscribed straightened notion! Call the world if you Please "The vale of Soul-making."' In this letter he sketches a teleological theodicy. 'Do you not see,' he asks, 'how necessary a World of Pains and troubles is to school an Intelligence and make it a Soul?' (*The Letters of John Keats*, ed. by M. B. Forman. London: Oxford University Press, 4th ed., 1952, pp. 334-5.)

[10]Thus Irenaeus said that 'the creation is suited to (the wants of) man; for man was not made for its sake, but creation for the sake of man' (A.H. v. xxix. I), and Calvin said that 'because we know that the universe was established especially for the sake of

mankind, we ought to look for this purpose in his governance also.' (*Inst.* I. xvi. 6.)

[11]Revelation xxi. I.

[12]Romans viii. 21-22.

Discussion Questions

1. Hick seems to be saying that evil is necessary in order for good to exist. Is he saying this? Do you agree that evil is necessary to good?

2. In the essay which precedes this one the author contends that there is no contradiction in saying that God could have made persons such that they would always freely choose the good. What would this mean to Hick's case? Do you agree that God could have so created?

3. If God wishes to create the types of beings Hick says he does, then certainly he will refrain from controlling their wills. But must he do so always? Why should he not leave men free to will the good, but intervene whenever they want to choose evil?

4. Hick says the justification of evil in God's universe lies in the magnitude and type of good to which it leads. Consider some of the abhorrent evils of our history and ask yourself whether freedom is worth the price paid.

    a. Can some evils never be righted, no matter what good emerges later?

    b. Would the punishment of those who inflict evil really "make it right" for those who suffered?

5. What are the implications of Hick's soul-making theodicy for our understanding of natural evil?

RETROSPECTIVE

Our theologies of creation and providence are very much dependent on the concept of purposiveness. A doctrine of creation must affirm the ultimate dependence of all finite being on God. Whether this requires the kind of theology of scripture which Carl Henry advocates is doubtful. Gilkey may be much more helpful when he insists that evolutionary theory, properly understood, is not antithetical to the faith. To be sure it may undermine a certain theology of scripture, but a meaningful creation doctrine may be possible on some other theology of scripture which is also compatible with evolutionary theory.

It is certainly possible that a theologian may allow his creation doctrine to be too much determined by scientific theory, and that is to be avoided. So also he must not allow the challenge of evolutionary science to shape completely his theology of scripture. Scientific data is only a small part of one of the source-norms for theology--that of human experience.

At the same time, however, a theologian must not ignore science. Those whom Henry calls creation scientists are performing a valuable corrective function. They remind us that even overarching paradigms of science are open to question. However, the extent to which their findings contribute anything like a vindication of Henry's theology of scripture is very questionable. And it is important to remember that the issue at stake here is not a doctrine of creation but a doctrine of the scriptures.

There is an important level at which creation scientists and theistic evolutionists agree. Indeed, it may be that they agree on the essential elements of creation doctrine. Their disagreements are more pronounced when one examines their theologies of scripture. Authentic scientific questions should be left to scientists.

The far more critical issue in this section is the question whether reality is a cosmos rather than a chaos. Is reality ordered by God? Is it moving toward his goals? Is he active in natural and history? If so, is he active only in the sense that he sustains the natural laws of reality, or does God sometimes intervene in special providences called miracles? And finally, if God orders reality how is it that there can be such evil?

Purposiveness is not perceivable by external observation, and thus imperceptibility should not count as evidence against it. If I am observed plowing my yard, you cannot discern my purpose simply by observation. I may be planning to plant a garden. Or, I may only wish to uproot the weeds which choke my grass. Or, I may be taking out my frustrations over my freshmen students. However, if I choose to reveal my purposes to you, then your observations will be filled with a deeper understanding.

There seems to be no reason to exclude special providences out of hand; nor even that the whole of reality is providential. Indeed, the Christian faith maintains that God has revealed that he has a purpose for what happens. But it is the very fact of this revelation which makes evil such a formidable problem for our faith. Its resolution may require an eschatological vision.

PART FOUR

HUMAN BEING AND SIN

HUMAN BEING AND SIN

There is a sense in which all theology begins
from an understanding of what it means to be a human
being. Theology is the answer which faith gives to
the questions posed by human existence. Accordingly,
the way in which one understands the nature of what it
is to be human and the problems and distortions of
the human situation will dramatically influence one's
emerging theological system.

For example, one may ask whether human life is
what it should be, and if not one must ask what went
wrong and what may be done to remedy the situation.
In the Christian faith such concerns refer first to
the doctrine of sin and then to salvation.

To be sure, changes in the prevailing views of
man effect the communication and reception of the
Christian message. During the Reformation period
persons seemed to relate to a deep sense of alienation
from God. They knew what Calvin meant when he spoke
of man's rebellion, his sin and depravity. Today's
cultural *Geist* seems different. There is less emphasis on sin, less consciousness of sin, and perhaps
less certainty about what sin is.

At the same time, the world view of Western
culture since the sixteenth century has made it
increasingly more obvious that traditional under-
standings of man are seriously questioned by the degree to which humans are now recognized as rooted in
nature. The gulf between humans and animals has been
greatly reduced. Physio-psychology has shown that
both consciousness and personality are very dependent
on chemical and organic factors. Scientists have
shown how drugs, electrical stimulation of the brain,
and surgical procedures can be used to alter the

character of persons. Does this mean that man is no more than a highly complex bioelectronic machine?

The essay by Pierre Teilhard de Chardin addresses this question directly, and by implication it deals with the uniqueness of human nature. This uniqueness he anchors in the human ability for reflection, which he considers the tremendous advance necessary to move toward personalization.

Sociologists and psychologists have amassed an impressive array of evidence which shows how much human decision is a product of environment, genetic coding, and behavioral conditioning. This may imply not only that it is difficult to distinguish human nature but also that human moral actions are biologically caused. If human conduct is effected dramatically by biology, then where can one locate the important religious concept of responsibility before God, and to one's neighbor?

The essays which follow represent attempts to guide theologians through the maze of questions which complicate a theology of the human being (anthropology) which can speak to modern man. The essays deal both with the question of human nature and with the identification and nature of sin.

G. C. Berkhouwer has long been occupied with the doctrine of the human being. In his essay he examines several proposals for a theology of the image of God. And he considers such a theology to be the key to restoring the uniqueness of humanity in the modern world. Berkhouwer realizes that this symbol must be intelligibly explicated. But he is quite critical of approaches such as Teilhard's which seek to isolate some higher quality found in humans as the focal point for their uniqueness. In contrast, Berkhouwer holds that the image of God cannot be given content apart from what is revealed in scripture. He turns particularly to the New Testament, affirming Christ as the embodiment and definition of the image of God.

Both Berkhouwer and Teilhard, however, locate man's uniqueness at the interface between nature and what might be called spirit. And neither of them succumb to a reductionism that makes man only natural. It is precisely at this interface that Reinhold Niebuhr locates the precondition for sin. His essay is an attempt to clarify how anxiety as the precondition eventuates in the sins of pride and sensuality. Such

sin effects other humans. Sin is also the clearest
evidence of humanity's lack of trust in God. Certainly the most controversial of his positions is Niebuhr's
contention that sin is inevitable, but that humans are
nonetheless responsible. While Niebuhr's essay deals
with individual sin, Rosemary Ruether deals with
corporate and institutional sin.

THE PHENOMENON OF MAN

It is rare indeed that the modern world produces
Renaissance men. The days are gone when a person can
master many disciplines. Specialized knowledge and
rapidly advancing research make it nearly impossible
to master even one field, much less more than one.

Nevertheless, among the modern candidates for the
label of Renaissance man one must include Pierre
Teilhard, a French Catholic theologian, philosopher,
and paleontologist. In the essay which follows Teilhard struggles to demark the leap that makes the human
being more than a mammal, although still a part of
nature.

According to Teilhard, the threshold crossed only
by humans is the phenomenon of reflection. Reflection
is not merely the capacity to think or know. Other
species may have such a trait; indeed we can now speak
of artificial intelligence. But to be able to reflect
is to know that one knows.

Reflection gives rise to invention, abstraction,
logic, reasoned choice and other valuable activities
of the inner life including also anxiety and moral
perplexity. Teilhard argues that this critical
transformation occurs without any intermediary being
between human and mammal. Either a being has not
reached or has already passed beyond this stage into
humanness.

Throughout the essay Teilhard writes as though
the ascent to consciousness was a purely natural
phenomenon. He even says that psychogenesis has led
to man. But Teilhard is a theistic evolutionist. He
believes that the process is providentially ordered.
In man the earth has a being which makes this place no

longer merely a biosphere. There is now a noosphere;
souls exist.

THE PHENOMENON OF MAN*

In one well-marked region at the heart of the
mammals, where the most powerful brains ever made by
nature are to be found, they become red hot. And
right at the heart of that glow burns a point of
incandescence.

We must not lose sight of that line crimsoned by
the dawn. After thousands of years rising below the
horizon, a flame bursts forth at a strictly localised
point.

Thought is born.

From a purely positivist point of view man is the
most mysterious and disconcerting of all the objects
met with by science. In fact we may as well admit
that science has not yet found a place for him in its
representations of the universe. Physics has succeeded in provisionally circumscribing the world of
the atom. Biology has been able to impose some sort
of order on the constructions of life. Supported both
by physics and biology, anthropology in its turn does
its best to explain the structure of the human body
and some of its physiological mechanisms. But when
all these features are put together, the portrait
manifestly falls short of the reality. Man, as
science is able to reconstruct him today, is an animal
like the others--so little separable anatomically from
the anthropoids that the modern classifications made

*Source: Abridged from pages 160-174, 181-184
from *The Phenomenon of Man* by Pierre Teilhard de
Chardin. Translated by Bernard Wall. Copyright 1955
by Editions du Sevill. Copyright 1959 in the English
translation by William Collins Sons and Co. Ltd. and
Harper and Row, Publishers, Inc. Reprinted by permission of Harper and Row, Publishers, Inc.

by zoologists return to the position of Linnaeus and include him with them in the same super-family, the hominidae. Yet, to judge by the biological results of his advent, is he not in reality something altogether different?

Morphologically the leap was extremely slight, yet it was the concomitant of an incredible commotion among the spheres of life--there lies the whole human paradox; and there, in the same breath, is the evidence that science, in its present-day reconstructions of the world, neglects an essential factor, or rather, an entire dimension of the universe.

I. THE THRESHOLD OF REFLECTION

A. *The Threshold of the Element: the Hominisation[1] of the Individual*

a. *Nature.* Biologists are not yet agreed on whether or not there is a direction (still less a definite axis) of evolution; nor is there any greater agreement among psychologists, and for a connected reason, as to whether the human psychism differs specifically (by 'nature') from that of man's predecessors or not. As a matter of fact the majority of 'scientists' would tend to contest the validity of such a breach of continuity. So much has been said, and is still said, about the intelligence of animals.

If we wish to settle this question of the 'superiority' of man over the animals (and it is every bit as necessary to settle it for the sake of the ethics of life as well as for pure knowledge) I can only see one way of doing so--to brush resolutely aside all those secondary and equivocal manifestations of inner activity in human behaviour, making straight for the central phenomenon, *reflection*.

From our experimental point of view, reflection is, as the word indicates, the power acquired by a consciousness to turn in upon itself, to take possession of itself *as of an object* endowed with its own particular consistence and value: no longer merely to know, but to know oneself; no longer merely to know, but to know that one knows.[2] By this individualisation of himself in the depths of himself, the living element, which heretofore had been spread out and divided over a diffuse circle of perceptions and activities, was constituted for the first time as a

249

centre in the form of a point at which all the impressions and experiences knit themselves together and fuse into a unity that is conscious of its own organisation.

Now the consequences of such a transformation are immense, visible as clearly in nature as any of the facts recorded by physics or astronomy. The being who is the object of his own reflection, in consequence of that very doubling back upon himself, becomes in a flash able to raise himself into a new sphere. In reality, another world is born. Abstraction, logic, reasoned choice and inventions, mathematics, art, calculation of space and time, anxieties and dreams of love--all these activities of *inner life* are nothing else than the effervescence of the newly formed centre as it explodes onto itself.

This said, I have a question to ask. If, as follows from the foregoing, it is the fact of being 'reflective' which constitutes the strictly 'intelligent' being, can we seriously doubt that intelligence is the evolutionary lot proper to man and to man *only?* If not, can we, under the influence of some false modesty, hesitate to admit that man's possession of it constitutes a radical advance on all forms of life that have gone before him? Admittedly the animal knows. *But it cannot know that it knows:* that is quite certain. If it could, it would long ago have multiplied its inventions and developed a system of internal constructions that could not have escaped our observation. In consequence it is denied access to a whole domain of reality in which we can move freely. We are separated by a chasm--or a threshold-- which it cannot cross. Because we are reflective we are not only different but quite other. It is not merely a matter of change of degree, but of a change of nature, resulting from a change of state.

Life, being an ascent of consciousness, could not continue to advance indefinitely along its line without transforming itself in depth. It had, we said, like all growing realities in the world, to become different so as to remain itself. Here, in the accession to the power of reflection, emerges (more clearly recognisable than in the obscure primordial psychism of the first cells) the particular and critical form of transformation in which this surcreation or rebirth consisted for it. And at the same moment we find the whole curve of biogenesis reappearing summed up and clarified in this singular point.

b. Theoretical Mechanism. This being said, and I am
merely presenting in a different light what has already
been revealed in our study of life, the upholders of
the spiritual explanation have no need to be discon-
certed when they see, or are obliged to see, in the
higher animals (particularly in the great apes) ways
and reactions which strangely recall those of which
they make use to define the nature and prove the
presence in man of 'a reasonable soul.' If the story
of life is no more than a movement of consciousness
veiled by morphology, it is inevitable that, towards
the summit of the series, in the proximity of man, the
'physical' make-ups seem to reach the *borders of intelligence.* And that is exactly what happens.

Hence light is thrown on the 'human paradox'
itself. We are disturbed to notice how little 'anthro-
pos' differs anatomically from the other anthropoids,
despite his incontestable mental pre-eminence in certain respects--so disturbed that we feel almost ready
to abandon the attempt to distinguish them, at least
towards their point of origin. But is not this extraordinary resemblance precisely what had to be?

When water is heated to boiling point under
normal pressure, and one goes on heating it, the first
thing that follows--without change of temperature--is
a tumultuous expansion of freed and vaporised mole-
cules. Or, taking a series of sections from the base
towards the summit of a cone, their area decreases
constantly; then suddenly, with another infinitesimal
displacement, the surface vanishes leaving us with a
point. Thus by these remote comparisons we are able
to imagine the mechanism involved in the critical
threshold of reflection.

By the end of the Tertiary era, the psychical
temperature in the cellular world had been rising for
more than 500 million years. From branch to branch,
from layer to layer, we have seen how nervous systems
followed *pari passu* the process of increased complication and concentration. Finally, with the primates,
an instrument was fashioned so remarkably supple and
rich that the step immediately following could not
take place without the whole animal psychism being as
it were recast and consolidated on itself. Now this
movement did not stop, for there was nothing in the
structure of the organism to prevent it advancing.
When the anthropoid, so to speak, had been brought
'mentally' to boiling point some further calories
were added. Or, when the anthropoid had almost

251

reached the summit of the cone, a final effort took
place along the axis. No more was needed for the
whole inner equilibrium to be upset. What was previously only a centred surface became a centre. By a
tiny 'tangential' increase, the 'radial' was turned
back on itself and so to speak took an infinite leap
forward. Outwardly, almost nothing in the organs had
changed. But in depth, a great revolution had taken
place: consciousness was now leaping and boiling in a
space of super-sensory relationships and representations; and simultaneously consciousness was capable
of perceiving itself in the concentrated simplicity of
its faculties. And all this happened for the first
time.[3]

Those who adopt the spiritual explanation are
right when they defend so vehemently a certain transcendence of man over the rest of nature. But neither
are the materialists wrong when they maintain that man
is just one further term in a series of animal forms.
Here, as in so many cases, the two antithetical kinds
of evidences are resolved in a movement--provided that
in this movement we emphasise the highly natural
phenomenon of the 'change of state.' From the cell
to the thinking animal, as from the atom to the cell,
a single process (a psychical kindling or concentration) goes on without interruption and always in the
same direction. But by virtue of this permanence in
the operation, it is inevitable from the point of view
of physics that certain leaps suddenly transform the
subject of the operation.

c. *Realisation.* If the threshold of reflection is
really (as its physical nature seems to require, and
as we have ourselves admitted) a critical transformation, a mutation from zero to everything, it is
impossible for us to imagine an intermediary individual
at this precise level. Either this being has not yet
reached, or it has already got beyond, this change of
state. Look at it as we will, we cannot avoid the
alternative--either thought is made unthinkable by a
denial of its psychical transcendence over instinct,
or we are forced to admit that it appeared *between* two
individuals.

The terms of this proposition are disconcerting,
but they become less bizarre, and even inoffensive,
if we observe that, speaking strictly as scientists,
we may suppose that intelligence might (or even must)
have been as little visible externally at its phyletic
origin as it is today to our eyes in every new-born

child at the ontogenetical stage: in which case every
tangible subject of debate between the observer and
the theorist disappears.

Without trying to picture the unimaginable, let
us therefore keep hold of one idea--that the access
to thought represents a threshold which had to be
crossed at a single stride; a 'trans-experimental'
interval about which scientifically we can say nothing,
but beyond which we find ourselves transported onto an
entirely new biological plane.

d. *Prolongation*. It is only at this point that we
can fully see the nature of the transit to reflection.
In the first place it involved a change of state; then,
by this very fact, the beginning of another kind of
life--precisely that interior life of which I have
spoken above.

Obviously by the effect of such a transformation
the entire structure of life is modified. Up to this
point the animated element was so narrowly subject to
the phylum that its own individuality could be regarded as accessory and sacrificed. It received,
maintained, acquired if possible, reproduced and
transmitted. And so on ceaselessly and indefinitely.
Caught up in the chain of succeeding generations, the
animal seemed to lack the right to live; it appeared
to have no value for itself. It was a fugitive foot-
hold for a process which passed over it and ignored it.
Life, once again, was more real than living things.

With the advent of the power of reflection (an
essentially elemental property, at any rate to begin
with) everything is changed, and we now perceive that
under the more striking reality of the collective
transformations a secret progress has been going on
parallel to individualisation. The more highly each
phylum became charged with psychism, the more it
tended to 'granulate.' The animal grew in value in
relation to the species. Finally at the level of man
the phenomenon gathers new power and takes definitive
shape. With the 'person,' endowed by 'personalisation'
with an indefinite power of elemental evolution, the
branch ceases to bear, as an anonymous whole, the
exclusive promises for the future. The cell has become 'someone.' After the grain of matter, the grain
of life; and now at last we see constituted the *grain
of thought*.

Does that mean that the phylum loses its function

from this moment and vanishes in thin air, like those animals who lose their identity in a veritable dust of spores which they give birth to in dying? Above the point of reflection, does the whole interest of evolution shift, passing from life into a plurality of isolated living beings?

Nothing of the sort. Only, from this crucial date the global spurt, without slackening in the slightest, has acquired another degree, another order of complexity. The phylum does not break like a fragile jet just because henceforward it is fraught with thinking centres; it does not crumble into its elementary psychisms. On the contrary it is rein-forced by an inner lining, an additional framework. Until now it was enough to consider in nature a simple vibration on a wide front, the ascent of individual centres of consciousness. What we now have to do is to define and regulate harmoniously an ascent of consciousnesses (a much more delicate phenomenon). We are dealing with a progress made up of other progresses as lasting as itself; a movement of movements.

Let us try to lift our minds high enough to dominate the problem. For that, let us forget for a moment the particular destiny of the spiritual ele-ments engaged in the general transformation. It is, in point of fact, only by following the ascension and spread of the whole in its main lines that we are able, after a long detour, to determine the part reserved for individual hopes in the total success.

We thus reach the personalisation of the indivi-dual by the 'hominisation' of the whole group.

'The biological change of state terminating in the awakening of thought does not represent merely a critical point that the individual or even the species must pass through. Vaster than that, it affects life itself in its organic totality, and consequently it marks a transformation affecting the state of the entire planet.'

Such is the evidence--born of all the other testimony we have gradually assembled and added to-gether in the course of our inquiry--which imposes it-self irresistibly on both our logic and observation.

We have been following the successive stages of the same grand progression from the fluid contours of the early earth. Beneath the pulsations of geo-

chemistry, of geo-tectonics and of geo-biology, we
have detected one and the same fundamental process,
always recognisable--the one which was given material
form in the first cells and was continued in the construction of nervous systems. We saw geogenesis pro-
moted to biogenesis, which turned out in the end to
be nothing else than psychogenesis.

With and within the crisis of reflection, the
next term in the series manifests itself. Psychogenesis has led to man. Now it effaces itself,
relieved or absorbed by another and a higher function--
the engendering and subsequent development of the mind,
in one word *noogenesis*. When for the first time in a
living creature instinct perceived itself in its own
mirror, the whole world took a pace forward.

As regards the choices and responsibilities of
our activity, the consequences of this discovery are
enormous. As regards our understanding of the earth
they are decisive.

The recognition and isolation of a new era in
evolution, the era of noogenesis, obliges us to distinguish correlatively a support proportionate to the
operation--that is to say, yet another membrane in the
majestic assembly of telluric layers. A glow ripples
outward from the first spark of conscious reflection.
The point of ignition grows larger. The fire spreads
in ever widening circles till finally the whole planet
is covered with incandescence. Only one interpretation, only one name can be found worthy of this grand
phenomenon. Much more coherent and just as extensive
as any preceding layer, it is really a new layer, the
'thinking layer,' which, since its germination at the
end of the Tertiary period, has spread over and above
the world of plants and animals. In other words,
outside and above the biosphere there is the noosphere.

With that it bursts upon us how utterly warped
is every classification of the living world (or,
indirectly, every construction of the physical one) in
which man only figures logically as a *genus* or a new
family. This is an error of perspective which de-
forms and uncrowns the whole phenomenon of the universe. To give man his true place in nature it is
not enough to find one more pigeon-hole in the edifice
of our systematisation or even an additional order or
branch. With hominisation, in spite of the insignificance of the anatomical leap, we have the beginning of
a new age. The earth 'gets a new skin.' Better still,

it finds its soul.

Therefore, given its place in reality in proper dimensions, the historic threshold of reflection is much more important than any zoological gap, whether it be the one marking the origin of the tetrapods or even that of the metazoa. Among all the stages successively crossed by evolution, the birth of thought comes directly after, and is the only thing comparable in order of importance to, the condensation of the terrestrial chemism or the advent of life itself.

The paradox of man resolves itself by passing beyond measure. Despite the relief and harmony it brings to things, this perspective is at first sight disconcerting, running counter as it does to the illusion and habits which incline us to measure events by their material face. It also seems to us extravagant because, steeped as we are in what is human like a fish in the sea, we have difficulty in emerging from it in our minds so as to appreciate its specificness and breadth. But let us look round us a little more carefully. This sudden deluge of cerebralisation, this biological invasion of a new animal type which gradually eliminates or subjects all forms of life that are not human, this irresistible tide of fields and factories, this immense and growing edifice of matter and ideas--all these signs that we look at, for days on end--to proclaim that there has been a change on the earth and a change of planetary magnitude.

There can indeed be no doubt that, to an imaginary geologist coming one day far in the future to inspect our fossilised globe, the most astounding of the revolutions undergone by the earth would be that which took place at the beginning of what has so rightly been called the psychozoic era. And even today, to a Martian capable of analysing sidereal radiations psychically no less than physically, the first characteristic of our planet would be, not the blue of the seas or the green of the forests, but the phosphorescence of thought.

The greatest revelation open to science today is to perceive that everything precious, active and progressive originally contained in that cosmic fragment from which our world emerged, is now concentrated in a 'crowning' noosphere.

And what is so supremely instructive about the origins of this noosphere (if we know how to look) is

256

to see how gradually, by dint of being universally
and lengthily prepared, the enormous event of its
birth took place.

Endnotes

[1]French: *hominisation*--a word coined by the
author.

[2]*Non plus seulement connaître, mais se connaître;
non plus seulement savoir, mais savoir que l'on sait.*

[3]Need I repeat that I confine myself here to the
phenomena, i.e. to the experimental relations between
consciousness and complexity, without prejudging the
deeper causes which govern the whole issue? In virtue
of the limitations imposed on our sensory knowledge by
the play of the temporo-spatial series, it is only,
it seems, *under the appearances* of a critical point
that we can grasp experimentally the 'hominising'
(spiritualising) step to reflection. But, with that
said, there is nothing to prevent the thinker who
adopts a spiritual explanation from positing (for
reasons of a higher order and at a later stage of his
dialectic), *under the phenomenal veil* of a revolutionary transformation, whatever 'creative' operation or
'special intervention' he likes. Is it not a principle universally accepted by Christian thought in its
theological interpretation of reality that for our
minds there are different and successive planes of
knowledge?

Discussion Questions

1. In your judgment has Teilhard said enough about
man's unique nature to do justice to Genesis' description of the creation of man?

2. Teilhard is sometimes criticized for the near
poetic language he uses. Do you think this is a fair
criticism? Does his use of this style serve a purpose?

3.   Do you think that Teilhard's position might leave room to call human any other species that crossed the threshold of reflection?

    a.   Is this a necessary openness?

    b.   What theological arguments could be offered against the hominisation of other species?

4.   Does Teilhard's position have any implications for the understanding of what it means to be a person as this relates to the contemporary ethical questions of abortion and euthanasia?   If so, what are they?

THE MEANING OF THE IMAGE OF GOD

In Christian doctrine no symbol is more important to an understanding of the uniqueness of human being than that of the Image of God. Genesis 1:26 describes the pivotal decision in God's creative activity to make a being in his own image and likeness. Human being is pictured as the climax of creation. Because man is in God's image, he is given dominion over the birds and beasts. He too becomes a creator of his own world and its history.

In this essay G. C. Berkouwer reminds us that the biblical materials provide no systematic explication of the meaning of the symbol of the image of God. It is for this reason that many theories have been offered as explanations. Berkouwer covers the now famous historical debate over whether the image of God and the likeness of God (Gen. 1:26) refer to the same thing. He demonstrates the exegetical improbability that two factors are meant. Both terms are used interchangeably, and thus Genesis 1:26 is an example of parallelism. For Berkouwer, then, the theologian should eschew any theological model based on the dubious distinction between these terms.

Berkouwer discusses several theological approaches to the explication of the image concept. He denies that the image of God means merely the human ability to dominate other life forms and nature. Neither does he have confidence in the method which finds the content of the image in various human categories. This criticism includes in its purview Teilhard's thesis. Berkouwer rejects this approach because it reads the biblical text in light of a particular view of humanity not scripturally derived.

A significant point made by Berkouwer is that any

259

attempt to understand the image of God must include
some reference to the human body, it cannot be merely
spiritual. He rests this position on the Hebraic use
of the term "image." But of course his viewpoint may
also be strengthened by the consistent picture of the
human being as a psycho-physical unity which is found
not only in the Scripture, but in modern anthropology
as well. And as an extended aside Berkouwer explains
the implications of this view for the use of anthropomorphic language in describing God.

As for his constructive theology of the image of
God, Berkouwer holds that there is little Old Testament
information on the image concept because the image is
shattered in the Fall (Gen. 3). Accordingly, any
theology of the image must be built of its restored
embodiment. This can be found, Berkouwer says, only
in Christ.

What this essay maintains is that Christ was the
only true human. All other humans are fragmented,
partial and marred representatives of humanity. Thus
the image of God is identified with Christ's life.
He is the content of the image. He is true human
nature. Human uniqueness is that we are such beings
capable of being redeemed to be like Christ. It is
not reflection, as Teilhard suggests; nor is the image
personality, or any other trait. The image is the
fullness of the person Jesus of Nazareth. No other
creature has the potential to be like that one, and
in our capacity for such being therein lies our
uniqueness.

THE MEANING OF THE IMAGE OF GOD*

If we examine the Biblical witness regarding man,
we soon discover that it never gives us any kind of
systematic theory about man as the image of God. It
is indeed rather striking that the term is not used
often at all, and that it is far less "central" in the
Bible than it has been in the history of Christian
thought.[1] This apparent discrepancy vanishes, however,
when we note that Scripture's references to the image
of God, whenever there are such, have a special urgency
and importance. Furthermore, there is the possibility
that Scripture often deals with the concept of the
image of God without using those exact words, so that
we surely should not a priori limit our investigation
of the concept to considering only those places where
the term itself is used.

It is understandable enough, however, that attention has always been directed first of all to those
Biblical passages where the creation of man in God's
image and the restoration of the image in Christ are
dealt with specifically, or where Christ as the image
of God is directly considered.

We shall begin, then, with an examination of the
passage which speaks of God's original decision
(Gen. 1:26) to "make man in our likeness, after our
image," and the following passage: "God created man
in his own image, in the image of God he created them;
male and female he created them." These passages are
shortly followed by Genesis 5:1, "When God created man,
he made him in the likeness of God," and Genesis 9:6,
where the shedding of man's blood is forbidden "*for*
God made man in his own image."

Special note has always been taken of the fact
that in Genesis 1:26 two words are used; "image" and
likeness," "*tselem*" and "*demuth*." This has led to
various views of the image of God which were based on

*Source: *From Studies in Dogmatics: Man, The
Image of God* by G. C. Berkouwer, copyright 1962,
used by permission of the publisher William B. Eerdmans
Co.

a fairly strong distinction between "*tselem*" and "*demuth*." Bavinck refers to a naturalistic view and a supernaturalistic view which both appeal to the distinction between image and likeness. The former sees man as created only in God's image, and as gradually evolving into God's likeness. The latter sees in the likeness something added to the image, a *donum superadditum*.[2]

We have already noted the fact that it is today generally agreed that earlier theologians who drew far-reaching conclusions from this dual terminology in Genesis were on the wrong track. There are not many today who would follow Origen, for example, when he writes that Genesis mentions man's creation in the image but is silent about any creation in the likeness, in order to indicate that man in creation received the dignity of the image, but that its fulfillment in the likeness was reserved for the future, and is reached through works and exertion.[3]

There has been a long tradition of such ideas,[4] related to the Septuagint translation "*eikona kai homoioosin*" (Vulgate *imaginem et similitudinem*), i.e., image *and* likeness. This tradition was broken with by both Luther and Calvin,[5] and today there is a strong convergence of opinion which rejects this tradition, in exegetical as well as in dogmatic literature.[6]

This convergence of opinion[7] is closely related to the increased appreciation of the variety of ways in which Genesis speaks of the image. Genesis 1:26 uses both "*tselem*" and "*demuth*," "image" and "likeness"; Genesis 1:27 and Genesis 9:6 use only "*tselem*." And if God's plan for man (that man should have both image and likeness) was only partially realized by man's creation in His image (as Origen and others claimed), then it is difficult to explain Genesis 5, which speaks of man's creation in God's likeness (*demuth*). And it goes on to speak of Adam's begetting a son "in his own likeness (*demuth*) and after his image (*tselem*)." Because of the variable usage of the two terms in Genesis, it is difficult to escape the conclusion that it is impossible to hold that "*tselem*" and "*demuth*" refer to two different things. As Bavinck says, the two terms "are used promiscuously and one is used in place of the other for no special reason."[8]

Both terms, obviously, refer to a relation between man and his Creator; a "likeness" between man and God, with no explanation given as to exactly what this likeness consists of or implies. When, for example, Von Rad speaks of man's "similarity, resemblance, correspondence" to God, this still does not explain in what the likeness lies.[9] It is clear enough that the likeness does not remove the difference between man and God, and that the insistence on this likeness at the same time witnesses to the uniqueness of man in comparison with other creatures. This last is clear enough from the story in Genesis, which refers to God's decision, His plan, in creating man: "let us make *man*. . . ." This creation, this creative act of God, is the high point of the whole creation, the aim, the purpose of the creation described in the preceding verses of Genesis.[10] And it is thus understandable that the image of God in man has been equated with that which makes man unique among created things. In this connection, attempts have sometimes been made to find some evidence as to the content of the image of God in man in the Scriptural text itself: e.g., by reference to Genesis 1:26, where God's making man "in our image, after our likeness" is directly related (some say) to the following words, "let them have dominion over the fish of the sea, and over the birds of the air, and over the cattle, and over all the earth, and over every creeping thing that creeps upon the earth." Some would conclude from this that Genesis itself clearly indicates that the image of God consists in man's *dominium*, his lordship over the other creatures which surround him, and which are subject to him. This view, which we find, for example, in the Socinian *Catechismus Racoviensis*,[11] has aroused a great deal of opposition, which also appeals to the very text to which this view looks for support. It is true that Genesis 1:26 does indicate that man, who is to be created in God's image, is intended for a unique status and task in the created world (his *dominium*). But this does not imply that the content of the image of God should be sought in this lordship, or that Genesis 1 is concerned with this *dominium* over other creatures as an image or representation of the complete and absolute sovereignty of God. It can be objected, and rightly so, that Genesis 1:28, in a special word from God, endows created man with this mandate (i.e., *dominium*): "fill the earth and subdue it," which is in itself a strong argument against equating image and *dominium*.[12]

To support this equation of image and *dominium*, an appeal is often made to Psalm 8:6-7 as illuminating what is the place occupied by man in the cosmos. And, indeed, the passage does refer in emphatic terms to the lordship of man: "Thou hast made him little less than God, and dost crown him with glory and honor. Thou hast given him dominion (*dominium*) over the works of thy hands; thou hast put all things under his feet." This indicates clearly enough the unique position of man in the created cosmos, but this in no sense implies that this *dominium* especially reveals the content of the image of God. To begin with, the term "image" is not used in Psalm 8, and this should be enough to arouse some caution. Ridderbos discerns an echo of Genesis 1 here, but still will not equate Psalm 8's *dominium* with the image of Genesis 1. He sees the passage as meaning "thou has created him a little lower than a god," not God, in distinction from *God*, in whose image man according to Genesis 1 was created.[13] In any event, Psalm 8 gives no support to an identification of *dominium* and image, even though the meaning of man's *dominium* and the special place which man occupies in the created world are strongly expressed.[14] And thus our question as to the specific meaning of the image remains unanswered, a fact which reminds us of Bavinck's remark: "the full meaning of the image of God is nowhere unfolded for us."[15]

Attempts to understand the riddle of the image of God have produced numerous proposed solutions. Most of these do not depend primarily--as did the interpretation of the image as *dominium* or *analogia relationis* --on certain Scriptural passages, but are attempts on more general grounds to arrive at the specific differentia of man. We can hardly say that the methods employed by most of these varied attempts arouse much confidence. One line of approach, for example, is to seek the content of the image in various anthropological categories. Thus Eichrodt sees it as lying in man's "spiritual superiority," which manifests itself in man's "self-consciousness and . . . personality," though the writer of Genesis could hardly be expected to use such abstract terminology to explain his meaning. Such approaches are opposed by those theologians, e.g., Von Rad, who would stress the real, the concrete meaning of the image. He considers it unfaithful to the Old Testament intention to read the texts in the light of the categories of a particular anthropology, and to use such concepts as spiritual being or essence, personality, ability to will. Von Rad would not rule out man's body as part of the image in man; quite to the contrary, he thinks that the idea of the image sets out from corporeality as something *visible*. According to the story in Genesis, the whole man is

264

made in the image of God, and Genesis certainly does
not imply that certain "higher" qualities exclusively
make up the content of the image.[16]

We can say that contemporary theologians rather
generally lean more to this line of approach, which is
related to a strong consciousness of the integral
unity of man, producing an opposition to any "division"
of man into "spiritual" and "bodily" aspects and
viewing the content of the image as lying exclusively
in the former aspect.[17] It is very noteworthy, in
this connection, that there has been increasing reluc-
tance to exclude man's body from the image of God--an
exclusion generally supported previously, when theologians sought the content of the image in man's
"higher" qualities, in contrast to the "lower" bodily
qualities, which should not be considered in connection with the image. It is clear enough that involved
in this change of attitude is not merely some subtle
nuance of meaning, but a change which raises questions
of decisive importance for our whole notion of the
content of the image.

Theologians, in their search for the meaning of
the image, often sought various similarities or
analogies between God and man, without thereby giving
up the difference between God and man. In the search
for such analogies, it often happened that man's body
was excluded from the image of God (since man's body
could hardly be similar to God's body!). The image
was sought in the higher aspects of man, the spiritual,
since it was thought that these could be thought of as
being similar to qualities possessed by God. This
"division" also has in its background the stress on
the incorporeality of God, *incorporalitas Dei,* which
seemed for many to imply that man could resemble or
image God in his spirit, but not in his body. Man's
body was excluded from the image, and it was believed
that if this exclusion was not firmly upheld, the
theologian would be supporting the naive *anthropomorphism* of earlier eccentric sects.[18]

The opposition against the exclusion of man's
body from the image of God arises, again and again,
from the Scripture's reference to the image of God as
in man, not in man's higher or spiritual attributes,
his self-consciousness or his person. Such opposition
was especially marked in periods when the dualism between soul and body was rejected, but the decisive
factor was that with reference to the image, not the
least Scriptural warrant could be found for the

division of man into soul and body. And thus the
traditional view, which was surely not without its
dangers, slowly crumbled, and the feeling grew that
the older view did not do justice to the image of God.

Scripture's emphasis on the whole man as the image
of God has triumphed time and time again over all
objections and opposing principles. Scripture never
makes a distinction between man's spiritual and bodily
attributes in order to limit the image of God to the
spiritual, as furnishing the only possible analogy
between man and God.[19]

Gunkel refers to various objections that modern
man brings against any bodily "analogy" between man
and God, such as "God can have no form, since He is a
spirit," and replies to such objections that the concept of the incorporeality of God is an abstract concept of which there is absolutely no trace in the
earlier Old Testament, as is shown (he says) by the
anthropomorphic ways in which God is described in the
Old Testament. This explains, he says, why early
Israel took no offense at the idea that man was
created in God's image. But, in contrast, says Gunkel,
the prophets deemed it blasphemy to picture God, an
idea which grew stronger as the God-concept became
more transcendent.[20]

Clearly, such a view as Gunkel's introduces an
unwarranted contrast in suggesting that there was a
conflict between Israel's idea of man as the image of
God and the sharp criticism levelled by the prophets
against making images of God, against picturing God.
The real question which might be asked here, however,
is a quite different one. Are the two not in harmony?
Does not the criticism depend on the *exclusive* way in
which man images God? A relation has constantly been
sought, and understandably so, between man as the
image of God and the Old Testament forbidding of
images.[21]

When Moses and the elders of Israel ascended the
mountain, they saw God, but "there was under his feet
as it were a pavement of sapphire stone, like the
very heaven for clearness" (Ex. 24:9-10). If we
would seek for an image or likeness of Jahwe, we must
listen to Isaiah's question, "To whom then will you
liken God, or what likeness compare with him?" (Isa.
40:18), and "To whom then will you compare me, that I
should be like him, says the Holy One" (Isa. 40:25).
An image is impossible and is forbidden because it is

a violation of Jahwe's incomparability. "Therefore
take good heed to yourselves. Since you saw no form
on the day that the Lord spoke to you at Horeb out of
the midst of the fire, beware lest you act corruptly
by making a graven image for yourselves" (Deut. 4:15-16,
cf. 4:25).

This emphatic prohibition has often been interpreted against a background of a supposed contrast
between material and non-material, and of Jahwe as
"spirit." Volz, for example, understands it thus; he
is opposed, and rightly so, by Zimmerli, who pointed
out that the stress on Jahwe's "sublime spirituality"
goes hand in hand with anthropomorphic references to
Jahwe and His real acts in visible history. Zimmerli
correctly judges that the contrast between "spiritual
and invisible" and "material and visible" is a contrast not drawn from the Biblical outlook but rather
from idealistic philosophy. Gispen notes the significant fact that Exodus 20:5 gives as the motive for the
prohibition not "I am Spirit," but rather "I the Lord
thy God am a jealous God." This is not in conflict
with Jer. 23:23, as its context makes clear.

The second commandment deals with a prohibition
against the arbitrariness with which man tries to
have God at his beck and call, tries high-handedly to
control God's presence in the visible world. It is
undeniable, for the Old Testament, that God through
His revelation is present in this created world, and
does not show Himself only as a God from afar. There
is thus no contradiction between the second commandment and the theophanies in which God "appeared" to
Israel, and Israel could speak of God in innumerable
anthropomorphic ways without having the idea that the
majesty of God was thereby in any way violated. In
all such anthropomorphisms, Israel carefully respected
the boundary beyond which God would be "humanized,"
subject to all the ambiguous, capricious, dark and
changeable aspects of man. Anthropomorphism is useful
in speaking about God, and useful in God's revelation
in the world. By means of it we can almost immediately intuit and understand what God's revelation has to
say to us. Meanwhile we hardly notice the "anthropomorphism" as such; as for example, when Mary says, in
her song of praise, "He has shown strength with his
arm" (Luke 1:51). God's revelation is made understandable to us not only through such striking anthropomorphisms as God's organs and feelings, but also in
connection with God's speaking, seeing, and hearing
(He who hears prayers!). Of central importance is

what Scripture says to us regarding the living and active God, in the forms and images of active men.[22]

Thus we can hardly see anthropomorphism as something which clouds our view of God, which should be conquered and surpassed, in order to gain a more "spiritual" view of God.[23] We should rather see it as a manner of speaking which gives full perspective to our view of the living and active God, though we must never forget that this manner of speaking is and must always be inadequate.[24] And hence it is not the danger that God will be anthropomorphically compared to some part of man (e.g., his body) which produced the limitations on anthropomorphism, but rather the danger that unlimited use of it might be wrongly understood in the context of the religious ideas of the heathen world surrounding Israel. In any case, the point of the second commandment is not a spiritualistic point, a protection of Jahwe's spirituality and transcendence, against anthropomorphism, in which, actually, we are shown God in His acts and dealings, in His mighty acts, through use of the forms of living and acting--and to us familiar--man. This is an annoyance and a scandal only to those who think in the categories of an abstract idea of God, of an "unqualifiable and pure spirituality of God."[25] Anthropomorphism finds a meaningful place in Biblical religion, which finds its expression in the personal relations between God and man, in which He comes and goes, sees and hears and speaks, and in which He reveals Himself to His people as the living God. It is in and by means of this Biblical anthropomorphism that His "spirituality," freedom and sovereignty, His mercy and compassion, are shown. And it is this which makes it impossible for man to seek in man-made things that which he cannot find in man, and which comes to him only through God's activities, in a constant presence which is vouchsafed to him by God through various human analogies, in anthropomorphic manner, as an irrefutable and comforting reality.[26]

We have already noted that while the account in Genesis does say that man was created in the image of God, it does not give us any further details. As Kuyper remarked, the picture given is "not very clear." It is indeed evident that Scripture sees man as a creature in a certain relationship to God, his Creator, and that it speaks of a "likeness" of some sort between man and God; but always the question arose wherein this likeness consists. Though dismissing the attempts to delineate the image by means of various

anthropological distinctions such as ego, personality,
self-consciousness, and the like, we must not fail to
notice a certain "method" for answering the question,
one which is frequently encountered. We refer to the
attempt to give more clarity to our picture of the
image by paying special attention to the witness of
the New Testament regarding the image. Perhaps we
may might gain a clearer insight, some said, with this
approach; not so much because the New Testament might
add something to what the Old Testament has said, but
rather because the New Testament speaks of the restoration of the image of God. Perhaps we could, by examining this restoration, arrive at a deeper understanding of the mystery of the image of God.

This "method" is used already by Calvin. He
notes that it appears we can give no complete description of the image of God unless it becomes clearer
which are the characteristics by which man excels
and wherein he reflects the glory of God. In this
connection, he arrives at what we might call a "hermeneutic method."

When we, with Calvin and Bavinck, refer to the
significance of the knowledge of man to be gained from
considering man's salvation in Christ, we do not mean
to restore to honor the sort of "reading off" which
Barth condemns, but we do wish to emphasize the
importance of the Biblical witness to Christ as the
image of God and to the renewal in communion with
Christ, of man according to that image[27] spoken of in
the New Testament. We shall begin with what the Bible
tells us regarding this renewal. Scripture pictures
the new man in contrast to the old man, lost in "the
vanity of their mind, having the understanding darkened,
being alienated from the life of God." Replacing the
dissoluteness and impurity of the old man there now
stands the new life, the new man, who has put away
the old man and who has learned to know Christ, has
been instructed in Him and has thus "put on the new
man" in righteousness and true holiness (Eph. 4:17-24).
In this life, the image of God becomes visible. The
New Testament sheds the fullness of its light on the
newness of this life, and it appears that this newness
does not merely refer to a new aspect in the life of
an individual but that it includes and indeed brings
about the community. Thus Paul calls Christ "our
peace, who hath made both one, hath broken down the
middle wall of partition between us . . . to make in
himself of twain, one new man, so making peace"
(Eph. 2:17; cf. 18-22). So deep is this community

that it does not arise from men who having individually been renewed now seek each other out; it is a peace[28] which is proclaimed and which is *actuality* in Christ, through the Cross.

In this newness, barriers are (not, will be) taken away, as two are made into one. In this community and this peace, the wonderful newness of man's humanness is manifested; thus Colossians 3:10, directly after speaking of the renewal of man in God's image, goes on to say that "there is no difference now between Greek and Jew, circumcised and uncircumcised, barbarian and Scythian, slave and free, but Christ is all, and all are in Christ." The remark that the community referred to here and in Galatians 3:28 does not mean a giving up of differences is correct: this newness does not mean a leveling process, a removal of differences, but a community, which reveals its wonderful and hitherto unknown newness precisely in these differences. But the point of Paul's words is not the retention of differences, but the newness of the *community,* which may never be relativized or made secondary by the differences.

The new man--that is the mighty change which in Christ comes over human nature. It is not a change in the sense of a "transubstantiation," a change from one essence to another. Rather, man comes to his true nature, his nature as God intended it to be, a nature in which true community is no longer threatened, in which one man is no longer a danger for the other. No matter how deep-seated the differences between men may be, *in* Christ the tension and convulsiveness vanish before the new nature. Thus when we consider the image of God in man as it is restored in Christ, we are not concerned with some "analogy" of ego or personality or self-consciousness, but rather with the fullness of the new life, which can be described as a new relationship with God, and *in* this relationship as the reality of salvation.[29] It should not surprise us, therefore, that Paul treats sanctifying in the context of the renewal according to the image of the Creator: the new man is knowable in the new direction of his life as over against "evil concupiscence and covetousness," lies, "anger, wrath, blasphemy, filthy communication" (Col. 3:5,8). These are the practices of the old man, which also affected his fellow man. Before the reference to "the new man which is renewed in knowledge" according to the image of God, Paul issues the warning: "Lie not one to another" (Col. 3:9). This disruption of the community in man's existence is the opposite of what the new creation in Christ is, in which the believers are God's "workmanship, created in Jesus Christ unto good works" (Eph. 2:10; cf. Jas. 1:18). There can be no doubt whatsoever as to the source of this renewal. Not only in general, but also in specific manifestations in human life, the source is clear: in Christ. The reality of renewal can be shown in various manners. Paul can say (Gal. 6:15), "neither circumcision availeth any thing, nor uncircumcision, but a new creature," and "neither circumcision availeth anything nor uncircumcision but faith which worketh by love," (Gal. 5:6), and in another context surprise us with the parallel "circumcision is nothing, and uncircumcision is nothing, but the keeping of the commandments of God" (I Cor. 7:19).

Endnotes

[1]Cf. H. Gunkel, *Genesis* (1902), pp. 99ff. He says, "The primary difference between the O.T. and Christian dogmatics as regards this point is that in the latter it plays an important role--it has sometimes served as occasion for developing a complete anthropology--while in the former it has no special importance; in the Prophets and the Psalms, for example, it is wholly absent."

[2]See Bavinck, *Gereformeerde Dogmatiek*, II, 494, 499. The supernatural view, says Bavinck, actually did not derive from the distinction, but was later tied in with it.

[3]See Origen, "De Principiis," III, IV, 1, *Opera Omnia*, ed. De la Rue, p. 375. Note the passage "*indicat quod imaginis quidem dignitatem in prima conditione percepit, similitudinis vero perfecto in consummatione servata est; scilicet. . . .*" Cf. further H. Crouzel, *Theologie de l'image de Dieu chez Origene* (1955), pp. 217ff.; A. Struker, *Die Gottebenbildlichkeit des Menschen in der Christliche Literatur der ersten zwei Jahrhunderte* (1913); R. Bernard, *L'image de Dieu d'apres St Athanase* (1952).

[4]Emil Brunner, *Der Mensch im Widerspruch* (1937), p. 523. He speaks of "the standard distinction, from

Irenaeus on, between image and likeness." Cf. also
the *Theologisch Woordenboek*, I (1952), *s.v.*, "*Beeld
Gods.*" It says that the Fathers distinguished between
image and likeness and that "this may have also been
the intent of the sacred writer, who wrote these words
under God's guidance," and then follows with a distinction between natural and supernatural image.

[5]See Calvin, *Institutes*, I, XV, 3. He says that
the traditional commentators sought a distinction
between the two words which is not really there, since
"likeness" is added to "image" simply for purposes of
clarification, and he refers to the Hebrew use of
parallelism. Cf. also his *Commentary on the Penta-
teuch*, *s.v.*, Gen. 1:26. Here he also denies the
distinction. Brunner notes Luther's similar views.

[6]For exegetical literature, see the following;
e.g., O. Procksch, *Die Genesis* (1913), p. 432; E.
Konig, *Die Genesis* (1919), p. 156; J. Skinner,
"Genesis," *International Critical Commentary* (1930),
p. 32; B. Jacob, *Das erste Buch der Tora, Genesis*
(1934), p. 58; G. von Rad, *Das erste Buch Mose* (1953),
p. 45; Th. C. Vriezen, "La creation de l'homme d'apres
l'image de Dieu," *Oud Testamentische Studien*, II
(1943), 92; W. Eichrodt, *Theologie des Alten Testaments*, II/III, p. 60. The Septuagint, the Greek
translation of the Hebrew, uses a copula to connect
the two terms, while the Hebrew does not. Eichrodt
comments that the Hebrew shows that there are not two
separate terms expressed here, but one. All the
authors cited above see "image" and "likeness" either
as referring to the same thing, or see "likeness as
further explaining "image."
For works in dogmatics, see, e.g., Bavinck, *op.
cit.*, p. 492; O. Weber, *Grundlagen der Dogmatik*, I
(1955), 625; E. Brunner, *Dogmatik*, II, 90. The
creedal *Synopsis* (Disp. 13, 27) already makes the
same point, following Calvin.

[7]Cf. E. Osterloh, "Die Gottebenbildlichkeit des
Menschen," *Theologia viatorum* (1939), pp. 9-32. He
is one of the exceptions; he even speaks of the
"contrast" between the two terms, and further feels
that there are grounds for holding to the two aspects
of the image, as earlier theologians felt. Osterloh's
view is a fairly isolated one in contemporary theology,
and, in our opinion, his argument is not valid.

[8]Bavinck, *op. cit.*, pp. 492-493. It should also
be noted that the prepositions involved are used

indifferently: after His image, in His image, after His likeness, in His likeness. Cf. Gen. 1:26, Gen. 5:3. Cf. also Ch. Aalders, *Genesis*, 2nd ed., I, 178. It is interesting to note that this point came up in the discussions of the Neo-Kohlbruggian interpretation of the image of God. Cf. also Bohl, *Dogmatik* (1887), p. 154; Bohl saw this preposition as showing the "various spheres in which and for which man was created." Cf. Bavinck, *loc. cit.*

[9]Bavinck, *loc. cit.* Cf. L. Kohler, "Die Grund-stelle der Imago Dei-Lehre, Gen. 1:26," *Theologische Zeitschrift*, IV (1948), 21. Kohler sees in *demuth* (likeness) a weakening sort of qualification; "similar-ity" as contrasted to "representation or close similar-ity." Kohler does not, however, support a double aspect of the image. Cf. also K. L. Schmidt, "Homo imago Dei im Alten und Neuen Testament," *Eranos-Jahrbuch*, XV (1948), 165ff. He stresses the indiffer-ent use of the two prepositions (*hendiadyoin*), but does not see the two terms as tautological; he agrees with Kohler in seeing *"demuth"* as added in order to clarify the possibly ambiguous connotation of *"tselem"* as implying very close similarity. Cf. also P. Hum-bert, *Etudes sur le recit du paradis et de la chute dans le Genese* (1940), pp. 160, 172. He refers to Ezek. 1:26--a likeness (*demuth*) which appeared as a man--as helping to clarify the sense of Gen. 1:26, i.e., as stressing that "likeness" does not imply substantial identity.

[10]Von Rad, *op. cit.*, p. 45. Cf. Vriezen, *loc. cit.* He says "the author does not say where this image shows itself."

[11]*Catechismus Recoviensis*, ed. G. L. Oederus (1739), p. 48. It says that the image consists of man's *"potestas et dominium in omnes res a Deo condi-tas supra terram,"* as Gen. 1:26 patently affirms. Cf. also regarding the remonstrant Arminians' views on the image, K. Schilder, *Heidelbergse Catechismus*, I, 233.

[12]Cf. Skinner, *op. cit.*, p. 32; Koning, *op. cit.*, p. 159; Gunkel, *op. cit.*, p. 99; Vriezen, *op. cit.*, p. 98; Schmidt, *op. cit.*, p. 174; Humbert, *op. cit.*, p. 164. All these see the image as the basis for the *dominium*.

[13]J. Ridderbos, *De Psalmen*, I (1955), 68, 75. The Hebrew of Psalm 8 refers to man as made a little lower

than *Elohim*. The Septuagint translates this as
aggelous, angels; cf. Heb. 2:7, "lower than the angels."
Cf. also Heb. 2:9, taken over from the Septuagint,
which, according to Ridderbos, is not thereby authen-
ticated. The problems involved here are, in our
opinion, not simple. In Hebrews 2, the "a little
lower than" of vs. 7 becomes "for a little while" in
v. 9, with reference to the temporary humiliation of
Christ. Cf. besides the usual commentaries on Hebrews,
G. Harder, "Die Septuaginta-zitate des Hebraerbriefs,"
Theologia viatorum (1939), p. 35.

[14]Eichrodt, *op. cit.*, p. 63; Calvin, *Institutes*,
I, XV, 4.

[15]Bavinck, *op. cit.*, p. 494.

[16]See Eichrodt, *op. cit.*, p. 62, and Von Rad's
demurrer in Kittel's *Theologisches Worterbuch*, II,
388-389: "the image of God does *not* lie in man's
'personality,' nor in his 'free ego,' nor in his
'human worth,' nor in his 'free use of moral tendencies.'" He sees arguments as to whether the image
relates to the spiritual or the bodily aspect of man
as "unpromising." Cf. also has *Das erste Buch Mose*
(1953), p. 45. Here he attacks view "based on one or
another set of anthropological concepts alien to the
O.T. writer," which define the image limitedly and
onesidedly in terms of the "spiritual essence" of
man.

[17]See, e.g., E. Konig, *Die Genesis*, p. 158. He
lists man's capability for abstract thinking, his
ability to form religions and world-outlooks, his
ego-consciousness, his moral aspect, and his freedom
to will.

[18]Cf. any theological dictionary s.v., Anthropomorphism.

[19]Cf. *Synopsis* (XII, XXXVI). Already the image is
"*et anima et corpore*." Cf. Schilder, *op. cit.*, I, 263.
He says we "should stop racking our brains trying to
analyze how an incorporeal God can be imaged through a
bodily man." Cf. also L. van der Zanden, *De Mens als
Beeld Gods*, p. 60.

[20]Gunkel, *op. cit.*, p. 99.

[21]Cf. F. Michaeli, *Dieu a l'image de l'homme* (1950),
p. 72, and also Kittel, *op. cit.*, II, 378-379.

[22]See extensively J. De Groot and A. R. Hulst, *Macht en Wil. De Verkondiging van het O.T. aangaande God* (1952), pp. 189-208; E. Jacob, *Theologie de l'Ancien Testament* (1955), pp. 30ff.; F. Michaeli, *op. cit.*

[23]See *Theologisch Woordenboek*, H. Brink, et al., ed., I (1952), 157. It says that anthropomorphism devaluates the idea of God; and it perennially threatens theology. Cf. A. Chollet, *Dictionnaire de Theologie Catholique*, I, 1369-70. He is much more careful. H. G. Groenewould, *Christelijke Encyclopedie*, I (2d ed., 1956), 249. He attacks the idea that anthropomorphism devaluates the idea of God. Cf. also Vriezen, *Hoofdlijnen der Theologie van het Oude Testament* (2d ed., 1954), pp. 183ff.

[24]Scriptural anthropomorphism goes hand in hand with frequent specific references to the difference between God and man, e.g., Hos. 11:9, Num. 23:19, Prov. 5:1, Job 10:4-5; and for further listings, see Michaeli, *op. cit.*, p. 115.

[25]Cf. De Groot and Hulst, *op. cit.*, p. 201. They refer to the important article by Hempel; "Die Grenzen der Anthropomorphismus im A.T.," *Z.A.W.* (1939), pp. 75-85. For theriomorphism, see De Groot and Hulst, *loc. cit.*; and Jacob, *op. cit.* p. 30. Both note the sobriety of theriomorphic imagery. In our opinion, the structures of theriomorphism and anthropomorphism are different, since the former always contains a comparison, a *tertium comparationis*.

[26]See also De Groot and Hulst, and Jacob, as cited above. Cf. Zimmerli, *op. cit.*, p. 561.

[27]Cf. R. Prenter, *op. cit.*, pp. 217-222. It is in this sense also that he accepts the basing of anthropology on Christology, and he says that this was already done by Luther and Irenaeus. When he places the Reformation (or at least Lutheran) contrast between "old" and "new" man over against Barth's "correspondence" and "likeness," the dilemma is not valid since, as we shall see, the New Testament uses "likeness" in very profound contexts.

[28]Cf. on Eph. 2:14 also E. Best, *One Body in Christ* (1955), pp. 152ff. Cf. also in this connection Prov. 4:7-12, "two are better than one," which emphasizes the richness of community as over against solitariness.

[29]Cf. Kittel, *op. cit.*, III, 1033.

Discussion Questions

1. Does Berkouwer's position provide us with a sufficiently clear criterion for identifying the uniqueness of human nature?

2. Do you think that Berkouwer's position excludes that of Teilhard, or does it add to it?

3. Is the statement "Jesus was the only true human, while we are fragmented and partial humans" a faith statement or a descriptive statement? How would you go about answering which it is? Could you use scientific or historical data?

4. Is it theologically important that humans be unique in God's creation? Why?

5. Would it be possible to realize the fullness of the image of God by our own strength alone? Why or why not?

MAN AS SINNER

In 1939, Reinhold Niebuhr was invited to deliver
the prestigious Gifford Lectures at the University of
Edinburgh. The essay which follows is an excerpt from
these lectures. No theological education in this era
is complete without a reading of the book form of these
lectures entitled *The Nature and Destiny of Man*. Of
all of the important contributions of this book, none
is more significant than Niebuhr's analysis of the
Christian understanding of sin. While reading, it is
important to remember that this essay deals more with
the nature of sin than with the forms of sin, although
Niebuhr also treated the latter theme.

Niebuhr begins the essay with what he considers a
crucial theological observation. He says that the
Christian approach to the human contradiction of being
a part of nature and yet above nature is to emphasize
that this is a problem of sin and will, not a problem
of man's finitude. The fact of human existence as finite, free and self-transcending is not evil in and
of itself.

If Niebuhr is correct, then sin is not just a religious way of speaking about our inevitable natural
fallibility. We cannot be excused with the observation, "Well I am only human."

According to Niebuhr, sin originates in the anxiety womb formed by our limitations (finitude) and our
freedom to choose. But even this situation would not
be a temptation were it not falsely interpreted.
Niebuhr takes the devil seriously, but not literally.
In the Fall account (Gen. 3) the serpent's role means
that there is a force of evil that is antecedent to

human action. Humans do not face their situation in
existence in a vacuum. But the exact nature of this
evil force is a mystery incapable of rational explication (similiar to Gabriel Marcel's notion of mystery).

The value of this point lies not only in its recovery of satanology for modern theology, but it also
prohibits any naive approach to the human situation.
Approaches which suggest that humans can overcome sin
by education, technology, or other contrivances simply
underestimate the mysterious presence of evil which the
Christian insists upon. Niebuhr holds that his position on this controversial notion is descriptive before
it is ontological. What this means is that he thinks
that no honestly exhaustive analysis of the human situation can omit reference to this mysterious tempting
force. Satan becomes a symbol for an ontological reality only after he is descriptively required.

In his situation man is anxious and anxiety is the
precondition of sin. Insecure humans are tempted to
overstep their bounds and be like God. However, according to Niebuhr it is not logically or ontologically
necessary that humans sin. Of course, Niebuhr differs
at this point with those who believe sin is inherited
and is thus ontologically necessary.

But it is important to note just how Niebuhr differs from the traditional understanding of original sin
as inherited sin. To be sure, Niebuhr does not argue
that man inherits either guilt or some internal defect
from an historical Adam: This difference alone is considerable.

Niebuhr is more concerned to show how sin grows
out of the present situation, not out of humanity's
prehistoric past. However, he does have a doctrine of
original sin. Niebuhr suggests that the Christian
doctrine of original sin means that human's will sin
inevitably, not that they will sin necessarily. He
makes this distinction because he believes that without
it sin becomes inescapable because of human nature, and
thus it becomes theologically problematic to assign responsibility.

Niebuhr again claims to be making a descriptive
observation when he says that man's examination of his
actions gives rise to remorse and repentance. Honest
contemplation always discloses our inner rationalizations and self-deceptions. Remorse and repentance at-
test to the responsibility we feel for our actions.

Accordingly, humans have all sinned, and all will sin,
but not because of some natural or even supernatural
necessity. The inevitability of sin is the meaning of
original sin, and it is a descriptive observation.
There is no possibility that humans alone will attain
righteousness (Pelagianism). And it is sin from which
humans must be saved, not their natural finitude.

MAN AS SINNER*

"In every religion," declared Albrecht Ritschl,
the most authoritative exponent of modern liberal
Christianity, "what is sought with the help of the superhuman power reverenced by man is a solution of the
contradiction in which man finds himself as both a part
of nature and a spiritual personality claiming to dominate nature." It is perfectly true that this problem
of finiteness and freedom underlies all religion. But
Ritschl does not appreciate that the uniqueness of the
Biblical approach to the human problem lies in its sub-
ordination of the problem of finiteness to the problem
of sin. It is not the contradiction of finiteness and
freedom from which Biblical religion seeks emancipa-
tion. It seeks redemption from sin; and the sin from
which it seeks redemption is occasioned, though not
caused, by this contradiction in which man stands. Sin
is not caused by the contradiction because, according
to Biblical faith, there is no absolute necessity that
man should be betrayed into sin by the ambiguity of
his position, as standing in and yet above nature.
But it cannot be denied that this is the occasion for
his sin.

*Source: From *The Nature and Destiny of Man,*
Vol. 1 by Reinhold Niebuhr. Copyright 1941, 1964 by
Charles Scribner's Sons. Used by permission of
Charles Scribner's Sons.

Man is insecure and involved in natural contingency; he seeks to overcome his insecurity by a will-to-power which overreaches the limits of human creatureliness. Man is ignorant and involved in the limitations of a finite mind; but he pretends that he is not limited. He assumes that he can gradually transcend finite limitations until his mind becomes identical with universal mind. All of his intellectual and cultural pursuits, therefore, become infected with the sin of pride. Man's pride and will-to-power disturb the harmony of creation. The Bible defines sin in both religious and moral terms. The religious dimension of sin is man's rebellion against God, his effort to usurp the place of God. The moral and social dimension of sin is injustice. The ego which falsely makes itself the centre of existence in its pride and will-to-power inevitably subordinates other life to its will and thus does injustice to other life.

While the Bible consistently maintains that sin cannot be excused by, or inevitably derived from, any other element in the human situation it does admit that man was tempted. In the myth of the Fall the temptation arises from the serpent's analysis of the human situation. The serpent depicts God as jealously guarding his prerogatives against the possibility that man might have his eyes opened and become "as God, knowing good and evil." Man is tempted, in other words, to break and transcend the limits which God has set for him. The temptation thus lies in his situation of finiteness and freedom. But the situation would not be a temptation of itself, if it were not falsely interpreted by "the serpent." The story of the Fall is innocent of a fully developed satanology; yet Christian theology has not been wrong in identifying the serpent with, or regarding it as an instrument or symbol of, the devil. To believe that there is a devil is to believe that there is a principle or force of evil antecedent to any evil human action. Before man fell the devil fell. The devil is, in fact, a fallen angel. His sin and fall consists in his effort to transcend his proper state and to become like God. This definition of the devil's fall is implied in Isaiah's condemnation of Babylon, in which the pride of Babylon is compared or identified with "Lucifer's" pride: "How art thou fallen from heaven, O Lucifer, son of the morning! how art thou cut down to the ground. For thou hast said in thine heart, I will ascend into heaven, I will exalt my throne above the stars of God. Yet thou shalt be brought down to hell."[1]

It is not necessary to trace the intricate relation between Old Testament satanology and its source in
Babylonian and Persian myths. The importance of Biblical satanology lies in the two facts that: (1) the
devil is not thought of as having been created evil.
Rather his evil arises from his effort to transgress
the bounds set for his life, an effort which places
him in rebellion against God. (2) The devil fell before man fell, which is to say that man's rebellion
against God is not an act of sheer perversity, nor does
it follow inevitably from the situation in which he
stands. The situation of finiteness and freedom in
which man stands becomes a source of temptation only
when it is falsely interpreted. This false interpretation is not purely the product of the human imagination. It is suggested to man by a force of evil which
precedes his own sin. Perhaps the best description or
definition of this mystery is the statement that sin
posits itself, that there is no situation in which it
is possible to say that sin is either an inevitable
consequence of the situation nor yet that it is an act
of sheer and perverse individual defiance of God.

Sin is not merely the error of overestimating human capacities. St. Paul rightly insists that "their
foolish heart was darkened" and that "they became vain
in their imagination." Neither the devil nor man is
merely betrayed by his greatness to forget his weakness, or by his great knowledge to forget his ignorance. The fact is that man is never unconscious of his
weakness, of the limited and dependent character of his
existence and knowledge. The occasion for his temptation lies in the two facts, his greatness and his weakness, his unlimited and his limited knowledge, taken
together. Man is both strong and weak, both free and
bound, both blind and far-seeing. He stands at the
juncture of nature and spirit; and is involved in both
freedom and necessity. His sin is never the mere ignorance of his ignorance. It is always partly an effort to obscure his blindness by overestimating the
degree of his sight and to obscure his insecurity by
stretching his power beyond its limits.

This analysis proves the impossibility of either
eliminating the element of conscious perversity from
sin or of reducing it merely to error. But it also reveals that both freedom and necessity, both man's involvement in nature and his transcendence over it must
be regarded as important elements in the situation
which tempts to sin. Thus man is, like the animals,
involved in the necessities and contingencies of na-

ture; but unlike the animals he sees this situation and
anticipates its perils. He seeks to protect himself
against nature's contingencies; but he cannot do so
without transgressing the limits which have been set
for his life. Therefore all human life is involved in
the sin of seeking security at the expense of other
life. The perils of nature are thereby transmuted into the more grievous perils of human history. Or
again: man's knowledge is limited by time and place.
Yet it is not as limited as animal knowledge. The
proof that it is not so limited is given by the fact
that man knows something of these limits, which means
that in some sense he transcends them. Man knows more
than the immediate natural situation in which he stands
and he constantly seeks to understand his immediate
situation in terms of a total situation. Yet he is unable to define the total human situation without col-
ouring his definition with finite perspectives drawn
from his immediate situation. The realization of the
relativity of his knowledge subjects him to the peril
of scepticism. The abyss of meaninglessness yawns on
the brink of all his mighty spiritual endeavours.
Therefore man is tempted to deny the limited character
of his knowledge, and the finiteness of his perspectives. He pretends to have achieved a degree of knowledge which is beyond the limit of finite life. This
is the "ideological taint" in which all human knowledge
is involved and which is always something more than
mere human ignorance. It is always partly an effort to
hide that ignorance by pretension.

In short, man, being both free and bound, both
limited and limitless, is anxious. Anxiety is the inevitable concomitant of the paradox of freedom and finiteness in which man is involved. Anxiety is the
internal precondition of sin. It is the inevitable
spiritual state of man, standing in the paradoxical
situation of freedom and finiteness.[2] Anxiety is the
internal description of the state of temptation. It
must not be identified with sin because there is always
the ideal possibility that faith would purge anxiety of
the tendency toward sinful self-assertion. The ideal
possibility is that faith in the ultimate security of
God's love would overcome all immediate insecurities
of nature and history. That is why Christian orthodoxy
has consistently defined unbelief as the root of sin,
or as the sin which precedes pride.[3] It is significant
that Jesus justifies his injunction, "Be not anxious"
with the observation, "For your heavenly Father knoweth
that ye have need of these things." The freedom from
anxiety which he enjoins is a possibility only if per-

fect trust in divine security has been achieved. Whether such freedom from anxiety and such perfect trust are an actual possibility of historic existence must be considered later. For the present it is enough to observe that no life, even the most saintly, perfectly conforms to the injunction not to be anxious.

Yet anxiety is not sin. It must be distinguished from sin partly because it is its precondition and not its actuality, and partly because it is the basis of all human creativity as well as the precondition of sin. Man is anxious not only because his life is limited and dependent and yet not so limited that he does not know of his limitations. He is also anxious because he does not know the limits of his possibilities. He can do nothing and regard it perfectly done, because higher possibilities are revealed in each achievement. There are, of course, limits but it is difficult to gauge them from any immediate perspective. There is therefore no limit of achievement in any sphere of acitivity in which human history can rest with equanimity.[4]

Anxiety, as a permanent concomitant of freedom, is thus both the source of creativity and a temptation to sin. It is the condition of the sailor, climbing the mast (to use a simile), with the abyss of the waves beneath him and the "crow's nest" above him. He is anxious about both the end toward which he strives and the abyss of nothingness into which he may fall. The ambition of man to be something is always partly prompted by the fear of meaninglessness which threatens him by reason of the contingent character of his existence. His creativity is therefore always corrupted by some effort to overcome contingency by raising precisely what is contingent to absolute and unlimited dimensions. This effort, though universal, cannot be regarded as normative. It is always destructive. Yet obviously the destructive aspect of anxiety is so intimately involved in the creative aspects that there is no possibility of making a simple separation between them. The two are inextricably bound together by reason of man being anxious both to realize his unlimited possibilities and to overcome and to hide the dependent and contingent character of his existence.

When anxiety has conceived it brings forth both pride and sensuality. Man falls into pride, when he seeks to raise his contingent existence to unconditioned significance; he falls into senuality, when he seeks to escape from his unlimited possibilities of freedom from the perils and responsibilities of self-determination, by immersing himself into a "mutable good," by losing himself in some natural vitality.

The temptation to sin lies, as previously observed, in the human situation itself. This situation is that man as spirit transcends the temporal and natural process in which he is involved and also transcends himself. Thus his freedom is the basis of his creativity but it is also his temptation. Since he is involved in the contingencies and necessities of the natural process on the one hand and since, on the other, he stands outside of them and foresees their caprices and perils, he is anxious. In his anxiety he seeks to transmute his finiteness into infinity, his weakness into strength, his dependence into independence. He seeks in other words to escape finiteness and weakness by a quantitative rather than qualitative development of his life. The quantitative antithesis of finiteness is infinity. The qualitative possibility of human life is its obedient subjection to the will of God. This possibility is expressed in the words of Jesus: "He that loseth his life for my sake shall find it." (Mt. 10:39).

But the self lacks the faith and trust to subject itself to God. It seeks to establish itself independently. It seeks to find its life and thereby loses it. For the self which it asserts is less than the true self. It is the self in all the contingent and arbitrary factors of its immediate situation. By asserting these contingent and arbitrary factors of an immediate situation, the self loses its true self. It increases its insecurity because it gives its immediate necessities a consideration which they do not deserve and which they cannot have without disturbing the harmony of creation. By giving life a false centre, the self then destroys the real possibilities for itself and others. Hence the relation of injustice to pride, and the vicious circle of injustice, increasing as it does the insecurity which pride was intended to overcome.

The sin of the inordinate self-love thus points to the prior sin of lack of trust in God. The anxiety of unbelief is not merely the fear which comes from ignorance of God. "Anxiety," declares Kierkegaard, "is the dizziness of freedom,"[5] but it is significant that the same freedom which tempts to anxiety also contains the ideal possibility of knowing God. Here the Pauline psychology is penetrating and significant. St. Paul declares that man is without excuse because "the invisible things of him from the creation of the world are clearly seen, being understood by the things that are made, even his eternal power and Godhead" (Romans 1:20). The anxiety of freedom leads to sin only if the prior sin of unbelief is assumed. This is the meaning of Kierkegaard's assertion that sin posits itself.[6]

The idea that the inevitability of sin is not due merely to the strength of the temptation in which man stands by reason of his relation to both the temporal process and eternity, is most perfectly expressed in the scriptural words: "Let no man say when he is tempted, I am tempted of God: for God cannot be tempted with evil, neither tempteth he any man: But every man is tempted, when he is drawn away of his own lust, and enticed. Then when lust hath conceived, it bringeth forth sin: and sin, when it is finished, bringeth forth death."[7] But on the other hand the idea that the situation of finiteness and freedom is a temptation once evil has entered it and that evil does enter it prior to any human action is expressed in Biblical thought by the conception of the devil. The devil is a fallen angel, who fell because he sought to lift himself above his measure and who in turn insinuates temptation into human life. The sin of each individual is preceded by Adam's sin: but even this first sin of history is not the first sin. One may, in other words, go farther back than human history and still not escape the paradoxical conclusion that the situation of finiteness and freedom would not lead to sin if sin were not already introduced into the situation. This is, in the words of Kierkegaard, the "qualitative leap" of sin and reveals the paradoxical relation of inevitability and responsibility. Sin can never be traced merely to the temptation arising from a particular situation or condition in which man as man finds himself or in which particular men find themselves. Nor can the temptation which is compounded of a situation of finiteness and freedom, plus the fact of sin, be regarded as leading necessarily to sin in the life of each individual, if again sin is not first presupposed in that life. For this reason even the knowledge of inevitability does not extinguish the sense of responsibility.

The fact of responsibility is attested by the feeling of remorse or repentance which follows the sinful action. From an exterior view not only sin in general but any particular sin may seem to be the necessary consequence of previous temptations. A simple determinism is thus a natural characteristic of all social interpretations of human actions. But the interior view does not allow this interpretation. The self, which is privy to the rationalizations and processes of self-deception which accompanied and must accompany the sinful act, cannot accept and does not accept the simple determinism of the exterior view. Its contemplation of its act involves both the discovery and the reassertion of its freedom. It discovers that some degree of conscious dishonesty accompanied the act, which means that the self was not deterministically and blindly involved in it. Its discovery of that fact in contemplation is a further degree of the assertion of freedom than is possible in the moment of action.

The remorse and repentance which are consequent upon such contemplation are similar in their acknowledgement of freedom and responsibility and their implied assertion of it. They differ in the fact that repentance is the expression of freedom and faith while remorse is the expression of freedom without faith. The one is the "Godly sorrow" of which St. Paul speaks, and the other is "the sorrow of this world which worketh death." It is, in other words, the dspair into which sin transmutes the anxiety which precedes sin.

There are of course many cases in which the self seems so deeply involved in its own deceptions and so habituated to standards of action which may have once been regarded as sinful that it seems capable of neither repentance nor remorse. This complacency is possible on many levels of life from that of a natural paganism in which the freedom of spirit is not fully developed, to refined forms of Pharisaism in which pride as self-righteousness obscures the sin of pride itself. It is not true, however, that habitual sin can ever destroy the uneasy conscience so completely as to remove the individual from the realm of moral responsibility to the realm of unmoral nature.[8]

The vertical dimension of the experience of remorse and repentance explains why there is no level of moral goodness upon which the sense of guilt can be eliminated. In fact the sense of guilt rises with moral sensitivity: "There are only two kinds of men," declares Pascal, "the righteous who believe themselves sinners; the rest, sinners, who believe themselves righteous." Pascal does not fully appreciate, at least as far as this statement is concerned, how infinite may be the shades of awareness of guilt from the complacency of those who are spiritually blind to the

sensitivity of the saint who knows that he is not a
saint. Yet it is obviously true that awareness of
guilt arises with spiritual sensitivity and that such
an awareness will be regarded as morbid only by moral-
lists who have no true knowledge of the soul and God.
The saint's awareness of guilt is no illusion. The
fact is that sin expresses itself most terribly in its
most subtle forms. The sinful identification of the
contingent self with God is less crass on the higher
levels of the spiritual life but it may be the more
dangerous for being the more plausible. An example
from the realm of political life may explain why this
is true. The inevitable partiality of even the most
impartial court is more dangerous to justice than the
obvious partiality of contending political factions in
society, which the impartiality of the court is intended to resolve. The partiality of the contending
forces is so obvious that it can be discounted. The
partiality of the court, on the other hand, is obscured
by its prestige of impartiality. Relative degrees of
impartiality in judicial tribunals are important
achievements in political life. But wihout a judgment
upon even the best judicial process from a higher level
of judgment, the best becomes the worst.[9]

The fact that the sense of guilt rises vertically
with all moral achievement and is, therefore, not assuaged by it nor subject to diminution or addition by
favourable and unfavourable social opinion, throws a
significant light on the relation of freedom to sin.
The ultimate proof of the freedom of the human spirit
is its own recognition that its will is not free to
choose between good and evil. For in the highest
reaches of the freedom of the spirit, the self discovers in contemplation and retrospect that previous actions have invariably confused the ultimate reality
and value, which the self as spirit senses, with the
immediate necessities of the self. If the self assumes that because it realizes this fact in past actions it will be able to avoid the corruption in future actions, it will merely fall prey to the Pharisaic
fallacy.

We cannot, therefore, escape the ultimate paradox
that the final exercise of freedom in the transcendent
human spirit is its recognition of the false use of
that freedom in action. Man is most free in the discovery that he is not free. This paradox has been
obscured by most Pelagians and by many Augustinians.
The Pelagians have been too intent to assert the integrity of man's freedom to realize that the discovery

of this freedom also involves the discovery of man's guilt. The Augustinians on the other hand have been so concerned to prove that the freedom of man is corrupted by sin that they have not fully understood that the discovery of this sinful taint is an achievement of freedom.

The paradox that human freedom is most perfectly discovered and asserted in the realization of the bondage of the will is easily obscured. Unfortunately the confusion revealed in the debate between Pelagians and Augustinians has been further aggravated by the literalism of the Augustinians. In countering the simple moralism of the Pelagians they insisted on interpreting original sin as an inherited taint. Thus they converted the doctrine of the inevitability of sin into a dogma which asserted that sin had a natural history. Thereby they gave their Pelagian critics an unnecessary advantage in the debate, which the latter have never been slow to seize.[10]

While Augustinian theology abounds in doctrines of original sin which equate it with the idea of an inherited corruption and which frequently make concupiscence in generation the agent of this inheritance, it is significant that Christian thought has always had some suggestions of the representative rather than historical character of Adam's sin. The idea of Adam as representative man allowed it to escape the historical-literalistic illusion. The very fountain-source of the doctrine of original sin, the thought of St. Paul, expresses the idea of original sin in terms which allow, and which possibly compel the conclusion that St. Paul believed each man to be related to Adam's sin in terms of "seminal identity" rather than historical inheritance. The Pauline words are: "Wherefore as by one man sin entered the world and death by sin; and so death passed to all men *for that all have sinned.*"[11] The idea of a mystical identity between Adam and all men is found in Irenaeus and is explicitly formulated in Ambrose.[12] Even Augustine, who insists on the theory of an inherited corruption, inserts an interesting qualification which points in the same direction when he quotes the Pauline passage, Roman 3:23, so that it reads: "'For all have sinned'--*whether in Adam or in themselves--*'and come short of the glory of God.'" The same idea struggles for, and achieves partial, expressions in some of the explanations of original sin in Calvin, even while he insists on the idea of inheritance.[13]

It is obviously necessary to eliminate the literalistic illusions in the doctrine of original sin if the paradox of inevitability and responsibility is to be fully understood; for the theory of an inherited second nature is as clearly destructive of the idea of responsibility for sin as rationalistic and dualistic theories which attribute human evil to the inertia of nature.[14] When this literalistic confusion is eliminated the truth of the doctrine of original sin is more clearly revealed; but it must be understood that even in this form the doctrine remains absurd from the standpoint of a pure rationalism, for it expresses a relation between fate and freedom which cannot be fully rationalized, unless the paradox be accepted as a rational understanding of the limits of rationality and as an expression of faith that a rationally irresolvable contradiction may point to a truth which logic cannot contain.

The Christian doctrine of orginal sin with its seemingly contradictory assertions about the inevitability of sin and man's responsibility for sin is a dialectical truth which does justice to the fact that man's self-love and self-centredness is inevitable, but not in such a way as to fit into the category of natural necessity. It is within and by his freedom that man sins. The final paradox is that the discovery of the inevitability of sin is man's highest assertion of freedom. The fact that the discovery of sin invariably leads to the Pharisaic illusion that such a discovery guarantees sinlessness in subsequent actions is a revelation of the way in which freedom becomes an accomplice of sin. It is at this point that the final battle between humility and human self-esteem is fought.

Kierkegaard's explanation of the dialectical relation of freedom and fate in sin is one of the profoundest in Christian thought. He writes: "The concept of sin and guilt does not emerge in its profoundest sense in paganism. If it did paganism would be destroyed by the contradiction that man becomes guilty by fate. . . . Christianity is born in this very contradiction. The concept of sin and guilt presupposes the individual as individual. There is no concern for his relation to any cosmic or past totality. The only concern is that he is guilty; and yet he is supposed to become guilty through fate, the very fate about which there is no concern. And thereby he becomes something which resolves the concept of fate, and to become that through fate! If this contradiction is wrongly understood it leads to false concepts of original sin. Rightly understood it leads to a true concept, to the idea namely that every individual is itself and the race and that the later individual is not significantly differentiated from the first man. In the possibility of anxiety freedom is lost, for it is overwhelmed by fate. Yet now it arises in reality but with the explanation that it has become guilty."[15]

Endnotes

[1]Is. 14:12, 13, 15. In the Slavonic Enoch the fall of the devil is similarly described: "And one from out of the order of angels, having turned away with the order that was under him, conceived an impossible thought, to place his throne higher than the clouds above the earth that he might become equal in rank with my [God's] power. And I threw him out from the height with his angels, and he was flying continually in the air above the bottomless [abyss]." ii Enoch, xxxix, 4.

[2]Kierkegaard says: "Anxiety is the psychological condition which precedes sin. It is so near, so fearfully near to sin, and yet it is not the explanation for sin." *Der Begriff der Angst*, p. 89. Kierkegaard's analysis of the relation of anxiety to sin is the profoundest in Christian thought.

[3]Martin Luther, in conformity with the general Christian tradition and quoting Sirach 10:14, writes in his *Treatise on Christian Liberty*: "The wise man has said: The beginning of all sin is to depart from God and not trust Him." Luther frequently defines the state of perfection before the Fall as being completely free of all anxiety. Here, as frequently in Luther's thought, he overstates the case. Ideally anxiety is overcome by faith but a life totally without anxiety would lack freedom and not require faith.

[4]Heidegger calls attention to the significant double connotation of the word "Care," *Sorge*, *cura*, that is a double connotation revealed in many languages. He writes: "The perfection of man, his becoming what in his freedom he can become according to his ultimate possibility, is a capacity of care or anxiety (*Sorge*). But just as basically care points to his being at the

mercy of an anxious world, of his contingency (*Gewoh-
fenheit*). This double connotation of *cura* points to a
basic structure in man of contingency and potentiality"
(*gewohfenen Entwuhfs*). *Sein und Zeit*, p. 199.

This double connotation according to Heidegger, is
clearly revealed if *Sohgfalt* is juxtaposed to *Sohge*,
that is care as carefulness to care as anxiety. Unfortunately the English language makes the distinction between *Angst* and *Sohge* impossible. Both of them must be
translated as *anxiety*.

[5]*Beghiff deh Angst*, p. 57.

[6]*Ibid.*, p. 27.

[7]James 1:13-15. This word succinctly expresses a
general attitude of the Bible which places it in opposition to all philosophical explanations which attribute the inevitability of sin to the power of temptation. One of the most ingenious of these is the theory
of Schelling, who, borrowing from the mystic system of
Jacob Boehme, declares that God has a "foundation that
He may be"; only this is not outside himself but within
him and he has within him a nature which though it belongs to himself is nevertheless different from him.
In God this foundation, this "dark ground," is not in
conflict with His love, but in man it "operates incessantly and arouses egotism and a particularized will,
just in order that the will to love may arise in contrast to it." Schelling, *Human Freedom*, tran. by J.
Gutman, pp. 51-53. Thus in this view sin is not only
a prerequisite of virtue but a consequence of the divine nature.

[8]James Martineau erroneously regards the state of
habitual sin as a reversion to natural necessity. He
writes: "The forfeiture of freedom, the relapse into
automatic necessity, is doubtless a most fearful penal-
ty for persistent unfaithfulness; but once incurred
it alters the complexion of all subsequent acts. They
no longer form fresh constituents in the aggregate of
guilt but stand outside in a separate record after its
account is closed. . . . The first impulse of the
prophets of righteousness when they see him thus is,
'he cannot cease from sin' and perhaps to predict for
him eternal retribution; but looking a little deeper,
they will rather say, 'he has lost the privilege of sin
and sunk away from the rank of persons into the destiny
of things." A *Study of Religion*, II, 108.

[9]Surely this is the significance of the words of Isaiah: "He maketh the judges of the earth as vanity" (Is. 40:23). In one of the great documents of social protest in Egypt, "The Eloquent Peasant," the accused peasant standing in the court of the Grand Visier declares: "Thou hast been set as a dam to save the poor man from drowning, but behold thou art thyself the flood." Cf. J.H. Breasted, *The Dawn of Conscience*, p. 190.

[10]One can never be certain whether Pelagian and Semi Pelagian criticisms of the Pauline doctrine are primarily directed against the literalistic corruptions of it or against its basic absurd but profound insights. A good instance of such a criticism is to be found in a modern Anglo-Catholic treatise on the subject: "Nor is it necessary to do more than point out the absurdity of the theory of 'original guilt,' which asserts that human beings are held responsible to an all-just Judge for an act which they did not commit and for physiological and psychological facts which they cannot help. . . . Those (if there be any such) who demand formal disproof of the belief that what is *ex hypothesi* an inherited psychological malady is regarded by God in the light of a voluntarily committed crime, may be referred to the scathing satire of Samuel Butler's *Erewhon*." N. P. Williams, *Ideas of the Fall and Original Sin*, p. 381.

[11]Cf. C. H. Dodd, *Epistle to the Romans*, p. 79.

[12]He writes: "So then Adam is in each one of us, for in him human nature itself sinned." *Apol. David altera*, 71.

[13]Cf. *Institutes*, Book II, Ch. i, par. 7. "We ought to be satisfied with this, that the Lord deposited with Adam the endowments he chose to confer on human nature; and therefore that when he lost the favours he had received *he lost them not only for himself* but for us all. Who will be solicitous about a transmission of the soul when he hears that Adam received the ornaments that he lost, *no less for us* than for himself? That they were given, not to one man only, *but to the whole human nature*." It must be admitted that Calvin confines Adam's identity with human nature to the original endowments. The loss of these endowments is conceived in terms of an hereditary relation between Adam and subsequent men, for Calvin continues: "For the children were so vitiated in their parent that they became contagious to their descen-

dants; there was in Adam such a spring of corruption that it is transfused from parents to children in a perpetual stream."

14Harnack declares: "The doctrine of original sin leads to Manichean dualism, which Augustine never surmounted, and is accordingly an impious and foolish dogma. . . His doctrine of concupiscence conduces the same view." *History of Dogma*, Vol. V, p. 217. Harnack's criticisms must of course be discounted, as those of other Christian moralists, because he is as unable to understand the doctrine of original sin, when stripped of its literalistic errors, as when stated in its crude form. His assertion that "turn as he will, Augustine affirms an evil nature and therefore a diabolical creator of the world" is simply not true.

15*Begriff der Angst*, p. 105.

Discussion Questions

1. Niebuhr does not think that a belief in an historical Adam and Eve is necessary in order to explicate the Christian doctrine of sin. Do you agree? Why or why not?

2. Can something, such as sin, be inevitable and yet not naturally or ontologically necessary?

3. Do you think that Niebuhr's position on the mysterious tempting influence (the devil) accurately portrays what occurs in the commission of sin?

4. Niebuhr says that the idea that sin is inherited from Adam destroys the notion of responsibility. Explain how.

THE PRINCIPALITIES AND
POWERS OF EVIL

Contemporary theologians have a keen appreciation
for the corporate nature of sin. Many thinkers have
devoted entire works to the principalities and powers
of this world; to how institutions and nations commit
sin and stand in need of redemption. In an early era
Walter Rauscenbusch wrote a surprisingly modern analysis of forces of evil that transcend the individual.
In the tradition of Rauscenbusch, Rosemary Ruether
writes of the corporate nature of sin and challenges us
to be liberators.

Many theologians and churchmen are concerned only
with individuals. Indeed, some do not think that it
is meaningful to speak of institutions as having a
life or character of their own. Most philosophers
would say that such language commits a "category mistake." It takes language which correctly refers to
individuals and uses it of organizations made up of
individuals as though the organization existed apart
from the persons who compose it.

Ruether holds that the Christian tradition
mandates through the biblical witness some theology
of corporate personality and corporate sin. She believes that if theologians fail to recognize this sort
of reality, then they are guilty of an extreme reductionism in their understanding of sin--not to mention
the neglect of a clear biblical motif. It is widely
recognized that substantial Old Testament passages
suggest a solidaristic vision of the nation as a
gigantic personality which stands before God. Equally
true is that the New Testament speaks of the Church
in this way.

Ruether emphasizes how an organization or institution garners authority over the individuals within it and imposes its standards on them. She would include among these groups such examples as fraternities, military organizations, corporations, political parties, governments, and even races. These she calls the principalities and powers of evil.

Ruether argues that organizations fall just like individuals do. And she holds that the greatest evils can be performed by institutions whose rationales and purposes for existence were the most noble. You may have surmised that this means that Ruether considers the Church's potential for evil to be the greatest of all. One is reminded of Luther's observation that the Church is the right place to meet God, but that it can also be the best place to hide from him.

Super-personal forces of evil, the corporate powers of this world, stand as much in need of redemption as do individuals. Indeed, individuals have little chance of experiencing full healing and renewal unless human social institutions are also engaged in these processes.

THE PRINCIPALITIES AND
POWERS OF EVIL*

The Biblical prophetic view, inheriting some of the unities of tribal religion, did not pull apart the individual from the community and the cosmos, but held these together within a holistic view of creation and its future promise of redemption. In Israel there was a development from tribal collectivism to a greater

*Source: From *Liberation Theology* by Rosemary Ruether. Copyright 1972 by the Missionary Society of St. Paul the Apostle in the state of New York. Used by permission of Paulist Press.

awareness of the participation and responsibility of the individual within the promise of the group, to be sure. But, even in St. Paul, the personal movement of conversion and reconciliation with God, cannot be separated from his ingathering into the community of reconciliation and promise, for these are two sides of one and the same thing. By the same token it is clear that, for St. Paul, the state of sin, alienation and brokenness between man and God, does not result simply in individual "bad acts" but stands within a corporate structure of alienation and oppression which has raised up a social and cosmic "anti-creation." This is what St. Paul calls "the Powers and Principalities" or the "Elementary Principles of the Universe." The individualistic concept of sin ignores this social-cosmic dimension of evil. A concentration on individualistic repentance has led, in Christianity, to a petty and privatistic concept of sin which involves the person in obsessive compunction about individual (mostly sexual) immorality, while having no ethical handle at all on the great structures of evil which we raise up corporately to blot out the face of God's good creation. In our "private confession" we have, in effect, involved people in a process of kneeling down to examine a speck of dirt on the floor while remaining oblivious to the monsters which are towering over their backs. Indeed privatistic religion systematically excludes attention to these corporate and social monsters by excluding them from their very definition of sin and repentance in a "religious" framework; i.e., "politics has nothing to do with religion."

A prophetic sense of sin might indeed acknowledge that sin begins in the personal "*cor curvum in se*," but its expression is corporate, social and even cosmic. Sin builds up a corporate structure of alienation and oppression which man, individually, cannot overcome, because he has fallen victim to his own evil creations as the very social fabric of his "world." This corporate structure of sin distorts the character of man in community and in creation so fundamentally that it can be visualized as a false "world"; an anti-society and anti-cosmos where man finds himself entrapped and alienated from his "true home," and he cries out for a transcendent liberation which will overcome "this world" and bring him back to his "original home in paradise." But "this world" is *not* God's creation, and so the solution to this dilemma is not a flight from creation to "heaven," but an overthrowing of this false world which has been created out of man's self-alienation, and a restoration of the world to its proper destiny as "the place where God's will is done on earth, as it is in heaven."

Nature and Grace

Liberation begins in grace and moves from this foundation in grace to the possibility of self-judgment and repentance. Liberation is not a fruit or reward of repentance, so much as it is the ground and possibility of repentance. Liberation begins in a gratuitous mystery of freedom that happens within our situation, yet beyond the capacities of the alienated situation itself. It is experienced as a free gift "from above." It is only in that gratuitous and transcendent mystery of freedom, that dawns upon us without our "deserving" it, and before we have articulated our need for it, that we find ourselves able to enter into this articulation and transformation. Repentance then is simply the power to disaffiliate our identity from the false and oppressive power systems of fallen reality. But the gift of liberation, although alien and transcendent to the situation of sin, is not alien to "our natures," but springs from the same "ground" as man's original foundation. So it is not properly seen as "supernatural," but as a restoration of man to his true self, and a reintegration of creation with its true destiny as "God's Kingdom."

Because Christianity adopted in its early formation a gnosticizing separation of redemption from creation, it has created a false dilemma of "nature and grace" which was foreign to the Hebraic perspective. (It has also projected upon Judaism the negative side of this dichotomy by defining its view of salvation as "carnal" and "materialistic." Thus Christian anti-Semitism and Christian gnosticism are two sides of a similar distortion.) Today we must strive for a perspective on liberation that overcomes these dichotomies. We must recognize that the movement of revolt against false and oppressive worlds of "Powers and Principalities" is integral to the renewal of the world whereby creation and bodily existence become the vehicle and theophany of God's transcendent appearing; i.e., creation becomes the place for the appearance of God's *Shechinah*. It is around such an interpretation of God's *Shechinah* that Christianity might be able to reestablish with Judaism some new dialogue about the meaning of "incarnation." God's presence does not appear just in one time and place "once for all," but wherever reconciliation is established and man glimpses his unity and the unity of the world with its transcendent foundation and meaning. A religious culture may pick out a particular place where this appearing is seen "normatively"; i.e., Jesus or the Torah or Buddha, but this doctrine of "incarnation" is not just "about" this one place or person, but this one place or person operates as a norm for discerning the nature of this "presence" wherever it happens.

The Oppressor and the Oppressed as a Model
for Liberation Theology

Recent theologies of liberation have stressed the role of the "oppressed community" as the primary locus of the power for repentance and judgment. God's liberation is seen as coming first to the "poor." God liberates the slaves from the oppressive system of power, symbolized by Egypt. God comes to overturn the oppressive reign of imperial power symbolized by Babylon (Rome; Amerika).

It is true that such a dualism of the "children of light" and the "children of darkness" can be extracted from prophetic thinking. However, this dualism, in its polarized form, appears primarily in the literature of apocalypticism. The thinking of the prophets addressed Israel as, simultaneously, the community of Promise and the community which must repent and be judged. Liberation, therefore, cannot be divorced from a sense of self-judgment and an identification with the community which is judged. It cannot be merely a movement of revolt against and judgment of an "alien community" for which one takes no responsibility. The paranoid projection of all evil upon the "nations," whereby Israel is seen simply as the "suffering saints," distorts this prophetic dialectic. Indeed such a total polarization is not found even in the apocalyptic writings, which never fail to address Israel itself as the one which must repent and be judged and return to obedience. Christianity inherited, through apocalyptic sectarian Judaism (further accentuated by the break between the sectarian apocalyptic community and ethnic Israel), the possibility of a one-sided distortion of the prophetic dialectic that would locate one community as the "oppressed saints," and the heirs of the Promise, while projecting upon the oppressors (Rome) and the rejectors (ethnic Israel) all evil and condemnation.

Such a viewpoint which judges "God's people" and "God's enemy" from the standpoint of the oppressed and oppressors has, nevertheless, a real theological

validity to it. Contextually, this historical situation
does indeed become the primary place of prophetic
discernment. Marxist systems, Black theology and Latin
American theologies of liberation, constructed on
this apocalyptic sectarian model, can carry a process
of judgment and liberation a considerable distance.
But, at a certain point, this model for the theology
of liberation begins to reveal the limitations and
disabilities inherent in its inadequate foundations.

There is a sense in which those who are primarily
the victims of an oppressive system are also those who
can most readily disaffiliate their identities with it,
for they have the least stake in its perpetuation.
In their revolt against it, they can thus become the
prophetic community, which witnesses against the false
empire of the "beast" and points to "God's Kingdom."
But, in their very situation as victims, they have
also been distorted in their inward being in a way
that does not immediately make them realized models of
redeemed humanity; i.e., the victims are not "saints."
They have a very considerable task of inward liberation
to do. They have been victimized by their powerlessness, their fear and their translation of these into
an internal appropriation of subservient and menial
roles. They have internalized the negative image projected upon them by the dominant society. They cower
before the masters, but are also filled with a self-
contempt which makes them self-destructive and fratri-
cidal toward their fellows within the oppressed community. Typically the oppressed turn their frustration
inward, destroying themselves and each other, not the
masters.

Liberation for the oppressed thus is experienced
as a veritable resurrection of the self. Liberation
is a violent exorcism of the demons of self-hatred and
self-destruction which have possessed them and the
resurrection of autonomy and self-esteem, as well as
the discovery of a new power and possibility of community with their own brothers and sisters in suffering.
Anger and pride, two qualities viewed negatively in
traditional Christian spirituality, are the vital
"virtues" in the salvation of the oppressed community.
Through anger and pride the oppressed community receives the power to transcend self-hatred and recover
a sense of integral personhood. Anger, here, is felt
as the power to revolt against and judge a system of
oppression to which one was formerly a powerless and
buried victim. Pride is experienced as the recovery
of that authentic humanity and good created nature

"upon which God looked in the beginning and, behold, it was very good." Anger and pride thus stand initially within the context of a prophetic dialectic of judgment and the renewal of creation.

However, at that point where all evil is merely projected upon an alien community, so that judgment is seen merely as rejection of that "other" group of persons, and salvation simply as self-affirmation, *per se*, (without regard to a normative view of humanity), then what is valid in this initial perception is quickly distorted. The leaders of the oppressed community are not incorrect when they recognize that they have, as their primary responsibility, the leading of their own people through a process of self-exorcism and renewed humanity. So there is a sense where it is true that they "do not have the time" to be worried about the humanization of the oppressor. Yet they must also keep somewhere in the back of their minds the idea that the dehumanization of the oppressor is really their primary problem, to which their own dehumanization is related primarily in a relationship of effect to cause. Therefore, to the extent that they are not at all concerned about maintaining an authentic prophetic address to the oppressors; to the extent that they repudiate them as persons as well as the beneficiaries of false power, and conceive of liberation as a mere reversal of this relationship; a rejection of their false situation of power in order to transfer this same kind of power to themselves, they both abort their possibilities as a liberating force for the oppressors, and, ultimately, derail their own power to liberate themselves. Quite simply, what this means is that one cannot dehumanize the oppressors without ultimately dehumanizing oneself, and aborting the possibilities of the liberation movement into an exchange of roles of oppressor and oppressed. By projecting all evil upon the oppressors and regarding their own oppressed condition as a stance of "instant righteousness," they forfeit finally their own capacity for self-criticism. Their revolt, then, if successful, tends to rush forward to murder and self-aggrandizement, and the institution of a new regime where all internal self-criticism is squelched. Seven demons return to occupy the house from which the original demon has been driven, and the last state of that place is worse than the first. Such has been the tendency of modern revolutionary movements patterned on the apocalyptic, sectarian concept.

The oppressor community, of course, has a similar

301

problem in finding who it is and what it should do in relationship to the judgment and revolt of the oppressed. The first tendency of the oppressors is, of course, to respond to the liberation movement simply by projecting upon it the negative side of their own self-righteousness. Since they have already identified their own false power with the "Kingdom of Righteousness," their initial tendency is simply to identify those in revolt against this power as the "evil ones" who are ever at work to undermine the security of "God's Elect." Within this paranoid framework, each side merely sees itself as the "saints," and the others as the "beast," and no authentic communication takes place. This paranoid view, by the way, is not merely true of traditional clerical and sacral societies, such as Christendom of the European *ancien régime*. It is equally true of revolutionary societies, which have likewise been founded upon the appropriation of messianic self-imagery, such as the USSR and the USA. These modern revolutionary societies have virtually reestablished the traditional problem of Constantinian societies, although it is the opinion of this author that the USSR has a deeper problem since it passed directly from Byzantine Caesaro-papism to Marxist sectarian apocalypticism, as its political identity, without having assimilated the fruits of liberalism that could provide a theory and an institutional base for on-going self-criticism and self-correction.

Yet there are also elements in the dominant society that *are* ready to respond sympathetically to the revolt of the oppressed and to make this revolt the occasion for their own self-judgment. It is this prophetic element in the dominant society, what is usually seen as the "alienated intelligentsia," that has been, typically, the crucial mediating force for translating the protest of the oppressed into an opportunity for repentance in the dominant society. But this mediating role is also fraught with dangers and possibilities of self-delusion. The vitality of this mediating role becomes aborted when this "alienated intelligentsia" becomes concerned primarily with its own self-purification through disaffiliation with its own class, race or nation; when it seeks primarily a parasitic identification with the oppressed, who are viewed, idealistically, as the "suffering saviors," who can do no wrong or in whom all is to be excused. The prophet in the dominant society, thus becomes involved in an endless movement of self-hatred and a utopian quest for identification with and acceptance by the victims, making it impossible for him to see either

302

side of the social equation as it really is.

Instinctively the victimized community rejects such a person, no matter how vehement his repudiation of his own people, because they sense that, in seeking to identify with them, he is taking over a leadership role which they need to learn to do for themselves. From his very social background he brings to them so much knowledge, in the way of self-confidence, expertise and familiarity with power, that he easily drowns their own feeble attempts to learn these things for themselves. Thus he interferes with their own self-discovery. Moreover, the alienated oppressor can never disaffiliate himself enough from his own society, as long as it continues in power and he automatically remains the beneficiary of that fact, to be seen by the oppressed as anything other than an extension of that fact of power over their lives in a novel form. Their own responses to the alienated oppressor who seeks to "help" them are doubtless very confused. This confusion reflects their own lack of inward liberation that makes it impossible for them to see him as other than a continuing symbol of oppression. This reflects the fact that they have not yet broken the hold of this power over their lives, and so they cannot deal with him as simply a "person" or an "exception to the rule," but react to him as a symbol of that power despite his protestations to the contrary. Yet they also discern, in a confused but valid way, that in merely adopting the echo of their own sectarian paranoia, in merely repudiating his own people and seeking identification with them, the alienated oppressor is also aborting the role of mediatorship to his own community, which is the only role in which he can be useful to them. In other words, they do not need him primarily to join what they are doing, but to play a complementary role in relation to that struggle for self-determination, by helping to get his own community off their backs so they can have a place in which to breathe. In seeking primarily to join their struggle and to move away from contact with his own people, he fails to play this vital mediating role which he alone can do for them and which they cannot do for themselves, short of successful violence.

Only when protest and response remain in dialogue in such a way that the society which is condemned is also addressed as a community which has fallen away from its own authentic promise, can there be a liberation without ultimate violence; a liberation that can end in reconciliation and new brotherhood. This cannot

easily be proclaimed as a possibility before the conditions for its realization have begun to appear. It
can happen only on the other side of "Black power" and
"Black pride" in the black community and repentance and
surrender of unjust power on the part of the white
community. This hope for a new community is aborted
when the black prophet refuses to have any part with
liberating the oppressor as a part of his own self-
liberation. It is also aborted when the white prophet
seeks merely self-exculpating identification with the
victims, rather than remaining in repentant and suffering identification with his own people, until he
can translate this judgment to them as their own self-
judgment. This was the vision of Martin Luther King.
King never forgot to address Amerika, the oppressor, as
also the land of promise for black man and white man
alike. This vision, declared obsolete, when King was
murdered, was not so much over and done with as it
represented a proleptic reaching for a prophetic wholeness, for which neither black Americans nor white
Americans were ready at that time. King's vision
pointed to a Black ideology beyond black racism, and
beyond white paternalism or white self-exculpation,
to the only validly prophetic way of doing an American
theology. All theologies of liberation, whether done
in a black or a feminist or a Third World perspective,
will be abortive of the liberation they seek, unless
they finally go beyond the apocalyptic, sectarian
model of the oppressor and the oppressed. The oppressed
must rise to a perspective that affirms a universal
humanity as the ground of their own self-identity, and
also to a power for self-criticism. The alienated
oppressor must learn what it means to be truly responsible for whom and what he is.

Discussion Questions

1. Do you agree that institutions, organizations and
nations can become corporate personalities, taking on
a life of their own? If so, what are some examples?

2. Ruether holds that the church can be the most evil
of all institutions. Do you agree? Why?

3. Corporate personalities are supported by myths.
What are some myths about your nation, your denomina-

tion, your race? Do these stand in need of reform?

4. Can an individual within a corporate entity be
guilty of its sinful policies or decisions? Compare
Ezekiel's teaching on individual responsibility to
the passages in Joshua 7:1-26 and Exodus 32.

5. What is your opinion of the liberation concept as
Ruether outlines it? Is liberation a legitimate theme
of Jesus' ministry?

RETROSPECTIVE

Intensified technological and medical progress hold forth the possibility that future generations will differ significantly from the present. The differences will be in native intellectual ability and other psychological, chemical and genetic phenomena capable of alteration. What if these changes reduce or eliminate the anxiety of the human situation? What if humans no longer commit traditional moral violations such as stealing, killing, etc.?

At the same time, how are humans to retain significance if machines not only think, but become reflective? And what if animals develop language and thought skills--naturally or artificially--which enable them to claim personhood?

Scientific accounts of the human being are incomplete. They neither establish the Christian understanding of man, nor disprove it. Christian theologians will go on affirming the uniqueness of humans among other created beings. Furthermore, the doctrine of sin prohibits Christians from becoming utopian about humanity--even if tremendous advances in genetics and biology do occur. Humans will sin, derailing even the most promising advances this history has proven time and again. And responsibility for action, no matter what we learn about the biological causes of value preference, will always be a socially required notion.

The two most serious inadequacies of the modern era are its failure to recognize the sinfulness of humanity and yet, secondly, its tremendous sense of inferiority. Although these may appear to be contradictory, they are actually integrally related. Humans in the modern world are very much aware of the small

gap between themselves and other mammals. The result
has been that human purposes, values, and even human
life itself has depreciated devastatingly. Theologians cannot restore dignity by means of a doctrine of
the human being which ignores or denies the scientific
data. Rather, Christian doctrine must seek what David
Tracy calls a critical correlation with science.

This inferiority complex of contemporary man
contributes to the failure to recognize human sinfulness and weakness. In earlier centuries theologians
called attention to the human subterfuge and rationalization that denied sin, or at least never admitted
that the root of moral chaos lay in humanity itself.
Today, however, the reason why sin is so little
recognized is different. The prevailing response is,
"Oh, I am only human." The close relation to other
species supported so thoroughly by human science has
provided a ready rationalization for sin.

Certainly the most valued of anthropological
doctrines is the promise of a new humanity. The
reduction of humanity toward a higher destiny is
related to the doctrine of salvation and it is to
that subject we now turn.

PART FIVE

CHRIST AND SALVATION

CHRIST AND SALVATION

In the Gospel according to Matthew (Mt. 16:13) Jesus of Nazareth asks his closest followers, "Who do men say that I am?" Since that time the main tradition of Christian believers has been united in the answer. They regard Jesus as the divine-human Savior of the world, the person in and through whom God reconciled a rebellious world to himself. Calendars are dated *Anno Domini* or *Anno salutis humani* (in the year of human salvation).

The task of Christology (the doctrine of Christ) is not exclusively theoretical or metaphysical. The primary responsibility of the Christian theologian is not to explain how divinity and humanity can dwell in a particular person who lived at a specific time and in a specific place. Of course, such explanation is important and necessary. However, it is not primary. The most important task of Christology is to explicate why the particular person, Jesus of Nazareth, is understood to be significant.

Accordingly, Christology is inseparably tied to Soteriology (the doctrine of salvation). This inseparable tie also provides a clue to the method for doing Christology. Both Christology and Soteriology grew out of the experience of the earliest followers of Jesus. The words and deeds of Jesus gave new life and brought reconciliation to God. This was true not just of his death but of his pre-Passion life as well. These words and deeds implied a Soteriology and Christology, and these emerged together.

It has been customary to speak of the person of Christ and then of the work of Christ. The former topic is concerned with who Christ was. The latter topic is concerned with what Christ has done for us.

But this is an artificial and misleading distinction.
Many Christologies begin with an understanding of
Christ's person on the assumption that his unique
identity made possible his works. "Because Jesus was
divine he could work miracles," is a popular way of
expressing this model. But historically, the movement
was different. The works of Christ were witnessed,
and his redeeming presence experienced, and then some
explication was made about what kind of a person he
must be. In technical terms this means that earliest
Christology was functional, not ontological. Or, to
use Wolfhart Pannenberg's distinction, Christology
originated "from below," from human encounter with
Christ, not "from above," handed down from on high.

This does not mean that any particular understanding of Christ, his person or role in redemption,
has enjoyed unqualified acceptance in Christian tradition. The Christological debate became so intense
during the first four centuries of Christian history
that the unity of both Church and Empire was threatened.
In a series of conciliar decisions, climaxing in the
Council of Chalcedon (451), the traditional *two-nature*
Christology was formulated. These church fathers
affirmed that Christ was

> . . . one and the same Son, our Lord Jesus Christ,
> at once complete in Godhead and complete in man-
> hood, truly God and truly man, . . . of one sub-
> stance with the Father as regards his Godhead, and
> at the same time of one substance with us as
> regards his manhood. . . . As regards his Godhead,
> begotten of the Father before all ages, but yet as
> regards his manhood, begotten for us men and for
> our salvation, of Mary the Virgin . . . ; one and
> the same Christ, Son, Lord, only begotten, recog-
> nized in two natures, without confusion, without
> change, without division, without separation. . . .

Historically, there has been a remarkable unity
of allegiance to the two-natures doctrine in Christianity. In practice, of course, theologians and laymen
alike fail to balance the two-natures of Christ as
delicately as does the creed. Donald Baillie discusses this recurring and even endemic problem with all
Christology. In doing so, he introduces the various
heretical traditions. Baillie maintains that Christians must recognize the inherent paradox of the
incarnation and admit that human reason and language
are not capable of explicating the person of Christ.

It was Friedrich Schleiermacher who first laid
the axe to the two-natures doctrine. He argued that
the word "nature" means *what a thing is*. Thus, no
thing or person could be said to have two natures.
His critique marked the beginning of a sustained
examination of Christology by modern theologians.
Baillie's approach which appeals to paradox has been
the common solution.

Of late, however, another path is being followed.
A growing number of contemporary thinkers have appropriated a new metaphysic which may be more helpful
to theology than the substance philosophy upon which
Chalcedon is based. In this collection the essay by
Peter H. Hamilton uses process philosophy to explicate
an understanding of Christ which avoids the appeal to
paradox. Hamilton argues that "God was in Christ" is
not a mythological statement. He believes this affirmation corresponds to an ontological reality which can
be opened to understanding through the use of process
philosophy. He attempts to make this intelligible
and, at the same time, to offer an understanding of
Jesus' uniqueness.

As examples of two fundamental Christological
problems I have included the essays by Raymond E.
Brown and Wolfhart Pannenberg. Brown is probably
the preeminent New Testament scholar in America,
certainly he has no peer among his Roman Catholic
colleagues. His essay deals with the Virginal Conception of Jesus and he presents dogmatic and scriptural arguments on both sides of the question of its
historicity.

Pannenberg's essay, which first appeared in
English in 1965, is an analysis of the resurrection
narratives. It is a fine example of doing Christology
from below. The essay also contains a well developed
position on the significance of the resurrection for
the pre-Easter activity of Jesus.

In an important discussion of Soteriology (atonement) from his *Systematic Theology*, Gordon Kaufman's
essay is an attempt to show how Christology and
Soteriology are inseparable. Beginning with Jesus,
Kaufman observes, there is a creative process that is
actually going on in history. God is penetrating
history, reshaping human rebellion into obedience to
God. In Jesus, the at-one-ment of God and man really
began. Jesus was one with God, and without him men
cannot become at-one with God. This is the sum of

Christology and Soteriology.

CHRISTOLOGY AT THE CROSSROADS

When it became increasingly evident that the
Gospels were not mere biographies of Jesus, but that
they were faith interpretations of his life, a crisis
developed in Christological understanding. Donald
Baillie sets the stage for a discussion of this crisis
when he briefly summarizes the history of Christological inquiry from the late nineteenth century. Those
theologians not content with the Christ of Faith
reported in the Gospels began a Quest for the Historical Jesus. They wanted to penetrate behind the layers
of theological understanding to Jesus' actual words
and deeds.

It was Rudolf Bultmann who used the tools of
biblical criticism to establish his contention that
the historical Jesus could never be recovered. Indeed,
he maintained that the search itself was a sign of
unbelief and lack of faith. Salvation was experienced
through one's trust in the Christ of Faith, not the
Jesus of History.

Bultmann's own students rejected their mentor's
approach as too subjective. They held that some
historical foundation for faith was necessary and
recoverable--at least with probability. It is this
latter interest in a New Quest for the Historical
Jesus which Baillie thinks informs contemporary
Christology.

Baillie believes this movement has led to a new
appreciation of Jesus' humanity, and that it provides
a necessary corrective to the heresy of Docetism which
overemphasizes Jesus' divinity. Baillie discusses
the limits of Jesus' knowledge and ability. He also
offers an explanation of the senses in which Jesus
can be said to have needed a religious life, and to

315

have undergone genuine moral struggle.

At first sight such a discussion may appear heretical, but Baillie reminds the reader that the Christian doctrine of Christology does not mean that Jesus was not a man but a God. He discusses the numerous heresies about Christ, and each student should make an effort to master the definitions of Arianism, Apollinarianism, Adoptionism and Docetism.

For Baillie the key to Christology is not just the Chalcedonian creed. He encourages the theologian to pursue Jesus' self-understanding as it can be reconstructed through the Gospels. And he considers it very important that Jesus himself expresses his self-consciousness in the most paradoxical of ways: "I, . . . yet not I, but the Father." Paradox is the only proper explication of Christology, Baillie contends. And this he considers to be the *mysterium Christi* (mystery of Christ).

CHRISTOLOGY AT THE CROSS-ROADS*

About half a century ago a distinguished British theologian spoke of the recovery of the historical Christ as the most distinctive and determinative element in modern theology, and went on to speak of the rejuvenescence of theology which was the result. That was by no means a peculiar or merely individual judgment, but may be taken as fairly representative of its age, and every student of theology to-day understands exactly what was meant. But every wide-awake student knows also that the theological scene has changed again in the most unexpected way; so that if a theo-

*Source: From *God Was In Christ* by Donald M. Baillie. Copyright 1948 by Charles Scribner's Sons. Used with permission of Charles Scribner's Sons.

logian of the 'nineties or the early nineteen-hundreds
were to play Rip van Winkle and come alive again today, he would rub his eyes in bewilderment at the new
orientation of the problem of Christology. Theological
thought has largely left behind the movement which we
may symbolize by the phrase 'the Jesus of history';
and it is highly important for us to understand the
ways in which that has been done, if we are to grasp
the Christological problem of to-day.

But at the same time, and even in the same circles, there has emerged another tendency which may
seem to point in an opposite direction, and which
certainly carries us far away from what I have called
the 'Jesus of history' movement: the tendency to lose
interest in the reconstruction of the historical human
figure of Jesus. This tendency may be found both in
the historical criticism and in the dogmatic theology
of the present time, and the two are closely connected.
In the historico-critical realm the determinative fact
is the emergence of the relatively new method which is
called *Formgeschichte,* Form Criticism; and its application to the Gospels is a movement of immense significance; raising some old theological problems in a new
and acuter form, and presenting to Christology a
challenge which has not yet been fully faced. It
does all this because it constantly seems to be questioning whether, and how far, the Gospels can be, or
ought to be, used as means of recapturing the historical Jesus. By shaking confidence in the possibility,
Form Criticism tends to shift the interest. In this
way it plays into the hands of the contemporary movement in dogmatic theology which subordinates the Jesus
of history to the Christ of dogma, and whose voice
would say not only 'No more docetism,' but also 'No
more historicism.' It is indeed a new variety of
historical scepticism about the Gospels as sources
for a 'life of Jesus' or a reconstruction of His
personality. This is the second of the two factors
that go to make the Christological situation and
problem of to-day.

The End of Docetism

It may safely be said that practically all schools
of theological thought to-day take the full humanity
of our Lord more seriously than has ever been done
before by Christian theologians. It has always, indeed, been of the essence of Christian orthodoxy to
make Jesus wholly human as well as wholly divine, and
in the story of the controversies which issued in the

317

decisions of the first four General Councils it is impressive to see the Church contending as resolutely for His full humanity as for His full deity. But the Church was building better than it knew, and its ecumenical decisions were wiser than its individual theologians in this matter. Or should we rather say that it did not fully realize the implications of declaring that in respect of His human nature Christ is consubstantial with ourselves? At any rate it was continually haunted by a docetism which made His human nature very different from ours and indeed largely explained it away as a matter of simulation or 'seeming' rather than reality. Theologians shrank from admitting human growth, human ignorance, human mutability, human struggle and temptation, into their conception of the Incarnate Life, and treated it as simply a divine life lived in a human body (and sometimes even this was conceived as essentially different from our bodies) rather than a truly human life lived under the psychical conditions of humanity. The cruder forms of docetism were fairly soon left behind, but in its more subtle forms the danger continued in varying degrees to dog the steps of theology right through the ages until modern times.

But now the belief in the full humanity of Christ has come into its own.

It seems worth while to illustrate this in some further detail.

(a) *The human limits of our Lord's knowledge.* Right through the Patristic and medieval periods there was a shrinking from the idea that Jesus' *knowledge* was limited by human conditions, and often even a docetic explaining away of such passages in the Gospels as seemed to deny His omniscience.[1] It is a long time now since theology, not only 'rationalistic' but 'catholic,' began to recover from this weakness and to learn that Jesus' knowledge was essentially the limited knowledge of a man. I need only refer to Charles Gore's celebrated essay on 'The Consciousness of our Lord in His Mortal Life,'[2] in which the Bishop found it necessary deliberately to part company with Patristic and Scholastic views of this matter and to return to the impression gained from the New Testament that Jesus' knowledge was limited by human conditions. This line of thought is carried much farther in Professor Leonard Hodgson's book, *And Was Made Man,* where it is boldly, yet most reverently, maintained that even our Lord's knowledge of His unique relationship to God came to Him empirically as He moved about among men, and it is suggested that, e.g., His knowledge of the past history of the woman of Samaria in John iv, 17, 18, if we are to credit such a detail at all, may be rendered credible not by the ascription to Jesus of omniscience or superhuman ways of knowledge, but by the fact that Orientals do seem even to-day to have sometimes a mysterious gift of insight into what is going on in other people's minds. 'His knowledge was limited to that which could find a channel into His human mind.'[3]

(b) *The human character of our Lord's miracles.* If there is one particularly fruitful insight that has been gained in the modern world in the interpretation of the Gospel story, it is this: that the problem of the 'mighty works' can be disposed of neither by denying them out of hand as unhistorical, nor by accepting them as sheerly supernatural portents because a divine Christ can do anything, but is to be met only by regarding them as works of faith, wrought by the power of God in response to human faith for which all things are possible. There was a time when the miracles were regularly used by Christian apologetics as 'signs and wonders' to prove the divinity of Christ. But there has been a growing awareness that this interpretation is quite at variance with the mind of our Lord Himself. He condemned the desire to have 'signs and wonders' as a basis for faith, and He plainly thought of His works of healing as manifestations of God's love and power which are at the disposal of all men if only they will believe. They were works of God's power, but they were also works of human faith. 'Your faith has cured you.'[4]

(c) *The human character of our Lord's moral and religious life.* This follows from what has just been said. Our Lord's life on earth was a life of faith, and His victory was the victory of faith. His temptations were real temptations, which it was difficult and painful for Him to resist. His fight against them was not a sham fight, but a real struggle. When we say *non potuit peccare,* we do not mean that He was completely raised above the struggle against sin, as we conceive the life of the redeemed to be in heaven, *in patria.* In the days of His flesh our Lord was *viator.* And when we say that He was incapable of sinning, we mean that He was the supreme case of what we can say with limited and relative truth about many a good man. 'He is incapable of doing a mean or under-hand thing,' we say about a man whom we know to be honourable; and so we say in a more universal and absolute way about Jesus: *Non potuit peccare,* without in any way reducing the reality of His conflict with His temptations. 'He overcame them exactly as every man who does so has overcome temptation--by the constancy of the will.'[5] Christians might have learnt this lesson about our Lord from the Epistle to the Hebrews from the start, but it is only in the modern world that it has been fully realized.

The same thing is even truer when we come to what we may call our Lord's own personal religion. H. R. Mackintosh wrote in 1912: 'Attention has recently been drawn, in a special manner, to the perfectly human quality of our Lord's religious life,'[6] and he went on to develop this sympathetically, dwelling especially upon Jesus' habit of prayer to God. To our forefathers of earlier ages the phrase 'our Lord's religious life' would have sounded quite incongruous. 'The personal religion of Jesus!' How could God incarnate have a religious life, a personal religion? To speak of Jesus as a religious man would have astonished them. Yet Jesus was a religious man, and we should now say that this is implied in the reality of the Incarnation, that if His life was really a divine *incarnation,* it *must* have been a life of human religious experience, human faith in God. Hardly any school of Christian thought would now deny this, though some would maintain, as we shall see, that the significance of Jesus for us as the Word made flesh has nothing to do with His 'religious experience.'

The Christian doctrine of the Incarnation does not mean that Jesus was not a man but a God. The New Testament writers knew very well that He was a man, and spoke of Him quite unequivocally as such; and few theologians now would make the distinction of saying that He is rather 'Man' than 'a man,' though that distinction has sometimes been made in the past. Moreover, Christianity does not teach that Jesus was 'a God.' Indeed if we are using language in a truly Christian way, there is no such entity as 'a God.' There is only one God, and in the Christian sense there could not conceivably be more. Tertullian said: *'Deus, si non unus est, non est.'*[7] And Peter Damiani, the medieval divine, commenting on the words uttered by the serpent in Eden ('Ye shall be as gods,' Gen. iii, 5) remarked that the Devil was the first grammarian when he taught men to give a plural to the word 'God.'[8] It should have neither a plural nor the indefinite article. It is a proper name.

320

Again, Christianity does not teach that Jesus was some kind of intermediate being, neither God nor man in the full sense, but something between. That mythical kind of being is quite familiar in ancient pagan religion, not to speak of Christian angelology; and so far as Christology is concerned, that is very much the conception of Christ that constituted the greatest of the heresies, Arianism. That is something quite different from the Christian doctrine of the Incarnation. When a New Testament writer tells us that 'there is one God and one Mediator between God and men,' he does not mean that the Mediator belongs to some intermediate type of being, for he goes on at once to describe the Mediator as 'a man, Christ Jesus.'[9] Jesus was not something between God and Man: He was God *and* Man.

But, again, this does not mean that Jesus was simply God or the eternal Son of God inhabiting a human body for thirty years on earth, so that while the living physical organism was human, the mind or spirit was divine. That is another of the great heresies, the Apollinarian.[10] It would mean that Jesus was not truly and perfectly human, but that it was a case of God having a partly human experience, or even taking a temporary human disguise; which is much more like the old pagan stories of divine theophanies than like the Christian idea of Incarnation. It would mean that in the experience of Jesus we could draw a line between the divine and the human element, a boundary where the human ceased and the divine began, so that each was limited by the other. But Christianity teaches that there was no such boundary or limit to either the one or the other. Each covered the whole field on different planes. Jesus is God and Man ἀχωρίστως, without boundary.

But further, it does not mean that Jesus began by being a man, and grew into divinity, became divine. That is another idea that has often emerged in Christological thought but has never satisfied the Church. It is broadly what is known as Adoptionism. Christian theology has indeed sometimes, both in the early Greek Fathers and in the Eastern Orthodox tradition down to the present day, conceived the salvation of each one of us as a sort of deification, by which we are changed into the divine nature. But it has never said this about Jesus Christ. It has taught that what He is by nature we can become by adoption; or even that He became man in order that we might become God. This last expression itself must be suspect, because if taken

321

strictly it would seem to imply either a pantheistic conception or the idea that there can be more gods than one. But even to speak of a man becoming *divine* involves us in manifest errors. It is not an accident that the adjective 'divine' hardly occurs in the New Testament.[11] The word belongs to quite a different world.[12] Indeed it seems alien to the New Testament writers, in all the varieties of their Christology, not only to say that Jesus *became* divine, but even to say that He was or is divine. That is not how they would have put it, because in the world of the New Testament, even though it is written in Greek, the word God is a proper name, and no one could be divine except God Himself. Therefore it is more congenial to Christian theology to say that Jesus is God (with the further refinements of meaning provided by the doctrine of the Trinity) than to speak of Him as divine; and certainly it will not say that He *became* divine.

Does Christianity, then, teach that God changed into a Man? Is that the meaning of 'and was made man?' That at a certain point of time God, or the Son of God, was transformed into a human being for a period of about thirty years? It is hardly necessary to say that the Christian doctrine of the Incarnation means nothing like that. Such a conception bristles with errors. God does not change, and it would be grotesque to suggest that the Incarnation has anything in common with the *metamorphoses* of ancient pagan mythology. Moreover, it is highly important to remember that, according to Christian teaching, the deity and the humanity of Christ are not merely successive stages, as if they could not co-exist simultaneously. If no boundary can be drawn between them by way of analysing the constituents of His make-up (ἀδιαιρέτως, ἀχωρίστως), neither can temporal boundaries be drawn, as if He had been first God, then Man, and then, after the days of His flesh were past, God again, with manhood left behind. These are all travesties of what Christian faith has to say about the Incarnation.

The misinterpretations that I have been rejecting in the last few pages are so crude and elementary, and the disclaimers are so familiar and obvious, that these pages must seem absurdly superfluous in a theological essay. Yet this rudimentary critique of old heresies has its own uses even to-day, as we may see in the chapters that follow. The total effect of the disclaimers is to repudiate every possible over-simplification of the doctrine of the Incarnation.

But the procedure has been entirely negative, and now
we are left with an immense paradox upon our hands,
the paradox of the God-Man. Some will maintain that
this is as far as theology can ever go, and that it
is vain for us to try to penetrate the mystery of *how*
Jesus is both God and Man, since we are only men ourselves and not God. But it is impossible to acquiesce
in the idea that nothing can be said about the Incarnation except in negatives, or that nothing more can
be said than what was said in the great Creeds, which
enshrined the mystery without explaining it.

True God and True Man

A very great deal has been written by biblical
scholars during the last century on the question as
to what Jesus held and taught about Himself and His
place in God's purpose, and a common phrase which
figured as the title of many discussions a generation
ago was 'the (messianic) self-consciousness of Jesus.'
The phrase was doubtless legitimate and useful.[13] And
yet it has a somewhat unnatural sound, because in the
Jesus of the Gospels it is not 'self-consciousness'
that strikes us, but God-consciousness. Throughout
the story we get the impression of one who, with all
His high claims, kept thinking far less of Himself
than of the Father. Even in Him--or should we say,
supremely in Him?--self-consciousness was swallowed up
in His deep and humble and continual consciousness of
God. When He worked cures, it was to His heavenly
Father that He looked up for aid, and it was to God
rather than to Himself that He expected people to give
the glory when they were cured.[14] As regards goodness,
He was not conscious of possessing it Himself independently, but looked away from Himself to God for it.
When once a man addressed Him as 'Good Master,' he
replied: 'Why do you call me good? No one is good
except God.'[15] If we take the reply seriously, we
shall surely find in it the supreme instance of that
peculiar kind of humility which Christianity brought
into the world. It was not self-depreciation: it was
rather a complete absence of the kind of self-consciousness which makes a man think of his own degree of
merit, and a dominating sense of dependence on God.
The Man in whom God was incarnate would claim nothing
for Himself as a Man, but ascribed all glory to God.

It is, however, when we turn to the Fourth Gospel
that we find on the lips of Jesus the most remarkable
expressions of this central paradox of Christian
experience. I cannot in this place discuss the

question as to how far the great Johannine discourses give us the *ipsissima verba* of Jesus; but it is in any case sufficiently impressive that in the Gospel which gives us the most transcendently high Christology to be found in the New Testament, Christology is more than anywhere else interwoven with the paradoxical human confession: 'I, . . . yet not I, but the Father.' On the one hand there is Jesus making His human choice from moment to moment, a choice on which in a sense everything depends. 'He that sent me is with me: he hath not left me alone; for I do always the things that are pleasing to him.'[16] 'Therefore doth the Father love me, because I lay down my life, that I may take it again. No one taketh it away from me, but I lay it down of myself. I have power to lay it down, and I have power to take it again. This commandment received I from my Father.'[17] But on the other hand, all His words and all His choices depended on the Father. 'I can of myself do nothing: as I hear, I judge: and my judgment is righteous, because I seek not mine own will, but the will of him that sent me.'[18] Verily, verily, I say unto you, the Son can do nothing of himself, but what he seeth the Father doing: for what things soever he doeth, these the Son also doeth in like manner.'[19] 'My teaching is not mine, but his that sent me. . . . He that speaketh from himself seeketh his own glory: but he that seeketh the glory of him that sent him, the same is true, and no unrighteousness is in him.'[20] 'I am not come of myself, but he that sent me is true, whom ye know not. I know him; because I am from him, and he sent me.'[21] 'I spake not from myself; but the Father which sent me, he hath given me a commandment, what I should say, and what I should speak.'[22] 'The words that I say unto you I speak not from myself: but the Father abiding in me doeth his works.'[23]

In these remarkable passages we find Jesus making the very highest claims; but they are made in such a way that they sound rather like disclaimers. The higher they become, the more do they refer themselves to God, giving God all the glory.

Thus the dilemma disappears when we frankly recognize that in the doctrine of the Incarnation there is a paradox which cannot be rationalized but which can in some small measure be understood in the light of a 'paradox of grace.' Somebody may wish to press the question in another form: Would *any* man who lived a perfect life be therefore and thereby God incarnate? But such a questioner would indeed be a

Pelagian, showing by his very question that he regarded the human side of the achievement as the prevenient, the conditioning, the determinative. When we really accept the paradox of grace, when we really believe that every good thing in a man is wrought by God, when we have really understood the confession: 'I . . . yet not I, but God,' and have taken that divine priority in earnest, the question loses its meaning, and, like the proposed dilemma, fades away into the paradox of the Incarnation. And if we take these things in earnest, we have, as it appears to me, at least an approach to the *mysterium Christi* which will enable us to combine the most transcendent claims of a full and high Christology with the frankest recognition of the humanity of the historical Jesus.

Endnotes

[1]Doubtless this was partly due to the strong tendency in the Greek Patristic period to identify the sin and evil of humanity with its ignorance, its finite limited knowledge. On this latter, see Reinhold Niebuhr, *Human Nature*, p. 172.

[2]In *Dissertations on Subjects connected with the Incarnation*, first published in 1895.

[3]L. Hodgson, *And Was Made Man* (1928), pp. 40f., 50-6, 159, 192f.

[4]Mark v, 34; x, 52; Luke xvii, 19.

[5]William Temple, *Christus Veritas*, p. 147.

[6]*Doctrine of the Person of Jesus Christ*, p. 399.

[7]Tertullian, *Adv. Marc.*, i, 3 (quoted by Barth).

[8]I owe this to G. G. Coulton, *Studies in Medieval Thought*, p. 87.

[9]I Tim. ii, 5.

[10]In maintaining that the $\sigma\tilde{\omega}\mu\alpha$ and the $\psi\upsilon\chi\acute{\eta}$ of Jesus were human, Apollinaris was surely using in the Aristotelian sense of 'life' or the 'vital

principle' in a biological reference, so that he made the living body of Jesus to be human, and the mind or spirit ($\nu o \tilde{v}_{5}, \pi \nu \epsilon \tilde{v} \mu a$) to be identical with the eternal Logos.

[11]In Acts xvii, 29, $\tau \grave{o}$ $\theta \epsilon \tilde{\iota} o \nu$ is practically a substantive, meaning 'the Godhead,' 'the Deity.' The only other passage is the very late 2 Pet. i, 3, 4, where the adjective appears twice: '. . . seeing that his divine power and virtue hath granted unto us all things that pertain unto life and godliness . . . that ye may become partakers of the divine nature. . . .'

[12]Cf. F. H. Brabant: 'We cannot but feel that the very wide employment of the adjective "divine" (in the age of Plotinus) was one of the things against which Christianity had to make a stand, in order to secure any real meaning for a "personal God."' Essay on 'Augustine and Plotinus,' in the symposium, *Essays on the Trinity and the Incarnation*, p. 311.

[13]It was, of course, a translation of *Selbstbewusstsein*, which in this kind of usage seems more at home in the German language than its translation does in the English.

[14]Mark vii, 34; v, 19; Luke xvii, 18.

[15]Mark x, 17f.

[16]John viii, 29.

[17]John x, 17, 18.

[18]John v, 30.

[19]John v, 19.

[20]John vii, 16, 18.

[21]John vii, 28, 29.

[22]John xii, 49.

[23]John xiv, 10.

Discussion Questions

1. Define the following: Docetism, Arianism, Apollinarianism, Adoptionism, Quest for the Historical
Jesus, New Quest for the Historical Jesus.

2. Discuss what evidences are in the Gospels which
tend to confirm that they are not biographies of
Jesus.

3. Do you agree that it is necessary to establish the
words and deeds of the Jesus of History before proceeding with a doctrine of Christ?

4. Do you believe that it is acceptable to resolve
theological difficulties by an appeal to paradox?
Why or why not?

SOME PROPOSALS FOR A MODERN
CHRISTOLOGY

Like Baillie, Peter Hamilton also believes that
Christology must begin with the actual words and deeds
of the historical Jesus. He holds that it is not
possible to reconstruct a biography of Jesus. Neither
can the theologian obtain a picture of Jesus that
requires no interpretation. Yet, Hamilton thinks that
the interpretations placed on Jesus can be refined and
improved by a new metaphysic known as Process philosophy.

Some students will immediately question Hamilton's proposals because he makes use of philosophy.
But it is important to remember that the scriptures
require interpretation. Interpretation requires the
use of some kind of explanation that uses categories
which may be called philosophical. We should not
forget that Chalcedon's Creed is very dependent on
the philosophical concepts of the fifth century--
particularly those relating to nature or substance.
What Hamilton recommends in the use of Process philosophy is not new, theology has always used philosophical
categories of some sort. But, of course, whether his
explication of Christology is acceptable must remain
to be seen.

Hamilton's intention is to penetrate beyond the
impasse of paradox which traditional Christological
formulations embody. He offers a consistent, but
probably not comprehensive, Christology.

Using Whitehead's theory of prehension, Hamilton
maintains that one entity may be actually, not just
metaphorically, immanent in another entity. By that
he means that one entity can be present to another

329

entity in such a way as to contribute and constitute the other. If I can make as my own an element or feeling that originally belonged to your subjectivity, then a part of you becomes objectively immanent in me. Hamilton holds that Jesus "prehended" God in this way. He actually felt as God, thought as God, acted as God, lived as God.

It is important to understand that Hamilton insists that "God was in Christ" is not a mythological or symbolic statement. Instead, it is an ontological statement explicated by the use of the notion of prehension. Jesus' obedience and feeling for God make it possible for God to be objectively present in Jesus' actions and words.

Hamilton addresses two objections to his Christological proposal. The first is that he places too little emphasis on God's action, opening his Christology to the charge of adoptionism, that because Jesus was so attuned to God, God adopted him. Hamilton recognizes that there is ample scriptural attestation to the priority of God's act in the incarnation. Hamilton's reply to this charge is that God's priority is in the giving of an "initial aim," or in his will for Jesus. God wills for Jesus to be the full expression of his being, but Jesus must co-operate.

This leads naturally to the second criticism Hamilton considers; the charge of having failed to maintain the uniqueness of Jesus. Hamilton does not accept any theology of Jesus' uniqueness which begins with the assumption that God indwelled Jesus in a different kind of way than he indwells any human. To advocate this view, Hamilton holds, would require the denial of Jesus' humanity.

Jesus is unique because God's initial aim or will for him is that he will be the fullest expression of God's self-revelation. God does not will this for anyone else. But Jesus is unique also in the sense that a difference in degree may produce a difference in kind. Hamilton never quite says this, but Whitehead certainly did. And if this is true, then the fact that Jesus' response to God's presence in his life was so comprehensive and deep may justify the position that Jesus became a different kind of being.

My own opinion is that Hamilton avoids this position because it could open his Christology to the charge that he makes Jesus a *tertiam quid*; neither man, nor God, but some third kind of being. The student must decide for himself if Hamilton preserves the uniqueness of Jesus to an acceptable degree.

SOME PROPOSALS FOR A MODERN
CHRISTOLOGY*

The term Christology is used in two senses. It can be confined to the doctrine of the Person of Christ; but for reasons that will soon emerge I will take it in the wider sense of the *Shorter Oxford English Dictionary*: 'that part of theology which relates to Christ.' 'Christ' is, of course, a title: used on its own, it lacks a referent. I therefore prefer to speak of 'Jesus' or 'Jesus Christ,' bearing in mind Paul Tillich's precise but cumbersome phrase, 'Jesus whom men call the Christ.' As Tillich thus reminds us, this combination of proper name and title must include in its scope the *response* to Jesus as well as his personality, teaching, and manner of life--and at least those aspects of the history and religion of Israel that are relevant to Jesus, to this response, and to the title Christ. And since the response includes the belief in his resurrection and ascension, the scope of the term 'Jesus Christ' must include the coming into being of this resurrection-faith and of the Church. Indeed this entire sequence of events possesses a unity such that we can meaningfully speak of it as 'the event Jesus Christ.' I here largely confine myself to its central core: the life, death, and resurrection of Jesus, and the initial response to this.

I shall seek to distinguish three constituents alike of the wider event and of this central core:

*Source: From *Christ for Us Today*, ed. Norman Pittenger. Copyright 1968, SCM Press. Used by permission of SCM Press.

331

history, mythology, and divine activity. These interpenetrate and overlap, but the main burden of this
lecture is the assertion that the third constituent
cannot be wholly subsumed under the other two. Theists
who speak of God acting in or through some event often
qualify this by saying that since God transcends both
space and time he cannot be said to 'act' in any
literal sense. We cannot here embark on the doctrine
of God, but I would wish to affirm both God's transcendence in one aspect of his being and his temporality in another aspect, and to say that God does act
within our temporal history, and that the response of
faith--itself a part of history, affecting what fol-
lows--is a response to the *ontological reality* to
which it points in saying God *has acted*.[1] I affirm
that God so acted within the wider event 'Jesus Christ,'
and in particular in his resurrection.

It may be helpful to begin by considering this
claim in connexion with an event that we can perhaps
view more dispassionately, the escape from Egypt under
Moses. We need not concern ourselves with the mecha-
nics of this, but rather with its religious status and
sequel. For the atheist, the escape must have been
due to good luck, good leadership, or Egyptian incom-
petence. The theist can say that God acted, either by
a physical miracle or by so guiding the Jews that they
benefited unwittingly from a sudden change of wind and
tide; or he can deny that God acted and say rather
that God's strengthening influence upon the Jews and
their leaders--for example, as they turned to him in
prayer--inspired but did not arrange their escape. Any
of these views, including the atheist one, is an
admissible interpretation of the evidence: a tribal
nationalism, belief in their tribal god, and an unexpected and improbable escape *could* account for the
rise of the exodus-faith and its subsequent centrality
in the religio-political history of the Jews.

I do not believe that a parallel statement can be
made about the birth of the resurrection-faith among
the disciples of Jesus. Unlike the Jews on the East
side of the Sea of Reeds, the disciples were not confronted with a sudden improvement in their fortunes--
precisely the reverse. It may be that we sometimes
exaggerate the disciples' despair at their master's
death, and that in its very nature this despair was
only temporary. It is also undeniable that a person's
closest friends often see him in a new light immediately after his death. It may be possible to develop
these and similar lines of thought to establish what

332

for brevity's sake I will call a self-generated or psychological theory of the disciples' belief that their leader was in some sense still alive and present with them.

My first difficulty is that this runs counter to elements in the New Testament which seem to survive rigorous critical analysis and 'demythologizing'; I have particularly in mind the disciples' surprise, their experience of being unexpectedly accosted by the risen Lord: neither the evangelists nor their sources had any motive for introducing this element, which is also found in Paul's own references to his experience of the risen Christ. Secondly, any naturalistic explanation of the rise of the Easter faith raises the further question why such a belief should have arisen once, and only once, in all recorded history. I believe that any modern Christology must be very wary of asserting claims to uniqueness, and I shall decline to affirm traditional uniqueness-claims as to the nature of God's indwelling in the person of Jesus. But the birth and continuance of the resurrection-faith is a historical phenomenon so strikingly unique as to query the adequacy of any naturalistic explanation, and to suggest that that faith includes what I have called an ontological element and was, and is, a response to a unique act and presence of God.

In thus presenting a theistic interpretation of Jesus and his resurrection, insisting upon an ontological element where others see only myth, I will be held by some to have abandoned all claim to offer proposals for a modern Christology. If in this connexion modern be synonymous with atheistic, and if the scope of Christology includes the resurrection-faith, then--for the reasons just given--I have no proposals to offer.

I continue this lecture because I do not accept-- and I sincerely hope that many of you would not accept --so narrow an interpretation of the adjective 'modern' in this connexion. I regard a Christology as modern if it uses every relevant insight of modern knowledge to differentiate the historical element in its inter- pretation of the event Jesus Christ from the mytholog- ical, and remembers that the actual event comprises only history and the ontological reality of God's presence and action within that history--whilst the mythology expresses that reality in ways which may indeed convey deep truth, yet have in themselves the status not of ontological reality but of poetry. In saying this I assume that the starting-point for such a Christology will be, not the historic creeds and formularies of later centuries, but the attempts of the New Testament writers both to describe and to interpret the life, death, and resurrection of Jesus.

Our starting point is the New Testament, but this itself needs to be interpreted if it is to point us, as I believe it can, to the person of Jesus and the initial response first to him and later to his resurrection. These form the datum; the later insights, including the proclamation or *kerygma* in the New Testament itself, are highly significant for Christology, but must be assessed in relation to our attempts to reconstruct that datum. In the words of Ernst Fuchs: 'Formerly we interpreted the historical Jesus with the help of the kerygma. Today we interpret the kerygma with the help of the historical Jesus.'[2]

I must here quickly re-tread ground covered in previous lectures. I take the view that the principles of form criticism have been established beyond question, but that some of the more negative conclusions drawn from them are unjustified. Detailed comparative analysis of individual sections or pericopae in the synoptic gospels has confirmed the hypothesis that during the lengthy period before the writing of our earliest gospel individual sayings and incidents in Jesus' ministry were--note the verb--*used*: as they were worked over and adapted, their context and wording may have been altered beyond recall. This analysis shows all the gospels to be deeply theological interpretations of Jesus. They are all so impregnated with belief in Jesus as Messiah, and as eschatological and pre-existent Son of Man, that it seems probable that these beliefs arose early in the pre-New Testament period. Indeed the evangelists and their source-material are alike so suffused with this post-Easter faith as to make impossible any attempt to construct either a biography of Jesus or a 'definitive edition' of his teaching.

The methods of form criticism help us to pick out aspects of the gospel accounts of Jesus' conduct and teaching which are in sharp contrast to the current practice and teaching of his day, and which it would not have been in the earliest church's interest to introduce into the material: for example, Jesus' attitude to women, his table-fellowship with 'tax collectors and sinners,' his refusal of the epithet 'good,' and Mark's comment--altered by Matthew--that

334

in Nazareth 'he could do no mighty work.' That the
gospel narratives do include actual historical memories is most clearly seen in their treatment of the
disciples. Consider first the repeated references,
particularly in Mark, to their lack of understanding.
Of course the cynic can say that in attributing pro-
digious miracles and claims to the earthly Jesus,
Mark is forced to exaggerate the disciples' failure to
understand: to insert the messianic secret in order
to compensate for unhistorical messianic claims. (He
could add that the disciples' lack of understanding
is most pronounced in the Fourth Gospel, where Jesus
is portrayed as virtually identifying himself with
the divine 'I AM.') But it would have been just as
easy--indeed more likely, if the evangelists and
their sources paid no regard to historicity--to describe Jesus' immediate entourage as being swept along
on this flood-tide of claims to, and acts of, divine
authority, whilst emphasizing the lack of understanding of everyone else. There was no need to emphasize
the disciples' failure to understand, nor their surprise at the resurrection, nor to record that one of
the twelve betrayed Jesus, that they all fled at his
arrest, and that Peter denied him to a servant-girl.

Such honest reporting shows that the synoptic
evangelists and their sources did attach some value
to history. This makes it the more significant that
there is no hesitation in attributing to the lips of
Jesus sayings that can only belong historically to the
post-resurrection period. I see this as evidence
that 'the early Church absolutely and completely
identified the risen Lord of her experience with the
earthly Jesus of Nazareth.'[3]

The tentative nature of the findings of form
criticism has already been stressed. But these findings are valuable in precisely those areas which most
concern us if we seek the same sort of understanding
of the historical Jesus as we have come to have of
man in general--an understanding or image succinctly
expressed in Dr. Dillistone's lecture: 'This image
is a "dynamic, temporal one that sees man as first of
all an agent, a self," who stands self-revealed only
in the midst of the density of temporal decisions.'

We are sometimes told by New Testament scholars
that we are in no position to enter into--let alone to
psychoanalyse--the mind of Jesus in order to establish
the primary motivation for certain decisions or sayings, in particular the decision to go to Jerusalem at

Passover-time which led to his death.[4] I am myself
uncertain how sharply one can differentiate between a
person's decisions and the motivation that lies behind
them. In any case this does not affect the point I
wish to make as to the application of Dr. Dillistone's
words to Jesus. For even if analysis of the individual
pericopae in the gospels does not reveal the primary
motivation of Jesus, such analysis does reveal his
decisions, some at least of the competing pressures
between which these decisions were made, and the still
greater pressures they engendered. We find a striking
unity between Jesus' decisions and actions and his
teaching. He not only practised what he preached but
also preached or proclaimed his own practice: 'Jesus'
conduct was itself the real framework of his proclamation.'[5]

I would agree with Fuchs and others that it was
Jesus' conduct, thus closely reinforced by his proclamation, that led the Jewish leaders to destroy him.
Jesus both proclaimed God's love and forgiveness and
lived this out in his repeated table-fellowship with
'tax collectors and sinners,' Jews who were regarded
as having 'made themselves as Gentiles.' This must
have been bitterly resented, as the gospels record.
Is it fanciful to see a close parallel between this
resentment and that of the prodigal son's elder
brother, as also of the labourers who had borne the
burden and heat of the day in the vineyard? Both
parables proclaim that God loves and forgives all men,
including the idler and the waster who becomes a
swineherd, and precisely in thus proclaiming God's
universal love they also justify Jesus' own conduct,
grounding this in the very nature of the love of God.
Here indeed is cause for the hierarchy to take strong
offence: here also, as yet only by implication, is
deep ground for the later belief that 'God was in
Christ.' 'There is a tremendous personal claim
involved in the fact that Jesus answered an attack
upon his conduct with a parable concerned with what
God does!'[6] Some find a similar claim in his characteristic opening 'Amen, I say unto you.'

In analysing the gospel accounts of Jesus' teaching, form criticism attributes greatest reliability
to those elements that contrast with the outlooks of
both Judaism on the one hand and the early church on
the other. It must suffice to mention one complex of
such elements, all closely inter-related. The Kingdom
(or Reign) of God, Jesus' 'comprehensive term for the
blessing of salvation,' is an eschatological concept

which shows that 'Jesus stands in the historical context of Jewish expectations about the end of the world and God's new future'[7]--yet his teaching also contrasts with that context. He dispenses with the customary apocalyptic 'signs of the end' (found only in secondary material). The Kingdom of God--the phrase itself is distinctive, being rare in the contemporary literature --is 'at hand,' quietly and unobtrusively breaking through in the everyday situations of life. Jesus' emphasis is not on nations or groups (as in the Old Testament prophets), but on the individual as confronted in and through his daily life by God's demand upon him as summed up in the two commands 'love God' and 'love your neighbour as yourself.'

This direct relating of God to everyday situations is epitomized by the way Jesus addresses God, not as 'O Lord God, Creator of the Universe,' but simply as 'Abba,' 'Daddy.' The relating of God to particular situations is also seen in Jesus' words of healing and exorcism: 'Your sins are forgiven'; 'Your faith has saved you.' In all of this Jesus stands in sharp contrast to his contemporaries.

In what has been so briefly outlined we find Jesus proclaiming the concern and love and forgiveness of God and living out that same concern and love and forgiveness amongst those he met, and those he went out of his way to meet. As Jesus called men to 'radical obedience,' so he lived out that obedience, 'intensifying his obedience to the call of God as every successive challenge in life makes its impact upon him.'[8] To Dr. Dillistone's description of the historical Jesus intensifying his obedience to God's call must be added St. John's 'the Word became flesh and tabernacled among us.' Personification of the Logos belongs not to history but to mythology: the immense significance of this way of expressing that power of God which men sensed in Jesus--even if they sensed it only dimly before his death and resurrection --is perhaps brought home to our modern minds by Norman Pittenger's fine paraphrase 'the Word or Logos or Self-Expressive Activity of God.'[9]

We have now reached a point at which, in my view, the 'philosophy of process' of Alfred North Whitehead and others has something of value to contribute: I therefore make an apparent digression in order to give the briefest outline of that philosophy. Whitehead is best known in English academic circles for his work with Bertrand Russell in the field of mathematical logic. For the nonspecialist, the most prominent feature of Whitehead's philosophical writings--like those of Teilhard de Chardin--is their fundamentally evolutionary viewpoint. But Whitehead was a mathematician, not a biologist: he was acutely aware of the two great discoveries in physics made while he was teaching mathematics, the theories of relativity and the quantum. Whitehead was also greatly concerned with aesthetics. As his mind turned increasingly to philosophy, the physicist in him sought to understand the whole of reality and not only man, whilst the aesthete in him interpreted all reality by extrapolation from human experience, thus finding aesthetic value in all actuality.

I here make two comments: that the resulting interpretation of the nature of the world is far easier to reject than to make one's own; and that it is peculiarly vulnerable to attack by linguistic-analysis philosophy. (This because it extrapolates the usage of such terms as 'feeling' and 'mind' even into the inorganic realm.) Both comments apply equally to Christian theology, which also stretches the meanings of words.

Charles Hartshorne resembles Whitehead in having had the privilege, or the misfortune, to be the son of an Anglican clergyman. He has certainly had the misfortune of being too often labelled the 'leading exponent of Whitehead,' whereas in fact Hartshorne is a significant philosopher-theologian who evolved his own principal positions prior to his contact with Whitehead. Hartshorne's main importance for Christian theology is his application of modern logic to the doctrine of God. The discipline of rigorously logical thinking has proved its value in many philosophical fields and should be more used--less feared, perhaps-- in Christian theology. Highly significant for Christology are these two quotations from Hartshorne's *The Divine Relativity*.[10] In the first he refuses to allow 'paradox' to cover up illogicality: 'A theological paradox, it appears, is what a contradiction becomes when it is about God rather than something else. . . .' In the second he applies this to the relation between God's power and our human decisions: 'For God to do what I do when I decide my own act, determine my own concrete being, is mere nonsense, words without meaning. It is not my act if anyone else decides or performs it.'

Throughout this lecture I have assumed that

whatever else we may believe about Jesus we accept
that he was, inwardly as well as outwardly, a man: I
need not spend time showing that this assumption is to
be found in every part of the New Testament.   Hartshorne's statement about human acts and decisions
applies, therefore, to Jesus: we must not say that
his acts and decisions were 'also'--still less, that
they were 'really'--God's.   If we feel that the concept of Jesus intensifying his obedience to God's call
does not adequately express the divinity of Jesus,
then we must seek to express this in ways that neither
compromise his humanity nor rely upon contralogical
paradox.

One such way is suggested by Whitehead's philosophy of nature and in particular its central feature,
which he calls 'the theory of prehensions.'   Whitehead
sees all actuality in terms not of substance but of
process, not of being but of becoming.   The process *is*
the reality: every entity is the process of growing
together into a unity of its 'prehensions' or 'impressions' of everything in its environment.   But 'impression' is primarily a passive term, and therefore not a
good paraphrase for 'prehension':   'grasping at' is
better.[11]   A novel entity 'becomes' by grasping at
the influences surrounding it: in grasping at each
such influence it incorporates something of its environment.   Thus a viewer's impression of a painting is
the growing together into a single unified experience
of his impressions of all its elements, impressions
which he does not passively receive like incoming
telephone calls, but grasps at in his own distinctive
manner.

In what follows, the person and resurrection of
Jesus Christ are treated not as exceptions to, but
as the chief exemplifications of, metaphysical principles.   The principle applicable to the person, the
divinity, of Jesus is that of immanence: incarnation;
'in him all the fullness of God was pleased to dwell.'
Whitehead's theory of 'prehensions' here offers a
significant contribution: it attempts to describe
the manner in which one entity is actually, not just
metaphorically, immanent in another--actually immanent
in that it contributes to and is constituent in the
other's subjectivity.   For Whitehead there is actual
immanence, yet each entity, each experience, retains
its own subjectivity.   He saw experience--and therefore everything--as divisible, not continuous: drops
of experience, like the frames of a cinematograph
film.   (There is a clear parallel here with the quantum

theory, the discovery that radiant or electromagnetic energy consists of minute, discrete pulses or *quanta* of energy.) Each drop of experience enjoys its own subjectivity during its brief 'process,' the growing together of its constituent 'prehensions.' Only thereafter, when it has 'perished' as a subject, moved away from in front of the lens, is it available as an object to be grasped at by other subjects. Thus when a new subject, a new moment of experience, 'A,' grasps at an object 'B' (itself, so to speak, an ex-subject, a moment of experience that has perished), what happens is that A makes its own an element or 'feeling' which formerly belonged to the subjectivity of B, wherein it was perhaps an insignificant, perhaps a decisive, element. Thus a part of B's moment of experience becomes objectively immanent in the experience of A.

This is so crucial to one of my Christological proposals that I venture the personal illustration of my relationship with my wife. In common parlance, in so far as I am a good husband I enter into her joys and sorrows—as she certainly enters into mine. To take an instance that is perhaps unimportant, and certainly infrequent, consider my wife's first wearing of a new dress. As I 'prehend' her evident enjoyment of this I enter into her joy—or rather, I make something of her joy my own. At that moment my wife's enjoyment is central to her experience, to her self, and in so far as I make this my own I make an element of her—strictly, of the 'she' of a moment ago, since my senses are not instantaneous—to become an element constitutive of me. Thus she becomes partially and objectively immanent in me. The more *sympatique* I am, the more vivid, and accurate, will be my impression of her enjoyment, making her—her experience—more fully immanent in me.

In general, the extent to which the experience of one person, A, enters into that of a new subject, B, depends both upon how *sympatique* B is to A and how compatible A is to B. Thus the belief that God's self-expressive activity was supremely present in the person and the decisions of the historical Jesus implies the belief that Jesus was supremely *sympatique* to God, and that God is supremely compatible to Jesus.

It may be that during Jesus' ministry his disciples did not fully or consciously think of him as divine, as Son or Servant of God, as Son of Man, or as Messiah: it may also be that Jesus did not explicitly

340

see himself in any of these terms. Indeed there are
a small number of very significant passages in the New
Testament which depict Jesus as completely human up to
his death, at or after which God raised him to superhuman dignity: 'descended from David according to the
flesh and designated Son of God in power . . . by his
resurrection from the dead.'[12]

The belief that 'in Christ God was reconciling
the world to himself' belongs to mythology: however
significant they may be, sin and reconciliation are
mythological terms. The four opening words perhaps
should not be separated from the rest of Paul's sentence, but if they are so separated the phrase 'God
was in Christ,' still more 'God was in the historical
Jesus,' is not a mythological statement: it corresponds to what I earlier called ontological reality.
The further statement that Jesus' disciples were at
least dimly aware of that reality during his ministry
belongs, as I have just suggested, to history--as does
the fact that he was fully human.

Christian theology has always sought to affirm
these three statements: process philosophy offers a
framework within which they can be affirmed without
either impairing their true status or resorting to
paradox. God's indwelling in Jesus is the chief
exemplification of this philosophy's principle of
immanence: as Jesus intensified his obedience to the
call of God so, without impairing Jesus' humanity and
human freedom, God was supremely, yet objectively,
immanent in Jesus. Thus the two 'natures' of Jesus
Christ are affirmed, whilst Jesus remains--as yet God
objectively present in such high degree that Jesus'
decisions and actions supremely reveal, through the
self of the historical Jesus, the 'Self-Expressive
Activity of God.'

What has just been said may be regarded as true,
but inadequate; inadequate firstly in failing sufficiently to affirm the *priority* of God's will and act in
the whole event Jesus Christ, and secondly in failing
to maintain the *uniqueness* of Jesus. These may well
be two ways of saying the same thing, but it is convenient to consider them separately.

The divine priority in the Incarnation is symbolized both by the Annunciation, God's messenger
announcing his plan in advance, and by the virgin
birth--more precisely, the virginal conception--of
Jesus; also by the concept of the pre-existence of

Christ, whether as Logos or Son of Man.

Even if he regards all of these as mythological, the Christian will find deep value in them and will wish to affirm them just as far as he can: the limiting factor is that nothing must impair our accompanying belief in the manhood of Jesus. One aspect of the Annunciation narrative is significant here: it depicts God's messenger, and therefore God's purpose, waiting upon Mary's consent: 'Be it unto me according to thy word,' God's will indeed has priority, but seeks to elicit Mary's consent rather than override her human freedom.[13]

A facet not yet mentioned of Whitehead's philosophy of process makes the same point. If each bud of experience is a growing together of its constituent elements, its own subjectivity arising with the process and not the precursor of it, then the process needs an initial aim or purpose, which must be given to it. Whitehead sees God as giving this 'initial aim. Thus we are free in each moment of experience either to conform to that initial aim or--within the limits of our freedom--to diverge from it. Once again, God's will has priority, but seeks to elicit our co-operation

We now turn to the charge of having failed to maintain the uniqueness of Jesus. Those who feel strong religious reasons for affirming this uniqueness may not appreciate that there are others, and other Christians, for whom claims to uniqueness are an inevitable barrier to relevance. Proclaimed as the chief exemplification of the potentiality of human life lived in utter obedience to God, the life and resurrection of Jesus could become meaningful for some who find them utterly irrelevant when proclaimed as unique acts of God.

Thus there are also strong religious reasons for not exaggerating the difference between Jesus and the rest of mankind: this is best avoided by not isolating Jesus from his historical context. I prefer to avoid the word 'unique,' with its several shades of meaning, but if it is to be used I wish to affirm the uniqueness of the whole event Jesus Christ, the whole Judaeo-Christian 'salvation-history,' as the supreme revelation and enactment of God's redeeming love: a unique event, with a unique effect. (To affirm this is not to deny that God also both acts and reveals himself in other ways and in other religions.) Within this whole unique event the life, death and resurrection of Jesus

342

occupies a uniquely central, indeed pivotal, position.
In his historical context, Jesus is thus doubly
'unique.'

Claims for the uniqueness of Jesus often take
two forms not covered by the above. God's presence
and indwelling in Jesus is said to differ not only in
degree but in kind from his indwelling in the greatest
of his saints, or in us. I can find no way of accepting this claim that does not impair, indeed deny,
Jesus' manhood. If religion has any meaning, a man's
conscious and unconscious relationship with God is a
vital aspect of his *self*. If this aspect differed in
kind in the case of Jesus from every other member of
the species man, then *in the present state of our
knowledge* it would seem impossible rightly to describe
Jesus as a man.[14] It may be the case that most Christians (and most Christian theologians) in most centuries *have* accepted this claim: but most have not
because either our modern sensitivity to the difference
between history and mythology or our concern for the
principles of logic. I emphasize the phrase 'in the
present state of our knowledge,' because it may well
be that in the future new insights will enable us to
affirm this claim: we should never assume that what
now seems impossible will always be so. But at this
present time I cannot affirm a difference in kind between Jesus and other men; indeed I find important
religious reasons for wishing to deny this.

The Christology of this lecture may also be
attacked on the ground that it sees every constituent
of the event Jesus Christ as contingent: Jesus'
obedience to God is a contingent concept, whereas it
may be claimed that God's redemption of the world in
Christ is not contingent but foreordained. My reply
is as before: if Jesus' obedience was not contingent,
it was not human obedience. I would add that I see
no need for this claim. That Napoleon was defeated at
Waterloo is a contingent fact, and also true. Where
religious truth is found enacted within history it
cannot avoid contingency, and loses nothing thereby.

The detailed framework of Whitehead's philosophy
is far less known than his aphorisms, for example:
'Christianity has always been a religion seeking a
metaphysic'[15]--with the implication that it never
rests in any one metaphysic, or philosophy. Whilst
our understanding of Christ can be deepened through
insights of process philosophy, Christology can never
rest in this philosophy, any more than in that accepted

by the early Fathers. In summing up, therefore, I would remind you of those parts of this lecture which do *not* rest upon process philosophy. The primary raw material of Christology is the New Testament documents. To study these I used the methods of form criticism. To interpret the results of that study I relied first upon logic. Hartshorne's criticism of paradox, and Whitehead's insistence that God is not an exception to all metaphysical principles but their 'chief exemplification,' are products of logical thought that in no way depend upon process philosophy: indeed the converse is the case, for this philosophy is largely built upon such principles of logic.

It is logic, not process philosophy, which insists that one cannot both describe Jesus as a man and also say that God's indwelling in him differs in kind from his indwelling in other men: since a study of the raw material confirms the first statement, logic demands a modification of the second. The further insight I then derive from process philosophy is that of seeing God's indwelling in Jesus as the supreme instance, the chief exemplification, of God's indwelling in his creatures--a divine indwelling which is itself the chief exemplification of this philosophy's concept of immanence. This insight closely corresponds to the disciples' experience--perhaps fully explicit only after the resurrection--that when they were with Jesus they were in some special sense in the presence of God.

Endnotes

[1]On being-ful reality: ontology is the study of being.

[2]From the foreword to his collected essays, which is unfortunately omitted from the English edition.

[3]N. Perrin, *Rediscovering the Teaching of Jesus*, 15.

[4]See Bultmann's recent essay in *The Historical Jesus and the Kerygmatic Christ*, eds. C. E. Braaten and R. A. Harrisville, (New York: Harper and Row, 1964).

[5]E. Fuchs, *Studies of the Historical Jesus*, 21.

[6]E. Linnemann, *Parables of Jesus*, 87.

[7]R. Bultmann, *Theology of the New Testament*, Vol. I, 4.

[8]From an earlier paper in *Christ for Us Today*, 96.

[9]*The Word Incarnate*, 187.

[10]Pp. 1, 134.

[11]I prefer 'grasping at' to Whitehead's own usage of 'feeling' as an alternative to 'prehension.'

[12]Romans 1:3,4 (RSV).

[13]I owe this insight to Dr. Norman Pittenger.

[14]This 'difference in kind' is also expressed by saying that Jesus is 'sinless' or 'perfect' man. Sin and sinlessness are mythological terms. I agree with John Knox that 'a perfect historical event is a contradiction in terms.'

[15]*Religion in the Making*, 50.

Discussion Questions

1. Discuss the use of philosophy in theology. Is it always necessary that we use some philosophy in explaining what the Bible or the creeds mean?

2. Try to name some of the criteria which Hamilton uses to determine whether a gospel account is authentic—that is, whether it tells of the Jesus of History vis-a-vis the Christ of Faith.

3. Do you agree that Hamilton avoids Adoptionism? Why or why not?

4. How necessary is it that Jesus be unique? Is it the historical person or his message that should be preserved as unique?

THE PROBLEM OF THE VIRGINAL CONCEPTION
OF JESUS

The virginal conception of Jesus, traditionally called the virgin birth, once occupied a key position in Christological doctrine. Both Ambrose and Augustine are numbered among the church fathers who relied on the virginal conception of Jesus in order to defend his sinlessness. They held that Jesus was free from original sin because he was conceived of a virgin. A number of other theologians used the virginal conception to support the Christian claim of Jesus' divine sonship.

Raymond Brown discusses the question whether the virginal conception of Jesus must be affirmed in order to preserve other valuable Christian beliefs. Those he examines are the doctrine of the sanctity of Mary, the sinlessness of Jesus, and the divine sonship of Jesus. He concludes that none of these doctrines necssarily requires that the theologian affirm the virginal conception.

Of course, one might suggest that certain theologies of the scripture could require a belief in the virginal conception. And this would be an important point to make. At the same time, however, the theology of scripture upon which this position rests would probably require as much defense as the virginal conception itself.

The doctrines Brown discusses which seem to undermine a belief in virginal conception are: the preexistence of Christ and the humanity of Jesus. To hold either of these doctrines would seem to conflict with

the doctrine of the virginal conception. But Brown
argues that the pre-existence of Jesus and his virginal
conception are not mutually exclusive. Jesus may have
existed prior to his incarnation in Mary. Brown reminds his readers of the skillful union of these ideas
found in Justin Martyr. And he also holds that the
natus de virgine (conceived of the virgin) was inserted
into the early creeds as an argument favoring Jesus'
humanity, with an anti-Docetic purpose.

Only after he treats the question of doctrinal in-
terdependence does Brown turn to the scriptures. Again
he examines the scriptural arguments which seem against
the historicity of the virginal conception, and those
which favor it.

Brown leaves the issue of the historicity of the
virginal conception unresolved. Neither historical nor
scientific data require a decision for or against the
claim.

Perhaps it is best now to make a few observations
about how this doctrine is an extremely unreliable
means of detecting departures from orthodoxy. Ebio-
nites, Arians, and even Muslims profess belief in the
virginal conception, and yet their Christologies seem
out of step with the Nicene-Chalcedonian tradition. On
the other hand, some theologians express the most ar-
dent faith in the Incarnation, and yet remain skeptical
about the historicity of the virginal conception.

Perhaps we need to be reminded that a virginal
conception does not necessarily make an incarnate Son
of God. If it does, then Buddha (Gautama), Zoroaster,
and Mahivira (founder of Jainism) would all have strong
claims to deity. And if we do not accept their birth
stories, then it seems incumbent upon us to say why.
It seems that the greatest miracle is the miracle of
the incarnation. And we have already seen that Christianity affirms Jesus' uniqueness in that respect.

THE PROBLEM OF THE VIRGINAL CONCEPTION
OF JESUS*

The Evidence from Interlocking Doctrines

We cannot consider the virginal conception of Jesus in isolation; it is related to other christological
and mariological tenets that are dear to Christianity.
Some of those tenets seems to favor the historicity of
the virginal conception, while for other tenets the
virginal conception is an obstacle. Let us consider
both.

(A) Doctrines That Seemingly Suppose
a Virginal Conception

(1) The sanctity of Mary.[1] All would recognize
that, if there was a virginal conception, this involved
an extraordinary intervention of God, so that Mary was
truly the *kecharitōmenē* of Luke 1:28, the "favored one"
of God. But the question raised here concerns more
than the consequences of the use of God's miraculous
power. There has existed in Christian thought the attitude, explicit or implicit, the virginal conception
is a more noble way of conceiving a child than is marital intercourse; and this attitude is tied in to the
thesis that virginity is the nobler form of Christian
life. Most often in Christian literature this attitude
was voiced not in immediate reference to Mary's virginal conception of Jesus but in reference to her remaining a virgin after Jesus' birth. Origen is the
first major theologian to bring this ascetical motif to
the fore: once overshadowed by the Holy Spirit, Mary
could not conceivably have submitted to marital intercourse with a man. She thus becomes the model of all
those who would choose virginity or celibacy as a way
of life for the sake of the kingdom of God.[2]

Most modern theologians (including many Roman
Catholics[3]) would not support an evaluation whereby the
witness of Christian virginity is deemed simply as
"better" than the witness of Christian married love.
And anti-sexual bias that occasionally colored the
theologizing of the past is not a dominant direction
today. But there is an even more fundamental difficulty in linking the "greater" sanctity of virginity to
the virginal conception, namely, that the infancy narratives do not make the slightest connection between
the virginal conception and the special value of the

*Source: The Virginal Conception and Bodily Re-
surrection of Jesus by Raymond E. Brown. (c) 1973 by
the Missionary Society of St. Paul the Apostle in the
State of New York. Used by permission of Paulist Press.

state of virginity (a theme that *does* appear elsewhere in the NT, e.g., I Cor. 7:8). Mary is depicted as having chosen the married state,[4] and the virginal conception is presented as God's intervention, not as Mary's personal choice. On the basis of the Gospel evidence it would be next to impossible to maintain that Mary would have been less holy if she had entered into normal marital relations with her husband and had borne Jesus through such relations.

(2) The sinlessness of Jesus. In Heb. 4:15 Jesus is described as "one who has been tempted as we are in every respect, *yet without sinning*," a description that Chalcedon (DBS #301) rephrased: "similar to us in all things *except sin*." Ambrose and Augustine, the Fathers of the Western Church who figured prominently in developing the theology of original sin, explained that Jesus was free from sin because he was conceived of a virgin.[5] Behind this explanation lies the thesis that the transmission of original sin is bound up with the sexual nature of human propagation and the sensual appetites aroused by procreation. Many modern theologians feel an urgency to reformulate the truth contained in the doctrine of original sin, but even the defenders of the traditional understanding of the concept have for the most part abandoned the "concupiscence theory" of the propagation of sin. Thus, while the virginal conception may enter into the mystery of Jesus' sinlessness, it is difficult to argue that in order to be free from original sin Jesus had to be conceived of a virgin.[6]

(3) The divine sonship of Jesus. The vehemence of conservative Christian feeling with regard to the virginal conception may best be explained by the fact that in the past the denial of virginal conception has often been accompanied by a denial that Jesus is the Son of God. Nevertheless, historical Christianity has resisted attempts to identify incarnation with divine filiation in any sense that would have the deity as the male element unite with Mary as the female element to produce the human Son of God--in other words, a form of *hieros gamos*.[7] In A.D. 675, for instance, the Eleventh Council of Toledo (DBS #533) rejected the contention that, since Mary conceived by the overshadowing of the Holy Spirit, the Spirit was the father of Jesus. And so, while the doctrine of the virginal conception draws attention to the fact that Jesus was not simply a man like all others and is God's Son in a unique way, it would be impossible to prove theologically that the Son of God could not have become incarnate as the product

of a marital union between Joseph and Mary. Both
Protestant and Catholic theologians have stated clearly
that the bodily fatherhood of Joseph would not have excluded the fatherhood of God.[8] Indeed, it is doubtful
that if there had been no infancy narratives of Matthew
and Luke (and thus there were no mention in the NT of
the virginal conception). Christian faith in Jesus as
God's Son would have been really different. The idea
of divine sonship is substantiated in the Synoptic accounts of the baptism and the transfiguration, and in
Pauline and Johannine christology; it is not dependent
upon the infancy narratives.

(B) Doctrines Seemingly Unfavorable
     to a Virginal Conception
     If theorizing about a natural conception does not
seem to raise insuperable difficulties in relation to
the doctrines discussed above,[9] we may now ask the converse question: Does retention of the virginal conception raise insuperable difficulties for other Christian doctrines *as they are understood in our times?*

     (1) Can the virginal conception be reconciled with
the pre-existence of the Son of God? Wolfhart Pannenberg has answered with a firm no: "In its content, the
legend of Jesus' virgin birth stands in an irreconcilable contradiction to the Christology of the incarnation of the preexistent Son of God found in Paul and
John."[10]

     In Matthew and Luke we have the christology moved
back to Jesus' infancy in Mary's womb, for an angel
proclaims that from the moment of his conception he was
already the Messiah and the Son of God. On the other
hand, in hymns quoted in the Pauline epistles (Philip
2:6-7; Col. 1:15-17), in Hebrews (1:2), and in John
(1:1; 17:5) the christology is moved toward pre-existence. The NT authors did not have the difficult task
of reconciling these two "pre-ministry" christologies,
one centered on conception, the other on pre-existence;
for we have no evidence that the proponents of one were
aware of the other.

     (2) On the other side of the coin, can the virgin-
al conception be reconciled with the true humanity of
Jesus? Does Jesus become docetic if he was not conceived in a truly human manner? Is he a Jesus "similar
to us in all things except sin?"[11] This question may
well be unanswerable in the abstract, since we are
dealing with something unique. We have said that Jesus
would still have been God's Son if he had two human

parents; how can we say that he would not be man's son if he had only one?[12] And, as we have seen, the *natus de virgine* was inserted into the creed with an anti-docetic purpose.

The Evidence from the Scriptures

Since our other forms of evidence ultimately refer back to the infancy narratives of Matthew and Luke, the value of the scriptural evidence for the virginal conception will have a great effect on any ultimate decision about historicity.

(A) Scriptural Arguments Against Historicity

(1) The "high" christology implied in a virginal conception. The most serious objection to historicity has already been mentioned. The explicit and high Christology of the infancy narratives centering on the virginal conception is hard to reconcile with the widely accepted critical theory of a gradual development of explicit NT christology, unless the virginal conception is considered to be a late christological theologoumenon. If the christology associated with virginal conception was known from the first moments of Jesus' earthly career, the whole critical theory falls apart. This difficulty is not insuperable if scholars can work out a distinction between *the fact* of virginal conception and *the christology* that surrounds it in the infancy narratives, but that has not yet been done in a satisfactory way. Further investigation in this direction is imperative if we are to resolve the principal modern objection to the virginal conception.

(2) The dubious historicity of the infancy material in general. I have already pointed out that we know little of the sources from which the various infancy traditions were drawn and thus the infancy narratives differ from the rest of the Gospels. But our problems deepen when we compare the two infancy narratives, one to the other; for, despite ingenious attempts at harmonization, the basic stories are virtually irreconcilable (cf. Matt 2:14 and Luke 2:39). They agree in so few details that we may say with certainty that they cannot both be historical *in toto*. Even the lists of Jesus'ancestors that they give are very different, and neither one is plausible.[13]

If we consider them separately, Matthew's account is redolent of the folkloric and imaginative: e.g., angelic appearances in dreams, guiding birth star, treasures from the East, the machinations of a wicked king, the slaughter of innocent children.[14] Luke's account has less of the folkloric, even though it reports several angelic appearances and a miraculous punishment of Zechariah. Yet Luke shows signs of considerable literary artistry and organization; e.g., a delicate balance between two annunciations and two births, joined by the visitation--obviously this is not the atmosphere of purely historical reporting. Moreover, some of the Lucan details are of dubious historicity, namely, a family relationship between the Baptist and Jesus;[15] or a census of the Roman world that affected Galilee and occurred before the death of Herod the Great.[16]

Once again the difficulty is not insuperable. Most scholars today would agree that each infancy narrative is composite: information or stories from different sources have been combined and edited by the two evangelists. Thus it is possible that some of the sources wore folkloric or non-historical, while other sources or items of tradition came down from genuine family memories. Virginal conception through the power of the Holy Spirit could have been in the latter category, precisely because it is common to the two evangelists. Nevertheless, one must admit that the general context of the infancy narratives, in which the virginal conception is preserved, does nothing to increase our confidence in historicity.

(3) The silence of the rest of the NT. The questionable historical character of the infancy narratives makes the silence of the rest of the NT about the virginal conception all the more significant. The NT material that rests in some way on apostolic witness (Pauline letters; Gospel traditions of the ministry) offers no support for the virginal conception; indeed not even all the infancy traditions support it. Let us try to evaluate the silence in each instance as to whether it implies ignorance or rejection of the virginal conception.

Paul. The Pauline letters are the earliest Christian writings; yet their problem-oriented character makes it very difficult to judge if Paul's silence on this question is accidental or significant.[17] That Paul described Jesus as "born of a woman" (Gal. 4:4) rather than as "born of a virgin" is scarcely probative;[18] and his reference to Jesus as the "seed of David" (Rom. 1:3) and the "seed of Abraham" (Gal. 3:16) is no more specific in its information about the "how"

of Jesus' conception than is Matthew's description (1:
1) of Jesus as "son of David, son of Abraham," a description that Matthew found reconcilable with virginal
conception. More important is the tension already mentioned between the pre-existence motif in hymns cited
by Paul and the christology of virginal conception. On
the other hand, scholars[19] have detected close vocabulary parallels between Rom. 1:3-4 and Luke 1:31-35, indicating a possible relation between a Pauline creedal
formula and the Lucan tradition of virginal conception.
Ultimately, however, there seems to be no way to establish persuasively whether or not Paul knew of the virginal conception.

Mark. The virginal conception is not mentioned by
the earliest Gospel, which paradoxically, however, is
the only Gospel that does *not* refer to Jesus as the
"son of Joseph" or the "son of the carpenter."[20] (Indeed, as we shall see, it is significant that Mark refers to Jesus as "son of *Mary*.") Some interpreters
deem the omission of an infancy narrative sufficient
proof that Mark new nothing about Jesus' birth. Yet,
in Mark's time would a birth tradition, even if well
known, have already been considered part of the public
proclamation of the Good News and hence something in
the category of Gospel? Others point out that Marcan
christology is not so "high" as that of the infancy
narratives. For instance, in Mark 8:29-30 Jesus reacts
against a confession that he is the Messiah. But the
same reaction is found in Luke 9:20-21, a Gospel that
has an infancy narrative where we are told that Jesus
is the Messiah.[21] If Mark's account of the baptism of
Jesus (1:11) *can* be interpreted as an adoption of Jesus as God's Son at that moment (probably a wrong interpretation) and thus as a negation of the christology
of the infancy narratives, so can Luke's account of the
baptism[22]--and Luke *did* accept the christology of the
infancy narratives. Exegetes who join Mark 3:21 to 3:
31-35 would have Jesus' "mother and brothers" (3:31)
thinking that Jesus was "out of his mind" (3:21)--an
attitude scarcely reconcilable with Mary's knowledge of
the uniqueness of her son's conception--but the relation of the two texts is not lucidly clear in Mark. In
general, then, Marcan silence may well mean Marcan ignorance of the virginal conception, but the evidence
leaves much to be desired.

John. The last of the Gospels is also silent on
the virginal conception. The third-person singular
reading in John 1:13: "*He who* was begotten, not by
blood, nor by carnal desire, nor by man's desire, but

of God," is considered by most[23] an early patristic change from the original plural in order to make the text christologically useful. Jesus is called "son of Joseph" in John 1:45 and 6:42 (but see n. 92). Some would find John's ignorance of the virginal conception made more likely by his seeming ignorance of Jesus' birth at Bethlehem (John 7:42; but see n. 88). I have already explained that a tension exists between John's thesis of Jesus' pre-existence and the christological direction taken by the infancy narratives. Overall, the scales tip in favor of Johannine ignorance of the virginal conception; and that means the ignorance of it in a late-first-century Christian community that had access to an early tradition about Jesus.[24] On the other hand, some suggest that the Fourth Gospel stems from the region of Antioch; and it is interesting that less than twenty years after the Gospel's composition, Ignatius, the bishop of Antioch who reflects certain Johannine ideas (whether or not he knew the Gospel), was firmly convinced of the virgin birth.

As a summary reflection on the silence of these various NT documents in relation to the virginal conception, I would have to insist that, even when this silence indicates ignorance, it does not disprove the historicity of the virginal conception. Such a conception would not have been part of the early proclamation, for it opened Jesus' origins to ridicule and calumny. One might theorize, then, that a family tradition about the virginal conception circulated among relatively few in the period A.D. 30-60 before it spread and became known by communities such as those for whom Matthew and Luke wrote. On the other hand, the silence of the rest of the NT enhances the *possibility* of the theologoumenon theory whereby sometime in the 60's one or more Christian thinkers solved the christological problem by affirming symbolically that Jesus was God's Son from the moment of his conception. According to the theory, they used an imagery of virginal conception whose symbolic origins were forgotten as it was disseminated among various Christian communities and recorded by the evangelists.

(B) Scriptural Arguments Favoring Historicity

The evidence is not one-sided and the theologoumenon theory leaves at least two knotty problems unsolved.

(1) The origins of the idea of a *virginal* conception. It is well attested that tales of marvelous

355

births are created post-humously for great men, especially religious leaders; this is a way of showing that
Providence had selected these men from the beginning.
Undoubtedly, such a tendency influenced the formation
of the infancy stories concerning Jesus; but our immediate concern is whether such a process explains one
precise point: the Christian contention that Jesus was
conceived virginally. If the Christian narrative of
the conception of Jesus were like the Lucan story (1:
5-20) of how the Baptist was conceived, namely, through
divine assistance that made aged and barren parents
fertile, there would be little difficulty in accepting
the theologoumenon theory--the conception could be explained as a symbolic, theological construction imita-
ting similar birth narratives in the OT, e.g., of Isaac
and of Samuel. But the story of Jesus' conception has,
in fact, taken a form for which, to the best of our
knowledge, there is no exact parallel or antecedent in
the material available to the Christians of the first
century who told of this conception.

The wealth of comparative material almost defies
summary.[25] Without sufficient concern as to whether
they would have been known by or acceptable to early
Christians, *non-Jewish parallels* have been found in the
figures of world religions (the births of the Buddha,
Krishna, and the son of Zoroaster), in Greco-Roman
mythology, in the births of the Pharaohs (with the god
Amun-Ra acting through the father)[26] and in the marvelous births of emperors and philosophers (Augustus,
Plato, etc.). But these "parallels" consistently involve a type of *hieros gamos* where a divine male, in
human or other form, impregnates a woman, either
through normal sexual intercourse or through some substitute form of penetration. They are not really similar to the non-sexual virginal conception that is at
the core of the infancy narratives, a conception where
there is no male deity or element to impregnate Mary.[27]

More logically others have turned to seek parallels in the Jewish background. In pre-Christian *Hebrew
or Aramaic sources*, however, no expectation or description of virginal conception has yet been found, even in
reference to the coming Messiah.[28] The allusion to a
divine begetting of the Messiah or Anointed One that
appears in the Qumran documents[29] involves no more than
the divine adoptive begetting (coronation) of the
anointed king in the royal psalms (Ps. 2:7).

Hellenistic Judaism has seemed a more fertile
field for search because Matthew makes reference to the

Greek (LXX) text of Isa. 7:14, "The *virgin* shall conceive."[30] But we have no evidence that in Alexandrian Judaism the LXX of Isa. 7:14 was understood to predict a virginal conception, since it need mean no more than that the girl who is now a virgin will ultimately conceive (in a natural way). Moreover, it is dubious that Isa. 7:14 was the *origin* of Matthew's tradition of a virginal conception; elsewhere, including chapter 2, it is Matthew's custom to add fulfillment or formula citations to existing traditions.[31] And, indeed, there is no proof that Isa. 7:14 played any major role in shaping the Lucan account of the virginal conception.

(2) The charge of illegitimacy. Matthew tells us of the rumor that Mary's pregnancy was adulterous. The explanation given by the angel may have set Joseph's mind at ease; but in the implicit logic of Matthew's account there would have been no way to disguise the fact that Jesus would be born indecently early after Mary was taken to Joseph's home. Obviously Matthew is facing a story that is in circulation and factual data that he cannot deny: he does not and seemingly cannot reply that Jesus was born at the proper interval after Joseph and Mary came to live together. Traces of the rumor of irregularity of birth and illegitimacy appear elsewhere in the NT. The reference to Jesus as "son of Mary" (Mark 6:3) is strange, for generally sons were not called by their mother's name unless paternity was uncertain or unknown.[32] Illegitimacy may be implied in the retort of "the Jews" in John 8:41, "We were not born illegitimate," if the Greek *hēmeis* is emphatic by way of contrast. And certainly, from the time of Origen through the Talmud and the medieval legends of the *Toledoth Yeshu*, the constant Jewish refutation of Christian claims about Jesus' origins has not been that he was an ordinary child, the legitimate son of Joseph, but that his mother committed adultery with another and he was born illegitimate.[33] Since it is not easy to dismiss such a persistent charge, which may be as old as Christianity itself, those who deny the virginal conception cannot escape the task of explaining how the rumor of illegitimacy and irregularity of birth arose and how they would answer it without accepting a very unpleasant alternative.

Endnotes

357

[1] I list the doctrines in an order of ascending importance. The mariological tenet is lowest in the scale because originally the virginal conception was a christological concept, not a mariological one.

[2] Origen, *Comm. in Matt.* 10, 17 (GCS 40, 21). In *De institutione virginis* 5, 36 (PL 16, 328), Ambrose of Milan states, "By Mary's example all are summoned to the service [*cultus*] of virginity." Mary's virginity becomes one of the prominent reasons why God has so favored her. Pope Siricius, *Epistle* 9, 3 (PL 13, 1177), in the late fourth century, argues that if one denies the perpetual virginity, one plays into the hands of scoffers who say that Jesus could not have been born of a virgin.

[3] The Council of Trent (*DBS* #1810) stated, "If anyone says ...that it is not better or holier to remain in virginity or celibacy than to be joined in marriage, let him be anathema." Yet, in the context of the sixteenth century, the real point of this was to defend the value of virginity against the attacks of some of the Reformers. The tendency among Roman Catholics today is not to compare virginity and marriage in terms of better or worse but to recognize that each has its uniqueness as a Christian witness. Because the choice of lifetime virginity for religious reasons is much less frequent than the choice of marriage, and because it is a choice that visibly renounces family continuity, the uniqueness of virginity is often thought to be centered in the eschatological challenge it presents to the world.

[4] Few today interpret the "I do not know man" of Luke 1:34 as a vow or a resolve of virginity, *pace* G. Graystone, *Virgin of All Virgins* (Rome: Pio X, 1968). In the long run, as Graystone admits on pp. 147-51, the interpretation depends on whether Mary is to be considered a pious Jewish girl of her times (a situation that militates against a vow or resolve of virginity) or whether, by a special impulse of grace and in view of her future vocation, she broke out of the limitations of her surroundings and resolved to remain a virgin. Nevertheless, if most take the former alternative and think that Mary entered matrimony with the same intentions as any other girl, one cannot agree with Thomas Boslooper, *The Virgin Birth* (Philadelphia: Westminster, 1962), who uses Mary's choice to polemicize against what he deems a perverse Roman Catholic emphasis on virginity. On p. 235 he contends, "In the narrative of Jesus' birth a preview glimpse is given of

the Savior's own teaching on sex and marriage. . . .
Those who receive this story with faith accept premarital chastity, heterosexuality, and monogamous marriage as a divinely ordained way of life." This is an example of eisegesis (in an otherwise perceptive book). The infancy narratives are not meant to praise either marriage or virginity but the greatness of God's action.

[5]See the texts in Von Campenhausen, pp. 79-84. Thus the virginal conception becomes almost a theologoumenon of sinlessness. While the Greek Fathers did not deal with this matter in terms of original sin, they too related the moral perfection and sinlessness of Jesus to his virginal conception. Irenaeus, *Adv. Haer.* I, 30, 12 (PG 7, 702) seems to think of this as a Gnostic view; but see Hippolytus, *In Ps.* xxii (GCS 1[2], 146-47).

[6]K. Barth, *Church Dogmatics* 1[2] (Edinburgh: Clark, 1956), 188-92, makes a sophisticated connection between the lack of original sin and virginal conception. W. Pannenberg, *Jesus--God and Man* (Philadelphia: Westminster, 1968), p. 149, firmly disagrees with Barth.

[7]Of note is the Mormon belief that God the Father is human and corporeal (and masculine) in form--since we were created in His image and likeness--and that He begot His son of Mary.

[8]A conflict between the two fatherhoods was suggested by Tertullian, *Adv. Marcion* 4, 10 (CSEL 47, 446). It is rejected by P. Althaus, a Protestant theologian quoted with approval by Pannenberg (n. 54 above), p. 148, and by the Catholic theologian, J. Ratzinger, *Introduction to Christianity* (New York: Herder and Herder, 1969), p. 208. Ratzinger, who is relatively conservative, states: "According to the faith of the Church the Sonship of Jesus does not rest on the fact that Jesus had no human father: the doctrine of Jesus' divinity would not be affected if Jesus had been the product of a normal human marriage. For the Sonship of which faith speaks is not a biological but an ontological fact, an event not in time but in God's eternity." We may add that in the relationship between virginal conception and incarnation, it is not the first that is essential for the second; it is the second that makes the first credible.

[9]I speak, of course, on the level of logical conflicts. But man does not live by logic alone; and it

may be that while there is no logical conflict between a natural conception of Jesus and these doctrines, *existentially* there is a conflict. For instance, abandoning the idea of a virginal conception, once it has been held, may very well have a deleterious impact on devotion to Mary and belief in the divinity of Jesus, despite the careful explanations of theologians. As I shall indicate in the conclusion to this chapter, I do not think such existential relationships can be discounted; but I am not clear on how decisive an argument they constitute in theology.

[10]Pannenberg (n. 54 above), p. 143. To discuss this question fully one would have to deal with sophisticated modern attempts to reinterpret pre-existence. See a Catholic attempt by P. Schoonenberg, *The Christ* (New York: Herder and Herder, 1971), pp. 80-91. In private correspondence H. Riesenfeld has suggested to me an argument that stands in direct contradiction to Pannenberg's thesis. According to Riesenfeld if one take seriously the pre-existence of Christ *as a person*, then one has a real conflict in positing a natural generation. When a human being is begotten by a father and mother, a new personality comes into existence; but in classical Christian thought the conception of Jesus involved a pre-existent person. How this argument would fare in a theology that is non-Chalcedonian (as some modern theologies are tending to become) I shall have to leave to the systematic theologians to discuss. What is true is that a denial of the virginal conception has more often favored an adoptionist christology rather than a pre-existent christology.

[11]Some have wondered if such a conception would not have made Jesus asexual, and they have related it to his remaining unmarried. This is another form of the connection made between virginal conception and lifetime virginity, a thesis rejected above when it was applied to Mary. Its application to Jesus goes back to Tertullian, *De carne Christi* 20 (CSEL 70, 241).

[12]Since the same evangelists who tell us about the virginal conception also give us genealogies of Jesus, they did not think that the conception ruptured the chain of human descent.

[13]The Matthean genealogy with its three groupings of fourteen generations is obviously artificial; it contains well-known confusions in the first two groupings and is impossibly short for the third or post-exilic period; moreover, it records a priestly name

like Zadok which is not expected in a Davidic list.
The Lucan genealogy also follows a numerical pattern
(probably 77 names) and may have duplications (compare
3:23-24 to 3:29-30); it attributes names of a definite
post-exilic type to the pre-exilic period.

[14]While the raw material is folkloric, the accounts are remarkably brief; they have been pruned down
to the bare storyline and to suit the evangelist's
pedagogical interests in OT fulfillment. See the analysis by A. Vögtle, *Bibel und Leben* 6 (1965), 246-79,
especially 263-65.

[15]Such a relationship could not even be suspected
from any other NT evidence and certainly was not known
by the fourth evangelist (John 1:31).

[16]See the superb summary of the evidence by G.
Ogg, "The Quirinius Question Today," *Expository Times*
79 (1967-68), 231-36, who shows how difficult it is to
avoid the conclusion that Luke has confused the dating
of the Roman census.

[17]To argue that, if Paul knew of the virginal conception, he would have mentioned it in the course of
his observations on virginity is to make an unwarranted
connection between virginal conception and virginity as
a life-style, a connection never made in the NT.

[18]Indeed an argument *for* the virginal conception
has been based on Paul's phrase "born of a woman." It
has been pointed out that in Gal. 4 Paul uses "born"
(*genomenon*; also Rom. 1:3; Philip. 2:7) in refering to
Jesus' origins but "begotten" (*gegennētai* or *gennē-
theis*) in referring to the origins of Ishmael and
Isaac. See W. C. Robinson, "A Re-study of the Virgin
Birth of Christ," *Evangelical Quarterly* 37 (Oct.-Dec.
1965), published as a *Supplement to the Columbia Theological Seminary Bulletin* (1966), pp. 1-14.

[19]J. Orr, *The Virgin Birth of Christ* (New York:
Scribners, 1907), pp. 120-21; G. A. Danell, *Studia
Theologica* 4 (1950), 94-101. This argument is independent of the unverifiable assumption that Luke,
Paul's companion, was the evangelist, an assumption
that vitiates much of R. J. Cooke's *Did Paul Know of
the Virgin Birth?* (New York: Macmillan, 1926).

[20]These designations are found in Matthew (13:55)
and in Luke (five times), evangelists who clearly believe in the virginal conception; and thus they need

imply no more than Joseph's legal or "public" paternity. Of course, they may have been taken over by Matthew and Luke from an earlier usage where there was no knowledge of virginal conception; yet it remains true that the designations themselves tell us nothing about the user's attitude on this question. It is striking that Mark 6:3, if we accept the best textual witnesses, refers to Jesus as "the carpenter," while Matt. 13:55 refers to him as "the carpenter's son." If the usage were the reverse, there would be exegetical unanimity that "the carpenter's son" in Mark (implying Joseph's natural fatherhood) was the original reading, changed by Matthew to "the carpenter" to favor virginal conception. Unfortunately, facts get in the way of theory.

[21]There is an unreconciled conflict in Luke between the two christologies (of the ministry and of the infancy), as we have previously insisted; but the fact that they can coexist in Luke makes it difficult to be sure what Mark's attitude would have been.

[22]Indeed, more so if one accepts the Western reading of Luke 3:22: "You are my Son; *today* I have begotten you"--a reading, however, that may be just a later scribal "improvement," smoothing out a mixed citation (Ps. 2:7 and Isa. 42:1), in favor of citing only Ps. 2:7.

[23]Although not found in a single Greek Gospel ms., this reading is still accepted by a surprising number of French-speaking exegetes: M.-E. Boismard, F.-M. Braun, D. Mollat (in the "Bible of Jerusalem"), and exhaustively defended by J. Galot, *Être né de Dieu: Jean 1:13 (Analecta Biblica 37;* Rome: Pontifical Biblical Institute, 1969).

[24]This is the least one can conclude from C. H. Dodd, *Historical Tradition in the Fourth Gospel* (Cambridge University, 1963).

[25]A competent survey is provided by Boslooper, pp. 135-86.

[26]This is stressed as an antecedent for the Christian stories by E. Brunner-Traut, *Zeitschrift für Religions-und Geistesgeschichte 12* (1960), 99-111. But the best parallels she offers are to the general (and often folkloric) details of the infancy narratives, and she does not resolve the main difficulty that the Pharaohs were thought to have been conceived by intercourse.

[27]Let me call attention to a few seeming exceptions: (a) Plutarch, *Life of Numa, 4*: "The Egyptians believe, not implausibly, that it is not impossible for the spirit of a god to approach a woman and procure in her certain beginnings of parturition." Yet he argues that it ought to work the other way around and that a man ought to be able *to have intercourse* with a goddess. (b) Aeschylus, *Suppliants*, vv. 17-19, speaks of Zeus making Io a mother "with a mystic breath" (which could be interpreted as spirit). But a few lines on we hear that Io was "quickened with Zeus' veritable *seed*," and Hera becomes jealous. (c) Plutarch, *Table-Talk*, VIII 1, 2-3 (Loeb, *Moralia* 9, 114-19), has Apollo engender Plato not by seed, but by power; but the sequence seems to imply a form of intercourse, for it leads into the motif mentioned above regarding Egyptian belief. (d) The cult of Dusares at Petra and Hebron (and sometimes associated with Bethlehem) which is related to the mystery-cult acclamation of the virgin-mother goddess who has brought forth a son. See T. K. Cheyne, *Basic Problems and the New Material for Their Solution* (New York: Putnam, 1904), pp. 74-75. W. K. L. Clarke, *New Testament Problems* (London: Macmillan, 1929), pp. 1-5. This is another form of the Oriental fertility cult (Tammuz/Ishtar; Osiris/Isis), and the real parallels are to the Christian liturgical development of the Magi story into an epiphany celebration. No truly virginal conception is involved.

[28]I assume the common scholarly agreement that the Hebrew of Isa. 7:14 has nothing to do with virginal conception. See pp. 15-16 above. D. Flusser, "The Son of Man," in *The Crucible of Christianity*, ed. A. Toynbee (London: Thames and Hudson, 1969), p. 229, calls attention to *Slavonic Enoch* and its statement that the mother of Melchizedek conceived her child through or from the Word of God. While this claim is interesting in the light of Qumran (and therefore pre-Christian) speculation about Melchizedek as a heavenly figure, *Slavonic Enoch* was written in the Christian period and so does not offer any real proof of a purely Jewish thesis of a virginal conception.

[29]See O. Michel and O. Betz, "Vom Gott gezeugt," *Judentum Urchristentum und Kirche*, ed. W. Eltester (J. Jeremias Festschrift; Berlin: Töpelmann, 1960), pp. 3-23. The banquet scene in 1QSa 2:11, at which the Messiah might appear, is scarcely the occasion for a virgin to conceive and bring forth a messianic child.

[30]See also the LXX rendering of Ps. 110(109):3,

"From the womb before the morning I have begotten you."
Some think the LXX translators may have been influenced
by the Egyptian ideas of royal birth (n. 103 above).

[31]K. Stendahl, *The School of St. Matthew* (rev.
ed.; Philadelphia: Fortress, 1968), pp. vii-viii; W.
Rothfuchs, *Die Erfüllungszitate des Matthäus-Evangel-
iums* (*BWANT 88*; Stuttgart: Kohlhammer, 1969), pp. 99-
100.

[32]E. Stauffer, "Jeschu ben Mirjam," *Neotestamentica
et Semitica*, ed. E. E. Ellis and M. Wilcox, in honour
of M. Black (Edinburgh: Clark, 1969), pp. 119-28.

[33]The Samaritan Chronicle of A.D. 1616, just published by J. Macdonald and A. J. B. Higgins, *New Testament Studies 19* (1971-72), 54-80, constitutes an exception since it reports the Jewish adversaries as saying that Jesus was the son of Joseph--but still his
illegitimate son because he lay with Mary before the
proper time. The value of the evidence is dubious because there is clear dependence on Matthew's Gospel.

Discussion Questions

1.   Do you consider it essential to affirm the
virginal conception in order to be a Christian?   If
not, what is the importance of this doctrine?   If so,
is such an affirmation something that you would be prepared to include as a condition for salvation?

2.   Discuss Brown's methodology for studying this
doctrine.   Why doesn't he begin with scripture first?
Does it matter where he begins so long as all the
source-norms of the faith are allowed to contribute to
the final formulation?

3.   What weight do you attach to the silence of
the rest of the New Testament on the virginal conception?

4.   Brown says that anyone who denies the virginal
conception must explain how the change of illegitimacy
arose.   How could this be done?   Suppose a theologian
held that Jesus was illegimiate and that this was part
of his identification with the poor, disinherited and
oppressed masses (much like his eating with publicans
and sinners).   Could this theologian construct a viable
Christology on Jesus' illegitimacy?

5. Is the doctrinal of virginal conception reconcilable with Hamilton's theology of Christ? How?

DID JESUS REALLY RISE FROM THE DEAD?

It would be difficult to conceive of the beginnings of the church apart from the resurrection of
Jesus. The resurrection played a major role in the
development of Christological doctrine. It should
come as no surprise then that the intellectual difficulties which have gathered around this concept have
been quite disturbing. Biological and historical
criticisms of the idea of Jesus' resurrection are too
numerous to mention here, although some are treated
by Wolfhart Pannenberg in the essay to follow.

Pannenberg argues that the resurrection of Jesus
should not be treated apart from his whole course of
life. It is not just any person that is raised. It
is Jesus, the man who has said the words and done the
works of God. He is whom God has chosen to raise.
The verdict of the world has been reversed by God, and
God's approval is written over the life of Jesus.

How do we know Jesus arose? Well, Pannenberg
rejects the idea that this is known by faith alone,
apart from any historical basis. He argues that faith
without a basis cannot be distinguished from superstition.

Pannenberg holds that the question of the resurrection is open to historical examination. To those
who follow such a course he offers two cautions.
First, he defines what is meant by resurrection, cau-
tioning us that the failure to understand what is
meant can create great misunderstanding. In so doing
he denies that resurrection is the revivification of a
corpse. Instead, he speaks of it as a radical kind of
transformation, unlike anything witnessed in past
experience. His second caution concerns the nature of
historical inquiry itself. He maintains that the

historian must not hold presuppositions such that he
would be required to deny an event reported with high
probability just because his assumptions tell him such
events do not happen.

Pannenberg begins with an analysis of the two
strands of Easter traditions: the appearance strand
and the empty tomb strand. He examines the appearance
traditions first, and he mentions several difficulties
present in every attempt to explain the Easter appearances by appealing to the psychological or historical
situations of the disciples. The empty tomb narratives
are likewise subject to several interpretations and
Pannenberg considers them each in turn.

Pannenberg notes that the historicity of the
resurrection in itself, even if established, would
tell us little about Jesus. It is left to theology to
explicate the meaning of this most unique of events.
Such a theology must not ignore the pre-Easter activity
of Jesus. But neither should a doctrine of the resurrection fail to state the meaning of this event for the
present and the future. If Christ is risen, then
Christians have nothing to fear--neither pain nor
death. Christians may live boldly in the firm assurance that the risen Jesus is the victor over the
principalities and powers of this world. The end of
history has had its pre-actualized occurrence, and
all who are under Jesus' Lordship will share in his
victory.

DID JESUS REALLY RISE FROM THE DEAD?*

The answer to this question is absolutely decisive
for any Christian proclamation and for the Christian
faith itself. This was the case from the very beginning of Christianity. And it cannot be expressed more
distinctly than it was by Paul in I Corinthians 15:14:
"If Christ has not been raised, then our preaching is
in vain and your faith is in vain." It could be shown
in detail that the early Christian traditions, preserved in the New Testament writings, were formed from
the experience of the risen Lord appealing to the
apostles. Neither the message of Jesus' cross as a
medium of salvation nor the Synoptics' witness of the
pre-Easter activity of Jesus would have been developed
without the Easter event, nor the early Christian conviction that Jesus is the One by whose appearance the
expectation of God's messiah and of the future Son of
Man, who will come from Heaven to judge the living and
the dead, is fulfilled. Only because of the resurrection of Jesus were the Synoptics able to describe his
earthly cause to be the cause of the Messiah or of the
Son of Man.

Thus, the resurrection of Jesus is the decisive
ground for the proclamation and for faith; however, it
cannot be considered as a single event, for it has to
be considered in connection with Jesus' whole course
of life. It is only by this event that everything
else in Jesus' appearing is illuminated. Every previous event would have been something else than it is
now, but for Jesus' resurrection. The importance of
the question of whether or not Jesus really rose from
the dead should be clear enough. But how can it be
answered? Could the answer be left to a mere decision
of faith? This must be absolutely denied. Jesus'
resurrection is the basis of faith, but this again cannot owe its certitude to a decision of faith, otherwise faith would find its basis in itself. Faith
cannot exist by its own decision. It can only live

*Source: From "Did Jesus Really Rise from the
Dead," by Wolfhart Pannenberg, in _Dialog_ 4 (Spring
1965), used with permission of _Dialog_.

out of a reality which provides the basis and reason for faith. This must be the presupposition for a decision of faith. If the certitude of faith would not have its roots in a certainty of its presuppositions, it could scarcely be distinguished from superstition.

Thus, Paul in his first letter to the Corinthians, chapter 15, did not think a mere demand for faith was enough, but he gave the list of the witnesses of the resurrection of Jesus. This is a proof as it was commonly used in legal proceedings. The Greek historians, for instance Herodotus, also gave their proofs in such a way. Historical evidence was obtained by an interrogation of the eyewitnesses. It is not without reason that Paul emphasized the point that most of the witnesses were still alive and could still be submitted to an interrogation (I Corinthians 15:6). The proof Paul gave was for his time a historical proof, a first-hand proof beyond doubt. However, today this argumentation is no longer satisfactory for us without further explanation. We cannot hear these eyewitnesses any more to make sure that they were not deluded. But by means of modern historical research, we are able to gain positive knowledge of these events in the past, for which we have no witnesses. We examine the literary and archaeological witnesses in the same way as Herodotus interrogated his contemporaries. By doing this the modern historian tries to find out the tendencies in his sources, and from this conclusions are drawn. The real fact, then, is gained by that description of the events which covers in the best possible way all available evidences.

The question is whether we can, with the methods and criteria applied everywhere else today, achieve what Paul achieved by his first-hand proof for his time: a proven knowledge of the resurrection of Jesus as an event that happened at a certain time, a knowledge which can be the basis of our faith, as it was the basis for Paul and his congregations?

The Meaning of Resurrection

Before we can answer these historical questions in detail, we have to decide about the precise meaning of the expression, "resurrection from the dead." Only if we have a precise notion of this, will we know whether this question has any importance.

First it has to be stated that the expression

"resurrection from the dead" has a metaphorical character. This expression stands for something we can experience in our everyday life like a mountain or a tree, like waking or sleeping. It is rather a metaphor, a way of speaking in an image. Just as we arise from sleep in the morning, in a similar way those who are dead shall also rise. This is not a literal expression for a reality which can already be experienced, but something which normally cannot be experienced directly and, therefore, must be described by a metaphor, in analogy to our rising from sleep daily. This metaphorical sense of the expression could already be found when the notion of resurrection is first mentioned in the Old Testament (Isaiah 26:19). The terms "rise" and "awake" are used in parallel. The frequently used interpretation of death as sleep has similar implications. (Daniel 12:2; Paul; I Thessalonians 4:13,15; I Corinthians 11:36; 15:6,20,51.)

One could be tempted in following the analogy of sleep and rising to think that the resurrection of the dead is a simple revivification of the corpse, an arising and walking of those who formerly were dead. This certainly is not intended in the early Christian image of the resurrection of the dead; in any case, Paul does not follow this line. For him resurrection means the new life of a new body, not a return of life into the physical body that died but has not yet decayed. Paul explicitly discussed the question of the corporality of those who rose from death (I Corinthians 15:35-56). For him there is no doubt about the fact that the future body will be another body than our present body, not, as he says, a physical body but a spiritual body (I Corinthians 15:44). The relation between the imperishable spiritual body and the present perishable physical body is described by Paul as a radical transformation: "I tell you this, brethren: flesh and blood cannot inherit the kingdom of God, nor does the perishable inherit the imperishable" (v. 50). But on the other hand it is the present perishable body that will undergo this "transformation" according to Paul: "For this perishable nature must put on the imperishable, and this mortal nature put on immortality" (v. 53). On the one hand, the transformation of the perishable into a spiritual body will be so radical that nothing will be left unchanged. There is no substantial or structural continuity from the old to the new. But on the other hand, the physical body itself will undergo this transformation. Nothing else shall be produced in its place, but a historical continuity relates the old to the new.

Here Paul does not refer especially to Jesus' resurrection but to the resurrection for which all the Christians were waiting. But Paul must have had the same mental image of the resurrected Jesus, for he has described the resurrection of Jesus and that of the Christians to be completely parallel events in every item (e.g. Romans 6:8; 8:29; Philippians 3:21). Paul also understood the resurrection of Jesus to be a radical transformation, not a mere revivification of his corpse. This is especially important for the reason that Paul's report is the only one we have, written by a man who saw the resurrected Lord with his own eyes. The appearance of Christ which Paul experienced must have been of a kind that could not be mistaken for a revivified corpse, but could only be understood as a reality of a completely different kind.

From this we conclude that the resurrection of the dead in the Christian hope for the future and in the Easter faith has to be sharply distinguished from those resurrections from the dead which are reported elsewhere in ancient literature as miracles and also from those which Jesus himself accomplished according to the gospels, e.g. the raising of the widow's son (Luke 7:11-17; Matthew 8:5-13) and the raising of Lazarus (John 11:38-44). Quite apart from the question of the trustworthiness of these legendary reports --probably of a later period--there is no doubt that these reports were intended to describe events of quite another kind than that intended by the testimony about the resurrection of Jesus and by the early Christian eschatological hope. In the case of Lazarus and the widow's son, we have a transitory return to life of one already dead. There is not a moment's doubt for the narrator that these persons, who were raised in this way again to life, had to die again. In the resurrection of Jesus and in the Christian eschatological hope, life means quite another thing--an imperishable life not limited by any death, which must be in any case completely different from ordinary organic structures.

The Easter Appearances

Now we come to an examination of early Christian Easter traditions. They form two different lines independent of each other; the traditions of the appearances of the resurrected Lord and the traditions of finding the empty tomb of Jesus. It is only in the latest reports in the Gospel of John that both groups have fused. The oldest texts report either appearances only (I Corinthians 15) or a narrative of the empty tomb (thus the original report of Mark, in 16:1-8; Mark 16:9-20 is later attached as an appendix with reports from the other Gospels).

Both traditions thus have to be examined separately and I begin with the *Easter appearances*.

This historical question is completely concentrated on the Pauline report I Corinthians 15:1-11. The appearances reported in the Gospels, which Paul does not mention, have in their whole literary form such a strongly legendary character that it is hardly possible to find any particular historical root in them. Those reports of the Gospels which correspond to something in Paul have also been shaped by strong legendary influences, mainly by a tendency to underline the *bodily* appearances of Jesus, a tendency becoming stronger in the later reports.

In examining the Pauline reference to the Easter witnesses in I Corinthians 15:1-11, an argument which has the explicit intention of giving a proof, as is especially true of v. 6, we must first emphasize the following fact: this text is very close to the events. We can tell this by who the author is as well as by the formulation itself. The first epistle to the Corinthians was written in the spring of 56 (or 57) A.D. at Ephesus. But Paul speaks out of his own experiences which are to be dated even before this time. According to Galatians 1:18, Paul had been in Jerusalem about three years after his conversion. There he saw at least Peter and James. If Paul's conversion is to be dated in the year 33--according to Galatians 1--and Jesus' death in the year 30, it is evident that Paul arrived in Jerusalem, at the latest, six years after the event which took place in Jerusalem, and he certainly spoke with the other witnesses of the resurrection of Jesus about the appearances to them in comparison with the one which had happened to him. Thus, Paul had a first-hand knowledge of the events which the reports in the Gospels did not have.

Furthermore, we have to notice that in I Corinthians 15 the center of the enumeration is constituted by several pre-Pauline formulations: ". . . (that) Christ died for our sins according to the scriptures; And that he was buried, *and* that he rose again the third day according to the Scriptures, *and* that he was seen of Cephas, then of the twelve" (15:3b-5).

Paul put together these single pieces and completed them by the reports of the appearance in v. 6, perhaps according to the information he gathered in Jerusalem. From this it follows that the single pieces of the formulation must have been developed in the first years after Jesus' death, in any case before Paul's visit to Jerusalem, that is, during the first five years after Jesus' death. Thus, we have here quite a number of formulations that were given a fixed form and were verbally transmitted shortly after the events.

That the events reported by Paul really took place is doubted by hardly any of the present historians. Much more complicated, however, is the question of the real character of these events. First, we have to discuss the contents of the appearances; secondly, we have to ask about the character of the experiences corresponding to them.

For the contents we have to consult Paul again-- the Gospels with their tendencies to understand the incorporality of Jesus' appearance do not offer reliable grounds for historical considerations, and, moreover, at this point they contradict Paul. Paul evidently presupposes in I Corinthians 15 that the appearances he had had were of the same character as the appearances the other Apostles had experienced. Paul himself gives us some indications of the appearance which occurred to him near Damascus (Galatians 1:12 and 16).

A more detailed report was not written until thirty to forty years later in the Acts of the Apostles, in three different versions (9:1-22; 22:3-21; 26:1-23), which do not coincide with each other at several particular points.

In spite of this, these reports are not without value from the historical point of view. Earlier traditions can be recognized in them, because they stand in tension with Luke's own understanding which he gives of the Easter events in his Gospel. But they have to be used with caution and only as far as they coincide with Paul's own statements. For in any case, these reports seem to be stylized in a way similar to apocalyptic visions (as, for instance, Daniel 10). However, we will consider five points as probably true.

1. For Paul, the relation of the appearance which he had to the man Jesus was evident. He says

himself that he has seen the Lord Jesus Christ (I Corinthians 9:1), that God has revealed his Son to him (Galatians 1:16).

2. We have stated earlier that Paul must have seen a spiritual body, not a physical one, near Damascus.

3. Most probably this was not an encounter which took place on earth, but an appearance that came from heaven, from above. This point in the story of Damascus in Acts 9 corresponds to the observation that the earliest Christian testimonies did not distinguish between the resurrection and ascension (Philippians 2:9; Acts 2:36; 5:30 f.; Mark 14:62). The appearance of the resurrected Lord then could be understood only as an appearance from heaven. If one takes the last two points together, the glorified form and the appearance from above, the result is:

4. That the appearance near Damascus may well have been a phenomenon like a bright light, as Acts 9:13 f. reports. Perhaps Paul refers to this, when in II Corinthians 4:6, he speaks of the light of the glory of God in the face of Christ.

5. Certainly the appearance of Christ to Paul was connected with an audition, but it seems that, there as otherwise, the content of what was heard was identical with what the appearance itself meant to Paul in his particular situation. This is not less than the Pauline "gospel" of the freedom from the Law and of his mission to the Gentiles (Galatians 1:12).

These five points, perhaps with the exception of the first, hold also for the other appearances of the resurrected Lord. In every case, all the witnesses recognized Jesus of Nazareth in the appearances. That this strange reality, which occurred in these appearances, could be understood and proclaimed as an encounter with one resurrected from the dead can only be explained by the above-mentioned apocalyptic expectation of a general resurrection of the dead, and that in the near future.

The Mode of Appearance

I shall come now to the mode of the Easter appearances. Evidently they were not events which could be seen and understood by everybody, but they were exceptional visions. In any case, this must be

said of the Damascus event if it is to be understood
as it is reported in the Acts, that is, that those who
were in Paul's company either only saw something and
did not hear anything (22:9; 26:13 f.), or only heard
something and did not see anything (9), but in any
case without understanding the appearance. There are
many reasons for holding that we have to understand
what really happened in a similar way.

But then the question arises as to whether such
an event should not be considered as a vision, if
the appearance in question could not be seen in the
same way by all who were present. Certainly we hear
that Paul's companions noticed something that fright-
ened them, but without understanding it. The notion
of "vision," however, is not sufficiently clear. If
it implied nothing but an extraordinary view, nothing
could be said against its application here. But
generally one understands by a vision a sort of illusion, an event rooted only subjectively in the visionary, and that does not correspond with reality. In
this sense, and also in the psychiatrical sense, the
notion of a vision cannot be used for the Easter
appearances of the resurrected Lord.

Again and again persons have tried to explain
these experiences of the appearance of the resurrected
Lord which the disciples had by psychological and
historical circumstances of those experiences, without
accepting a specific reality of resurrection which
here was experienced. Historical-critical thinking
must certainly try this way again and again. But
precisely the failure of all these subjective theories
about visions secures the historical credibility of
speaking about the "resurrection of Jesus." It
becomes evident that a presentation can do justice to
those events, only if it takes the specific reality
into account which is signified by the symbolical
expression "resurrection of the dead."

I shall mention the two most important difficulties for all attempts which try to explain the Easter
appearances by the psychic and historical situation
of the disciples:

(a) That the appearances may have been caused by
the enthusiastic imagination of the disciples is, in
any case for the first and basic appearances of Jesus,
not convincing. All constructions holding that the
faith of the disciples of Jesus remained unshattered
after Jesus' death are problematical even from a

psychological point of view. This is also true if one considers the anticipation of an imminent end of the world, which Jesus must have had when he died and in which his disciples lived. That the death of Jesus exposed the faith of the disciples to an extreme stress cannot be doubted. In this situation one can hardly suppose that the disciples of Jesus produced these appearances through their enthusiastic imaginations.

(b) The second basic difficulty of the "subjective vision hypothesis" consists in the plurality of the appearances and in their being distributed over a long time. One would have to maintain that the disciples of Jesus were men with a special visionary gift and explain the plurality of appearances by a sort of psychic chain reaction arising out of the enthusiastic atmosphere after Peter's experience. But the image of a chain reaction is questionable here because "the single appearances did not succeed each other so quickly" (Grass). The enthusiastic experiences of the early Christians were--as far as we can see--only the effects of the appearance of the resurrected Lord. That the appearances of the resurrected Lord were different in kind from those later enthusiastic and visionary experiences, common in early Christianity, is already expressed by Paul. According to I Corinthians 15:8, such an encounter with the resurrected One occurred only once to Paul, and this was at the same time the very last appearance. However, even later on Paul had "visions and revelations of the Lord" (II Corinthians 12:1).

The Empty Tomb

Now we have to examine the traditions of the empty tomb of Jesus. Paul does not mention anywhere the empty tomb. This, however, does not necessarily mean that these reports which appear in their earliest form in Mark 16:1-8 are not at all reliable. For the empty tomb is not among those features of Jesus' destiny which Paul thought believers shared with Jesus, and yet it seems that Paul was only interested in just such parallel items. The empty tomb, *if* it is a historical fact, belongs only to the unique aspects of Jesus' destiny.

We can take it for granted that Paul counted on the emptiness of the tomb, whether he knew the Jerusalem tradition of the tomb or not. In the apocalyptic text of the resurrection, it is held throughout

377

that the earth will return the dead. For the early
community in Jerusalem, the situation was quite different in comparison to Paul's silence concerning the
empty tomb. We have only to try to imagine how Jesus'
disciples could proclaim his resurrection if they
could constantly be refuted by the evidence of the
tomb in which Jesus' corpse lay. Without having a
reliable testimony for the emptiness of Jesus' tomb,
the early Christian community could not have survived
in Jerusalem proclaiming the resurrection of Christ
(P. Althaus). Otherwise, the Easter message would
have taken a thoroughly spiritualistic character, and
it could not have been proclaimed precisely in Jerusalem. On the other hand, the Jewish anti-Christian
polemics would have had a great interest in the preser-
vation of the report of the tomb, which would have
still contained Jesus' corpse. But nothing of this is
to be found in the tradition. On the contrary, the
Jews agreed with their adversaries that the tomb was
empty.

Thus, out of general historical considerations
regarding the resurrection-kerygma in Jerusalem, the
supposition is inevitable that Jesus' tomb was empty.
In this case the mere analysis of the text of Mark 16
is not decisive. It is justified to lay stress on the
fact that (because of several legendary motives) one
cannot with certainty infer from this text the historical reality of the empty tomb. But even more decisive
here is the consideration of the historical situation
of the first community in Jerusalem, which cannot be
understood without the tomb having been found empty.
This general historical consideration, however, will
be justified rather than called into question by the
analysis of Mark 16.

There is a theory, however, that reconstructs
the cause of the events in the following way. The
disciples of Jesus had returned to Galilee after
Jesus' arrest already before his death. Only several
weeks after they had seen the resurrected Lord in
Galilee did they return to Jerusalem to proclaim the
Messiah. The lapse of several weeks meant, according
to this hypothesis, that precise information about the
place where Jesus' corpse could be found was no longer
available, and no special efforts were made to find
it, "because one was certain of the resurrected Lord
through the appearances" (Grass, 184). But this
recent hypothesis is extremely unlikely, as I have
shown above. Moreover, no vain search for the tomb
of Jesus is mentioned nor is there anything that could

be understood as an indication in this direction, not even in the Jewish polemics, and this again is very important. The Jewish polemics had only the intention of proving that the disciples themselves had carried away the corpse, but they did not emphasize the fact that the tomb of Jesus was unknown. However, the hypothesis about stealing the corpse can only be judged as adventurous. The enthusiasm of an ultimate devotion in the face of all obstacles which leads to sacrificing one's own life could not arise out of deceit.

Of great importance for the historical judgment is the question of the connection between the finding of the empty tomb and the appearances of the resurrected Lord. Today it is widely accepted that the basic appearances took place in Galilee, while the empty tomb naturally was found in Jerusalem. Now we have to see how these two things are connected: whether the discovery of the empty tomb was the reason the disciples of Jesus went to Galilee in the hope of meeting the resurrected Lord there (thus Campenhausen) or whether the disciples returned to the Galilean home because their journey to Jerusalem had come to such a catastrophic end (perhaps already before the execution of Jesus?) so that they met the resurrected One in Galilee, while in the meantime women (as we find everywhere in the tradition) discovered that Jesus' tomb was empty. This latter version is very probable because of the original independence of each of the two traditions, the finding of the empty tomb, on the one hand, and of the appearances of the resurrected Lord, on the other hand. Furthermore, this is supported by the fact that, according to the earliest reports, the disciples were not present at the execution nor at the burial and that they were not interested at first in the empty tomb, according to Mark 16. It would be difficult to explain these facts if one maintains that the disciples were still in Jerusalem. On the other hand, one cannot see why they should have gone to Galilee after the discovery of the empty tomb, because Jesus evidently thought Jerusalem would be the place of God's final decision regarding the imminent end of the world. And just for this reason the disciples did come back to Jerusalem in order to form, precisely in this city, the first community. Therefore, it is very likely that the appearances and the discovery of Jesus' empty tomb happened independently of each other and became connected only in later stages of the tradition. The independence from each other of the two traditions forms a last and weighty reason for the fact that the Easter events were not only imaginations of disturbed men, but the starting point in a unique but real event which occurred prior to all human experience of it.

The Historicity of the Resurrection

I now come to the conclusion. We saw that something happened in which the disciples in these appearances were confronted with a reality which also in our language cannot be expressed in any other way than by that symbolical and metaphorical expression of the hope beyond death, the resurrection from the dead. Please understand me correctly: Only the *name* we give to this event is symbolic, metaphorical, but not the reality of the event itself. The latter is so absolutely unique that we have no other name for this than the metaphorical expression of the apocalyptical expectation. In this sense, the resurrection of Jesus is an historical event, an event that really happened at that time.

Up to a very recent date it has repeatedly been said that this would violate the laws of nature. But contemporary physicists have become much more careful before making such statements, not because of special microphysical results, but because of more precise consciousness of the fact that general laws do not make possible an absolutely certain prediction about the possibility or impossibility of single events, except in the case where all possible conditions can be taken into account. This might be possible in an experiment, but not in the process of the world as a whole.

If resurrection would mean revivification of the corpse, then we must really say this would hardly be thinkable from the point of view of the natural sciences. The range of the possible conditions in this model could be surveyed, so that such an event, although not entirely impossible theoretically, must practically be excluded. The beginning and end of an event which is understood in this way lie in the realm of the world known to our experience. After life has ceased for several seconds, or in special cases, for several minutes, irreversible processes of dissolution have begun. The concept of transformation is different, however, since we only know the starting point, but not the final point of this process. We speak of this on the basis of the appearances and, indeed, only in a metaphorical language.

380

Now, someone may ask: Even if the resurrection of Jesus is certain as an event that really happened, what would that mean? Would it be possible to recognize by this that Jesus was the Son of God, that he was the One who died on the cross for the sins of all men? This is precisely the case. If the resurrection of the dead really happened with Jesus and if one understands the meaning of this event in connection with the pre-Easter activity and destiny of Jesus, then all the assertions of the early Christian message of Christ are only a development of the meaning included in this event--also expressed in a way relative to that time. That can be proved and shown step by step, if one follows the way in which the message of Christ developed out of the proclamation of the resurrection of Jesus, thus expressing the inner meaning of this event in its original context. That this event has such an absolute meaning consists in the fact that the resurrection of Jesus stands in a close connection with the final destiny of man. With the resurrection of Jesus, what for all other men is still to come has been realized. Therefore, now man's attitude toward Jesus as a man is decisive for his future destiny, this was the claim made by Jesus before the events in Jerusalem. Thus, man has a hope beyond death through community with Jesus. In his destiny the final destiny of all men became an event, and through this Jesus proclaimed that the destiny of all people will be decided by the attitude they have toward him.

Thus, Jesus is the final revelation of God and, therefore, he himself is God. This doctrine adds nothing essential to the events of the resurrection of Jesus; it only makes clear the inner meaning of that event.

Discussion Questions

1. Is it necessary for faith to rest on some basis which is historical or factual?

2. Do you think that our presuppositions sometimes enable us to see only what we want to see?

3. Explain in your own words what God's raising of Jesus means about Jesus' pre-Easter life and teachings.

381

4. Sometimes persons hold that the reason they know Jesus is alive is that he lives within them. What do you think this means? Is it a valid approach to resurrection doctrine?

THE ATONEMENT

No single atonement theology has ever won its way to the general acceptance enjoyed by the Nicene-Chalcedonian theory of the person of Christ. Indeed, it may be said that the history of Christian thought is saturated with theories that seek to elucidate the connection between Jesus' life, death and resurrection, and our salvation. It is important to note that each approach to the at-one-ment between man and God accomplished by Christ sought to express what was believed to be the scriptural witness. The history of the atonement doctrine reflects clearly that several theological viewpoints may be found in the scriptures.

Notable among atonement theories one must include the classical Ransom theory according to which atonement is accomplished external to man. God in Christ does the work of atonement and man is the recipient. A cosmic struggle occurred in the cross and resurrection, and man waited on the sidelines until God won the victory. A second theory, some version of which is found in most Christian traditions, is the Satisfaction (Propitiation) theory. This theory, expressed in its classic form by Anselm of Canterbury, was built on the interpretation that the problem which blocked atonement was within God. It was not so much that Satan had possession of man and a ransom had to be paid to him. Rather, the problem was the tension between God's love and his justice (honor). Human sin offended God's honor or justice, and God could not simply forgive without satisfaction. Christ died as the sacrifice to God's justice. Since Christ was sinless, and did not need to die because he never violated God's honor, then his willing sacrifice freed God to forgive all who would come to him through Christ.

A third major theory was advocated by Peter

Abelard, and it has come to be called the Moral Influence theory. According to Abelard atonement could be achieved only if something changed within humans. God loved humans and he wanted to forgive and accept them, but their hearts were cold and callous. It is the world (humanity) which must be reconciled to God, not vice versa. Abelard held that Christ's death on the cross did not appease God. He believed Anselm's theory was profoundly in error.

According to Abelard, Anselm's theory could not explain three crucial questions. It could not account for the forgiveness of sin before Christ. It could not explain how the death of any innocent person could satisfy justice. And finally, it could not explain how God could be satisfied with the death of the God-man. Such an act should have been more offensive than any other (c.f., the parable of the wicked husbandmen).

Abelard argued that Christ tried to soften the hearts of humans through his life and teachings. When this failed he submitted to the cross in a final effort to draw men. In the cross man sees the love of God and his egotism is broken. He turns back to God.

In Gordon Kaufman's analysis of the atonement he argues that we should set these classical theories aside as somewhat misleading. Each theory has some truth to convey, and thus it is erroneous to conclude that we should choose one or the other of them.

According to Kaufman, atonement is the process of transformation from the disharmony and chaos into which human existence has fallen, into the kingdom of God (Rule of God). He holds, therefore, that it is easy to understand why the early Christians employed the language of warfare and struggle (characteristic of the Ransom theory) to interpret the great atonement transformation.

In his reconstruction of atonement doctrine, Kaufman draws two insights from the *Christus Victor* theory. One of these is that any appropriate atonement doctrine must take the reality of human bondage seriously. The Ransom theory said humans are in bondage to the devil, and Kaufman understands this to mean that humans are under the grip of evil from which they cannot escape. Kaufman thinks that this kind of bondage is readily demonstrable and he calls attention to various contemporary processes of war, hunger, and alienation as evidence.

The second insight that must be incorporated into an atonement theory is that God is overcoming the powers of evil. The grounds for this confidence cannot be our observation of life. Simply looking at things we might conclude God is only holding his own. But our memory of the actions of God gives us confidence. The exodus, the giving of the land, the restoration of the nation, the coming of Jesus, all of these events suggest God is at work. Indeed, in the Christ-event we witness the apparent victory of the powers of evil in Jesus' death, but in reality what we witness is the creative beginning of a redemptive process by which God is reshaping man's rebellion. In this sense, Christ was the second Adam. He was the actual historical beginning of a new humanity, a new community destined to become God's people.

The following essay represents a statement of atonement theology by Professor Kaufman written before he had worked out his understanding of theology as "imaginative construction" (Cf. "Constructing the Concept of God" in this book). He continues to affirm the general lines of the historicist interpretation of the atonement sketched out here, but doubtless he would formulate all of this somewhat differently were he to write an article on this subject today.

THE ATONEMENT*

The central problem of salvation, as we have noted, is that man has turned away from God and toward himself; instead of pursuing God's will, he seeks his own selfish interests. In consequence, man has exchanged the possibility of a harmonious and creative community of love on earth, in which each self could find freedom and fulfilment--the kingdom of God--for a war of all against all; and the life of man has become, as Hobbes put it in a classic phrase, "solitary, poor, nasty, brutish, and short."[1] The problem, now, is how this condition can be rectified. How is this collection of self-centered men, warring against each other, each pursuing chiefly his own goals, to be

*Source: From *Systematic Theology: A Historicist Perspective* by Gordon D. Kaufman. Copyright 1968 by Gordon Kaufman. Used with the author's permission.

transformed into the kingdom of God, the community in
which God is acknowledged as sovereign and men love
each other?

Clearly, there are two dimensions to the problem.
(a) God's sovereignty itself must be fully confirmed
and established; it must in no way be weakened or
threatened by the solution. (b) Genuine love and self-
giving among men must become the characteristic actu-
alities of human intercourse. The several theories of
atonement each deal with both these dimensions, though
their respective emphases differ considerably. Sometimes these theories are classified into two groups
(corresponding roughly to the above two dimensions),
regarded as "objective" and "subjective" views,
according to whether the changed relation between man
and God is understood to depend principally on a change
in *God* or in *man*. The so-called orthodox doctrine of
propitiation is said to be the outstanding example of
the former; the "moral influence" view, of the latter.
For the purposes of the present analysis such classifications must be disregarded as more misleading than
helpful, and my suggestion that there are two *dimensions* involved in the atonement should not be understood to refer to this ordinary twofold classification
of theories. These dimensions are not alternatives
between which we may choose: both are required if
there is to be genuine atonement, and it would only
make misunderstanding inevitable were they to be tied
in some way to the "objective" and "subjective"
theories. We shall, then, view the doctrine of atonement as interpretation of the way in which the disharmony and chaos into which human existence has fallen is restored into the kingdom of God.

From the earliest period Christians were confident that the church was living in the midst of this
process of transformation. In the New Testament the
appearance of Christ was understood as the beginning
of the great change: "in Christ God was reconciling
the world to himself" (2 Cor. 5:19, RSV footnote).
Though the change was thus well under way, it had not
yet reached completion: "For as in Adam all die, so
also in Christ shall all be made alive. But each in
his own order: Christ the first fruits, then at his
coming those who belong to Christ. . . . he must
reign until he has put all his enemies under his
feet" (1 Cor. 15:22-23,25).[2] This process of at-one-
ment through which Christ was overcoming his enemies
will soon reach its climax: "When all things are
subjected to him, then the Son himself will also be

subjected to him who put all things under him, that God may be everything to every one" (1 Cor. 15:28). Thus, the early church was conscious of living through the turning point of the battle between God and his enemies; all existence was shortly to be brought under God's sovereignty.

It is not difficult to understand why the earliest church frequently interpreted this great transformation in terms of images drawn from the human experience of warfare. It was not uncommon in the ancient world for the cosmos to be visualized as a great battleground between God with his forces of light, and the demons and principalities and powers--the forces of darkness. In terms of this conception, man, who had for long been in bondage to these evil powers, was now being freed; in a great battle Christ is overcoming--has already overcome!--the power of the devil. The magnitude of the battle required to accomplish this work is made dramatically clear by the fact that God's mighty warrior, his own Son Jesus Christ, was himself killed in the fray.

> . . . you were ransomed from the futile ways inherited from your fathers, not with perishable things such as silver or gold, but with the precious blood of Christ.
>
> 1 Peter 1:18-19

> For in Christ our release is secured and our sins are forgiven through the shedding of his blood.
>
> Ephesians 1:7 NEB

> The children of a family share the same flesh and blood; and so he too shared ours, so that through death he might break the power of him who had death at his command, that is, the devil; and might liberate those who, through feat of death, had all their lifetime been in servitude.
>
> Hebrews 2:14-15 NEB

> For the Son of man . . . came not to be served but to serve, and to give his life as a ransom for many.
>
> Mark 10:45

Though the battle was fierce and the price tremendous, in the end the tragedy of Christ's death was itself a victory over the evil powers that held man in bondage.

Because Christ paid this supreme price for man's sake

> and became obedient unto death, even death on a
> cross . . . God has highly exalted him and be-
> stowed on him the name which is above every name,
> that at the name of Jesus every knee should bow,
> in heaven and on earth and under the earth, and
> every tongue confess that Jesus Christ is Lord,
> to the glory of God the Father.
>
> Philippians 2:8-11

Thus, the death which had seemed to be supreme tragedy
turned out eventually (i.e., in Christ's resurrection
from the dead) to be total victory. And it could be
said that though he was "delivered to death for our
misdeeds," he was "raised to life to justify us"
(Rom. 4:25 NEB).

The consequences of Christ's sacrificial victory
were twofold. (a) The sovereignty of the evil powers
to whom men had been subject was broken, and they
could now become obedient servants in God's kingdom.
"He has delivered us from the dominion of darkness and
transferred us to the kingdom of his beloved Son"
(Col. 1:13). No longer need men fear that any power
"in all creation, will be able to separate (them) from
the love of God" (Rom. 8:39). God's kingdom is well
on the way to being established. (b) Men no longer are
in bondage to self and sin, but are now free beings
who can live in genuine community with love for their
fellows. "For freedom Christ has set us free; . . .
only do not use your freedom as an opportunity for the
flesh, but through love be servants of one another"
(Gal. 5:1,13). A new life has thus opened up for man,
an "abundant" life (John 10:10) of authentic freedom
and creativity and love; man has become veritably a
"new creation" (2 Cor. 5:17). Thus, with the victory
over the demons won through Christ's death, God's full
sovereignty over his world was being reestablished even
while the possibilities of a life of genuine fulfilment and meaning were opening once again for man. In
the near future, when "the Lord himself will descend
from heaven with a cry of command, with the archangel's
call, and with the sound of the trumpet of God"
(1 Thess. 4:16), the forces of evil will be completely
wiped out and the great battle will be brought to its
end with victory for God and his mighty warrior, Christ.

For those who thought man's situation and problems resulted from his being caught in the middle of
a cosmic battle, the Christian proclamation must have

been exciting news indeed. For according to this
message God does not stand aloof from man's terrifying
situation. Rather, he girds on his mighty sword and
enters into the dangers of the battle in man's behalf.
The powers that hold man in slavery are sufficiently
strong that salvation is a difficult work even for the
Creator of the universe: he must finally sacrifice
his own Son in order to achieve the victory. But he
manages at last to outwit and overpower the devil and
to free man. And so now man, also, can join battle
against the demons, suffering as Christ suffered to
help release other captives (cf. 2 Cor. 5:19-6:13).
Inasmuch as man was himself responsible for his plight
and thus the world's chaos--since his guilty disobedience of God had brought him into bondage to the
powers of darkness (Rom. 1:18-3:20; Eph. 2:1-5, 6:12;
etc.)--how joyously could he now enter the fray, for
God himself, before whom he was guilty, had forgiven
him and acted to free him from bondage (2 Cor. 5:18-19;
Eph. 1:3-8, 2:4-8; Col. 1:12-14, 2:13-15; etc.).
These images have had great significance to those who
accepted the mythology of the cosmic battle and thought
they saw it finally drawing to a close in God's victory.
This was a meaningful way to understand both the present disorder, terror, and bondage--for what is more
chaotic than a bloody battlefield?--and the means
through which it was at last being transformed into
the kingdom in which God would be fully sovereign.
Since this view of salvation is the one most prominent
in the New Testament and the church fathers, we may
well refer to it, with Aulen, as the "classic" theory
of the atonement.[3]

The classic view has some very obvious limitations, two of which we may consider here. First, it
is heavily dependent on the mythology of the great
battle between light and darkness. As long as men
subscribed to this world-picture, the conception was
potentially relevant and meaningful. But if the
mythology changes, and men can no longer think in
these terms, what then? In the middle of the twentieth
century--indeed, long before--it has seemed simply
absurd to speak of literal demons and powers which
hold man and the world in bondage and which God must
overcome in a mighty battle. Unless it is possible to
demythologize this understanding of God's mighty act
so that it can be grasped also by those who no longer
think in such terms, the whole Christian message
appears a fantastic, if somewhat fascinating, product
of man's all too fertile imagination.

Second, the classic view is time-bound not only in the sense of being informed by prescientific conceptions of the world and human bondage. For its meaning depends not only on the conviction that there is a cosmic battle in process, but that that battle is now rapidly coming to its end, thus establishing once and for all God's full sovereignty. Only if it can be believed that the fight is nearly over and God's victory won does God's act in Christ retain its overwhelming significance. But if the end of the world does not come and seems never to come, what then? God's kingdom apparently is not established after all; the victory was not complete; the final stages of the battle drag on and on, and one wonders whether God has failed to defeat the devil in the moment of decisive encounter. Thus, this mythology, instead of proclaiming God's final sovereignty, only succeeds in making it appear problematic once again. Are the faithful in God's kingdom or not? Have they been freed from bondage to sin and the devil or not? As these questions arise and become increasingly insistent, the classic theory appears less and less adequate, for it no longer is an expression of the central conviction of Christian faith: that the kingdom of God is really breaking into history, and the church lives in the midst of the process of its establishment.[4]

What sort of restatement of the atonement is possible and necessary in order for men in the twentieth century to grasp how the chaos of history is being transformed into the kingdom of God? Let us recall the two dimensions necessary to any adequate Christian view of salvation, both included under the comprehensive biblical symbol, the *kingdom of God*. On the one hand, it must be *God's* kingdom, his authentic and full sovereignty over his world, which is being established; on the other hand, this kingdom must be seen not simply in transcendental or supernaturalistic or symbolical terms, but as the actual empirical establishment of a community of authentic love among men.[5] The doctrine of atonement is the interpretation of how this two-dimensional kingdom of God actually is coming to be. We can best develop the conception by beginning with the classic view of atonement, demythologizing and elaborating it in certain respects.

It goes without saying that demythologizing is required here. Few moderns could accept the mythology of the cosmic battle even if they wished to. No doubt some in our time (e.g., Jehovah's Witnesses) still claim to think in terms of a great struggle, soon to come to an end, between forces of light and darkness, but most find such a view utterly fanciful; the notions of demonic and angelic hosts seem to have no warrant. Even less credible is the claim that Jesus of Nazareth will soon return with these heavenly hosts to vanquish the foe. However, the problematic character of these mythological conceptions does not mean that the classic view is to be regarded as fallacious and outmoded in every respect.

Two points in the imagery of the cosmic battle must be noted. In the first place, the reality of human bondage or enslavement is taken seriously. In the conception of men being in the hands of God's enemies--the devil and other evil powers--is expressed awareness that human history has gotten into the grip of evils from which man cannot escape. Every attempt fails; men are unable effectively to grapple with the situation. This bondage involves suffering and continual frustration for man, and salvation from it can be purchased only at the cost of further suffering. The notion of the cosmic battlefield, with its gruesome images of chaos and destruction and frightful struggles culminating in bloodshed and death, expresses well the horror and evil of this situation: man is now suffering as prisoner of evil powers; later, when he is freed, it will only be to become a warrior in the battle against them. Thus man's suffering will continue until victory is finally won and God's kingdom comes. God himself must sacrifice much--his only Son!--to achieve victory; not even the almighty God can bring man's bondage to an end simply by a word.

In our own time we have once again become aware of the reality of human bondage. The course of history seems out of control. We do not know but what we may destroy not only ourselves but all civilization and possibly all mankind. It is not, of course, that anyone desires this. Rather, somehow we have gotten into the grip of powers which we cannot handle, which control us. The great wars of our century have shown that political processes are not directly subject to man's will; the persistence of poverty in wealthy America shows that economic processes cannot easily be managed, nor are they benevolent when left uncontrolled; the rise of urban industrial society, with the consequent appearance of "mass man" and all the related social, moral, and cultural problems, has created new fears that just in his "progress" man may be destroying the possibility of authentic personal existence. All of these, taken together with an exploding technological advance, mean that human existence has become more precarious than ever before (though, of course, it is also true that many middle-class individuals now lead lives with few physical hazards). Brainwashing and the H-bomb have become veritable apocalyptic symbols. In our time once again we know bondage to "principalities and powers" which seem to determine almost every facet of existence, tending it toward evil. And this is a bondage from which there seems no escape. The Anselmic doctrine of a substitutionary atonement[6] appears irrelevant to the problem; Abailard's hope for a mere changing of the hearts of men[7] seems pale and weak. Somehow men must be enabled to believe there can be and is occurring an actual historical process through which this present chaos is being brought into order. They must be able to hope that, despite all evidence to the contrary, *God is winning the battle proceeding in the very historical existence in which they are living.*

This brings us, in the second place, to the central contention of the classic view, that victory is assured, God is indeed overcoming the powers of darkness. Even though much misery and evil remains in human existence, "the sufferings of this present time are not worth comparing with the glory that is to be revealed . . . because the creation itself will be set free from its bondage to decay and obtain the glorious liberty of the children of God" (Rom. 8:18, 21). That is, it is not on the basis of the present empirical evidence in history--"the sufferings of this present time"--that Christians believe God will achieve victory. Such evidence appears to suggest all is going wrong; man's bondage is far from overcome. If one surveys the whole of history "objectively," there seems little evidence that God is winning the battle and the day of bondage is past; indeed, all of creation "has been groaning in travail together until now" (8:22). Nevertheless, "in this hope"[8] that God is in fact accomplishing his mighty redemptive act "we were saved" (8:24). What is the ground for such faith in God's sovereignty and deliverance?

If the overall context of man's existence is not a purposive movement and his history is not actually going anywhere, if there is no ontologically significant change occurring in the historical world, then that event of two thousand years ago can have little meaning today. It is but another tragic fact of human life, so distant from us as to remain largely abstract and irrelevant. However, *if that event can be under-*

*stood as beginning a historical process which is trans-
forming human existence into God's kingdom, then it
has significance for all time and direct relevance to
the contemporary situation.*

In certain respects the position suggested here
resembles the hope of liberal protestantism that God
is guiding present history into the historical realization of his kingdom.[9] If men could really believe
this--as the liberals did--then they could endure such
suffering as they might have to undergo, as well as
the most discouraging reversals, because in the light
of their hope all such would be apprehended as but
temporary and bound ultimately to fail. The meaninglessness and absurdity in present existence could be
tolerated "while we wait for God to make us his sons
and set our whole body free" (Rom. 8:23 NEB). Unfortunately, the faith of liberal protestantism did not
have a foundation adequate to withstand all reversals;
for it was rooted, at least in part, in what seemed
to be clear empirical evidence of the imminence of
God's kingdom: the supposed continuous progress
upwards of Western civilization. When that conclusion
had to be revised and even reversed because of new
data coming to light in the twentieth century, the
faith and hope based on it foundered also. Liberalism
should be criticized not so much for the content of
its hope--that the kingdom of God is indeed coming--
as for its grounding of that hope more on supposed
empirical evidence than on God's revelation, and for
its somewhat superficial belief that this coming could
occur without great suffering and struggle and even
terrible reversals. The classic view did not suffer
these limitations. It recognized that the battle in
which God and men were engaged was nothing less than
cosmic in scope; and it saw clearly, therefore, that
its hope had to be rooted in God, and him alone, if
it were to be securely grounded. But from such a
position it was possible also to say, "If God be for
us, who can be against us?" (Rom. 8:31 KJ). The
earliest Christians were thus able to place their
faith in the very Foundation of the universe, who had
revealed to them, as they believed, himself and his
purposes for history. This meant they could also
believe--experiential evidence to the contrary not-
withstanding--that God's kingdom was in fact coming;
and they could live and act on that belief in the
historical interim in which they found themselves,
regardless of the suffering they had to bear.

Let us now tie together some of these points.

It makes little sense to speak of a substitutionary
atonement (Anselm) as an event which occurred two
thousand years ago but somehow effects men's redemption today, or to preach of God's love manifest two
thousand years ago but somehow piercing men's hearts
today (Abailard). Such events are so historically
and metaphysically remote, both from the contemporary
sense of existential meaning and value and from the
form in which the human problem impinges on contemporary man, as to appear absurd abstractions or senti-
mental and irrelevant ways of escaping the harsh
historical realities of existence. However, one can
make significant sense of that event of two thousand
years ago if it is seen as the *creative beginning of
a redemptive process that is actually going on in
history,* reshaping man's rebellion and consequent
enslavement into obedience to the Lord of creation and
consequent freedom. Through this process--beginning
with Jesus of Nazareth and expanding outward (with
many reversals of course) through the centuries of
church history--God is penetrating human history with
his spirit, converting men's continuous "war of each
against all" into a community of love. Of course, the
belief that this is the real significance of the
church's history is scarcely to be inferred directly
from the somewhat sordid empirical facts of that
history itself; for the church has hardly been such a
community. Rather, the Christian hope and expectation
is that the church shall finally become this community
--not because the historical facts of her life give
warrant for such belief--but because this is God's
ultimate will.

For those who live by such faith, there can be no
easy optimism that the kingdom is about to be established. In this respect it is no longer possible to
share the view either of the early church or of
protestant liberalism. With Buchenwald and Hiroshima
as living memories, and the present racial and international situations a clear vision, our generation can
realize as perhaps not many before how hard it is for
God to change the hearts and communities of men.
Believers, desiring to be vehicles through which God
can transform this world, can properly anticipate only
suffering for themselves. There is no place for ease
or comfort in this view of the atonement: it involves
God's suffering and sacrifice, and man's, if the
troubled world we know is really to become his kingdom;
and there is no reason to suppose that either we or
our great-grandchildren will see the end. But at the
same time such suffering or sacrifice as one is called

to undergo is given new meaning, for he is able to apprehend it as a living symbol of--and thus historical participation in--that suffering through which God is redeeming the world.[10]

In this historically realistic and meaningful sense Christ was the "second Adam" (1 Cor. 15:45-49; Rom. 5:12-21). This suggestive title need not be understood in some esoteric or mystical sense as meaning that Christ stands before God in place of other men, or that he becomes the "representative man" before God.[11] It can be understood in a fully intelligible historical sense: he was the actual historical beginning of the new humanity, the new community destined to become God's very kingdom, as "Adam" stands for the actual historical beginning of the old.[12] In him atonement--the at-one-ment of God and man--really began; in his death and resurrection God's love succeeded in breaking into human history, becoming a new element in the on-going historical process. And thus without him, men could not become at-one with God, reconciled with him. But the atonement was not completed in this death and resurrection of a man of two thousand years ago, and it shall not be completed until the divisions which keep men from being at-one with God and with each other are overcome in the perfect community which is God's kingdom. It will not be completed, then, until the present course of history has run to its end, thus fulfilling God's purposes for it. It is in this hope that the church lives, and it is for the establishment of this kingdom that Christians struggle. The word "atonement" points to this on-going struggle in which Christians, under God's sovereignty, are participating.

Endnotes

[1]*Leviathan*, Ch. 13.

[2]Upon occasion the early Christians were not averse to spelling out in some detail the several stages of the historical process in which they were living (cf. 2 Thess. 2; Mk. 13; etc.).

[3]Gustaf Aulen, *Christus Victor* (London: S.P.C.K., 1953). Aulen, however, would not accept my designation

395

of the classic view as a "theory," because--in accordance with his anti-theoretical anti-philosophical bias--he regards this view less contaminated by human speculation than the other interpretations of the atonement; it is therefore to be regarded as an "idea" or a "motif" while the others are mere theories and doctrines (see pp. 174f.). One cannot help but wonder what kind of perverseness or anti-cultural admiration for the primitive leads some theologians to regard man's attempts at disciplined thought to be somehow wrongheadedly "speculative" in a way that his creation of fantastic mythologies is not.

[4]Anselm as early as the eleventh century sought a new interpretation of the atonement partly because he realized that the "classic" view of God's act, with its outmoded and somewhat crude mythology, gave far too much power to the devil and the other powers of evil, thus calling into question God's sovereignty in an intolerable way (*Cur Deus Homo*, Book I, Chs. 6-7). Moreover, the image of God engaging in conflicts and transactions of various sorts with the powers of the underworld was unseemly. (In some versions of the classic view, for instance, God was portrayed as paying a ransom /the death of his Son/ to the devil; or it was even suggested that God defeated the devil by deceitfully outwitting him: the devil, seizing on the bait of Christ's human nature "as it is with greedy fish," swallowed the fishhook of his divinity, and thus was destroyed /Gregory of Nyssa/.) Such images, Anselm argued, violated God's proper dignity in the most offensive manner. The mythology of the cosmic battle was thus inadequate and it was essential to find another analogy to understand the salvation which God had provided. But what was to be substituted for it?

The problem, as Anselm formulated it, was essentially that of the stained and strained relationship between lowly man and the Lord of the universe (rather than God in mortal conflict with the powers of evil). What analogy could be more fitting for this new formulation than the relationship between lord and serf as found in the contemporary social structure? Lowly man has violated God's holy will--a mere serf has defied the Lord of the universe--and this creates an intolerable situation (see, e.g., Bk. I, Chs. 11-15, 20-24; Bk. II, Ch. 5). God must assert his righteous lordship over the cosmos through punishing, even destroying, the evildoer. However, God is merciful and wishes to forgive man, reestablishing community with him. How, now, can God's righteousness and proper

396

honor be maintained, on the one side, while man is
forgiven and restored to fellowship with God, on the
other? Obviously, the problem is completely beyond
solution from the human side. God is the infinite
and absolute being, and this means that even the
slightest peccadillo is of immeasurable weight (Bk. I,
Ch. 21; here of course the feudal conception that the
measure of guilt increases in proportion with the
status of the one whose honor is violated is clearly
at work). It is, then, impossible for man ever to
make reparation for his disobedience to God, for it
is necessary that such a reparation be infinite. Here,
then, is the answer to the question, why God became
man: though perfectly innocent of any sin, by offering himself up for sacrifice on the cross, the God-man
Jesus was able to offer an infinite reparation, at
once satisfying God's honor and making it possible for
God, for Jesus' sake, to remit to other men as reward
what Jesus had won and wished to bestow upon them (Bk.
II, Ch. 18). Thus, through an ingenious chain of
reasoning, Anselm resolved one of the principal problems of the classic view of the atonement through
proposing a theory in which God's sovereignty and
initiative is clearly maintained throughout; and at
the same time he explained the necessity of the orthodox paradoxical beliefs about the Incarnation.

However, there are problems with Anselm's view of
man's at-one-ment with God quite as serious as those
of the classic view. Not the least of these is its
contrived and artificial appearance. While to a
medieval mind who took for granted the truth of the
Christian dogmas Anselm's explanation might appear
rational and clear, to a modern, dubious in any case
about the Christian claims, it seems an outrageous
play of concepts and words. What is a "God-man?" Is
Gos so divided that one "part" of him (the Son) can be
conceived as doing something for another (the Father)?
How can such a transaction within the Godhead have
anything to do with my load of guilt and sin, which is
a *personal* burden I must bear? What can it possibly
mean to say that the righteousness of another man is
somehow transferred to me or my account? Moreover,
even so far as it is comprehensible, Anselm's formulation has misleading implications. Guilt and sin appear
not so much as qualities of a personal relationship
between God and man which require to be removed by
personal forgiveness, as "things" which can be transferred away from man through a complex transaction
within the Godhead. In an interpersonal situation,
how, after all, can another make reparation for my
guilt? Even God's sovereignty, though central to

Anselm's concern, is hardly given its due in his theory. For God's love and honor are so set over against each other that it appears impossible for him to act in genuine and straightforward personal forgiveness of man. Instead of proposing an interpretation of the way in which the death of Christ altered the interpersonal relation between God and man and made it possible for man to find the personal and communal fulfilment God had intended for him--thus simultaneously realizing God's objectives and man's--Anselm developed an intricate theory explicating a dubious dogma about two metaphysical natures in the one person Christ. And God's *personal* sovereignty over the *personal subjects* in his kingdom tended to be forgotten.

[5]With respect to this secomd emphasis in particular, the interpretation of the coming of God's kingdom in the next pages (and in this work as a whole) is similar to that of the sixteenth-century Anabaptists (cf., e.g., Robert Friedmann, "The Doctrine of the Two Worlds," in *The Recovery of the Anabaptist Vision*, ed. G. F. Hershberger /Scottdale, Pennsylvania: Herald Press, 1957/, pp. 105-118). The full significance of the views of these men of the "radical reformation" for our contemporary "post-Christian" situation is only very belatedly becoming realized.

[6]See above, n. 4.

[7]For Abailard (a younger contemporary of Anselm) the important problem was not so much the threat to God's sovereignty raised by man's sin (Anselm) as the actual fact of lovelessness in human existence. Men were in bondage to themselves. How could they be freed to love God and neighbor? We should note here certain affinities with the classic view of the atonement. Once more the problem is thought of as human bondage, though this is no longer conceived in the mythological terms of the earlier view, but rather psychologically. How now does God's act in Christ free man from this self-slavery and make it possible for him to love? Abailard's answer is at once simple and profound. Somehow genuine love must break into the circle of man's lovelessness, for only this can evoke from man the response of love which he otherwise could not generate. And this in-breaking of God's love is precisely what is proclaimed in the Gospel. It is through a "unique act of grace manifest to us" that "we have been justified by the blood of Christ and reconciled to God." This is an act which "frees us from slavery to sin . . . (and) wins for us the true

liberty of sons of God" by evoking from us a "deeper
affection . . . so that we do all things out of love
rather than fear--love to him who has shown us such
grace that no greater can be found." (*Exposition of
the Epistle to the Romans* /Second Book/, commentary on
Rom. 3:19-26; trans. from *Library of Christian Classics*,
X /Philadelphia: Westminster Press, 1956/, 283-284.)
In Abailard's view, God transforms man, not in any
mechanical or heteronomous or impersonal way, but by
so dramatically manifesting his own love to man that
man's heart of stone is thawed and replaced by a
heart of flesh (Ezek. 36:26). The magnitude of God's
love has become visible in the sending of his Son,
and in his death on the cross at men's hands. When
this fact is appropriated, that the King of the universe gives himself for men, suffers for them, their
self-centered shells are broken through and a response
of gratitude and love to God is evoked, along with the
desire really to serve him through loving their fellows and sacrificing for them as Jesus did. Thus, in
Abailard's view what is necessary is that men become
genuinely aware of God's great love for them, for "if
they . . . see the glory prepared for them by God's
mercy, at that moment, along with discernment, the
love of God is born in them" (ibid., p. 287). In this
way, through Christ's teaching and death, God's "express purpose of spreading this true liberty of love
amongst men" (p. 284) is accomplished.

Abailard's theory is strong where Anselm's is
weak, for atonement remains an abstract and empty
conception unless one can see how human existence is
actually changed concretely and empirically by God's
act in Christ; and Abailard tried to show how precisely
that act makes possible the appearance of genuine love
among men. But his view is also weak where Anselm's
is strong, for it focuses attention so much on man's
need and man's redemption that it tends to overlook
the other evil wrought by sin, namely, that God's
sovereignty is threatened. With this anthropocentric
emphasis it is but a short step to a view of God as
nothing but man's servant, a kindly old gentleman who
pulls men out of difficult situations but has little
other function or meaning. If this humanistic tendency
is carried to an extreme, God as a genuinely active
agent may drop out of the picture entirely, the un-
breakable bondage to sin and self may be forgotten,
and the Gospel interpreted largely as an exhortation
to follow Jesus' moral example of self-sacrifice.
Certainly this was not Abailard's intention, but developments along this line occurred in the liberal protestantism which found his view preferable to either

the classic or the Anselmic view.

⁸It should be noted that Paul makes very clear
that what he is affirming here does not have the kind
of certainty characteristic of empirical knowledge,
but is rather a matter of hope, the self's venture or
stance of confidence in face of an open (and unknown)
future: "Now hope that is seen is not hope. For who
hopes for what he sees? But if we hope for what we
do not see, then, in waiting for it, we show our
endurance" (Rom. 8:24-25; vs. 25 adapted from NEB).

⁹It could be argued that liberalism, a perspective
often supposed to have ignored such matters as the
atonement altogether, in fact subscribed to what we
might call a "progress view" of God's act. The atonement is concerned with the becoming at-one of God and
man, with the conversion of the chaos of human affairs
into the kingdom of God; every theory has developed
this theme in its own way. Only the earliest or classic view, however, portrayed the kingdom as actually
to be established on earth with the imminent coming of
the end of the world. As this mythology became
increasingly unbelievable, it dropped out of succeeding interpretations, which portrayed the atonement as
occurring in God himself (Anselm) or in the individual
soul (Abailard), rather than in the movement of history.
To the nineteenth-century progress theologians, however, the notion of the kingdom of God on earth once
again seemed somewhat tenable; so for them the expectation of the establishment of a real community of love
among men in history reappeared also. However, though
in this respect there was a return to certain emphases
of the classic view, the old mythology had now disappeared entirely. No longer was there belief in Christ''s
imminent conquest of the demons from below; rather,
now God's (or Christ's) conquest of the self-centered-
ness of the human heart (cf. Abailard) was proclaimed,
and with it the kingdom would really be established
among men.
Above all, the progress theologians insisted
that the atonement must have genuine relevance to the
actual social structures and institutions of human
history, and not simply to individual souls isolated
from the community. They saw the atonement as a
process now going on, a process in which men participate in the present but which will not be completed
until God's kingdom is the context in which human life
is actually lived. And they were able to hope, therefore, that God was actually guiding the movement of
empirical history toward the ultimate goal of his

kingdom. Unfortunately, however, the technological progress of the nineteenth and twentieth centuries was so impressive to the men who thought in these terms that they obscured the very real strengths of their position by certain additional convictions. Not only did they somewhat naively believe the kingdom's full establishment in history to be imminent (here also their view can be compared with the earliest Christians), but they often failed to recognize the depth of hard suffering (classic view, Anselm, Abailard) required to usher it in. It thus became possible-- and this was theologically most disastrous of all--for them to believe that perhaps man himself, through his own efforts, was really the one bringing in the new community of love. And thus the kingdom of God became watered down to a humanistic utopia, and the necessary ontological foundation for this hope for history--the loving purposes of the Creator of the heavens and the earth--tended to drop out of view.

10Cf. the remarks of Kazoh Kitamori: "By serving as witness to the pain of God, our pain is transformed into light; it becomes meaningful and fruitful. By the pain of God which overcomes his wrath, our pain, which had hitherto been the reality of the wrath of God, ends in salvation from this wrath. By serving the pain of God which is the glad news of salvation, our pain ends in sharing the salvation. By serving him through our pain, the pain of God rather saves and heals our own pain. When the pain of God heals our pain, it already has changed into love which has broken through the bounds of pain--'the love rooted in the pain of God.' By this love, whoever follows the Lord, bearing his own cross and losing his life for Christ's sake, will find life. Through our service in the pain of God, the wounds of our Lord in turn heal *our* wounds, thus our pain can actually be relieved by serving the pain of God. All kinds of pain experienced in this world remain meaningless and fruitless as long as they do not serve the pain of God. We must take care not to suffer human pain in vain" (*Theology of the Pain of God* [Richmond: John Knox Press, 1965], pp. 52, 53).

11In the past this term has often been understood in quasi-platonistic terms. Jesus was held to be no mere individual but the *form of man* as such, or he was regarded as the "representative man," so that whatever affected him necessarily affects all, his actual relationship to God becoming the possibility of a new relationship for every man. But for most moderns, with their conviction of the reality of the individual person, such conceptions are no longer intelligible. Even were they able to think in these terms, there would remain serious problems--e.g., how can one particular man be at once the form of man and still a particular exemplification of that form? To questions of this sort platonistic orthodoxy has never been able to give a clear and convincing answer. The historicist interpretation of Christ has the advantage of preserving a genuine metaphysical primacy and uniqueness for Jesus in terms intelligible to historically oriented moderns while avoiding the metaphysical difficulties into which platonistic interpretations fall.

12Cf. Schleiermacher: "The appearance of the first man constituted at the same time the physical life of the human race; the appearance of the Second Adam constituted for this nature a new spiritual life, which communicates and develops itself by spiritual fecundation" (*The Christian Faith* /Edinburgh: T. & T. Clark, 1928/, Sec. 94).

Discussion Questions

1. Try to find several passages of scripture which you think support the three main theories of the atonement discussed in this essay.

2. Do you think that Kaufman's theory preserves any of the concept that Christ's death was a sacrifice? If so, in what senses does it do so?

3. Is Kaufman's theory of the atonement compatible with any theories of Christ's person or human nature and sin which we have studied? If so, which?

4. For some traditions it has been important to stress that atonement is a once-for-all accomplished fact. Is this a necessary element to a Christian atonement theory? Can Kaufman's theory preserve this truth, if it needs to be preserved?

RETROSPECTIVE

As with the other doctrines we have studied it is
always easier to know the errors to be avoided in
Christology and atonement theory than it is to risk a
constructive theory of our own. Nevertheless, no
Christian theologian can completely avoid this task,
particularly with regard to Christology and atonement.

Baillie has rightly criticized the prevalent
Docetism of much popular Christology. Docetic Christology may reflect the good intention of preserving
dignity and reverence for Jesus. Or, it may be a
confession of one's very low view of human being, such
that nothing attributed to humans can be true of Jesus
Christ. In any case, Docetic Christology fosters
numerous misconceptions and it undermines the potential
present when humans cooperate with God.

Provided one can avoid Adoptionism, Hamilton's
view is in my opinion preferable to both Docetism and
to Christologies which wind up affirming only the
concept of paradox. To be sure, there is the danger
that metaphysics will dominate revelation and that is
to be avoided scrupulously. But I think this danger
is preferable to the silence of paradox.

Hamilton's Christological suggestions interface
with Kaufman's atonement theory very well. But one
still wonders if some biblical emphases are not ignored by Kaufman. But whether a theologian must find
room for every scriptural emphasis is probably a moot
question. No theologian will be able to capture every
nuance of the biblical witness. Some theologians will
not even have this as a goal.

Still, the sacrificial motif seems to be a favorite interpretation of Jesus' death, and it is presented as necessary for atonement to occur. Kaufman seems very little concerned with this model. But I believe that both Kaufman's theory and the theme of sacrifice can be preserved if sacrificial religion is properly understood.

PART SIX

THE CHURCH AND THE CHRISTIAN LIFE

THE CHURCH AND THE CHRISTIAN LIFE

To be a Christian is to be involved with the
church. Most persons who claim the Christian faith
will confirm that faith was born in the church. Of
course, this does not mean that theologians have been
uncritical in their attitude toward the church. But
the norm has been not to advocate the destruction of
the church, but its reform and restoration.

In contemporary secular society the necessity of
the church is seriously questioned. The problem
reaches far beyond the practical noninvolvement of
modern members. There is now the belief that one can
be Christian without the church. Other critics hold
that the church has become secularized to such a degree that in order to be a Christian one must abandon
at least the institutional church and seek Christian
fellowship and support in another setting.

What is the church? Many theological viewpoints
can be found. Some theologians have held that the
church is the focal point through which God's grace
is mediated. The other extreme has regarded the
church as a human fellowship the *raison d'etre* of
which is mutual support and edification. The essay
by Colin Williams examines the traditional views of
the church. Williams explores the meaning of various
biblical images available to a theology of the church.
His essay clears the ground for those who wish to
recover a viable understanding of the church.

As we have seen when examining the doctrines of
Christ and salvation, some theological concepts seem
mutually interdependent. This is the case with the
doctrine of the church and any theological understanding of what it means to live the Christian life.
The most obvious way to demonstrate this connection is

406

expressed in William Willimon's essay. The liturgy, the worship of the church, helps form the Christian identity. Some worship acts demonstrate what is considered to be appropriate behavior for crises in life's situations. Other acts are repeated to maintain the message of the faith. The Story of the faith is acted and affirmed at Christmas, Easter and Pentecost. Worship helps Christians order life, and it expands their minds to envision a world transformed into the Kingdom of God.

There is no place where the Christian rituals are performed other than the church. And there are essential contributions made to the Christian life by Christian ritual without which the distinctives of the faith are left unformed. Such spiritual lives are truncated and atrophied. How we act, and what actions we take, are at least as important as what we say we believe. Ritual is theologically significant; it is as significant as language. This notion we must explore further in Willimon's essay and in retrospective.

Some theologies of the church include well defined criteria for deciding what is Christian lifestyle and what is not. Indeed, varying degrees of discipline may be used to exact conformity to these lifestyle norms. Ethics, then, is also a theological issue. And Hans Küng explores what it means to be a Christian in the essay included in this section.

Küng holds that no abstract principles or general norms can finally function as the ultimate criterion for deciding what is Christian. Instead, he advocates the concrete person of Jesus himself as the ultimate norm and he suggests Christian conduct for several modern scenarios.

As a follow-up to Küng's discussion, I have included an essay by a recognized spiritual mentor for many contemporary Christians. Thomas Merton's essay is in the form of counsel, and in some respects it is unique in this collection. At the same time, however, it is an attempt to elucidate what it means to be a Christian in the modern world and it should provoke considerable discussion.

THE CHURCH: TRADITIONAL VIEWS REEXAMINED

It may seem impossible to speak of any Christian consensus concerning the doctrine of the church. A maze of unresolved difficulties confronts the theologian when trying to explicate an understanding of the church. Questions arise over infant and adult baptism, open and closed communion, apostolic succession, salvation outside of the church, the necessity of having bishops, whether there are sacraments or only ordinances and how many there are, whether there is a correct church government and if so what it is. At all of these points, and others too numerous to mention, Christians have broken ties with other Christians.

Colin Williams begins his essay with a grouping of what he calls the ecclesiastical families of Christendom. The three streams of tradition he identifies are the Catholic (including Orthodox and Anglican), the classical Protestant (Lutheran and Reformed), and the free church Protestant (including a welter of various denominations and groups). Williams' contention is that a healthy ecclesiology will include the truths in all three of these emphases. He thinks that there is scriptural and traditional basis for each of the ecclesial families.

Williams holds that the response to Christ within varied situations led to the different forms of the church. He does not seek to harmonize the various theologies of the church into a unitary theory. He says that the variety of response is the message the church proclaims. At the same time, however, Williams does maintain that the scriptures disclose some common features that mark the life of the church throughout its different settings. Yet he cautions us not to treat these factors as abstract truths, since even these characteristics are bracketed into a particular historical setting.

This is a wise caution. The reconstructionist tradition which seeks to rediscover *the* New Testament pattern of the church is doomed to failure before it begins. The reason why this attempt must fail is that there is no single New Testament pattern of the church. There is a family resemblance in the way the church existed in the first century, but no single pattern nor understanding ever obtained. This can be shown by historical inquiry and it should not dismay us.

Furthermore, the characteristics that seem to predominate wherever we find churches in the first century, at least those which Williams isolates, do not lend themselves to the level of disputes which has caused most schism and fragmentation in Christianity. Thus, the images of the church in the New Testament may not really help us prove that our church government is preferable to another.

Also to be noted is that the traditional catalog of the church's characteristics in the historical creeds does not provide us an adjudicatory device either. The church is One, Holy, Catholic, Apostolic fellowship. But Williams' discussion of the notion of the apostolicity of the church is meant to show that creedal affirmations about the church cannot enable us to condemn patterns different from our own.

As long as the church pattern practiced brings us in touch with Jesus Christ, then the unity of the Christian mission is preserved and in some sense our church is consistent with the New Testament under- standing of the church's presence in the world. This does not mean that just any church pattern will do. Nor does it mean that all expressions of the church are equally edifying. It does mean that the particular historical situation of particular individuals and institutions may be the laws for God's activity. No historical configuration can exclude God and he is able to meet and create his people where they are.

THE CHURCH: TRADITIONAL VIEWS REEXAMINED*

"Comparative ecclesiology" was the order of the day in the first stage of the modern ecumenical movement. The churches probed their own self-understanding and sought to explain themselves to one another in the hope that as they compared their views they would be able to discover the tradition behind the traditions, the God-given original unity behind the historical disunities.

The Ecclesiastical "Families"

An attempt was inevitable to bring some order into our investigation of the many ecclesiological strands by classifying them into major "families." A rough consensus has emerged that we can usefully divide them into three major streams of tradition:

1. The *Catholic* view, sometimes called the "horizontal" view, seems to place its prior emphasis upon the "given continuity" of the life of the church within history. Its initial stress is upon the claim that Christ has given the church guaranteed historical characteristics by which he keeps the church continuously present in the world and through which he keeps his redemptive presence continuously available to man. There are vital differences of emphasis between the various representatives of this horizontal view-- Roman Catholic, Orthodox, Anglo-Catholic--but there is the common assertion that the true church must be found in the context of the visibly continuous ministry, creeds, liturgy, and Sacraments.

2. The *classical Protestant* view is sometimes called the "objective vertical" view, because it places priority of emphasis upon the way the church is continuously called into being "from above" through the preaching of the Word and sustained in being from above by the given life of the Sacraments. Again

*Source: Reprinted from *New Directions in Theology Today*, volume IV, *The Church*, by Colin W. Williams. Copyright MCMLXVIII, The Westminster Press.   Used by permission.

there are vital differences of emphasis among the various representatives of this view--Lutheran and Reformed--but there is the common emphasis that we must look first, not to historical continuities visible to the eye of man, but to the event of faith in which Christ continuously calls his church into existence through the true preaching of the Word and the due administration of the Sacraments.

3. The *free church Protestant* view is sometimes called the "subjective vertical" view, because it places priority of emphasis upon the free response of believers in the Spirit and upon the need for us to be open to the possibility that Christ will call out new forms of faith and obedience in apparent disregard of the niceties of visible continuity. There is a considerable range of differences between the wide assortment of free churches, and yet there seems to be an obvious family similarity that characterizes them in their differences.

Now it is easy (and undoubtedly justified) to insist that a healthy ecclesiology today will need to include all three emphases. It is illuminating, too, to suggest that these three emphases can be brought together in a Trinitarian reconciliation:[1]

--the Catholic horizontal view, representing the symbol of "God the Father" as the providential continuity of God's unbroken care for his creation;

--the classical Protestant objective vertical view, representing the symbol of "God the Son" as the One who constantly recalls the world to its true center and who summons it out of its false worldly continuities into the redeemed continuities of his original purpose;

--the free church Protestant subjective vertical view, representing the symbol of "God the Spirit" bringing unpredictable responses out of the sluggish stream of history, but in such a way that yesterday's stream of renewal becomes tomorrow's pool of inertia out of which yet new forms of obedience have to be drawn.

The Trinitarian Structure of the Church

This family view would seem to suggest that there is a Trinitarian reality of the church that has tended to fragment from time to time, but requires

that the rediscovery of unity be sought within the
wholeness of the Trinitarian work of God. To some it
has appeared that promising results could accrue if we
were to explore the traditional Trinitarian formulations for the light they can throw on the proper
relation between the three motifs which have become so
sadly separated over the course of the centuries.

For example, take the doctrine of "perichoresis"
--the teaching that the three persons of the Trinity
"interpenetrate" in the unity of the one life of God.
This suggests the way in which the three ecclesiological
emphases must interpenetrate in an adequate doctrine
of the church. But what does this have to say about
the right relation between these three emphases?
Here we may call in the doctrine of the "procession"
of the life of the Trinity, or perhaps (if we accept
the Western clause) also the "filioque." If the Son
"proceeds" from the Father, and the Spirit from the
Father and the Son, this may suggest that the objective vertical view has to be held within the prior
framework of the Father's concern for the whole created
order, with its created continuities and cosmic context,
and that the subjective vertical must be protected
from uncontrolled freedom by being placed under proper
Christological control.[2]

Hesitations enter concerning this speculative
line. What is the status of these Trinitarian formulations and how great is the interpretative value?
That they represent a highly creative "projection" of
the meaning of the Christ event into the Greek language
and classical thought forms we may allow. But before
we can use these insights with any measure of control
today, we have to translate them from those older
metaphysical categories into the historical categories
of our time.

"Start with Christ"

At this point a more historical starting point
suggests itself. The historical center of the doctrine of the Trinity lies in its concern with Jesus
of Nazareth. It was the conviction that the reality
of God, with its radical promises and demands, had
here broken through in history that impelled the church
along the path of Trinitarian speculation. Similarly,
the life of the church emerged out of that historical
center as a response to the Christ event.

It is this conviction which lies behind the

suggestion that emerged at the Faith and Order meeting at Lund in 1952 that the right place for the churches to begin their common search for the one church is with Christology. "The nearer we come to Christ," the suggestion ran, "the nearer we come to each other." Or, to put it another way, the church's true unity can be given it only when it looks beyond its own divided life to Christ, its head.

There can be little doubt that this approach has resulted in some important gains within Faith and Order.[3] One effect was the reminder that the path to true unity cannot be found by putting together the pieces of past tradition into an ecclesiastical jigsaw puzzle. The church of the present can be found not in its own past alone but in its Living Lord. While the traditions must be examined for the clues they can give us in the search for present obedience to Christ, we must not forget that the unity needed now is an event which occurs at the point of true response to Christ today. That this response will have common features with the responses of the past we can reasonably expect. The Christ event has a recognizable shape. We must search for the common features that mark the moments of past obedience, while being open to the mystery of how they will be taken up into a new form as the people of God seek to follow Christ into the servant tasks of the present.

Exploring the Biblical Picture

In this search for the common features of past church events and for characteristics of the ways in which these continuities are taken up in new forms in changing situations, what is the status of the New Testament picture of the church? In those pages we can see how the church in the first century took on a variety of forms. The response to Christ within varied situations led to the emergence of different forms of ministry, liturgy, preaching, doctrinal formulation. What does this have to say to the church of today about its search for unity?

By giving the Bible canonical status, the church has (in one sense) lifted this picture of the church above the continuing stream of tradition. It has given to the primal, formative moments of the tradition normative status in relation to the rest of the tradition. But we must not take that to mean that it constitutes a "timeless" norm, so that we should seek to reproduce that picture of the church in every time

414

and place. Instead, it is normative in the sense
that this first response to Christ within the stream
of history can provide the clues to future responses
to Christ within that stream.

This helps us to see what the interpretative task
is. We are to explore that first moving picture with
all its variety. We must not seek to harmonize that
variety into a single picture that would then provide
the basis for unity. The variety is the message. We
must seek for clues to our response to Christ within
the varied situation of our time within their response
to the varied situation of that time. This requires
us to shuttle back and forth between the two settings,
putting our questions to it and its questions to us,
and (with the help of the continuing story of the
church to check our intuitions) to seek to discern
from this encounter the forms and shapes of the
church's obedience today.

From the New Testament variety we ask: How much
continuity is needed in the life of the church from
one situation to another? What common features mark
the life of the church in those different first-
century settings? Is the relation between continuity
and freedom describable?

It is to this Biblical exploration that we now
turn. But a warning is needed. It is one thing to
point, as we have, to the way in which the New Testament pictures a living church in the process of obedience. But as we explore that picture, the temptation
still is to turn a movement, described in the process
of faithful response to particular situations, into a
series of isolated pictures from which we draw abstract
truths invested with timeless significance. We must
keep reminding ourselves that the pictures we are
seeing are relative to their own situation, and that
they will speak properly to us only if we explore the
question of response in our temporal setting in contrast with the responses the Biblical story records
in that temporal setting.

Titles and Images of the Church in
the New Testament

Paul Minear isolates over a hundred images of
the church in the New Testament, but an analysis of
the main group should be sufficient to introduce us to
the various facets of the church's life which the
images reveal.

415

1. *Ekklēsia.* This is the word that we translate as "church" in our English New Testament. It means simply, "called out." The church consists of those called out by God from among the mass of humanity to represent his purpose.

The Greek term originally denoted an assembly of people called together for a particular purpose, such as the political assemblies of the city-states. When the Old Testament was translated into Greek, *ekklēsia* was used to translate the Hebrew term *Qahal* which described Israel as the assembled people of God called out of the world to represent God's purpose among the nations. In the New Testament the followers of Christ take over the word. They see themselves as carrying on the purpose for which God called Israel out of the nations. They are now the *ekklēsia tou Kyriou* (the church of the Lord: I Cor. 2:12; Rom., ch. 16; Acts 20:28) or the *ekklēsia tou Theou* (the church of God: I Cor. 10:32; 11:22; Col. 1:18,24; Acts 10:28). As the followers of Christ they are the representative assembly in which the nations of the world are to see their destiny. The true family relationship which is God's purpose for all has been established through their brotherhood in Christ (*adelphoi*: I Cor. 1:10).

2. *The Israel of God.* Paul rings the changes on the relationships between the nation of Israel in its calling to be God's chosen people and Christ's disciples in their continuation of God's purpose for Israel. In his allegory of the olive tree in Rom., ch. 11, continuity is clearly intended. It is the same olive tree. But the tree surgery is so radical that the extent of the discontinuity is also clear. The dead branches of the old Israel are cut out of the tree and the grafting in of the Gentiles represents a major change in the look of the tree, to say the least! Paul's point is that there is continuity here, but the continuity of God's purpose can bring about major changes in strategy as the purpose unfolds. To interrupt the movement at any point and to make the way the church looks at that time normative for all time would be to misunderstand the mission of the church. The continuity is in Christ and his underlying purpose; the discontinuities are very considerable but can be understood within the total sweep of God's purpose.

3. *The Temple.* In the Old Testament the temple represents the place where God has chosen to dwell in the midst of his people--the place where his glory is made manifest and where the people gather to worship

him. It is the place set apart as the focus point for the total relationship between God and his people.

The attitude of Jesus toward the old temple is one of radical judgment. It no longer serves to focus this relationship of living obedience to the Lord of history. (See Matt. 21:13: "'My house shall be called a house of prayer'; but you make it a den of robbers." And Matt. 24:2 "There will not be left here one stone upon another, that will not be thrown down.") But that Jerusalem Temple with its fixed location as a separate holy place is to be replaced by a living temple which will enable disciples to celebrate God's Lordship in the context of the total human existence. When Jesus was on trial one of the charges was: "This fellow said, 'I am able to destroy the temple of God, and to build it in three days'" (Matt. 26:61). The radical change from their fixed conception was too great for them to understand. So John is forced to interpret the saying by explaining how Christ himself becomes the temple. "He spoke of the temple of his body" (John 2:21)--the body of his death and resurrection. The destruction of the old temple is final, as is the destruction of his own limited body. But the latter gives way to his resurrection presence and it is now in that presence that God dwells with his people.

This transformation of the fixed symbol is of great importance for us today. In the Christendom period the church again took on a fixed place in the world. Is its collapse a tragedy? Or does it free us to see the church in relation to the living presence of Christ within the total range of human existence? This temple symbol certainly suggests a positive answer. We have become used to the church's having fixed locations and fixed forms. How far is this expectation normative? This temple symbol as it is worked out in I Peter, where the church is likened to living stones growing up into the risen Christ, would suggest that the church has to be free to move with Christ within the structures of man's common life. Living stones are difficult for church extension architects, ecclesiastical bureaucrats, and doctrinal orthodoxists who work with fixed blueprints. Here their fixed views are called under radical question.

4. *The Body of Christ.* The symbol of the church as God's temple was radically transformed when the temple of stones was replaced by the temple of Christ's resurrection body. When Jesus died on the cross, says Matthew, the curtain of the old Temple was torn in two

417

(Matt. 27:51). The way of God's presence is now through the sanctuary of the risen body of Jesus. The true temple is the risen Lord; the church is the body of Christ.

We are not too certain about the origins of this favorite symbol of Paul. It may be related to the Stoic use of the term "body" ("the body politic"). It is probably related to the eucharistic practice of the early Christians in which Christ made himself known to them in the breaking of the bread ("my body"). It certainly seems to indicate the faith that the risen Christ gathers his disciples to himself in such a way that they are called by him to continue in history the work of his incarnate life. They are his body for his work in the world. The profundity of this term as it draws upon the resurrection promises of Christ to the church makes it a rich store of meaning. It is no wonder that it regularly finds a central place in treatments of the doctrine of the church--particularly in Roman Catholic works, but also in all the traditions.

Nevertheless, a problem emerges in this treatment. The term has often been translated into the saying, "The church is the extension of the incarnation." The church as a visible hierarchical institution, with its head, arms, body, feet, is seen as the continuing form of Christ's presence in history. But this is a misuse of Paul's metaphor. With Paul, certainly, it carries the suggestion that the body of believers is used by Christ for his resurrection presence. But the term has a careful dialectic. There is no identity of Christ and church. Christ is the head of the body; the members have to grow up into him (Col. 1:18-20; 2:19). Baptism, putting off our flesh and rising into his resurrection body, signifies the need for a daily death (I Cor. 15:31), and the continued participation in the Lord's Supper (I Cor. 10:16-17) reminds us that our life in the body of Christ needs continual renewal.

The continuity of the visible institution as the body of Christ cannot therefore be taken for granted. There is the continuity of the promises of Christ (Word) and the continuity of the symbols of his promise (Sacraments), but the life of the church as the fellowship of believers depends upon constant renewal.[4]

5. *The Fellowship* (koinōnia). The word *koinōnia* signifies "sharers in a gift." For the early Christian church this common gift was their life in the Spirit, given in fulfillment of the resurrection promise of

418

Jesus.

Pentecost is often called "the birthday of the church," the day the Spirit was given. The Spirit must be seen as Christ's alter ego in the church. Now that the incarnate Christ is not visibly present among his followers, the Spirit takes his place, incorporating the disciples into Christ's resurrection body, distributing the gifts of Christ (his truth, his way of life), and guiding the church in the way of obedience to him. These gifts are not complete. The members have to grow up into Christ as they are led toward the final fulfillment of Christ's purpose. But they now receive the "firstfruits" or "earnest" of this life through the Spirit.

In the Pentecost story this new life is shown as one that promises the final transformation of the full range of our worldly existence. There the Spirit created a community that broke through the barriers of language, culture, race, sex--even possessions. Here is the promise of new life for all the nations--a life in which the "walls of hostility" which divide our human communities are overcome by Christ. It is this life which is described by Paul (Gal. 3:28; Col. 3:11) when he says that "in Christ there is no Greek or Jew, no barbarian or Scythian, male or female, bond or free." The church is called to be the moving sign on the front wave of history, revealing to the nations the promise of their destiny.

This symbol stands in constant judgment over the reality of the empirical church! And in our day it serves as a summons for the church to risk its life on the promises of Christ in the Spirit, seeking to reveal this new community existence in the midst of the political and social realities of our time. The church happens as the people of God risk themselves upon the promises of Christ; it grows up into Christ as it receives the gifts for "edification" for the common good.

6. We have selected five of the more common terms to open up some of the rich symbolism that is used in the New Testament to point to the dimensions of the life of the church in the world. A few shorter references should be added however to indicate something more of the dynamic reality of the church's life.

The church is the *family and household of God,* sustained and disciplined by the Father through the Son,

419

and led on by him as it is nurtured toward maturity.
(John 1:12; Rom. 8:15; II Cor. 6:18; Gal. 4:5-6;
I John 3:1.)

The church is the *pilgrim people*, led by God out
of slavery through the wilderness of the world's life
on the way to the promised land of the Kingdom, with
Christ as its new Moses or expedition leader (*archēgos*).
(Heb. 2:10; I Peter 2:9-11; Titus 2:11-14; Heb. 8:
8-13). As a pilgrim people the church has to lead a
relatively rootless existence (in tents) so that it
can be free to move on with Christ as he fights his
way through history to the completed Kingdom.

In these terms we catch something of the reality
of the church as the visible servant of God's purpose,
called to be the body through which the risen Christ
reveals the shape of the new Kingdom in which the
restrictive limits of the world's communities are
broken through, and standing constantly under the call
of Christ to be ready for new forms of obedience.

It is interesting to compare the characteristics
here with the traditional catalog of the "notes" of
the church embodied in the creeds. The church is:

One. All the terms we have analyzed presuppose
unity. The church is the sign of the ultimate unity
of all things in Christ. Believers are growing up into
"one new man," and their growing unity is the promise
of final unity for the creation.

Holy. Holiness is a status given to the chosen
community because it is set apart by God for his
service. But the holiness of the church in the New
Testament is eschatological: It is set apart as a
sign of God's purpose to fill all creation with his
presence, and it must grow up into the life of holiness. Holiness is no longer the cultic quality of a
special place in life, but a gift to the church in the
midst of life. This gift is also a mission: The
church is called to be a sign of God's intention that
this gift is for all creation.

Catholic. This points in tradition to both the
wholeness of the church's life--the fullness of the
truth it has received--and the wholeness of its mis-
sion--it exists for all the world and so transcends
the narrow boundaries of all smaller communities.
The New Testament images we have explored certainly
confirm these meanings of the term. But it is clear

420

that "Catholic" must be understood historically--as a mission given to the church--rather than ontologically --in the sense of a status guaranteed to an institution. Catholicity is a gift of the Spirit, but it is a gift that has to be appropriated; it has to happen. The church is catholic as it reveals how Christ is drawing the world out of its brokenness.

Apostolic. The apostles were chosen by Christ to be his authoritative witnesses, and the church continues this primary apostolic task of witness to him. Within this term, however, there is concealed a major historical problem. Is there a particular unbroken institutional line of continuity with the apostles-- through Peter as primate to his successors in Rome and/or through the Twelve to their successors, the bishops? Or is the term "apostolic" satisfied by the continuation of the faithful witness begun by the apostles and carried on by the church through forms of order which can be properly varied according to different political and social situations in which the witness occurs?

Apostolic Succession

My belief is that we can value the symbol of apostolic succession--an episcopal line with visible continuity reaching out across space and back through time to the age of the apostles--as *a* valuable symbol of the unity of the church. But equally we must insist that such a continuity is no guarantee of faithfulness, and that the clear use of the other traditions by Christ for his apostolic witness must be confessed and recognized in the church's order.

A similar analysis of Peter's place of priority seems justified. In every list of apostles his name is first. In every key situation (Caesarea Philippi, transfiguration, Mount of Olives, Gethsemane), Peter is always in the small group separated from the rest and consistently acts as the spokesman. And it now seems clear that in Matt. 16:18-19 the words of Jesus giving to Peter the place of the rock and the gift of the keys must be taken as the recognition of a place of doctrinal and disciplinary authority in the community. Peter is the primary spokesman of the community to the world, and he exercised that function after Pentecost.

What are we to say then? That the church was given a primate and that the tradition of Peter's successor in Rome has solid roots in the Biblical story? It is not as simple as that. Peter's foundation role seems to be in the main complete after Pentecost. Paul then exercises authority in his area; James, in Jerusalem. When Paul challenges Peter's attitude over Jew-Gentile relationships the question is decided by a council (Acts, ch. 15). Similarly in John's Gospel (ch. 20:23) the apostolic authority given to Peter in Matthew is given to the whole community. The later hierarchical structure of Rome is obviously not authorized here.

However, our answer cannot be a simple no to the primacy tradition. The New Testament does take the visible institutional unity of the church seriously as an essential aspect of the church's witness among the institutions of the world. The representation of that unity under the Peter figure was then used by the church in an attempt to accomplish what the Roman Empire through its caesars had failed to do. We may now judge it as a glorious attempt which ultimately failed because it took over too easily the world's structures of power. The authority Peter exercised was a servant authority and was one that was shared with the whole body. Now the Roman Church is undertaking a painful reassessment of its authoritarian order. The authority of the laity is being gradually rediscovered along with the servant character of true authority.

But is there no value in personal expressions of the apostolic mission and of the unity of life in Christ in bishops, and even in one bishop symbolically representing all? The unity of the mission has its personal center in Jesus Christ, and personal expressions of that mission and of the unity of that mission are consistent with the New Testament understanding of the church's presence in the world.

Endnotes

[1] Lesslie Newbigin does this in his book *The Household of God* (London; SCM Press, Ltd., 1959). This same approach lies behind Dr. Blake's suggestion and largely explains the wide-spread acceptance.

[2] A good representative of this kind of ecclesiology is T. F. Torrance. See his two-volume work, which grew largely from the Faith and Order discussions in the first period after Amsterdam, *Conflict and Agreement in the Church* (London; Lutterworth Press, 1959, 1960).

[3] In Chapter IV, I will explore the usefulness of "the Christological analogy" in the church's self-understanding, and will refer to a little of the considerable literature evoked by this development in the Faith and Order story. A typical, direct outcome of this stage is found in the material for the subsequent meeting at Montreal in 1963. See particularly section VI, "Report of the Theological Commission on Christ and the Church," North American Section and European Section, in *Faith and Order Findings*, ed. by Paul S. Minear (London: SCM Press, Ltd., 1963).

[4] We have noted already that the Vatican Council document *De Ecclesia* drew the term "people of God" into primacy of place so that the historical character of the church could be affirmed in its pilgrim contingency, as over against the ontological fixed view of the church represented in the traditional body of Christ treatments.

Discussion Questions

1. Define *Ekklesia*.

2. Which of the New Testament images of the church predominates as a guiding paradigm for your church? Which is most neglected?

3. What do you think Williams means when he says that the Catholicity of the church is a mission to the church, rather than an ontological status of the church?

4. Williams holds that the New Testament takes the visible institutional unity of the church seriously. How does your church do this? Which communions do you think have the most appropriate models for this end?

WORSHIP AND THE CHRISTIAN LIFE

Acts of worship are primarily actions, not uses of verbal expression. Worship is performative communication. In many arenas of life some things cannot be known except by performance. This is true, for example, of swimming, riding a bike, learning to play an instrument. No amount of verbal instruction about these things can actually constitute knowledge. Likewise, there are some truths of the Christian faith, and many depth dimensions to its reality which cannot be known or experienced except through action, particularly acts of worship. When one says in prayer, "I am no longer my own, but Thine," he is performing an act of surrender to God, not just mouthing words.

Gestures, rituals, and the use of natural and sacred objects all serve as communicative signs. The great Old Testament prophets, and Jesus also, often proclaimed God's word through symbolic *acts*. Indeed, the works of Jesus were the announcement that the kingdom was present: he made the blind see, the deaf hear, the dumb speak, the lame walk, he ate with publicans and sinners, he preached forgiveness (Luke 7:18-23).

To be sure, the technical functions of theological reasoning refine our explication of the Christian message. But worship experiences are more supple expressions of communion with God. Theology is the verbal and rational reflection on experience with God. Worship ritual and action is one step closer to the reality experienced than is theological reflection.

Of course, rituals may be codified. Bodily actions, movement and the use of objects may be so rigidly prescribed that experience is lost. However, some persons witness to the fact that when theological language becomes confusing, misleading, or even bankrupt, meaning may be preserved to faith by continuing to worship. "Going through the motions" should not be depreciated, because doing so may be itself a channel for communion with God.

This essay by William Willimon is an exploration into the contribution worship makes to the Christian life. Of course Willimon recognizes that worship may be twisted and abused. But such abuse is not unique to worship. Our theology, polity, and even the scriptures may be abused and distorted. Accordingly, the theologian cannot ignore the significance of worship simply on the grounds that it is sometimes abused.

Willimon holds that Christian rituals provide a patterned way of confronting life by focusing the worshipper's attention on actions which reflect Christian beliefs, norms and sentiments. He divides Christian rites into two categories: crisis rites and cyclical rites.

Among the crisis rites Willimon includes marriage, baptism, confession and penance, the funeral, and ordination. The crisis rite of marriage, for example, should be done Christianly. The service of holy matrimony is what the church wants a couple to say and do in order to be married. The vows are performative. They are required by the church because they express what it is to be a Christian couple: to forsake others, to love and honor, etc. Attendance at a wedding may reinforce and renew one's commitment to his own marriage.

Cyclical rites include the major seasons of the Christian year: Advent, Easter, and Pentecost. But each week's worship is a cyclical rite too. Regular, sustained, rehearsing and reenacting of the faith we affirm. Praise, confession, presentation, hearing, witnessing—these are all elements of the cycle of faith which reinforces the Christian life.

Willimon identifies six ways in which worship influences Christian life.

1. Worship helps form Christian identity.
2. Worship creates a structure of reality under which life can be interpreted.
3. Worship experiences are the primary source of our language about the faith.
4. Worship releases our commitment to the status

426

quo.
5. Worship is our act of attachment to the values
of the faith.
6. Worship enables us to rise above the present
and envision the coming reality of God's
kingdom.

WORSHIP AND THE CHRISTIAN LIFE*

To be sure, worship can be used as a narcotic trip
into another world to escape the ethical responsibilities of living a Christian life in this world. Religious rituals easily lend themselves to corruption.
Most biblical scholars agree that the prophetic criticism of the cult was not an attack on sacrificial
worship as such, but rather upon sacrificial worship
that found no expression in social righteousness.
The prophets remind us that our rituals can become a
retreat from reality, crude attempts to compensate for
our moral misdeeds through cultic deeds, and a means
of avoiding the ethical cost of discipleship through
the ersatz discipleship of the cult. The essence of
idolatry is the easy certainty that our rituals and
cultic institutions are the sole custodians of what is
right and righteous.[1] Karl Barth deprecated our
"religion" as a culture-bound, sinful attempt at self-
salvation through self-appointed means.[2]

But surely this is an abuse rather than an inherent part of worship. *Any* aspect of the church's life--
scripture, polity, theology, even our good works, as
Paul so aptly noted--can be twisted into the service of
human sinfulness. The church's worship is not immune
from such abuse.

*Source: Excerpted from *The Service of God* by
William H. Willimon. Copyright 1983 by Abingdon
Press. Used by permission.

Ritual (patterned, purposeful, predictable, public behavior) is an integral part of all public worship. Ritual is a part of worship whether it be a Roman Catholic Pontifical Mass or a Holy Roller meeting. Human beings in groups--particularly groups that deal with potentially threatening aspects of life such as birth, death, sex, and God--do things in prescribed, patterned ways. While the primary purpose of these rituals is to praise, to placate, open oneself to God in the midst of life, rituals also have human consequences. At the risk of violating my own interpretive principle and conceiving of our liturgies in utilitarian fashion, it may be helpful to review their sociological/ anthropological function. How might the rites and rituals of Christian worship positively affect Christian moral development?

Anthropologist, Edward Norbeck, has noted two types of rituals in so-called primitive societies that have counterparts in the rites of Christendom.[3] These are *crisis rites* that occur during important times in the community (birth, death, puberty, war, famine) and *cyclic rites* that are periodically repeated for the maintenance of group life (regular cultic gatherings, memorial days, feast days).

(1) Ritual is "a complex act of self-protection from destructive, unintelligible, and immoral forces."[4] *Crisis rites* provide a patterned, predictable way of coping by focusing our attention upon norms, beliefs, and sentiments derived from those visions and values the community holds dear.

Any significant transition in life provokes an identity crisis in the person or group experiencing the transition. When faced with the limits of life, the "limnal" situations (death, birth, sickness, marriage),[5] we are required to move from one state of existence to another, shedding one identity for another. The crisis of transition threatens to overwhelm us. Crisis rites help us cope by giving us the knowledge, skills, and vision needed to negotiate the journey from one state of being to another.

For instance, marriage is the crisis in which two people make the passage from being single to being married. The wedding itself is the rite in which the couple says to each other, in the presence of "God and these witnesses," that their love for each other is appropriate in the sight of God and this company, that the values they affirm are shared by this commu-

428

nity, that their marriage is sanctioned and confirmed by the community of faith. All that talk about fidelity, "forsaking all others," "for better or worse," and "until death us do part" is an attempt by the Christian community to say what it believes at the time of marriage. The Service of Holy Matrimony is the church saying, "These are the things we want you to say and do in order to be married."

Similar observations could be made about other Christian crisis rites such as the funeral, baptism, penance, or ordination. If you want to know what a given community officially believes about these changes and crises in peoples' lives, you must look at what is said and done in these rites. The content of such rites—both verbal and symbolic—is an ethical statement about what the community considers appropriate behavior for those going through this change in status. In this way liturgy is a source for ethics. It tells us how we are expected to behave.

Rites of crisis not only provide ethical clues for those individuals who are currently experiencing the acute crisis of death or marriage or birth or other role changes; they are important for everyone in the community. Every time I attend a wedding, even though it is not my own wedding, I continue to live out the significance of my own marriage. Witnessing someone else's marital commitments may lead me to renewed commitment in my own marriage. The educational, formative value of these rituals continue long after the immediate, acute crisis of my own change has passed. Thus the church insists that a service of worship like a funeral or a wedding is not a private affair for the grieving family or the bride and groom. Every service of worship is for the whole church—those who are preparing for, or who are continuing to struggle with, the long-term implications of such transitions.

(2) *Cyclic rites* are periodically repeated for the maintenance of the group. They provide both the sustenance for and the judgment of the group's myth upon itself. Christmas, Easter, and Pentecost are examples of cyclic rites within the church. At such times we tell the Story again, passing it on to our young, confirming who we are by telling where we have been, rehearsing and reenacting the truth we affirm. We thus set limits on our community, define outsiders from insiders, and judge the adequacy of the community's present living out of its vision.

Each Sunday's worship is a kind of cyclic rite, a
time to gather and be reminded of who we are. Without
these regular, sustaining gatherings, a community
quickly loses its identity, breaks apart into subgroups
and cliques, confuses its Story with other stories,
and fails to integrate sufficiently its young or its
initiates into its life together.

Liturgical Contributions
to Christian Character Formation

Let us now be more specific about ways Christian
liturgy may influence Christian character.

1) *Liturgy helps form Christian identity.*

In the sixties and seventies, many theologians
emphasized that the true *Sitz im Leben* ("life situation") of Christians was in the world.[6] As far as
coming in for worship was concerned, it was said that
"we are inside only for the sake of those outside."[7]

Talk of this kind made some interesting assumptions
It assumed "the world sets the agenda" and, if God were
active, it was everywhere but inside the church (a
claim that could be easily disputed by empirically
examining the average congregation). This appealed to
the pragmatic, utilitarian, secularized American church
in particular, a church that was never sure about the
value of corporate worship. After all, what good does
all that singing and praying do anyone?

Even Vatican II, mapping the way for renewal of
Roman Catholicism, said on the one hand, that "the
liturgy is the outstanding means by which the faithful
can express in their lives, and manifest to others,
the mystery of Christ and the real nature of the
church";[8] but on the other hand, it gave such heavy
emphasis to God's actions outside the church and in
secular *diakonia,* that it implicitly cast doubt on the
importance of *leitourgia*--prayer, preaching, sacraments.

Admittedly, on many moral issues (the civil rights
movement, the women's movement) it seemed as if the
world had to reveal the gospel to the church rather
than the other way around. Sometimes God's will is
revealed, not through the church, but in spite of the
church. I fear that after two decades of this thinking,
the church finds it is losing its identity, its integrity and coherence in its marriage with the world. The
world has become the transformer of the church rather

than that which is being transformed. The church which let the world set the agenda has now forgotten why it came to the meeting.

Within my own denomination we celebrate a theology that affirms "pluralism" as a great theological virtue and social principles that speak much of "freedom of choice" and "personhood"--theology and social values without biblical foundation and without distinction from prevalent opinions within American society as a whole. While pluralism, freedom of choice, and self-affirmation may be important values for keeping things balanced and running smoothly in a multiracial, multi-ethnic, democratic society with nothing to hold it together but aggressive self-interest, it is doubtful whether such values are specifically Christian.

But how do we know? Cast adrift from our biblical roots, our tradition, our Story, our rites and rituals; we are left with few criteria for judgment.

In the rites of the church our Story is told and retold. This is where the Christian vision is seen and shared. The liturgy of the church thus becomes a primary source for a Christian's identity.

Any claim for the importance of Christian liturgy in moral formation rests upon certain anthropological assumptions. How are human beings made? Is the human being inevitably a creature who needs communal rituals and symbolic actions to express and effect the basic consensus a society needs for survival? If so, ritual is powerful. The rituals that exercise power over us may be Christian or not, but they will have their way with us. They may be the rituals of chauvanistic nationalism, communism, egocentrism, atavism, or some other secular faith. We are formed in countless ways by these secular "liturgies." The only way the church will remain distinctive and lively in this world is through close attention to her identity-forming liturgies and rites.

2) *Liturgy creates a world for the Christian.*

The human brain constructs a picture of the world, various interlocking bits of information, which is more than a mere data bank of shelved facts. Our picture of the world is the sum of the implications and inferences which we have drawn from our experiences with reality as well as our personal ordering, incorporation, and interlocking of these experiences.[10]

Liturgy creates a world for the Christian, world
in the sense that it is often used in the New Testament. When Paul refers to "the world" (*cosmos*) he is
not referring to the physical world, the planet, but
to the social reality; the world of values and institutions into which we have been socialized. We live
in this world, and it lives in us. It is thus an
inner and an outer experience. Our world is our unified structure of meaning, the result of our natural
human capacity to unify our experiences of reality and
to project this unified image. But this world is not
a merely subjective phenomenon, a fanciful tableaux.
It is the expression of the relationship between
humanity and the things-that-are.[11]

Liturgy reveals the world of the Christian faith,
which is not part of our natural, inborn perception.
It is rather something to which our eyes are gradually
opened. The liturgy is not merely an expression of
this particular world, it is an exposure of it. Unless
this "world" of faith is revealed, our ethics will
merely adapt to the contours of the status quo, conventional wisdom, and the safe confines of contemporary
values.

In the liturgy, we are enabled to see things as
they "really are"--as Christians see reality. How
often have Christians been told, in recent years, to
get out of the sanctuary and back into the "real
world." But this reverses the traditional order. In
past times, when the Christian entered the sanctuary
and its liturgy, it was not a matter of leaving the
world, but rather of entering the world as it *really*
looked in its full, transparent reality--as the place
of God's love and activity. That divine love and
activity takes place, of course, outside the "world"
of the liturgy, for the whole world outside is God's
world. But due to our defective vision, our inadequate
perception, sometimes it is difficult for us to see
that divine busyness. So, as Leo the Great once said
of the Eucharist, the liturgy "makes conspicuous" the
world as it is, a world to which we might otherwise be
blinded.

The liturgical endeavor to help Christians see
the world more accurately could be illustrated by
referring to the words, the choreography, or the music;
but I most often feel this cosmological function at
work through liturgical architecture.

This is not to say that the liturgical "world" is

always an accurate depiction of the Christian vision. The world that liturgical words, ceremonial, music, and architecture create must be judged and refined by using the Bible or church tradition or whatever criteria the church uses to test its visions.

3) *Liturgy is a primary source of the symbols and metaphors through which we talk about and make sense out of our world.*

Liturgy is a symbol-laden endeavor. The chalice, the loaf of eucharistic bread, the open Bible on the pulpit, the preacher in a black robe, the vivid language, the cross on the altar, all are powerful symbolic statements. Social change is primarily symbolic change. In order for us to change, our symbols must change. Our symbols must change because they determine our horizons, our limits, our viewpoints and visions.

When women were at last given leadership positions in the liturgy of many churches, we soon realized how much symbolic change needed to be made in order to adjust the metaphors and symbols to the church's clearer vision of the role of women in the church. We realized how limited many of our old, male-dominated, hierarchial images were—God the Father; the Heavenly King; Lord over All; Rise Up, O Men of God. There could be no basic change without change in the symbols and metaphors through which we attempt to grasp reality and reality grasps us.[12]

The liturgy reminds us that we are more image-making and image-using creatures than we think. We apprehend reality only through symbols, sacraments, gestures, and metaphor. Even our language—which we use to describe ourselves as abstracting, rational creatures—is a symbolic system. Through these symbols we make sense out of the dismaying multiplicity we encounter. This renders our world apprehensible and manageable.[13] We cannot even speak of symbol or metaphor without employing metaphor and symbol. By the use of these, we predetermine, to a great extent, what we will be able to see and say about reality.

With the loss of vitality of some of the historic symbols of the faith (when such things as sheep, crosses, and kings pass from our daily existence) Christians have often been unable to grasp some aspects of reality or have substituted inadequate secular images for traditional Christian ones.

433

Our character is relative to the kind of community from which we inherit our primary symbols and metaphors. The Christian expects to see and say things differently than the non-Christian for each will be employing different symbols of their world.

Because we say and see things differently, we have different characters. Without careful attention to the specific symbols and metaphors that the Christian community uses, we will be unable to form specifically Christian character.

4) *Liturgy aids in Christian imagination.*

One unique characteristic of humans is our ability to operate in the mind with images not present to the senses. This is our second language with which we carry on a continual discourse within ourselves, with which we debate, dream, argue, file away, and weigh what is happening to our lives. This is how humans rise above mere instinct--we imagine out of our remembered store of images, and we imagine beyond the present moment.

Liturgy is mind-expanding work on a Christian's imagination. It helps us to transcend our immediate situation, to see "a new heaven and a new earth," to release the tight grip of the status quo.

Bad liturgy, like bad art, merely confirms our warped vision, our truncated perspectives, our obsessive self-concern, soothing the "heart all curled in upon itself" rather than humbling us with love and truth.

So, through the imagination, liturgy, like art, may act upon a person to lead that person to goodness, not by direct command, but by a more subtle and complex interaction. Christian ethics, in spite of how it sometimes presents itself--a tidy, logical discipline of thought and problem solving--is a much more ambiguous, imaginative, interesting, mysterious, intuitive enterprise than we admit. There is no way to be free from the ambiguity of our ethics, to land in some pristine world of clear principles and directives for action. The task is ambiguous because we humans do not know everything, because we are limited and cannot see everything. To deny this fundamental ambiguity is the essence of sin itself.

5) *Liturgy is a primary source of the Christian*

vision.

"The moral life is a struggle and training in how to see."[14] Human beings differ from one another, not only because their vision is selective, seeing some things in the world as morally significant and other things as insignificant, but also because they see a different world. Our morality is made, not only of principles and choices, but also of vision. Jonathan Edwards describes the converted person as one who has been given "new sight."

The goal of liturgical revision, this painful and exciting venture of the past few decades, is literally re-vision: seeking appropriate language and forms to keep alive, in worship, the church's vision of God.

We must periodically withdraw from the world in order to worship because our vision needs the focus and concentration that occurs in worship. Such withdrawal is confrontation rather than escapism. Thus Bernard Haring sees the sacraments as *signs which sharpen our vision to the divine presence*, not exclusively in the sacraments themselves, but in the world. The sacraments thereby enable us to shape our deeds in configuration with Christ's deeds in the world so that we ourselves become sacraments to the world.[15]

A truncated liturgical life--in which "worship" is used to assuage our guilt by rationalizing and justifying our values and actions, or to confirm our delusions of self-control by moralizing about our need to save the world (since we believe that we are the only ones to save it)--corresponds to our truncated ethical life. Both the ethics and the worship are results of the myopic vision.[16]

Worship is a place of vision. "Worship is the place in which the vision comes to a sharp focus, a concentrated expression, and it is here that the vision has often been found to be most appealing."[17] Worship is not only a place to dream and envision a "new heaven and a new earth" where the deaf hear, the blind see, and outcasts come to a feast; worship is also a time set apart to focus our attention on and attach ourselves to something and someone outside ourselves.

We humans are inherently attaching creatures. We do not so much decide to be good or just or courageous, as we become attached to some object of love and

attention that refocuses and releases our energies so
these good things are done, not as an act of reason or
will or response to a command, *but as response to the
beloved.* We are obedient to whatever absorbs our
attention. If this be true, then Christian morality
should endeavor as much to focus our attention on the
beloved (Christ) and on gaining a clearer vision of
the beloved as to elucidate principles and decisions.

Christian worship or Christian ethics is thus a
matter of training in how to pay attention.[18] It is
practice in attentiveness of heart and mind. Until we
become sufficiently attentive to God, our selves will
be mired in the illusion, self-hate, self-defensiveness,
and anxiety that occurs when we are forced to create
and sustain our own significance.

Every time we worship, we should be reminded that
the Christian life is not a response to a code of moral
conduct or a response to the memory of a noble person
who once lived. The Christian life is response to a
reality, a personal reality, a presence which evokes--
not mere obedience--but an effective relationship.[19]

In beholding God's glory, we come to reflect it
in ourselves, (II Cor. 3:18). We now see "through a
glass, darkly," but one day we shall see "face to
face" (I Cor. 13:12). We shall then bear God's image
which, heretofore, we have only dimly reflected.

Sometimes, in worship, we receive certain codes
or guides for behavior--the recital of the Decalogue,
the hearing of scriptural commands, the affirming of
vows. Sometimes we hear and affirm certain guiding
principles and ideals for the Christian life--self-
sacrifice, justice, kindness, humility. But the main
"good" we receive in worship is a relationship with
God, the one who loves and is therefore loved.

6) *Liturgy is a major source of our Christian
tradition which enables us to rise above the present
and envision the future.*

One important way human beings differ from other
animals is that animals cannot reach back any distance
into their past. They have only habit to do the work
of memory. Only the human is truly personal, a person,
because only the human is able to carry in his mind
what he was. Only the human tells stories. Only the
human is able to conceive of a "future," because only
the human recalls the past.

Ritual, religious or otherwise, is an inherently traditionalist activity. Part of ritual's power is its sameness, its repetition, its predictability. It provides the rudder for our lives in the midst of a sea of change. The worship of the church strikes us as the most traditionalist of all the church's activities: the archaic language, repetition, outdated vestments, resistance to innovation, the same old stories again and again.

In recent years the church has been engrossed in liturgical change. I have been an advocate and active participant in such change. We must be open to the Spirit's leadings, keeping liturgy related to life, modifying the liturgy to meet the changing needs of people. But it is also important, particularly after these past two decades of rapid, unsettling liturgical change, to recognize the positive values--particularly for Christian ethics--of the liturgy as a repository of Christian tradition.

Somewhere Jaroslav Pelikan distinguishes between "traditionalism," which he calls "the dead faith of living men"; and "tradition," which he calls "the living faith of dead men." Liturgy is often a place for archaism and antiquarianism, a place to hold on to the cultic vestiges of a dead faith. These traditions can and should be dispensed with as an affront and a subversion to living faith. But tradition is another matter. Tradition is the origin, not in time, but origin in substance of the community, the wellspring of faith itself.[20] It is good that liturgy has a kind of inertia. The worship life of the church seems to hold doggedly to certain time-honored truths, repeating them over and over again in the face of new truth claims, making new revelation fight for itself.

The liturgical year, with its round of seasons, keeps the essential features of the Story before us. As we live through this year, we not only hear the Story, we enact it until it becomes our own. Those churches which do not observe the liturgical year often find that they suffer from a truncated story. Their worship fails to hit the full range of notes within the Christian narrative. The result can only be a truncated ethical life. It is important to tell the Story, the whole Story, again and again until it is our own.

In its sameness, liturgy gives the requisite identity, security and stability from which exploration can proceed. The liturgy must be the church's supreme skeptic in the face of change, that one aspect of the church's life which continually honors the past and respects the wealth of the church's experience, the complexity of the church's Story in the face of modern manipulators of the liturgy who claim the past was too limited. These innovators endanger the church by imposing only purely contemporary standards.

In affirming the wealth of the church's tradition, the liturgy is not only holding on to what is important in our past, but is also prodding us forward to ever-widening realms of importance. Memory is the major source of foresight. We push into the future mainly on the basis of inherited images from the past. Tradition is also the major critic of the church. Present detractors are never as tough on the church as our own story in its criticism of us. Tradition gives the church a fresh perspective which rises above the conventional folk wisdom of present culture and frees us from the tyranny of those who know only what they have personally experienced.

I heard a sermon recently in our university chapel which urged us to "put meaning in our lives" by "reaching out to touch other people, opening ourselves up to other people, and getting beside other people." On the way out, I asked a student what she thought of the sermon.

"Well, it was O.K. But it wasn't much different from the kind of thing you would have heard if you had stopped the average college Freshman and asked, 'What is the meaning of life?' I'm sure you would have heard all about 'reaching out' and 'touching' and 'being open' If the preacher had stuck with the Bible passage for today and preached from the Bible rather than ignoring it, he might have had something interesting to say-- even something shocking to say."[21]

A rich and multifarious tradition can be a great help to a church. Churches whose liturgies are less "rich," tend to have a paucity of images, themes, metaphors, and patterns to draw from when confronting present ethical dilemmas.

The identity, world, symbols and metaphors, imagination, vision, and tradition which the church receives through its liturgical life enable the church to be the church and enable individual Christians to engage in *diakonia* without forgetting why they are in service and whose service they are in. The memory and hope they receive in their *leitourgia* thrusts them into, and sustains them within, their *diakonia*. Their *diakonia* provides the context and the need for their *leitourgia* until, in *leitourgia* or *diakonia*, worship or service, it becomes difficult for the Christian to distinguish between the two. This may, after all, be the point of it all.

Endnotes

[1]See Jacques Ellul's opening chapter on deceitful prayer in his *Prayer and Modern Man*, trans. C. E. Hopkin (New York: The Seabury Press, 1973).

[2]Karl Barth, *Church Dogmatics*, I, 2, pp. 280-361. See also James F. Gustafson, *Ethics from a Theocentric Perspective: Theology and Ethics* (Chicago: University of Chicago Press, 1981), pp. 293-99.

[3]Edward Norbeck, *Religion in Primitive Society* (New York: Harper & Row, 1961), pp. 138ff.

[4]Edward Shils, "Ritual and Crisis," in Donald R. Cutler, ed., *The Religious Situation: 1968* (Boston: Beacon Press), p. 736. Of course, rituals can be dysfunctional as well as functional, keeping us from reality rather than aiding us in approaching reality.

[5]Victor W. Turner, *The Ritual Process: Structure and Anti-Structure* (Chicago: Aldine Publishing Co., 1969).

[6]J. C. Hoekendijk, trans. Isaac C. Rottenberg, *The Church Inside Out*, p. 54.

[7]Valyi Nagy, Ervin and Heinrich Ott, *The Church as Dialogue*, trans. Reinhard Ulrich (Philadelphia: Pilgrim Press, 1969), p. 56.

[8]*Constitution on the Sacred Liturgy*, # 2.

[9]George A. Lindbeck, *The Future of Roman Catholic Theology* (Philadelphia: Fortress Press, 1970), pp. 50, 55.
Jürgen Moltmann has characterized our current problem as the "Identity-Involvement Dilemma." When

the church becomes preoccupied with its identity, it becomes a religious club, removed from the struggles of the world. On the other hand, when the church involves itself in social and political struggle, it tends to get swallowed up by secular movements and lose its identity as the church. The blend which results is what Moltmann calls chamelion theology--adapting to blend with the secular surroundings. The separation of identity from involvement is a major problem for the church, in our time. "Christian Theology Today," *New World Outlook*, 62 (1972), pp. 483-90.

David Kelsey says, "The activities . . . of a Christian worshiping community should all be ordered to one end, viz., shaping the identities of its members. . . ." "The Bible and Christian Theology," *Journal of the American Academy of Religion*, 48 (1980) 387.

[10]Bronowski, *Identity of Man*, p. 35.

Obviously, in my stress on the church and its liturgy as the primary locus of moral formation, I am in agreement with James B. Nelson who says, in criticizing contemporary Christian ethics: "A serious shortcoming in most Protestant Christian ethics has been its tendency to speak of God's gratitude-eliciting work in ways which imply that the church is quite incidental to the process . . . a relational theology and ethics must recapture, but in a new and broad way, the Roman Catholic and Reformation Protestant claim *extra ecclesiam numma salus*--outside the church there is no salvation." *Moral Nexus* (Philadelphia: The Westminster Press, 1971), p. 44.

[11]Martin Heidegger, *Being and Time* (London: SCM Press, 1962), pp. 91-148.

[12]James F. White, "The Words of Worship: Beyond Liturgical Sexism," *Christian Century*, December 13, 1978, pp. 1202-6.

[13]As Suzanne Langer says, "Man can adapt himself somehow to anything his imagination can cope with; but he cannot deal with chaos. . . . Therefore our most important assets are always the symbols for our general orientation in nature, on the earth, in society and in what we are doing: the symbols of our *Weltanschauung* and *Lebenanschauung*." *Philosophy in a New Key*, 4th ed. (Cambridge: Harvard University Press, 1960), p. 287. See also Dykstra, *Vision and Character*, ch. 3.

[14]Hauerwas, *Vision and Virtue*, p. 20.

[15]Bernard Haring, *The Sacraments in a Secular Age* (Slough: St. Paul Publications, 1976). "Prayer consists of attention . . . the orientation of all the attention of which the soul is capable toward God." Simone Weil, *Waiting for God*, trans. E. Craufurd (New York: Harper & Row, 1973), p. 105.

[16]So John Macquarrie says, "the greatest obstacle in the way of our realizing the presence of God [in worship] . . . [is that] our horizons have been narrowed to considerations of production and consumption, our idea of the good life is built around the advertisements in the glossy magazines, and the only possible result of this unspirituality is an impaired vision." *Paths in Spirituality* (New York: Harper & Row, 1972), p. 124. In his book on ethics and pastoral care, Don S. Browning notes that one of the ways worship facilitates moral formation is, "by imparting the moral vision which is the substance of the Christian faith." *The Moral Context of Pastoral Care* (Philadelphia: The Westminster Press, 1976), p. 102.

[17]Geoffrey Wainwright, *Doxology* (New York: Oxford University Press, 1980), p. 3.

[18]John Macquarrie has described worship as "concentration," the recollecting or gathering of the self in a focal experience of encounter that is a compelling, formative center. *Principles of Christian Theology* (London: SCM Press, 1966), p. 434. Worship is thus a dialectical experience of concentration through consolidation and attentiveness to the "givens" of the faith and expansive envisioning through ecstatic attentiveness to the visions and dreams of the faith.

[19]Hauerwas, *Vision and Virtue*, p. 194.
Worship is the "enactment of the core dynamics of the Christian life . . . its central and focusing activity. It is paradigmatic for all the rest of the Christian life." Dykstra, *Vision and Character*, p. 106.

[20]A phrase suggested by Karl Barth's discussion of tradition in *Church Dogmatics*, IV, p. 705.

[21]Of course, the Bible itself is one of the traditions that worship constantly keeps before us. For more on this matter, see my *The Bible and Worship: The Sustaining Presence* (Valley Forge, Pa.: Judson Press, 1981).

Discussion Questions

1. If worship acts are as communicative of meaning as Willimon holds, then how could we account for the diversity in worship found in Christianity?

2. Some rituals of the faith have different theological explications. For example, some consider the Eucharist a *sacrament,* others an *ordinance* of remembrance. Does this explication effect the meaning derived by the worshipper? Does each explication have a truth to preserve?

3. Design a worship service for Advent or Easter. What *actions* need to be done and what *objects* used?

4. Study Jesus' worship life and describe the rituals he participated in and avoided.

5. Do you agree that faith may sometimes be sustained or recovered more easily through worship than through the technical functions of theological reasoning? Why or why not?

6. What worship reforms are needed in your tradition?

ON DECIDING WHAT IS CHRISTIAN

The following of Christ is what distinguishes
Christians from those of other ideologies. No Marxist
or Freudian would want to claim that he was ultimately
dependent on his teacher's life as well as his teachings. But Hans Küng contends that this is precisely
what Christians claim. The ultimate criterion for what
is Christian ethically and volitionally is not an abstract principle. Rather, it is the concrete person
of Jesus Christ.

Küng is not advocating a literal imitation of the
historic Jesus. Life's canvas has changed since Jesus
lived out his authentic union with God in *his lebens-
welt* (life-world). Küng is calling for practical
personal discipleship of spontaneity, creativity, and
innovation; a conduct the matrix of which is one's
immediate relationship with the living Christ. But
this is no mere subjective morality. The living
Christ moves us in directions, recognizably of the
same fabric as the incarnate Jesus.

According to Küng, following Christ is not merely
a matter of studying information and acting according
to norms drawn from it. Following Christ, being a
Christian, is a formation of a certain character; a
remaking of being. The story of Jesus provides inviting, challenging, obligatory examples and cases which
impress and transform his followers. New dispositions,
insights, intentions, are engendered and maintained by
following Jesus' example.

Küng offers suggestions for how this theory of the
Christian ethic applies to some of the basic problems
of modern life. He includes problems of peace and war,
the use of power for others, and the practice of inward
freedom from possessions.

Christian moral theologians often debate whether
there is a single principle for Christian life, or
whether there are many relevant norms. Theologians
like Joseph Fletcher hold that the only norm of Christianity is to act in order to maximize love in the
situation at hand. Past situations, rules and traditions may be helpful guides, but ultimately the context
of the situation must guide one in determining what is
the loving thing to do at that time and with the particular persons involved. Theologians like Paul Ramsey
generally give a larger role to moral rules than does
Fletcher. These various approaches are not completely
rejected by Küng; however, he is attempting to suggest
a more subtle, and yet more realistic, ethical norm.
Whether his suggestion carries the specificity needed
is an important question. But Küng would probably hold
that the request for specificity is misplaced. Specific rules create abstraction and they take away the
vitality needed in an ethic.

ON DECIDING WHAT IS CHRISTIAN*

What is specifically Christian therefore is the
fact that all ethical requirements are understood in
the light of the rule of the crucified Jesus Christ.
It is then not a question merely of what is moral.
The gift and the task coincide under the rule of Jesus
Christ; the indicative already contains the imperative.
Jesus, to whom we *are* subordinated once and for all in
baptism by faith, *must* remain Lord over us. "In following the Crucified it is a question of manifesting
the rule of the risen Christ. Justification and sanc-
tification go together in the sense that both mean
assimilation to Christ. They are distinguished, since
this does not happen once and for all, but must con-

*Source: Excerpt from *On Being a Christian* by
Hans Kung. Copyright 1976 by Doubleday and Co., Inc.
Reprinted by permission of the publisher.

stantly be freshly experienced and endured in varying situations from the time when it all began with baptism."[1] Thus Pauline ethics is nothing but "the anthropological reverse side of his Christology."[2]

Concrete Person Instead of Abstract Principle

Ideas, principles, norms, systems lack the turbulence of life, the vivid perceptibility and the inexhaustible, inconceivable richness of empirical-concrete existence. However clearly defined, simple and stable, however easy to conceive and express, ideas, principles, norms, systems appear to be detached, abstracted from the concrete and individual, and therefore colorless and remote from reality. Abstraction results in uniformity, rigidity, relative insubstantiality: all "sicklied o'er with the pale cast of thought."

A concrete person however does not merely stimulate thinking, critical-rational conversation, but also continually rouses fantasy, imagination and emotion, spontaneity, creativity and innovation: in a word, appeals to the whole man, of flesh and blood. We can depict a person,[3] but not a principle. We can enter into an immediate existential relationship with him. We can talk about a person and not only reason, argue, discuss, theologize. And just as a story cannot be replaced by abstract ideas, neither can narrating be replaced by proclaiming and appealing, images replaced by concepts, the experience of being stirred replaced by intellectual apprehension.[4] A person cannot be reduced to a formula.

Only a living figure and not a principle can *draw* people, can be "attractive" in the most profound and comprehensive sense of the term: *verba docent, exempla trahunt*, words teach, examples carry us with them. It is not for nothing that people speak of a "shining" example. The person makes an idea, a principle, visible: he gives it flesh and blood, "embodies" this idea, this principle, this ideal. Man then not only knows about it, he sees it in a living shape before him. No abstract norm is imposed on him, but a concrete standard is set up for him. He is not only given a few guidelines, but is enabled to take a concrete, comprehensive view of his life as a whole. He is not therefore expected merely to undertake a general "Christian" program or merely to realize a general "Christian" form of life, but he can be confident in this Jesus Christ himself and attempt to order his

life according to his standard. Then Jesus, with all
that he authoritatively is and means, proves to be far
more than simply a "shining example,"[5] proves in fact
to be the true "light of the world."[6]

The Basic Model

If someone commits himself to Jesus as the standard, if he lets himself be determined by the person of
Jesus Christ as the *basic model for a view of life and
a practice of life*, this means in fact the transformation of the whole man. For Jesus Christ is not only
an external goal, a vague dimension, a universal rule
of conduct, a timeless ideal. He determines and
influences man's life and conduct, not only externally,
but from within. Following Christ means not only
information, but formation: not merely a superficial
change, but a change of heart and therefore the change
of the whole man. It amounts to the fashioning of a
new man: a new creation within the always diverse,
individually and socially conditioned context of each
one's own life in its particularity and singularity,
without any attempt to impose uniformity.

We might then summarily define Jesus' unique
significance for human action in this way: with his
word, his actions and his fate, in his impressiveness,
audibility and realizability, he is himself *in person*
the *invitation*, the *appeal*, the *challenge*, for the
individual and society. As the standard basic model
of a view of life and practice of life, without a hint
of legalism or casuistry, he provides inviting, obligatory and challenging *examples, significant deeds,
orientation standards, exemplary values, model cases*.
And by this very fact he impresses and influences,
changes and transforms human beings who believe and
thus human society. What Jesus quite concretely conveys and makes possible both to the individual and to
the community who commit themselves to him may be
described as follows:[7]

> A *new* basic orientation *and* basic attitude, *a new
> approach to life, to which Jesus summoned men and
> whose consequences he indicated. If a man or a
> human community has in mind this Jesus Christ as
> concrete guiding principle and living model for
> their relations with man, world and God, they may
> and can live differently, more genuinely, more
> humanly. He makes possible an identity and inner
> coherence in life.*

New motivations, *new motives of action, which can be discovered from Jesus' "theory" and "practice." In his light it is possible to answer the question why man should act just in one way and not in another: why he should love and not hate; why—and even Freud had no answer to this—he should be honest, forbearing and kind wherever possible, even when he loses by it and is made to suffer as a result of the unreliability and brutality of other people.*

New dispositions, *new consistent insights, tendencies, intentions, formed and maintained in the spirit of Jesus Christ. Here readiness to oblige is engendered, attitudes created, qualifications conveyed, which can guide conduct, not only for isolated and passing moments, but permanently. Here we find dispositions of unpretentious commitment for one's fellow men, of identification with the handicapped, with the fight against unjust structures; dispositions of gratitude, freedom, magnanimity, unselfishness, joy, and also of forbearance, pardon and service; dispositions which are tested in borderline situations, in readiness for complete self-sacrifice, in renunciation even when it is not necessary, in a readiness to work for the greater cause.*

New projects, *new actions on a great or small scale, which in imitation of Jesus Christ begin at the very point where no one wants to help: not only universal programs to transform society, but concrete signs, testimonies, evidence of humanity and of humanizing both the individual and human society.*

A new background of meaning and a new definition of the goal *in the ultimate reality, in the consummation of man and mankind in God's kingdom, which can sustain not only what is positive in human life, but also what is negative. In the light and power of Jesus Christ the believer is offered an ultimate meaning, not only for man's life and action, but also for his suffering and death; not only for the story of man's success, but also for the story of his suffering.*

In a word: for both the individual human being and the community Jesus Christ in person, with word, deed and fate, is invitation ("you may"), appeal ("you should"), challenge ("you can"), basic model therefore of a *new*

447

way of life, a new life-style, a new meaning to life.

Freedom in the legal order

Jesus expects his disciples voluntarily *to renounce rights without compensation.* If any individual or group today wants to take this Jesus Christ as a guide to behavior, no renunciation of rights will be required in principle. But in the wholly concrete situation for the sake of the other person the possibility of renouncing one's rights will be offered as an opportunity.

The *problem of peace and war* may be taken as an example. For decades it has proved impossible to establish peace in certain areas of the world: in the Near East, in the Far East, but also in Europe. Why is there no peace? It is easy to say, because "the other side" does not want it. But the problem lies deeper. Both sides assert claims and rights, rights to the same territories, nations, economic opportunities. Both sides can also substantiate their claims and rights: historically, economically, culturally, politically. The governments on both sides have the constitutional duty to uphold and defend the rights of the state. It used to be said that they had the right even to extend them.

The power blocs and political camps have based and still base their foreign policy on stereotypes of the enemy which are supposed to justify their own positions. Hostile images which are shaped psychologically both by the individual's fear of everything foreign and by his prejudices against whatever is different, disparate, unusual. Hostile images which also have an identification and stabilization function in internal politics for society as a whole. Such hostile images and prejudices in regard to other countries, nations and races are congenial because they are popular. Just because they are rooted in man's deepest psychical strata, they are extraordinarily difficult to correct. The political situation of the power blocs is thus characterized by an atmosphere of suspicion and of collective insinuations: a vicious circle of mistrust which renders any intention of peace and any readiness for reconciliation dubious from the very outset, since these will be regarded as weakness or mere tactics on the part of the other side.

Seen globally the consequences are of considerable relevance: armaments competition against which all negotiations and treaties already contracted on the

on the limitation and control of armaments remain
ineffective. Spirals of violence and counterviolence
in international crises in which each side tries to
outmaneuver the other power-politically, economically,
militarily-strategically. Thus in different parts of
the world there is no genuine peace, because no one
sees why just he and not the other person should
renounce his legal rights and power. No one sees why
he should not occasionally make his standpoint prevail
even brutally, if he has the power to do so. No one
sees why he should not subscribe to a Machiavellian
foreign policy which involves the least possible risk
to himself. But what can Christians do? Here are
some brief suggestions:

> The Christian message provides no detailed informa-
> tion as to how--for instance--the Eastern frontiers
> of Germany, the borders between Israel and the
> Arab states or the international fishing limits
> should be drawn; how certain conflicts in Asia,
> Africa or South America, how in particular the
> East-West conflict should be settled. It makes no
> detailed suggestions for disarmament conferences
> and peace conversations. The Gospel is neither a
> political theory nor a method of diplomacy.

> But the Christian message says something funda-
> mental, something that statesmen could not so
> easily demand from their peoples, but which
> Catholic, Protestant and Orthodox bishops, Chris-
> tian Church leaders, theologians, pastors and lay-
> people in the whole world very well could say and
> certainly ought to say: that renouncing rights
> without expecting anything in return is not neces-
> sarily a disgrace; that Christians at least should
> not despise a politician who is prepared to make
> concessions. In fact, in very special cases--not
> as a new law--a renunciation of rights without
> recompense can constitute the great freedom of the
> Christian: he is going two miles with someone
> who has forced him to go one.

The Christian who takes this great freedom as the
standard and determining factor of his life is also, in
his small or large sphere of influence, a challenge to
all who do not want to understand why it is appropriate
in certain situations to renounce rights and advantages
for the sake of men and for the sake of peace. He is
a challenge to all who think that the use of power and
violence, getting one's own way and exploiting others,
whenever this is possible without risk to oneself, is

449

the most advantageous, the most shrewd and even humanly speaking the most rational policy.

The Christian message is decidedly opposed to this logic of domination which gambles with men's humanity for the sake of legality, profitability and violence. It is an offer to see something positive, authentically human, in renunciation: a guarantee of one's own freedom and the freedom of others.

Freedom in the struggle for power

Jesus appeals to his disciples voluntarily *to use power for the benefit of others.* Any individuals or groups who take Jesus Christ as their model will not today be required to do the impossible: to renounce all use of power. But in the particular situation they will see how they are called to use power for others.

We may recall, for example, the *problem of economic power.* Since the problems here are analogous to those already discussed in connection with war and peace, we can be more brief and confine ourselves to what is absolutely essential. The facts are well-known. There seems to be no way of halting rising prices and inflation. They continue to rise, affecting most seriously the poorest members of the community. The employers blame the unions and the unions the employers, and both blame the government. A vicious circle? What is to be done? Here too we can only offer some brief suggestions:

> *The Christian message does not give any detailed information as to how the problem should be tackled technically, how therefore the riddle of the magic square is to be solved: how full employment, economic growth, price stability and a favorable trade balance can be simultaneously achieved. Supply and demand, home market and foreign market seem to obey iron economic laws. And each and every one enters into the merciless struggle for power, trying to exploit them as far as possible to his own advantage.*

> *The Christian message says something which is not normally found in any economics textbook, either of the left or of the right, and which is extraordinarily important for the present context: namely, that in all the inevitable conflicts of interests it is no disgrace either for the industrialist or for the trade union leader if he does*

not always exploit to the full his power over the other. It is not a disgrace if the employer does not pass on every increase in production costs to the consumers, merely to keep his profit constant or if possible to increase it. Nor is it a disgrace if the union leader occasionally does not insist on an increase in wages even if he could do so and the union members are perhaps expecting him to do so. In brief, despite all the tough discussions, it is no disgrace if those who have power in society do not always use it to their own advantage, but in certain situations are prepared completely freely--again, not as a universal law--to use that power for the benefit of others: being ready for once in the individual case to "give away" power, profit, influence, and to give his coat in addition to his cloak.

In this way something is made possible in the individual case which seems too much to demand of men belonging either to the capitalist or to the socialist society and which is nevertheless infinitely important for all human life together, of individuals and of nations, of different language groups, classes and even Churches: being able endlessly to forgive instead of off-setting the blame; to be able to make concessions unconditionally instead of maintaining positions; the better justice of love instead of continual litigation; peace surpassing all reason instead of the merciless struggle for power. A message of this kind does not become the opium of empty promises. It involves a much more radical commitment than other programs do to the present world. It aims at change where the rulers threaten to crush the ruled, institutions to overwhelm persons, order to exclude freedom, power to suppress law.

Wherever individuals or whole groups forget that power exists not for domination but for service, they contribute to the prevalence of power thinking and power politics in both the individual and the social sphere: to the dehumanization of man in the now unavoidable struggle for power.

But wherever individuals or whole groups remember that power exists for service and not for domination, they contribute to the humanizing of the all-round human competitive struggle and even in the midst of this struggle make possible mutual respect, respect for men, reconciliation and forbearance. They may then believe in the promise that mercy will be shown

451

to those who show mercy.[8]

Freedom from the pressure of consumption

Jesus invites his disciples *to practice inward freedom from possessions (consumption)*. If anyone wants his behavior to be inspired in the last resort by Jesus Christ, he will not be forced to renounce in principle possessions and consumption. But in the wholly concrete case he will be offered the opportunity to make this renunciation for the sake of his own and others' freedom.

We may recall, for example, the *problem of economic growth*. Despite all progress, our efficiency-oriented and consumer society is increasingly entangled in contradictions. Supported by an economic theory extolled on all sides, the slogan runs: increase production so that we can increase consumption, so that production does not break down but expands. In this way the level of demand is always kept above the level of supply: through advertising, models and bellwethers of consumption. Wants continue to increase. New needs are created as soon as the old are satisfied. Luxury goods are classified as necessary consumer goods, in order to make way for new luxury goods. The targets of our own living standard are raised with the improvement of the supply situation. There is now a dynamic expectation of prosperity and a satisfying life. The surprising result is that, with constantly increasing real income, the average citizen feels that he has scarcely any means completely at his disposal, that he is really living at a minimum of existence.

At the same time the industrial welfare society and the economists too to a large extent start out from the assumption that increasing prosperity creates increasing happiness, that the capacity to consume is the essential proof of a successful life. The consumption of goods becomes a demonstration of one's own status to oneself and to society, so that expectations mount up on all sides in accordance with the law of herd instinct, prestige and competition. We are what we consume. We are more when we have reached a higher standard. We are nothing if we remain below the standardized position of the generality of people. All things considered, if we want to reach a better future, production and consumption must continually increase: everything must become bigger, more speedy, more numerous. This is the strict law of economic growth.

452

On the other hand it is increasingly recognized today that the assumptions behind this law are largely out of date in the industrial nations. Our first and most important concern is no longer the conquest of poverty and shortage of goods: for these preconditions of a genuinely human life are normally fulfilled in the highly industrialized countries. So for many people the call for bread alone, for possessions and consumption alone, is no longer convincing. On the one hand efforts to eliminate poverty have now given way to the spiral of infinitely increasing demand (on the part of consumers) and continual stimulation of demand (on the part of producers). On the other hand certain groups in our society are making it increasingly clear that, in addition to the hitherto primary economic needs, there are now secondary and tertiary wants which can no longer be satisfied from the goods provided by the national economy. Even the propertied classes are no happier as a result of material prosperity alone. And, among young people particularly, habituated to consumption, there is a widespread feeling of boredom and profound disorientation, together with uneasiness about the one-sided orientation to constantly increasing consumption.

The law of uncontrolled economic growth however creates a continually widening gap between rich and poor countries and strengthens among the underprivileged part of mankind feelings of envy, resentment, deadly hatred, but also of sheer despair and helplessness. And, as outlined at the opening of this book, it is turned in the end against the well-to-do themselves. We are suffering increasingly from the apparently endless growth of cities, proliferating traffic, noise on all sides, pollution of rivers and lakes, bad air; we are worried about the disposal of butter and meat mountains, we are crushed under the waste and lumber of our own prosperity. The world's raw materials, ruthlessly and more and more extensively exploited, are becoming increasingly scarce; the problem of an ever more widely expanding world economy is becoming incomprehensible. But what is to be done? Again we give a brief summary:

The Christian message provides no technical solutions: not for environment protection, distribution of raw materials, town and country planning, noise abatement, elimination of waste; nor for any kind of structural improvements. Nor do we find in the New Testament any instructions about the possibilities of bridging the gap between rich and poor, between the industrialized and the industrially underdeveloped nations. Least of all can the Christian message offer any decision models or devices for solving the enormous problems which a change of policy would create: for instance, the problem of freezing the national and international economy to zero growth, without causing a breakdown of the different branches of industry, loss of jobs, chaotic consequences for the social security of whole population groups and for the underdeveloped countries.

But the Christian message can make something clear which is apparently not envisaged at all either in the economic theory or in the practical scale of values of the modern consumer- and efficiency-oriented society, but which perhaps could have a part to play: replacement of the compulsion to consume by freedom in regard to consumption. In any case there is some point in not constructing one's happiness on the basis of consumption and prosperity alone. But in the light of Jesus Christ it also makes sense not to be always striving, not always to be trying to have everything; not to be governed by the laws of prestige and competition; not to take part in the cult of abundance; but even with children to exercise the freedom to renounce consumption. This is "poverty in spirit" as inward freedom from possessions: contented unpretentiousness and confident unconcernedness as a basic attitude. All this would be opposed to all fussy, overbold presumption and that anxious solicitude which is found among both the materially rich and the materially poor.

What is the point? Not asceticism or an urge to self-sacrifice. Not a new, stringent law. But so that the normal cheerful consumer may remain free, may become free. So that he does not give himself up to the good things of this world, whether money or a car, alcohol or cigarettes, cosmetics or sex. So that he does not give way to the addictions of the welfare society. In other words, so that man in the midst of the world and its goods--which he must use and may use-- in the last resort remains human. Here too then it is not a question of possessions, growth, consumption, for their own sake. And certainly not men for the sake of possessions, growth, consumption. But everything for the sake of men.

Wherever individuals or whole groups overlook the fact that all good things of this world exist for the sake of man and not man for the sake of these things, they are not worshiping the one true God, but the many false gods--Mammon, power, sex, work, prestige-- and they surrender man to these merciless gods. They intensify the humanly destructive dynamism in which our economic processes are involved today. They strengthen the thoughtlessness with which the economy today is run at the expense of the future. They strengthen the inhuman selfishness with which the forces of the world economy assign too much to one half of mankind and too little to the other. Even if they are not aware of it, they are spreading inhumanity in the welfare and consumer society.

But wherever individuals or whole groups insist that the good things of this world in any case exist for the sake of man, they are contributing to the humanization of the now unavoidable welfare and consumer society. They are creating the necessary new elite, not tied to one class, which is learning to live with a new scale of values in this society and in the long run can initiate a process of reorientation. Even in this new age they make possible for themselves and others independence, supreme simplicity, an ultimate, carefree superiority, true freedom. To these also the promise applies that all those who are poor in spirit will possess the kingdom of God.[9]

Human existence transfigured in Christian existence

Being Christian cannot mean ceasing to be human. But neither can being human mean ceasing to be Christian. Being Christian is not an addition to being human: there is not a Christian level above or below the human. The true Christian is not a split personality.

The Christian element therefore is neither a superstructure nor a substructure of the human. It is an elevation or--better--a transfiguration of the human, at once preserving, canceling, surpassing the human. Being Christian therefore means that the other humanisms are transfigured: they are affirmed to the extent that they affirm the human reality; they are rejected to the extent that they reject the Christian reality, Christ himself; they are surpassed to the extent that being Christian can fully incorporate the human, all-too-human even in all its negativity.

455

Christians are no less humanists than all humanists. But they see the human, the truly human, the
humane; they see man and his God; see humanity, freedom, justice, life, love, peace, meaning; all these
they see in the light of this Jesus who for them is
the concrete criterion, the Christ, In his light they
think they cannot support just any kind of humanism
which simply affirms all that is true, good, beautiful
and human. But they can support a truly radical humanism which is able to integrate and cope with what is
untrue, not good, unlovely, inhuman: not only everything positive, but also--and here we discern what a
humanism has to offer--everything negative, even suffering, sin, death, futility.

Looking to the crucified and living Christ, even
in the world of today, man is able not only to act but
also to suffer, not only to live but also to die. And
even when pure reason breaks down, even in pointless
misery and sin, he perceives a meaning, because he
knows that here too in both positive and negative
experience he is sustained by God. Thus faith in
Jesus the Christ gives peace with God and with oneself, but does not play down the problems of the world.
It makes man truly human, because truly one with other
men: open to the very end for the other person, the
one who needs him here and now, his "neighbor."

So we have asked: why should one be a Christian?
The answer will certainly be understood now if we reduce
it to a brief recapitulatory formula:

*By following Jesus Christ
man in the world of today
can truly humanly live, act, suffer and die:
in happiness and unhappiness, life and death,
sustained by God and helpful to men.*

Endnotes

[1]E. Kasemann, *An die Romer*, Tubingen, 1973, p.166.

[2]Ibid.

[3]Cf. B I, 2: "The Christ of piety?"

[4]Cf. C VI, 1; "Limits to demythologization."

[5]Even the English expression, "The Paradigmatic Individuals," is not an adequate translation of Karl Jaspers' term, *die massgebenden Menschen.* Cf. the otherwise very sound article by A. S. Cua, "Morality and the Paradigmatic Individuals" in *American Philosophical Quarterly*, 6 (1969), pp. 324-29.

[6]Jn. 8:12.

[7]For a number of the following points I gained some valuable ideas from a conversation with J. M. Gustafson on the occasion of his lecture in Pittsburgh, "The Relation of the Gospels to the Moral Life," published in D. G. Miller/D. Y. Hadidan (eds.), *Jesus and Man's Hope*, Pittsburgh, 1971, Vol. II, pp. 103-17. Cf. the same author, *Christ and the Moral Life*, New York/London, 1968.

[8]Mt. 5:7.

[9]Mt. 5:3.

Discussion Questions

1. Can Küng's model for ethical decision avoid subjectivism? If so, how? Is Kung's model any more or less vulnerable to the charge of subjectivism than others you might think of?

2. What does Küng mean when he says that an authentic Christian ethical criterion requires the turbulence of life, the inexhaustible, inconceivable richness of concrete existence?

3. Do you think that Küng follows his own method when dealing with the several scenarios discussed in this essay?

4. What are the implications of Küng's position that being a Christian is a transfiguration of the human? Does this sound like Hamilton's essay? If so, in what senses?

5. Do you agree that "Christianity is at least a

humanism"? What does "humanism" mean in this context?

BEING A CHRISTIAN: THE INNER STRUGGLE

In many respects the disciplines of the Christian life are lost to modern Christians. This essay is a collection of musings by Thomas Merton. In the essay Merton speaks of the contemplative person. He speaks also of the saint. Readers should not interpret these titles too rigidly. Merton intends for his observations to have influence beyond the monastic orders. The saintly life is worthy of every Christian's commitment, according to Merton.

Merton considers superficiality to be a spiritual problem. He clearly believes the disciplines of the spiritual life to be for ordinary humans. Work may be a spiritual devotion. And he maintains that everything that is, is holy. Detachment from things is not an end in itself, he says. Rather, detachment from things is done in order to attach ourselves to God. He stresses that a Christian is able to use and enjoy possessions, and that Christians may be true to their inner commitment without any explicit reference to God. Indeed, Merton considers the loud and hackneyed use of religious language among the pseudo-pious to be repugnate to an authentic life of discipleship.

When Merton advises us to avoid the noise and business of men, to keep as far away as we can from the places where humans gather to cheat, exploit and mock one another, he is admonishing an interior solitude and removal. But he does not depreciate the need for external physical detachment either. Prayer and renunciation are concomitant traits of the disciplined life.

BEING A CHRISTIAN: THE INNER STRUGGLE*

How am I to know the will of God? Even where
there is no other more explicit claim on my obedience,
such as a legitimate command, the very nature of each
situation usually bears written into itself some
indication of God's will. For whatever is demanded by
truth, by justice, by mercy, or by love must surely be
taken to be willed by God. To consent to His will is,
then, to consent to be true, or to speak truth, or at
least to seek it. To obey Him is to respond to His
will expressed in the need of another person, or at
least to respect the rights of others. For the right
of another man is the expression of God's love and
God's will. In demanding that I respect the rights of
another God is not merely asking me to conform to some
abstract, arbitrary law: He is enabling me to share,
as His son, in His own care for my brother. No man
who ignores the rights and needs of others can hope to
walk in the light of contemplation, because his way
has turned aside from truth, from compassion and
therefore from God.

The requirements of a work to be done can be
understood as the will of God. If I am supposed to hoe
a garden or make a table, then I will be obeying God
if I am true to the task I am performing. To do the
work carefully and well, with love and respect for the
nature of my task and with due attention to its purpose, is to unite myself to God's will in my work. In
this way I become His instrument. He works through
me. When I act as His instrument my labor cannot become an obstacle to contemplation, even though it
may temporarily so occupy my mind that I cannot engage
in it while I am actually doing my job. Yet my work
itself will purify and pacify my mind and dispose me
for contemplation.

Unnatural, frantic, anxious work, work done under
pressure of greed or fear or any other inordinate

*Source: From Thomas Merton, *New Seeds of Con-
templation*. Copyright 1961 by The Abbey of Gethsemani,
Inc. Reprinted by permission of New Directions Publishing Corporation.

passion, cannot properly speaking be dedicated to God, because God never wills such work directly. He may permit that through no fault of our own we may have to work madly and distractedly, due to our sins, and to the sins of the society in which we live. In that case we must tolerate it and make the best of what we cannot avoid. But let us not be blind to the distinction between sound, healthy work and unnatural toil.

In any case, we should always seek to conform to the *logos* or truth of the duty before us, the work to be done, or our own God-given nature. Contemplative obedience and abandonment to the will of God can never mean a cultivated indifference to the natural values implanted by Him in human life and work. Insensitivity must not be confused with detachment. The contemplative must certainly be detached, but he can never allow himself to become insensible to true human values, whether in society, in other men or in himself. If he does so, then his contemplation stands condemned as vitiated in its very root.

Everything That Is, Is Holy

Detachment from things does not mean setting up a contradiction between "things" and "God" as if God were another "thing" and as if His creatures were His rivals. We do not detach ourselves from things in order to attach ourselves to God, but rather we become detached *from ourselves* in order to see and use all things in and for God. This is an entirely new perspective which many sincerely moral and ascetic minds fail utterly to see. There is no evil in anything created by God, nor can anything of His become an obstacle to our union with Him. The obstacle is in our "self," that is to say in the tenacious need to maintain our separate, external, egotistic will. It is when we refer all things to this outward and false "self" that we alienate ourselves from reality and from God. It is then the false self that is our god, and we love everything for the sake of this self. We use all things, so to speak, for the worship of this idol which is our imaginary self. In so doing we pervert and corrupt things, or rather we turn our relationship to them into a corrupt and sinful relationship. We do not thereby make them evil, but we use them to increase our attachment to our illusory self.

Those who try to escape from this situation by treating the good things of God as if they were evils

461

are only confirming themselves in a terrible illusion. They are like Adam blaming Eve and Eve blaming the serpent in Eden. "Woman has tempted me. Wine has tempted me. Food has tempted me. Woman is pernicious, wine is poison, food is death. I must hate and revile them. By hating them I will please God. . . ." These are the thoughts and attitudes of a baby, of a savage and of an idolater who seeks by magic incantations and spells to protect his egotistic self and placate the insatiable little god in his own heart. To take such an idol for God is the worst kind of self-deception. It turns a man into a fanatic, no longer capable of sustained contact with the truth, no longer capable of genuine love.

Some men seem to think that a saint cannot possibly take a natural interest in anything created. They imagine that any form of spontaneity or enjoyment is a sinful gratification of "fallen nature." That to be "supernatural" means obstructing all spontaneity with cliches and arbitrary references to God. The purpose of these cliches is, so to speak, to hold everything at arms length, to frustrate spontaneous reactions, to exorcise feelings of guilt. Or perhaps to cultivate such feelings! One wonders sometimes if such morality is not after all a love of guilt! They suppose that the life of a saint can never be anything but a perpetual duel with guilt, and that a saint cannot even drink a glass of cold water without making an act of contrition for slaking his thirst, as if that were a mortal sin. As if for the saints every response to beauty, to goodness, to the pleasant, were an offense. As if the saint could never allow himself to be pleased with anything but his prayers and his interior acts of piety.

A saint is capable of loving created things and enjoying the use of them and dealing with them in a perfectly simple, natural manner, making no formal references to God, drawing no attention to his own piety, and acting without any artificial rigidity at all. His gentleness and his sweetness are not pressed through his pores by the crushing restraint of a spiritual strait-jacket. They come from his direct docility to the light of truth and to the will of God. Hence a saint is capable of talking about the world without any explicit reference to God, in such a way that his statement gives greater glory to God and arouses a greater love of God than the observations of someone less holy, who has to strain himself to make an arbitrary connection between creatures and God

462

through the medium of hackneyed analogies and metaphors that are so feeble that they make you think there is something the matter with religion.

Learn To Be Alone

Physical solitude, exterior silence and real recollection are all morally necessary for anyone who wants to lead a contemplative life, but like everything else in creation they are nothing more than means to an end, and if we do not understand the end we will make a wrong use of the means.

We do not go into the desert to escape people but to learn how to find them; we do not leave them in order to have nothing more to do with them, but to find out the way to do them the most good. But this is only a secondary end.

There should be at least a room, or some corner where no one will find you and disturb you or notice you. You should be able to untether yourself from the world and set yourself free, loosing all the fine strings and strands of tension that bind you, by sight, by sound, by thought, to the presence of other men.

"But thou, when thou shalt pray, enter into thy chamber, and having shut the door, pray to thy Father in secret. . . ."

Once you have found such a place, be content with it, and do not be disturbed if a good reason takes you out of it. Love it, and return to it as soon as you can, and do not be too quick to change it for another.

City churches are sometimes quiet and peaceful solitudes, caves of silence where a man can seek refuge from the intolerable arrogance of the business world. One can be more alone, sometimes, in church than in a room in one's own house. At home, one can always be routed out and disturbed (and one should not resent this, for love sometimes demands it). But in these quiet churches one remains nameless, undisturbed in the shadows, where there are only a few chance, anonymous strangers among the vigil lights, and the curious impersonal postures of the bad statues. The very tastelessness and shabbiness of some churches makes them greater solitudes, though churches should not be vulgar. Even if they are, as long as they are dark it makes little difference.

463

Let there always be quiet, dark churches in which men can take refuge. Places where they can kneel in silence. Houses of God, filled with His silent presence. There, even when they do not know how to pray, at least they can be still and breathe easily. Let there be a place somewhere in which you can breathe naturally, quietly, and not have to take your breath in continuous short gasps. A place where your mind can be idle, and forget its concerns, descend into silence, and worship the Father in secret.

There can be no contemplation where there is no secret.

We have said that the solitude that is important to a contemplative is, above all, an interior and spiritual thing. We have admitted that it is possible to live in deep and peaceful interior solitude even in the midst of the world and its confusion. But this truth is sometimes abused in religion. There are men dedicated to God whose lives are full of restlessness and who have no real desire to be alone. They admit that exterior solitude is good, in theory, but they insist that it is far better to preserve interior solitude while living in the midst of others. In practice, their lives are devoured by activities and strangled with attachments. Interior solitude is impossible for them. They fear it. They do everything they can to escape it. What is worse, they try to draw everyone else into activities as senseless and as devouring as their own. They are great promoters of useless work. They love to organize meetings and banquets and conferences and lectures. They print circulars, write letters, talk for hours on the telephone in order that they may gather a hundred people together in a large room where they will all fill the air with smoke and make a great deal of noise and roar at one another and clap their hands and stagger home at last patting one another on the back with the assurance that they have all done great things to spread the Kingdom of God.

The Pure Heart

You will never find interior solitude unless you make some conscious effort to deliver yourself from the desires and the cares and the attachments of an existence in time and in the world.

Do everything you can to avoid the noise and the business of men. Keep as far away as you can from the

places where they gather to cheat and insult one another, to exploit one another, to laugh at one another,
or to mock one another with their false gestures of
friendship. Be glad if you can keep beyond the reach
of their radios. Do not bother with their unearthly
songs. Do not read their advertisements.

The contemplative life certainly does not demand
a self-righteous contempt for the habits and diversions
of ordinary people. But nevertheless, no man who seeks
liberation and light in solitude, no man who seeks
spiritual freedom, can afford to yield passively to
all the appeals of a society of salesmen, advertisers
and consumers. There is no doubt that life cannot
be lived on a human level without certain legitimate
pleasures. But to say that all the pleasures which
offer themselves to us as necessities are now "legitimate" is quite another story.

It should be accepted as a most elementary human
and moral truth that no man can live a fully sane and
decent life unless he is able to say "no" on occasion
to his natural bodily appetites. No man who simply
eats and drinks whenever he feels like eating and
drinking, who smokes whenever he feels the urge to
light a cigarette, who gratifies his curiosity and
sensuality whenever they are stimulated, can consider
himself a free person. He has renounced his spiritual
freedom and become the servant of bodily impulse.
Therefore his mind and his will are not fully his own.
They are under the power of his appetites. And
through the medium of his appetites, they are under
the control of those who gratify his appetites. Just
because he can buy one brand of whisky rather than
another, this man deludes himself that he is making a
choice; but the fact is that he is a devout servant of
a tyrannical ritual. He must reverently buy the
bottle, take it home, unwrap it, pour it out for his
friends, watch TV, "feel good," talk his silly unin-
hibited head off, get angry, shout, fight and go to
bed in disgust with himself and the world. This
becomes a kind of religious compulsion without which
he cannot convince himself that he is really alive,
really "fulfilling his personality." He is not "sinning" but simply makes an ass of himself, deluding
himself that he is real when his compulsions have
reduced him to a shadow of a genuine person.

In general, it can be said that no contemplative
life is possible without ascetic self-discipline. One
must learn to survive without the habit-forming

465

luxuries which get such a hold on men today. I do not
say that to be a contemplative one absolutely has to
go without smoking or without alcohol, but certainly
one must be able to use these things without being
dominated by an uncontrolled need for them. There
can be no doubt that smoking and drinking are obvious
areas for the elementary self-denial without which a
life of prayer would be a pure illusion.

I am certainly no judge of television, since I
have never watched it. All I know is that there is
a sufficiently general agreement, among men whose
judgment I respect, that commercial television is
degraded, meretricious and absurd. Certainly it would
seem that TV could become a kind of unnatural surro-
gate for contemplation: a completely inert subjection
to vulgar images, a descent to a sub-natural passivity
rather than an ascent to a supremely active passivity
in understanding and love. It would seem that television should be used with extreme care and discrimina-
tion by anyone who might hope to take interior life
seriously.

Keep your eyes clean and your ears quiet and your
mind serene. Breathe God's air. Work, if you can,
under His sky.

But if you have to live in a city and work among
machines and ride in the subways and eat in a place
where the radio makes you deaf with spurious news and
where the food destroys your life and the sentiments
of those around you poison your heart with boredom,
do not be impatient, but accept it as the love of God
and as a seed of solitude planted in your soul. If
you are appalled by those things, you will keep your
appetite for the healing silence of recollection. But
meanwhile--keep your sense of compassion for the men
who have forgotten the very concept of solitude. You,
at least, know that it exists, and that it is the
source of peace and joy. You can still hope for such
joy. They do not even hope for it any more.

If you seek escape for its own sake and run away
from the world only because it is (as it must be)
intensely unpleasant, you will not find peace and you
will not find solitude. If you seek solitude merely
because it is what you prefer, you will never escape
from the world and its selfishness; you will never
have the interior freedom that will keep you really
alone.

466

One vitally important aspect of solitude is its intimate dependence on chastity. The virtue of chastity is not the complete renunciation of all sex, but simply the right use of sex. This means, according to most of the great religious traditions of the world, the restriction of all sex to married life, and, within the married state, to certain ordinate norms.

Nowhere is self-denial more important than in the area of sex, because this is the most difficult of all natural appetites to control and one whose undisciplined gratification completely blinds the human spirit to all interior light.

Sex is by no means to be regarded as an evil. It is a natural good, willed by God, and entering into the mystery of God's love and God's mercy toward men. But though sex may not be evil in itself, inordinate attachment to sexual pleasure, expecially outside of marriage, is one of man's most frequent and pitiable weaknesses. Indeed, it is so common that most people today simply believe that sex cannot be fully controlled--that it is not really possible for a normal human being to abstain from it completely. Hence they assume that one should simply resign himself to the inevitable and cease worrying about it.

One must certainly agree that pathological guilt about sex is no help at all in helping men to get control of passion. However, self-control is not only desirable but altogether possible and it is essential for the contemplative life. It demands considerable effort, watchfulness, patience, humility and trust in Divine grace. But the very struggle for chastity teaches us to rely on a spiritual power higher than our own nature, and this is an indispensable preparation for interior prayer. Furthermore, chastity is not possible without ascetic self-sacrifice in many other areas. It demands a certain amount of fasting, it requires a very temperate and well-ordered life, modesty, restraint of curiosity, moderation of one's aggressivity, and many other virtues.

Perfect chastity establishes one in a state of spiritual solitude, peace, tranquillity, clarity, gentleness and joy in which one is fully disposed for meditation and contemplative prayer.

Distractions

Prayer and love are really learned in the hour

467

when prayer becomes impossible and your heart turns
to stone.

If you have never had any distractions you don't
know how to pray. For the secret of prayer is a hunger for God and for the vision of God, a hunger that
lies far deeper than the level of language or affection.
And a man whose memory and imagination are persecuting
him with a crowd of useless or even evil thoughts and
images may sometimes be forced to pray far better, in
the depths of his murdered heart, than one whose mind
is swimming with clear concepts and brilliant purposes
and easy acts of love.

That is why it is useless to get upset when you
cannot shake off distractions. In the first place,
you must realize that they are often unavoidable in
the life of prayer. The necessity of kneeling and
suffering submersion under a tidal wave of wild and
inane images is one of the standard trials of the
contemplative life.

The kind of distractions that holy people most
fear are generally the most harmless of all. But
sometimes pious men and women torture themselves at
meditation because they imagine they are "consenting"
to the phantasms of a lewd and somewhat idiotic bur-
lesque that is being fabricated in their imagination
without their being able to do a thing to stop it.
The chief reason why they suffer is that their hope-
less efforts to put a stop to this parade of images
generate a nervous tension which only makes everything
a hundred times worse.

If they ever had a sense of humor, they have now
become so nervous that it has abandoned them altogether
Yet humor is one of the things that would probably be
most helpful at such a time.

There is no real danger in these things. The
distractions that do harm are the ones that draw our
will away from its profound and peaceful occupation
with God and involve it in elaborations of projects
that have been concerning us during our day's work.
We are confronted by issues that really attract and
occupy our wills and there is considerable danger
that our meditation will break down into a session of
mental letter-writing or sermons or speeches or books
or, worse still, plans to raise money or to take care
of our health.

But in all these things, it is the will to pray that is the essence of prayer, and the desire to find God, to see Him and to love Him is the one thing that matters. If you have desired to know Him and love Him, you have already done what was expected of you, and it is much better to desire God without being able to think clearly of Him, than to have marvelous thoughts about Him without desiring to enter into union with His will.

Renunciation

The way to contemplation is an obscurity so obscure that it is no longer even dramatic. There is nothing in it that can be grasped and cherished as heroic or even unusual. And so, for a contemplative, there is supreme value in the ordinary everyday routine of work, poverty, hardship and monotony that characterize the lives of all the poor, uninteresting and forgotten people in the world.

Christ, Who came on earth to form contemplatives and teach men the ways of sanctity and prayer, could easily have surrounded himself with ascetics who starved themselves to death and terrified the people with strange trances. But His Apostles were workmen, fishermen, publicans who made themselves conspicuous only by their disregard for most of the intricate network of devotions and ceremonial practices and moral gymnastics of the professionally holy.

The surest asceticism is the bitter insecurity and labor and nonentity of the really poor. To be utterly dependent on other people. To be ignored and despised and forgotten. To know little of respectability or comfort. To take orders and work hard for little or no money: it is a hard school, and one which most pious people do their best to avoid.

The contemplative needs to be properly fed, clothed and housed. But he also needs to share something of the hardship of the poor. He needs to be able to identify himself honestly and sincerely with the poor, to be able to look at life through their eyes, and to do this because he is really one of them. This is not true unless to some extent he participates in the risk of poverty: that is to say, unless he has to do many jobs he would rather not do, suffer many inconveniences with patience, and be content with many things that could be a great deal better.

Discussion Questions

1. Do you agree that the spiritual disciplines Merton suggests are necessary in the modern world? Are they realistic?

2. Would it be possible to live these disciplines without being a Christian?

3. To what extent, if any, do Merton's recommendations promise such a change in degree as to produce a change in kind of human being?

4. There is a classic tension between withdrawal from the world, and engaging social change in the world. Where would you place Merton's type of disciple on this continuum?

RETROSPECTIVE

To be a Christian is to live a transformed existence within a new community (the church). But the
uniqueness of Christian life must not be identified
too readily with the addition of "religious" or
church duties. Churches do not exist as ends in
themselves, neither do religious duties. On this,
all the writers of the section are in agreement.

The character of a Christian is not defined by
his churchly or religious activities. It is marked
by his embodiment of the person of Jesus Christ, and
here Küng is correct. He is not precise, but he is
correct. Precision and utility are our demands of a
moral norm, and one must always ask "Do I want to know
exactly what is required in order to be obedient,
or in order to know how to circumvent the standard?"

The church as both a witnessing and a performative
community is the place where Christ meets the contemporary Christian. The disciplines and celebrations
of worship are deliberate attempts to form Christian
character. And spiritual discipline is not to be
embraced in order to appease God, but that one may
become like Christ.

With this summary as background, we may still
note that many questions remain unanswered. For
example, what should be our attitude toward church
unity? Is disunity in Christianity to be regarded as
normal and good; indeed, necessary? If unity is
sought, should it be the unity of a common spirit
rather than structural or doctrinal oneness?

The church's mission is to facilitate growth into
Christlikeness, but how does the church balance
evangelism and social activity under this mission

task? What may the church do to constitute a transfigured humanity? Is worship enough? What forms of
worship are needed?

Of course, no actual church embodies the definition of a transformed human community founded upon
Jesus Christ and constituted by the Spirit. And
every church must be consciously self-critical or
else succumb to privatistic idolatry of its own
institution. But bringing the real church into harmony with what the church is in its essence is a work
not left to humans alone, it is also God's work.

PART SEVEN

THE KINGDOM OF GOD AND THE LIFE EVERLASTING

THE KINGDOM OF GOD AND THE LIFE
EVERLASTING

The doctrine of eschatology is concerned with the "last things"; the expected consummation of individual existence and history in general. Theologians must make intelligible the meanings of resurrection and eternal life with respect to the individual, and they must explicate the symbol of the Kingdom of God in order to make clear the Christian understanding of history.

Many negative associations accompany any discussion of eschatology. Poor scriptural hermeneutic and wild speculations have marked the history of the doctrine. There has been no orthodox eschatology, at least not in the same sense that there has been an orthodox Trinitarian or Christological formula. There are many reasons why this is so. One reason is that the main scriptural sources for eschatology are among the most difficult to interpret in the canon.

A second reason is that these themes have to do with the future, and the future is always to some extent inaccessible. Related to this second reason is the fact that eschatology speaks of a future which is held to be radically different from our past or present.

A third reason is that the modern *geist* is one of widespread satisfaction with this life and a willingness to accept human mortality and finitude. Indeed, other-worldliness is sometimes taken as evidence of neurosis. Healthy persons accept their humanity and do not attempt to evade human responsibilities to their neighbors by pursuing another world.

474

A fourth reason is the difficulty in conceiving of a life after death. Moderns take more seriously the social origins of selfhood. I am nothing apart from what I have become as son, father, husband, teacher, and friend. How could I survive cut off from these relations? And strangely enough, I am a self that includes errors, prejudices, weaknesses, and so forth. Could I be myself if all these were eliminated in some future life? And finally, what could it mean to exist as a self after the body, upon which my consciousness is dependent, has returned to dust?

A fifth and final reason why there have been many views on eschatology is that many aspects of the biblical picture of eschatology are morally problematical. If I become a Christian merely to escape punishment, have I not dishonored Christ and deceived myself? If the hope of eternal life directs my actions away from creative and responsible social change in the here and now, have I truly understood the gospel?

Even more troubling is the biblical teaching on judgment and punishment. Can the sins which we commit in our finitude have eternal consequences? What end does punishment serve if it is eternal without educatory or redemptive intentions? Human standards of justice require a more moral perspective than some theologies of eschatology advocate. And it does not seem a proper response to say, "Oh, but you cannot judge God by human standards." The problem is that it seems God's actions must at least analogously approximate our puny standards. Can we worship a God who is less humane than we?

In spite of all these difficulties there is a growing emphasis on eschatology. But eschatology is no longer merely the final chapter in theology. It is characteristic of contemporary theology to recognize the eschatological impact of every theological statement. It is the promise of hope. And contemporary theologians recognize that the Christian hope is not fully explicated if it is related only to the individual. The social, political, economic and cultural realities of human life are also being transformed. Peace and justice are provisionally actualized, but the promised kingdom will bring them in fullness.

In the essays to follow, John A. T. Robinson sets the stage for the crisis facing theologians who formulate the doctrine of eschatology in the modern

world. He calls for a shift in the mental lumber of
theologians who attempt to translate the biblical and
historical symbols of eschatology into a meaningful
message for modern men.

I have included only two essays which attempt
the kind of reconstruction Robinson calls for. The
essay by Hans Schwarz deals with most features traditionally associated with Christian eschatological
expectations. The final essay in the collection is
the now famous article by John Hick on theology and
verification. In this work Hick discusses the notion
of the resurrection of the person and shows its relevance to the entire Christian message.

MODERNITY AND ESCHATOLOGY

John A. T. Robinson probably will not provoke any argument when he observes that the gulf between the biblical viewpoint and modern secularism is greatest in the matter of eschatology. What disturbs Robinson is that this divergence of world view has led to the eclipse of the entire Christian eschatological scheme.

Naturally Robinson is aware of the popular literature which offers some theology of the future. But Robinson believes most of these attempts are so spurious scripturally that they do not merit serious consideration.

But the main reasons modern man has difficulty with eschatological viewpoints are not scriptural or even hermeneutical. According to Robinson, there are two characteristics of modernity which make an appreciation of Christian eschatology problematical.

The first of these is that contemporary humans can conceive of the end of the world. But they conceive of its end as the result of human war and nuclear conflagration, not as the work of God. Robinson's claim is that instead of supporting Christian eschatology this fear of the end of history actually undermines it. The reason for this apparent contradiction may be found in the second characteristic of modernity treated by Robinson. Contemporary humans have no real sense that history is going anywhere. Since modern persons have lost the notion of purpose (teleology) in history, then eschatology can mean nothing.

Robinson holds that Facism, Nazism, and Communism are all eschatologies of history, but he does not believe that any of them have a strong sense of the

purpose or direction of history. These systems regard
nature only as process, he says, and process
alone cannot guarantee purpose. And it is left to the church,
Robinson holds, to recreate a belief in hope and purpose.

MODERNITY AND ESCHATOLOGY*

Nowhere, over the field of Christian doctrine, is
the gulf between the Biblical viewpoint and the outlook of modern secularism so yawning as in the matter
of eschatology. The whole New Testament prospect of
a return of Christ, accompanied by the transformation
of this world-order, a general resurrection, a final
judgment, and the vindication of the sovereignty of
God over heaven and earth, is regarded by the scientific humanist of the twentieth century as frankly fantastic. The Biblical narratives of the Last Things
seem to him as incredible as the Biblical narratives
of the First Things appeared to his grandfather a
century ago. Or, rather, they are more incredible.
For, whereas the Genesis stories, reinterpreted, could,
it was found, be harmonized with the evolutionary
picture, the Second Advent and its accompaniments
appear to the modern a simple contradiction of all his
presumptions about the future of the world, immediate
or remote. And yet, despite its incompatibility with
the modern outlook, the Biblical view of the Last
Things, unlike that of the First, has hardly stirred a
ripple of controversy. The entire Christian eschatological scheme has simply been silently dismissed
without so much as a serious protest from within the

*Source: Abridged from *In the End, God* by John
A. T. Robinson, Volume Twenty in the *Religious Per-
spectives Series*, planned and edited by Ruth Nanda
Anshen. Copyright 1968 by J. A. T. Robinson. Re-
printed by permission of Harper and Row, Publishers,
Inc.

ecclesiastical camp.

To appreciate why this is so, it is necessary to take account of two changes in the secular outlook which distinguish the mind of the twentieth century from that of the nineteenth.

The first change would appear perhaps to make the Christian teaching seem more rather than less relevant. It is the fact that it is very much easier to-day than it was for our grandfathers to reckon seriously upon the end of the world. The nineteenth-century scientists may have known well enough the chilling prospects for the future of this earth under the second law of thermo dynamics. But it was not a knowledge that modified in any serious way the general optimism of the Victorian outlook. The end of the world was far away, and human society had ample time to reach the goal of its progress before that need be reckoned with. Moreover, it was only a limited number of people who really believed that, in the most significant sense, this was the end. The majority retained enough of the Christian heritage to doubt, even if things should prove to go out 'not with a bang but a whimper,' whether it seriously mattered. But to a generation brought up, not merely to the conclusions of the laboratory, but, more importantly, to its perspectives and horizons, the picture of the last state of our planet colours, or pales, much of its more sober thinking.

But to-day, of course, it is nothing so gradual or remote as the cold processes of entropy (or the now-favoured probability of a scorched earth, as the sun converts more and more of its hydrogen into helium) that has forced men to reckon again with the end of the world as a serious possibility. Scientists may deny the likelihood of the disintegration of this planet, or even of the total annihilation of human life, as the result of uncontrolled chain reaction from atomic fissure. The layman is left to place what confidence he can in such assurances and to derive from them what comfort he may. But whether the eclipse of human history be total or merely partial, the live possibility, not to say probability, of such an event in the foreseeable future, has brought back the issues of eschatology not simply to the laboratory but to the lobby.

All this might, as was said, seem to betoken a new relevance and promise a new hearing for the

Christian message of the End. And there have not
lacked those who in their preaching and evangelism
have sought to turn the situation to account.[1] But
this is to reckon without the second great change that
has come over the nineteenth-century prospect.

Up to the end of the last century, and well into
this, men were convinced that it was natural to seek
the clue to the course of history in its final stage.
That was an assumption which was foreign to the ancient world, except to the Jews and to such as had
come under Zoroastrian influence. But with the spread
of Christianity it became one of the accepted axioms
of Western civilization. The modern belief in progress is, as has often been said, a Christian heresy,
a secularized version of Hebraic eschatology. As long
as this belief persisted, it was still to the end of
things that men looked to find the meaning and justification of the whole. So much was this so, that, from
the eighteenth century onwards, political theorists
were happy to speak, as Christianity with its dimension
of eternity had never done, as though every generation
except the last could be regarded as a means to an end,
provided that that last generation did obtain the
promise. The logical conclusion of this assumption
can be seen in Marxist thought, where the eschatological element is strong.[2] If every generation is a
means to an end, then so is every individual in it--
and so he can be treated. But, pursued ruthlessly to
its secular conclusion or not, the assumption that it
was legitimate to interpret history in terms of a goal
was all but universally accepted.

To-day that presumption is disappearing. The
final generation, far from being the favoured one, will
simply be the unlucky one, either as it is called upon
to endure natural conditions increasingly insupporta-
ble for human life, or as it has to witness the final
agonies of racial suicide. Special value or significance attaches to the last term of a process only when
the whole is thought to be purposive. Apart from a
belief in teleology there can be no true *telos* or
climax, but only a stopping, a cessation, a petering
out. In this case, any term in the series becomes as
important--or as meaningless--as any other. And in
so far as men to-day have lost a conception of the end
of history as more than cessation, whether lingering
or catastrophic, they must fail to see any relevance
whatever in a doctrine of last things. For the last
things, on this reckoning, have no more significance
for the understanding of the world than the penultimate

pre-penultimate, or any other. It is for this reason
that the gulf between the Church's teaching on eschatology and secular thought is wider to-day than ever
before. Men now may have a more lively expectation
of an end. But the decisive factor is whether they
think of that end as purposive, not whether they
believe it to be near. To the nineteenth century, the
Christian scheme may have seemed incredible--an
improbable answer to an intelligent question; to the
twentieth it appears blankly irrelevant--the question
itself has become meaningless. For, without some kind
of belief in teleology, there can be no eschatology.

In an attempt at communication especially designed to speak to him modern man would frankly not
expect to be presented with a book on the Last Things.
For, however well-disposed he may be towards Christianity as a whole, he regards this particular department of it for the most part as dead wood. He might
perhaps be prepared for a book on the future life,
which is the only part of the traditional content of
Christian eschatology in which the secular world
retains a flicker of interest. And it does that, in
so far as it does it, only because this doctrine has
in modern teaching been lifted entirely out of its
original framework of cosmic eschatology. How far
in consequence this isolated fragment has remained
recognizably Christian is another matter, and one that
will require further discussion.

But even such interest as attaches to the question of an after-life is notoriously weak in the modern
world, except when it is artificially stimulated in
time of war. And even here the second World War
differed from the first in revealing a much less active concern about the state of the departed and a
far more widespread spirit of fatalistic indifference.
About a question which touches every individual so
closely, and presses, one would think, yet the more
urgently in an age of destruction, the modern man is
blandly unconcerned. In his own jargon, he just
couldn't care less.

Short of the ultimate issue of belief or disbelief in the Christian God, the most fundamental fact
which a writer on Christian eschatology must face is
that men to-day have lost valid grounds for believing
any statement about eschatology in any form. Deep
down, contemporary scepticism may doubtless be traced
to irreligion; but to the sceptics themselves it is a
question of *evidence*. The initial problem for anyone

approaching the subject is, therefore, epistemological.

What grounds are there for making any assertions
about eschatology which may reasonably claim to be
true? Until a hundred years ago or so such statements
were thought to rest securely, like other theological
truth, on the twin foundations of revelation and
reason. Time was when the future prospects both of
the individual and of the world could be asserted
with confidence on the authority of infallible propositions of Holy Writ and the necessary postulates
of rational thinking. To-day that confidence has been
almost entirely shattered. In matters eschatological,
perhaps more than in any other department, the modern
generation believes neither in the inerrancy of
Scriptural statement nor in the validity of metaphysical thought. The whole edifice in which our forebears lived and hoped has collapsed with the crumbling
of its epistemological foundations. The dark paths of
the future have been abandoned to 'the astrologers,
the stargazers, the monthly prognosticators' (Is.
47.13), who, together with the Theosophists, Spiritu-
alists, Seventh Day Adventists, Jehovah's Witnesses,
British Israelites, Christadelphians, The Panacea
Society, and the rest have stepped in to answer for
the modern man Kant's third great question, 'What
may I hope for?', to which Kant himself first caused
men to doubt whether there might be a rational answer.
And even those who do not go all the way to Endor
have ceased to believe that assertions about the
hereafter comprise more than a web of speculation, in
which any statement is as likely, or as unlikely, to
be true as any other. You may not pay your money, but
you still take your choice. Christians themselves
have lost confidence in their ability to give a bottom
to their hopes which is more solid than sanctified
wishful thinking. Even to the theologian the field
of eschatology must appear the least amenable to those
canons of induction and verification whereby his
discipline, like any other science to-day, must substantiate its claim to give valid knowledge.

Before anything can be said, then, of the content
of Christian eschatology, it is necessary to enquire
afresh into its credentials. Ours is a day when the
most significant Biblical theology is soaked through
with eschatology. Its rediscovery has transformed
and quickened our understanding of the gospel of Jesus
and the apostolic church. If this new light is to
break through into Christian doctrine and have any
chance of touching secular thought, modern man has

first to be convinced that the whole eschatological
viewpoint, accepted without question by the New Testament writers, has any validity or relevance for the
twentieth century. Unless this task of apologetic
is successfully performed, we shall be left, as Albert
Schweitzer was, to make the best of a situation where
Biblical theology requires us to interpret the Gospel
in categories that are confessedly fantastic and false
for the modern world. And to rest there is either to
abandon the Gospel as dated and irrelevant, or to
sever it from all ties to its historical foundation.
And the latter, despite Schweitzer's heroic example,
is equally to sound its knell. For an unhistorical
mysticism of 'the spirit of Jesus' may be magnificent,
but it is hardly catholic Christianity.

Moreover, whether men hear or whether they for-
bear, the eschatology of the Christian gospel should
be capable of addressing this generation with a genuine
relevance. Never since the first century have men
been so conscious of living in the last times. '"We
live in an apocalyptic age"--one hears from people who
do not believe in any apocalypse whatsoever.'[3] But in
this century the Church has been faced by people who
do believe in apocalypses--the great secular myths of
Fascism, Nazism, and Communism, each with its own
eschatology of history. These myths have come up like
thunderstorms against the wind. In an intellectual
atmosphere slowly stifling all forms of teleology,
these vast, irrational cyclones have swept everything
before them.

For men have found that they cannot live without
an eschatology. This recognition has come as the
last stage of a progressive disillusionment. The age
which began at the Renaissance confidently believed
that it had overcome the choice of having to decide
between the Hebraic faith in a God of history and the
Classical acceptance of a God of nature, between, that
is to say, an ultimate interpretation of the world in
terms of *divine purpose* and an ultimate interpretation
of the world in terms of *natural process*. The one
gave goal and direction, but seemed indemonstrable;
the other looked scientific, but took the meaning out
of everything. With triumphant optimism, it put its
trust in the universe as itself a *purposive process*.
An immanent purposiveness could be relied on to see
history through to an end which would not put human
values to shame. This secular providence was understood in many forms: by some in terms of immanent
spiritual forces, by others in the evolutionary

categories of biology, by others again, including both
the Manchester and the Marxist schools, in terms of
economic law. But though the path of progress might
run straight or dialectically, it was generally assumed
that a pattern of advance was there to find, could men
but detect and obey it. Freedom, as Marx insisted,
lay in the recognition of necessity.

But the shattering of this confidence led to the
rediscovery that history purely as nature, as process,
could of itself guarantee no purpose. Spegler's
Decline of the West (1918), with its return to a
frankly naturalistic and cyclical interpretation of
the birth and decay of civilizations, itself marked
the end of a cycle. He spoke for a generation of men
upon whom it seemed that history had defaulted, who
had indeed seen the righteous forsaken and the poor
man begging his bread. But men were soon to find they
could not live in this waste land of resignation and
despair, without a god or hope in the world. Spengler
is himself symptomatic in that he was forced to go on
to write another book, less well known, but whose
title speaks for itself--*The Hour of Decision*. It was
written to welcome the Nazi revolution of 1933.

For twentieth-century man has not been able to
remain content with meaninglessness. If he cannot
find meaning, he must create it. 'We have created our
myth,' declared Mussolini at Naples in 1922. 'The
myth is a faith, it is passion. It is not necessary
that it shall be a reality. It *is* a reality by the
fact that it is a goad, a hope, a faith, that it is
courage. Our myth is the nation, our myth is the
greatness of the nation.'[4]

Here is the man-made substitute for an end of
history, which is no longer an attempt at a rational
interpretation of the direction of events, but a
pattern to mould them. The point is not whether it
is true, but whether it can be made to be true; it
will be true if it can enlist the emotional and
volitional drive necessary to turn it into a reality.
An age which had given up believing that its hope
would work because it was true (because, that is, it
was written into the universe or grounded in God)
succeeded in persuading itself that it must be true
if it could be made to work, if a particular pattern--
be it the New Roman Empire, the Reich that would last
for a thousand years, the great Experiment of the
U.S.S.R.--could be imposed upon events, and imposed by
any methods.

The end of all this was a final disbelief in providence, either divine or secular; it was an attempt to *be* providence, to stamp one's own pattern and end on history. It was a last catastrophic effort to stave off return from the discredited Baalim of nature to the God of history. The hour was at hand when Christian eschatology would reassert itself with pressing relevance. Out of the darkened skies the strange, familiar words of the New Testament came again like thunder-claps to the Churches of the persecution. 'The end of all things is at hand' (I Pet. 4.7); 'Little children, it is the last hour: and as ye heard that antichrist cometh, even now have there arisen many antichrists, whereby we know that it is the last hour' (2 John 1.18). Christians in cellars and concentration camps sensed again something of what it meant to live with the prayer, 'Amen: come, Lord Jesus.' There was a new expectancy and a new urgency abroad which might be felt wherever the Church was being the Church.

But if the Spirit is to be free to course men's minds, there is much mental lumber to be shifted and a deal of retranslation to be done.

Endnotes

[1]2 Pet. 3.10, for instance, provides an admirable 'atomic' text: 'The day of the Lord will come as a thief; in which the heavens shall pass away with a great noise, and the elements shall be dissolved with fervent heat, and the earth and the works that are therein shall be burned up.' To save a good deal of unprofitable labour I have kept the Biblical quotations in the older material in this book, where the sense is not affected, in the Revised Version (American Standard Version) in which I originally cited them. Writing today, I should naturally use the Revised Standard Version or the New English Bible.

[2]See my essay 'The Christian Hope' in *Christian Faith and Communist Faith* (ed. D. M. Mackinnon).

[3]Quoted from Berdyaev by E. Lampert, *The Apocalypse of History*, p. 12.

4Quoted by Charles Smyth in 'Christianity and the Secular Myths,' *Theology*, October, 1949. I have paraphrased some sentences from this in the following paragraph.

Discussion Questions

1. Do you agree that contemporary persons find it possible to conceive of an end to human history?

    a. Would the annihilation of human life by weapons of war be the Christian eschaton? Why or why not?

    b. Do you think God would allow humanity to destroy itself? Why or why not?

2. Discuss what Robinson means when he says that Marxism and Communism are mythic systems with their own eschatologies. Ask your professor for help in understanding this important point.

3. How could we know that an eschatological belief was true? Read Hick's essay in this section and consider if you wish to alter your answer.

4. Robinson says persons cannot live without some form of eschatology. Do you agree or not? Why or why not?

THE CHRISTIAN HOPE

Like Robinson, Hans Schwarz holds that some eschatology is required in order to be human. If it is not
a religious eschatology, it will be some secularized or
politicized one. Schwarz also holds that eschatology
is central to the Christian faith. He believes Christianity is built upon a proleptic awareness of the new
world to come. By that he means, that the end of history has already been manifested in Jesus. We are
awaiting its full realization.

The expectation and hope that the kingdom will be
fully realized frees all Christians to expend themselves unreservedly in discipleship. This motif
sounded often by Schwarz may also be found in the major
Theologies of Hope: Jürgen Moltmann, Wolfhart Pannenberg and Johannes Metz.

According to Schwarz, hope is not only the ground
for activity but also for creativity. An appropriate
eschatology he says, calls upon Christians to live as
though the kingdom were present. They have caught a
vision of the end of history in Jesus, and they actualize it at all cost.

Notable among the biblical symbols relevant to a
Christian eschatology is that of the anti-Christ.
Schwarz points out the way in which the symbol has been
used in history to point to the forces that claim the
human allegiance which properly belongs only to God.
The anti-Christ oppresses the work of Christians. The
anti-Christ is one and many, it is the symbol which reminds Christians that no theology of the inevitable
progress of mankind into the kingdom of God will ever
be true.

Schwarz takes the consummation of the world order seriously. He uses the resurrection of Christ as evidence that our categories of time, space, and matter are limited ones! He also reinterprets the symbol of the last judgment but he cautions us against speculation about the final destiny of others. Schwarz discusses in conclusion the meaning of heaven and hell.

THE CHRISTIAN HOPE*

It is not possible to dispense with the eschatological expectations of Christian faith and still maintain meaningful hope in the future. "And yet one must also recognize that these are simply *hopes* not yet realized, hopes with a foundation outside themselves."[1] Christians, however, do not simply sit there and hope. The very fact that they are Christians allows them to anticipate proleptically the new world to come.

Proleptic anticipation and the signs of the end

We remember that in referring to the Gospel of John, Bultmann has pointed out the *now* as the decisive eschatological moment in which our decision between life and death is made.[2] The last things are already anticipated in our present confrontation with the word of God. Jesus' whole life was the decisive question which was posed to the Jewish people and which asked them whether they wanted to live in conformity with God or to reject him. We hear Jesus say: "He who hears my word and believes him who sent me, has eternal life; he does not come into judgment, but has passed from death into life" (John 5:24), or "He who does not believe is condemned already" (John 3:18). These would

*Source: Reprinted by permission from *On the Way to the Future* by Hans Schwarz, copyright 1972. Augsburg Publishing House, Minneapolis, MN.

be difficult words to explain as a projection of man's desires in the fashion of Feuerbach. The present is decisive time, time which determines our future, not in a way of complementing, but as consolidation and clarification.

This emphasis on the now as the anticipatory moment of the end is not restricted to John. Paul devotes almost a whole chapter (Rom. 6) to clarify that we are now dying and rising with Christ, and he declares that "now is the acceptable time; behold, now is the day of salvation" (2 Cor. 6:2). This is not an attempt to comfort us with the hope for a better "hereafter." And already Jesus, referring to his actions, tells his inquirers: "But if it is by the finger of God that I cast out demons, then the kingdom of God has come upon you" (Luke 11:20; Matt. 12:28). Especially this remark, which was solicited by people who asked Jesus in whose name he performed his actions, shows that anticipation of the end does not make the end demonstrable. Eternity in time is only possible in disguise. Even the evident results of the encounter of the divine with our earthly sphere are subject to contrary interpretations. Although this holds true for Jesus himself as well as for the life and actions of Christians, it does not exempt the Christians from anticipating the end.

If Christians would refrain from anticipation, that would not only modify their present existence, but also their future one. This means that the present decision and the present attitude does not eliminate the final judgment, but it determines it. Thus the present is the decisive time for the Christians, because the whole future is at stake. Of course, it would be a gross misunderstanding to conceive of the present activity of a Christian as work righteousness and the final judgment as the big "awards day." Any anticipation of the end, whether in a positive or a negative way, is only possible because Christ has already anticipated the end in his resurrection and we are invited to share in this anticipation. Man's attitude can only be an attitude of response and not of initiative. Though Marxists are right in pointing out that, contrary to our own intentions, we have often not responded well enough to our eschatological situation, they have gone to the other extreme of exclusively emphasizing man's own initiative.

Jürgen Moltmann very rightly states that the Christian response is not only missionary proclamation of faith and hope and unrestricted gathering of believers, but also bodily obedience in worldly activity.[3] This response reflects a visible and creative discipleship, and results in productive obedience in society and is as important as proclamation and gathering of believers. "The expectation of the promised future of the kingdom of God which is coming to man and to the world to set them right and create life, makes us ready to expend ourselves unrestrainedly and unreservedly in love and in the work of reconciliation of the world with God and his future."[4]

The Christian thus is creative, because he accepts and anticipates the new world which will come by the provision of God.[5] No matter how much we emphasize the anticipatory character of eschatology, it is only proleptic anticipation and not the end itself. If it were otherwise, there would be no anticipation possible and we would understand our activities exclusively as the creative high point of evolution. But the anticipatory character of our activities is enabled by and points to the future fulfillment. Throughout the New Testament the now as the anticipated end points to and enables the future fulfillment and vice versa.[6] This becomes especially evident in the so-called signs of the end.

There are several major apocalyptic passages in the gospels (Matt. 24; Mark 13; Luke 21) which indicate the signs of the end: emergence of false prophets, climactic wars, catastrophes in nature, famines, persecution of the Christians, and the proclamation of the gospel to all people (Mark 13:10). The Gospel of John, which does not contain any long apocalyptic passages, is complemented by the Book of Revelation, where the signs of the end are especially dealt with in Chapters 6, 8, 13, and 16. Since many of these signs had already occurred when they were written down (cf. destruction of Jerusalem; Luke 21:20, 24), they are a theological evaluation of history in the light of the expected end and not a calendar according to which one can calculate when the end will come. Sentences such as "This generation will not pass away before all these things take place," with the following interpretation: "Heaven and earth will pass away, but my word will not pass away" (Mark 13:30f.), show that the evangelists did not want to enhance an apocalyptic fever in which people were convinced that they knew the course of world history, including its end.

The evangelists rather returned to Jesus' own message which culminated in the demand for immediate readiness. We hear Jesus say: "What I say to you I

say to all: Watch" (Mark 13:37), and "For as the
lightning comes from the east and shines as far as the
west, so will be the coming of the Son of man" (Matt.
24:27), and we hear him telling the parable of the five
wise and the five foolish maidens (Matt. 25:1-13), and
even Paul asserts: "The day of the Lord will come like
a thief in the night" (1 Thess. 5:2). These passages,
and many more, convey the demand for immediate readiness. To interpret them as an indication of an immediate expectation of the end by Jesus or the first Christian community, an expectation which proved to be
wrong, seems to miss the point.[7]

Immediate readiness, similarly to the decisive
character of the now, does not necessarily express belief in the near return of the Lord, but it shows that
our present attitude determine for us the outcome of
the future, the eschaton. The watchword of the Middle
Ages *memento mori* (be aware of your death) thus was
closer to the New Testament than the traditional belief
in the final end of history. *Memento mori* does not
just remind us that we never know when we will die, but
that death will make our present life attitude irreversible. This is why we are called to respond to the demand for immediate readiness with a life attitude of
preparing anticipation and not with a once-in-our-life-
time decision. That the demand for immediate readiness
stands next to and is interspersed with indications of
the end should also tell us that, no matter how carefully we interpret history, the coming of the end will
be a total surprise, it will be absolutely unexpected.
The consequence for a Christian is that he will live
his life in active anticipation, as if each moment
would be his last.

There is one sign of the end, however, which de-
serves special attention, the concept of the anti-
Christ.[8] The imagery which is incorporated in the concept of the anti-Christ is in part of Jewish origin.
For instance, in Daniel 9:27 we hear that someone, perhaps Antiochus IV Epiphanes, will come on the "wing of
abominations" and will make desolate the holy place
(the temple). In the New Testament it is said that in
the last days "false Christs and false prophets will
arise and show signs and wonders, to lead astray" (Mark
13:22). Paul warns of the "son of perdition, who opposes and exalts himself against every so-called god or
object of worship, so that he takes his seat in the
temple of God, proclaiming himself to be God" (2 Thess.
2:3f.). In the First Letter of John we hear that in
the last hour the anti-Christ is coming; therefore we

know that it is the last hour (1 John 2:18), and a few verses further on we hear that the anti-Christ denies the Father and the Son (1 John 2:22). In the Second Letter we read of the many deceivers who have gone out into the world, "men who will not acknowledge the coming of Jesus Christ in the flesh; such a one is the deceiver and the anti-Christ" (2 John 7). Finally, in the Book of Revelation the anti-Christian power is understood as being represented in the Roman State with its cult of the Emperor (Rev. 13:1-10), and the anti-Christ also signifies the false prophets who advocate this cult (Rev. 13:11-18).

This diversity of the concept of the anti-Christ shows us that the New Testament has no clear "doctrine" of the anti-Christ. The anti-Christ comes in disguise and power and will mislead many; he looks like a lamb, but talks like a dragon, and he wants to dethrone God and puts himself in God's place. Sometimes there is just one anti-Christ, at other times there are many. Sometimes the anti-Christ comes from within the Christian community, for instance when he denies the incarnation of God in Jesus Christ, sometimes he comes from outside.

The church accepted this idea of the anti-Christ and used it widely. For the early church the Roman emperors, especially Nero and Domitian, who persecuted the Christians, were called the anti-Christ. In the Middle Ages, during the papal schism, usually the counter-pope was declared the anti-Christ, and he in turn called the original pope the anti-Christ. The Franciscan Spirituals, who had followed the millennial ideas of Joachim of Fiore were also quick to declare the pope as anti-Christ, simply because he denied their claim for poverty. Later, the forerunners of the Reformation, John Hus and John Wyclif, sometimes extended the idea of the anti-Christ to the whole Catholic Church.

Luther was at first very reluctant in using the term anti-Christ.[9] However, under the impact of Laurentius Valla's discovery that the papacy had illegally usurped its supremacy over worldly authorities with the forgery of the Constantine Donation, Luther came to the conclusion that the papacy must be the anti-Christ. The papacy, not an individual pope, is the anti-Christ, because it puts its own authority beyond that of the word of God. With this conviction Luther, of course, regretted that the Augsburg Confession made no mention of the anti-Christ. Though in contemporary history many dictators, such as Stalin or Hitler, have been labeled as anti-Christ, the question for us is what we shall do with this concept. Shall we simply recognize its frequent and manifold use and then go on to more important business?

Without disregarding all diversity in the use of this concept, three features seem to be consistent and noteworthy. 1) Whereas in dualistic Parsiism, which undoubtedly influenced the emergence of the concept of the anti-Christ, there is a gradual disappearance of the anti-Godly powers, the Christian faith is aware of the threatening presence of the anti-Christ up to the final consummation of the world. This shows the conviction that mankind does not gradually work itself up to the kingdom of God with God sanctifying these human endeavors in declaring the goal of their work as his kingdom. The alienation from God and the usurpation of anti-Godly sovereignty seems to increase instead of decrease. 2) The anti-Christ is not a possibility of the future, but a reality of the present. The conviction that the anti-Christ is already here emphasizes that we must constantly be on alert. There is no neutral ground on which to stand and wait. Either we are engaged in active preparation, or we fall prey to the anti-Christ who will lead us to a different activism. 3) The activities of the anti-Christ do not result in events whose theological significance have to be shown, they already *have* theological significance. The anti-Christ, be it from within or from outside the Christian community, attempts to dethrone God and to place himself on God's throne. Belief in technology and progress instead of faith in God, belief in the essential goodness of man instead of faith in the love of God, hope for the Christianization of mankind instead of hope for the coming of the kingdom of God, are only a few alternatives which show us the anti-Godly tendency of the anti-Christ. Yet, realizing the seriousness of the *many* faces of the anti-Christ, we know that even he is subjected to temporality, and the last judgment will terminate all anti-Godly endeavors.

Last judgment and the love of God

Consummation of the world: In considering the concepts of time and eternity we have noticed that any kind of last judgment as a universal judgment demands the consummation or at least transformation of the categories of time, space, and matter, or of the world as we know it. This is also the conviction of the New Testament. "Immediately after the tribulation of those days the

sun will be darkened, and the moon will not give its
light, and the stars will fall from heaven, and the
powers of the heavens will be shaken; then will appear
the sign of the Son of man in heaven, and then all
tribes of the earth will mourn, and they will see the
Son of man coming from the clouds of heaven with power
and great glory" (Matt. 24:29f.). And the Second Letter of Peter tells us in even greater detail: "But the
day of the Lord will come like a thief, and then the
heavens will pass away with a loud noise, and the elements will be dissolved with fire, and the earth and
the works that are upon it will be burned up" (2 Peter
3:10).

Inquisitive spirits have always tried to investigate how such a consummation could be possible, and
modern scientific insights have paved the road for many
speculations. For instance, the possible collision of
our earth with other planets or planetoids would certainly darken the sun and the moon for us and might
perhaps lead to the extinction of life on earth. A
cosmic nuclear reaction could also dissolve the elements with fire, and if militarists would employ all
our presently available "overkill" they could even usher in the eschaton at their own wish. Also the looming
prospect of a global pollution of life could lead to
the end of life here on earth. But Teilhard de Chardin
already observed that such a sidereal disaster would
affect only part of the universe and not the total universe. Even the final heat death through an equilibrium of all energy levels, to which Karl Heim alluded,
would not lead to the consummation of this world, but
only to the end of life within it. At best, science
can tell us that our universe does not contain any
eternal life force. However, it cannot show us that or
how our universe will be consumed. Science, by its
very nature, is bound to work within the categories of
space, time, and matter, and this means with the universe we live in. But consummation of the world does
not just affect existence in the universe, it affects
the very existence of the universe.

According to the New Testament, the consummation
of the world is not primarily destruction. It is rather the universal incorporation into the creative and
transforming ᵃᶜᵗ of Christ's resurrection. No one has
expressed this clearer than Paul in his Letter to the
Romans where he writes that "the creation waits with
eager longing for the revealing of the sons of God,"
and that it will be "set free from its bondage to decay," and that we ourselves wait for adoption as sons,

"the redemption of our bodies." This is no vague or
uncertain hope, because "he who raised Jesus Christ
from the dead will give life to your mortal bodies
also" (Rom. 8:11, 19-23).

Salvation in the eschaton pertains to the whole
man, to the whole cosmos, and to the whole creation.
It is a salvation which is described as redemption
from transitoriness.[10] When our sonship, which we
have received in baptism, will be disclosed, this will
mean that we are not merely in anticipation, but in
reality no longer subjected to transitoriness. Consummation of the world is then perfection and completion.
It is completion of time[11] and perfection of our limiting forms of space, time, and matter.

A foretaste of this new world, as far as it
pertains to man, is already given to us in the witnesses of those who encountered the resurrected
Christ.[12] The biblical witnesses tell us that the
risen Lord was no longer limited in time, space, and
matter. The material and spacial bounds of a closed
room or of hunger could no longer confine him. But,
of course, he could appear in a room and he could eat.
In a similar way, he was no longer bound to the transitoriness of time, yet he could appear sooner, or
later, or now. Perfection of the forms of this world
also means the elimination of the anti-Godly distortion of this world, of sin, destruction, and death.
Again this is shown in the resurrected Christ who is
beyond the possibility of sinning and beyond the
possibility of dying.

Whenever we talk about the new world to come we
must mention Christ and his resurrection, because "all
things were created through him and for him" (Col.
1:16). There is no other goal of creation than Jesus
who, as the Messiah, enabled this creation to move
toward this goal.[13] The consummation is then the
disclosure of the new world which was enabled by and
has started in the resurrection of Jesus Christ.
Martin Luther, in his unique and picturesque language,
has expressed the point of the consummation very well
when he says:

This world serves for God only as a preparation
and a scaffolding for the other world. As a rich
lord must have a lot of scaffolding for his house,
but then tears the scaffolding down as soon as the
house is finished, . . . so God has made the whole
world as a preparation for the other life, where

finally everything will proceed according to the power and will of God.[14]

Last Judgment: The last judgment is a difficult subject to mention, because everybody wants to be saved but only a few are willing to accept the consequences. H. Richard Niebuhr's famous phrase about 19th century American liberalism: "A God without wrath brought men without sin into a kingdom without judgment through the ministrations of a Christ without a cross,"[15] is a vivid description of man in general. Man desires heaven, but he does not want to accept that the only way to heaven is through judgment. But the New Testament in all its witnesses makes it unmistakably clear that the only way to the new world to come is through judgment, and that the consummation of the world does not mean final evolution, but implies the parousia of the Lord and the final judgment.

"For the Son of man is to come with his angels in the glory of his Father, and then he will repay every man for what he has done" (Matt. 16:27). "When the Son of man comes in his glory, and all the angels with him, then he will sit on his glorious throne. Before him will be gathered all the nations, and he will separate them one from another as a shepherd separates the sheep from the goats" (Matt. 25:31 f.). "For the Lord himself will descend from heaven with a cry of command, with the archangel's call, and with the sound of the trumpet of God" (1 Thess. 4:16). "We must all appear before the judgment seat of Christ, so that each one may receive good or evil, according to what he has done in the body" (2 Cor. 5:10). "And I saw the dead, great and small, standing before the throne, and books were opened. Also another book was opened, which is the book of life. And the dead were judged by what was written in the books, by what they had done" (Rev. 20:12). The imagery of these quotes from the New Testament, which could easily be multiplied, betrays Old Testament and Jewish apocalyptic influences. The language is that of a past age and need not necessarily be reiterated, but the tendency of these passages is crystal clear: there is a final judgment.

Often this final judgment has been conceived as the great awards day. This is especially evident in the chiliastic hopes of a 1000 year's rule over and at the expense of others. Yet, the final judgment is not a judgment of our own merits, but of our response to God's grace which he has extended to us in Jesus

496

Christ. We are not awarded a certificate of loyalty, simply because we happened to be on the right side at the right time. Such cheap grace would neglect man's wrong doings. Voltaire was not right when he mocked: "God will forgive, because it is his job." Paul caught the seriousness of the final judgment much more appropriately when he cautioned: "For whatever a man sows, that he will also reap" (Gal. 6:7). Our Lord will take into consideration each of our individual situations and judge to what an extent we have attempted to respond to the promise he offers and to the exemplary life style which he had shown us.

The judgment is not a judgment where everybody will be sheared over the same comb, it is rather a judgment according to one's own possibilities. "Everyone to whom much is given, of him will much be required; and of him to whom men commit much they will demand the more" (Luke 12:48). This does not mean that we can take it easy, because we have to measure up to the possibilities of our own response and not to some ambiguous standards which we might adopt. Since this judgment will concur with the parousia of the Lord, it becomes evident that Christ will be the judge. In judging us in the name of God and as God, this judgment is irrevocable, final, and binding. There is no higher court of appeal possible.

Since Christ the savior is also the judge, the judgment in all seriousness has a comforting aspect. In confronting us with himself and his gospel Christ has shown us the direction of our life, and through his dying and resurrection he has enabled for us the direction of our life, to live in conformity and towards conformity with God. The first Christian community which preserved for us all the dreadful apocalyptic imagery of the final judgment was not scared by the prospect of this judgment. They knew that it was the necessary "entrance gate" to the new world to come. Thus *marana tha* ("our Lord, come!") was a familiar word in the first Christian community (cf. 1 Cor. 16:22),[16] and the Book of Revelation closes in a similar way with "Amen. Come, Lord Jesus!" (Rev. 20:20). Martin Luther has recaptured this New Testament confidence in the face of the judgment, when, contrary to the mood of the Middle Ages, he did not conceive of this day as a day of wrath, but as a day of the glory of God, a day he was looking forward to when he said in many of his letters: "Come, dear, last day."[17]

Paradox between justice and love of God: The option
for a universal homecoming becomes at no time more
urgent than when we are confronted with the final
judgment and when we realize that not everybody will
be saved. But Jesus, and with him the New Testament
witnesses, are convinced of a twofold outcome of this
final judgment.[18] "The gate is wide and the way is
easy, that leads to destruction, and those who enter
by it are many. For the gate is narrow and the way
is hard, that leads to life, and those who find it
are few" (Matt. 7:13 f.), we hear Jesus say. And we
read in the Gospel of John the same, only actualized
in the now: "He who believes in the Son has eternal
life; he who does not obey the Son, shall not see
life, but the wrath of God rests upon him" (John 3:36).
And the Book of Revelation expresses in typical apocalyptic fashion: "And the smoke of their torment goes
up for ever and ever; and they have no rest, day or
night" (Rev. 14:11).

To make the issue more confusing the New Testament also contains many assertions that God wants all
men to be saved. For instance, Paul in wrestling
with the destiny of Israel expresses the conviction
that "God has consigned all men to disobedience, that
he may have mercy upon all" (Rom. 11:32). The goal
of the cosmos and of all saving history is universal
salvation, a goal which embraces the destiny of all
individuals, Jews and pagans alike.[19] In a similar
way, to quote just one more reference, we hear that
God our savior "desires all men to be saved and to
come to the knowledge of the truth" (1 Tim. 2:4). All
this boils down to a final paradox which states on the
one hand that God's love wants all to be saved, and
which declares on the other hand that God's justice
requires all the disobedient to be punished.

Of course, we could attempt to solve the evident
paradox by asserting that God's justice is only preliminary, and justice and love are related to each
other like law and gospel. God threatens with his
justice in order that we might flee to his love.[20]
But this evidently anthropomorphic construct of a
pedagogic God, who punishes only in order to save
(cf. Schleiermacher!), does not take into account that
the judgment is disclosure and finalization of our life
attitude and not a transition to the universal love of
God. If our life attitude runs counter to the love
which God extends, the result is a dichotomy which
cannot be bridged through evolution or amelioration.

Another attempt to solve the paradox between God's justice and love, though only a half-hearted one, is to assert that the condemned will be annihilated and thus all (who are left) will be saved.[21] But how can there be an annihilation of anybody, if there is no escape from God, since God is everywhere, even in death and beyond death? The solution must rather be sought in what we mean when we talk about the justice and love of God. Do we really mean that we *describe* God with these terms, or do they not rather *disclose* certain aspects of God *for us*? We must remember that God's self-disclosure can only be expressed in human language and this means with necessarily anthropomorphic and inadequate conceptual tools.[22] Thus we can rightly conclude that God is in a similar way beyond justice and love as he is beyond being a person when we call him a personal God.

We must remember too that we are confronted with God's decision-demanding word which says: Repent and follow me. As we accept God's offer to direct our lives according to his eternal purpose, a universal homecoming will be meaningless for our salvation, since we will be saved according to the promise of his redemptive word. Ultimately, the idea of a universal homecoming can result only as a speculation about the final destiny of others. Even in our most sincere concern for them we have to acknowledge the ultimate hiddenness of God, a God who is beyond justice and love, and we can only hope that his never-ending grace will ultimately prevail.

The new world

When we finally attempt to make assertions about the new world, then it seems next to impossible to say something meaningful here without indulging in speculations. Yet Jesus and the New Testament invite us to put our trust in something concrete, something we can already to some degree anticipate in our present life. We also remember that the goal of history and of mankind has already started with Jesus' coming. These two facts, the New Testament's own insistence on a "concrete" future and the anticipatory aspect of this future, seem to provide enough room for positive assertions about the new world.

Disclosure of the kingdom of God: When Jesus entered our scene, it was announced: "The time is fulfilled, and the kingdom of God is at hand; repent, and believe in the gospel" (Mark 1:15). The kingdom of God or the new world to come has already started with Christ's coming. However, the kingdom also has a future, and admission into it demands a decision, because "not every one who says to me, 'Lord, Lord,' shall enter the kingdom of heaven" (Matt. 7:21).

All the parables of the kingdom seem to indicate that at one point it will become evident who has entered the kingdom of God and who has not, or in other words, good and evil will be separated (cf. Matt. 13:30, 49 ff.). Jesus even had to hold back enthusiastic disciples who demanded that, since the decision about entrance must be made now, the evidence of entrance or non-entrance must also be disclosed. But Jesus rejected any attempts to build a pure "Christian community" here on earth by pointing to the future dimension of such a perfection: "Let both grow together until the harvest; and at harvest time I will tell the reapers, Gather the weeds first and bind them into bundles to be burned, but gather the wheat into my barn" (Matt. 13:30). This future dimension will find its fulfillment with the final judgment. Then the already existing invisible separation will become visible and irreversible. The kingdom of God, or the new world which will be discovered, is described with the term heaven, while the exclusion from the new world is described with the term hell.

Heaven and hell: To talk about heaven or hell as the final destiny of man seems, at the first glance, a re-mythologization of eschatology. In most religions heaven is understood as the location of the gods, while hell is usually associated with the devil, with demons, and other figments of a world of fantasy. When looking at the New Testament we discover, however, that the term heaven is used at least as frequently, and not just primarily in the gospels, as the term kingdom of God. At some places the terms are even merged to a "kingdom of heaven" (cf. Matt. 3:2; 5:3; and others).

Already Luther mocked at the idea of picturing hell as built of wood or bricks so that it would have gates, windows, locks, and bars as a house does here on earth. And, of course, Christ did not destroy hell with a flag of cloth in his hands.[23] For Luther "hell means that death is accompanied by the feeling that the punishment is, at once, unchangeable and eternal. Here the soul is captured and surrounded so that it cannot think anything else except that it is to be eternally damned."[24] In a similar way Luther mocked

at the "Schwarmer" who understood God's dwelling place
in heaven in a local way. Because the visible heaven
or sky is constantly moving, Luther concludes that
this would mean that God cannot sit still for one
moment. It is, however, absurd to understand God's
realm in a local way so that one thinks of God as
sitting on high, somewhat like a stork in its nest.
But Luther was also aware that the Bible in its pre-
Copernican world view often uses the terms hell and
heaven in a local way.

Already in the Old Testament the term heaven is
not just used in a cosmological topography, but also
in a theological understanding in which heaven denotes
the dimension of God and his power, and of the source
of salvation.[25] In rabbinic literature heaven can
even become a paraphrase for God.[26] The differentiation between a cosmological and a theological understanding of heaven is intensified in the New Testament.
Theologically speaking heaven can be the dimension of
God, the source of salvation, and the integrating
focus for the present and future blessings of salvation in the new aeon.[27] That such a theological understanding demands a transcendence of the prevalent
three-story world view of the Bible is indicated in
such passages as the exclamation of David: "Behold,
heaven and the highest heaven cannot contain thee;
how much less this house which I have built!" (1 Kings
8:27) and the assertion of Paul: "He who descended
is he who also ascended far above all the heavens,
that he might fill all things" (Eph. 4:10).

Although in the earlier parts of the Old Testament sheol or "hell" is understood indiscriminately as
the shadowy existence of all who have died (cf. Ps.
89:48), it is at the same time the dimension of
alienation from God and the dimension of death. In
post-exilic times, perhaps through the influence of
Parsiism, sheol is conceived of as a temporary dwelling
place and as different for the righteous than for the
godless.[28] Gehenna, the New Testament word for hell,
already presupposes resurrection and final judgment.[29]
Total man with body and soul will be tormented in
Gehenna, where his "worm does not die, and the fire
is not quenched" (Mark 9:48). While hell does not
just originate in the eschaton (Matt. 25:41), it is
only after the resurrection and judgment that it will
be disclosed as the realm of eternal torment. In
apocalyptic thinking Gehenna was still associated
with the Hinnom valley near Jerusalem, where once King
Ahaz and King Manasseh had brought sacrifice to

foreign gods. This kind of localization was abandoned in the New Testament. In contrast to apocalyptic, the New Testament usually did not paint the torments of hell in drastic colors, and when it did, it did so to awaken the conscience of the listeners (cf. Matt. 10:28).

When we now attempt to draw a final conclusion, we realize that hell and heaven neither receive their peculiarities from any cosmological localities, nor from any imageries that are associated with them, but only from their respective relationship with God. Only in the world of fantasy is hell the domain of the devil. But according to the biblical witnesses even the anti-Godly powers are under God's control.[30]

In talking about hell, we talk about something we do not know. The allusions of the New Testament such as: "neither gloom of darkness" (2 Peter 2:17), "outer darkness," "weeping and gnashing of teeth" (Matt. 22:13), and "eternal fire" (Matt. 25:41), describe hell in terms of pain, despair, and loneliness. In so doing these words are taken from present negative experiences and attempt to transcend them. These negative experiences express the reaction to the disclosure and finalization of the discrepancy between the eternal destiny of man and his realization of this destiny. They express the anguish of knowing what one has missed without the possibility of ever reaching it. They witness to a state of extreme despair without the hope of reversing it. It becomes clear that such an anguish and despair will not just result from a local separation from God. It will be a dimensional separation from God and from the accepted. Yet God and the destiny of the accepted will be somehow present, present as a curse.

Since Christians do not confess faith in hell, but in "resurrection of the body and life everlasting," hell is of no ultimate concern to us. It serves for us only as an admonition to reach the eternal destiny of man and to appreciate even more the offer of such a destiny. In talking about life everlasting, or about heaven, we have to agree with Luther's fitting remark: "As little as children know in their mother's womb about their birth, so little do we know about life everlasting."[31] When we read about our habitation in the new Jerusalem, a city of gold, similar to pure glass, with walls of precious stones, and with twelve gates, each made of one pearl (cf. Rev. 21), then this apocalyptic picture resembles so much a world of fantasy that it looks more like an attraction in Disneyland than the eternal goal of our lives. Even the much more restrained assertion that once we have reached our final goal, we will see God "face to face" (1 Cor. 13:12) sounds unreal. And the promise that God will dwell with the elected "and they shall be his people and God himself will be with them; he will wipe away every tear from their eyes, and death shall be no more, neither shall there be mourning nor crying nor pain any more, for the former things have passed away" (Rev. 21:3 f.), and that God will be "everything to every one" (1 Cor. 15:28) looks like wishful thinking.

Union with God, abolition of anguish and sorrow, and permanent beauty and perfection seem so unreal to our life of alienation, pain and suffering, transition and change that we are about to discard these hopes as utopian dreams. We would be right in so doing if Jesus Christ had not shown us through his death and resurrection that this fulfillment is attainable. Because of Jesus Christ and because of the promise that is contained for us in the Christ event, the hope for a final realization of such a destiny is a realistic hope. It shows us that man's immanent and perpetual yearning for self-transcendence, for deification, for elimination of death, and for progress toward perfection is not a utopian dream, but will find its fulfillment in life everlasting. But it also poses the all-decisive question: Do we understand our attempts to fulfill our inborn yearning through pursuit of technological progress, peace for man, and between man and man in Marxist or Western materialistic fashion as an end in itself, and consequently exclude ourselves from any non-man-provided true fulfillment? Or do we understand our endeavors here on earth as proleptic anticipation of that which "God has prepared for those who love him" (1 Cor. 2:9), and consequently hope for a God-provided true fulfillment?

"Only he who is certain of his future can relax and turn to today's business."[32] It is necessary to check our life-attitude, and once again put our trust alone in Jesus who is "the pioneer and perfecter of our faith" (Heb. 12:2).

[1]Kaufman, *Systematic Theology*, p. 325.

[2]Bultmann, "The Eschatology of the Gospel of John" (1928), in *Faith and Understanding*, Vol. 1, p. 175.

[3]Moltmann, "Antwort auf die Kritik der Theologie der Hoffnung," in *Diskussion über die 'Theologie der Hoffnung,'* ed. by Wolfdieter Marsch, p. 231.

[4]Moltmann, *Theology of Hope*, p. 337.

[5]Cf. Moltmann, "Die Revolution der Freiheit," in *Perspektiven der Theologie: Gesammelte Aufsätze* (Munich: Chr. Kaiser, 1968), p. 210, in his discussion of Marxist anthropology.

[6]Cf. Gustav Stahlin, "nun," in *Theological Dictionary of the New Testament*, Vol. 4, pp. 1118 ff., where he mentions that the thought of a twofold fulfillment runs through the whole New Testament.

[7]At this point it is difficult for us to agree with the otherwise excellent presentation of Paul Althaus, *Die letzten Dinge*, p. 273 f., who states on the one hand that the expectation of the impending eschaton was not fulfilled and who claims on the other hand that the end is in essence near and is at each point a threatening possibility. This spiritualist interpretation seems to neglect the progressiveness of history and comes close to a dualism of time and eternity.
It is certainly true that there were people in the first Christian community and at many other points in the history of the Christian church who expected the immediate return of the Lord. It is also true that Jesus unmistakably emphasized the nearness of the eschaton, or in other words, he mentioned more than once that the end is close at hand. Yet he also consistently rejected any attempts to date the "point" at which the eschaton might come. This reservation would be unexplainable if he had expected the coming of the eschaton in connection with his death or with his resurrection, or after thirty or forty years (destruction of Jerusalem). Should Jesus not rather have meant: the hour of fulfillment has begun, the kingdom of God is manifesting itself already here and now, the final end will come soon, therefore, make use of the time as long as you can? But Jesus refused to

limit God's sovereignty by imparting to us an eschatological timetable (cf. the excellent treatment of the issues involved by Joachim Jeremias, *New Testament Theology*, Part 1, pp. 131-141).

[8]For the concept of the anti-Christ, cf. Regin Prenter, *Creation and Redemption*, pp. 555 f.; and Paul Althaus, *Die letzten Dinge*, pp. 282-297.

[9]Cf. for the following Ulrich Asendorf, *Eschatologie bei Luther* (Gottingen: Vandenhoeck & Ruprecht, 1967), pp. 173 ff.

[10]Otto Michel, *Der Brief an die Romer*, p. 171.

[11]Walter Kunneth, *The Theology of the Resurrection*, pp. 285 f. The term "consummation" which is used to translate the German *Vollendung* does not render the full meaning of this term.

[12]Karl Heim, *Jesus the World's Perfecter: The Atonement and the Renewal of the World*, trans. by D. H. van Daalen (Philadelphia: Muhlenberg, 1961), pp. 166 ff.

[13]Cf. Eduard Lohse, *Die Briefe an die Kolosser und an Philemon* (Gottingen: Vandenhoeck & Ruprecht, 1968), pp. 91 f., in his exegesis of Col. 1:16.

[14]WA TR II, 627, # 29-628, 4.

[15]H. Richard Niebuhr, *The Kingdom of God in America*, p. 193.

[16]Hans Conzelmann, *Der erste Brief an die Korinther*, pp. 360 f., claims in his exegesis of 1 Cor. 16:22, that it must be left open whether this phrase invokes God's participation in the Eucharist or his parousia. Since the Eucharist must be regarded as an eschatological meal the phrase in either way points to the coming eschaton.

[17]Cf. Althaus, *The Theology of Martin Luther*, pp. 420 f., in his excellent treatment of Luther's interpretation of eschatology.

[18]Joachim Jeremias, *New Testament Theology*, Part 1, p. 131, in exegeting Matt. 22:14, mentions that the invitation is unlimited, but the number is small of those who follow it and are being saved.

19Cf. Michel, p. 253, in his exegesis of Rom. 11:32.

20This misunderstanding seems to be implied in Emil Brunner's otherwise excellent book *Eternal Hope*, pp. 182 ff.

21This idea is, for instance, advanced by Joseph E. Kokjohn, "A Hell of a Question," in *Commonweal*, XCIII/15, p. 369. Maurice Carrez, "With What Body Do the Dead Rise Again?" in *Immortality and Resurrection*, ed. by Pierre Benoit and Roland Murphy, p. 101, is closer to the truth when he suggests that resurrection implies the entering into the fulness of life with a transformed body. While *all* will appear before the Lord on the day of judgment, there is only one resurrection, namely to eternal life.
But we must ask here, how can we meaningfully speak of a judgment of all, if we do not speak of a resurrection for all? Of course, resurrection to a "newness of life" and a subsequent damnation (of this newness) seems to be an obvious contradiction. The question, however, is, whether resurrection must be understood this way. Albrecht Oepke, "anhistemi," in *Theological Dictionary of the New Testament*, Vol. 1, p. 371, claims rightly that the predominant view of the New Testament is that of a twofold resurrection.

22Karl Rahner, "The Hermeneutics of Eschatological Assertions," in *Theological Investigations*, Vol. 4, pp. 344 f., points out very convincingly that each term conveys its own particular imagery, and that no new assertion *adequately* renders the real content of the assertion which it attempts to translate and interpret. This means that any new interpretation is not a better one which replaces the old, but it is a new and necessary attempt in our search for a more contemporary and adequate approximation in expressing God's relationship to us and to our final destiny.

23WA XXXVII, 65, 33. Cf. for Luther's understanding of heaven and hell Hans Schwarz, "Luther's Understanding of Heaven and Hell," pp. 83-94.

24WA V, 497, 16-19 (*Studies in Psalms*).

25Cf. Gerhard von Rad, "ouranos, B. Old Testament," in *Theological Dictionary of the New Testament*, Vol. 5, pp. 502-509.

26Cf. Helmut Traub, "ouranos, C. The Septuagint and Judaism," in Ibid., p. 512. The term "kingdom of heaven," frequently used in the Gospel according to Matthew, reminds us of this usage.

²⁷Ibid., p. 532.

²⁸Joachim Jeremias, "hades," in *Theological Dictionary of the New Testament*, Vol. 1, p. 147.

²⁹Cf. for the following Joachim Jeremias, "gehenna," in Ibid., pp. 657 f.

³⁰A dramatic dualism occasionally introduced by biblical writers to emphasize the threatening power of evil, cannot challenge their basic monotheistic outlook.

³¹WA TR III, 276, 26 f.

³²Pannenberg, *What Is Man?*, p. 44 (own translation).

Discussion Questions

1. Define the following:
   Proleptic
   Chiliasm
   Apocalyptic

2. What eschatological forces or institutions, if any, operate in the contemporary world? Remember to be self-critical in making your judgments.

3. Some scientists suggest that parallel dimensions may exist along side of ours but that we may not perceive them because of our limited perceptual categories. Does such a viewpoint have any relevance to eschatological truth or epistemology?

4. What criteria would you suggest for distinguishing mythological or symbolic eschatological statements from ontological ones?

   a. Can we make ontological statements about realities beyond our conceptual frameworks?

   b. Could ontologically significant realities be revealed to us if they were beyond our perception?

ESCHATOLOGY AND VERIFICATION

This essay is now quite a familiar one. Its merits have been debated by both theologians and philosophers. John Hick suggests a way in which he believes that the truth of the statement "the Christian God exists" may be verified. By "verified" he means that rational doubt concerning an assertion is excluded.

To help the reader better understand his case Hick tells a parable about two men travelling on a road. It is evident that the travelers are a believer and a nonbeliever. Throughout life these men make similar observations. The believer sees the same types of things the unbeliever sees. He does not have the benefit of any special or miraculous experiences. Throughout their journey the issue of faith seems to be only a matter of different "ways of seeing" things.

However, the key to Hick's parable is that both men must turn the final corner of the road; that means both must die. It will then be clear, according to Hick, which of the men was correct. Now, Hick is not saying that the future state can be used as evidence for theism. But he is saying that an eschatological vision serves to show that the choice between world views is a real choice, not merely a verbal or emotive one.

Hick contends that his model of eschatological verification can be acceptable only if something approximating the Christian belief in continued personal existence after death is intelligible. He carefully distinguishes the Christian belief in the resurrection of the body, from the idea of the immortality of the soul.

Hick argues that an intelligible explanation for
how one could be the same person after death can be
offered. In order to do so, one must have an identifi-
able resemblance to one's earthly body, although the
"resurrection body" need not be material. Secondly,
one must have memories and habits consistent with one's
pre-mortem life. Thirdly, in order to know that one
lived in a post-mortem state, one must meet members of
one's family and historical figures known to have died.
And finally, to have confidence that one's Christian
beliefs are confirmed one must experience a community
in some sense ruled by Jesus Christ.

Hick considers each of these conditions to be
plausible. But of course, they each depend on God's
activity in re-creating the individual as a spiritual
person. The best theological evidence for this hope
is the resurrection of Jesus and we are here reminded
again of the proleptic nature of eschatology.

ESCHATOLOGY AND VERIFICATION*

To ask "Is the existence of God verifiable?" is
to pose a question which is too imprecise to be capable of being answered.[1] There are many different concepts of God, and it may be that statements employing
some of them are open to verification or falsification
while statements employing others of them are not.
Again, the notion of verifying is itself by no means
perfectly clear and fixed; and it may be that on some
views of the nature of verification the existence of
God is verifiable, whereas on other views it is not.

Instead of seeking to compile a list of the
various different concepts of God and the various

*Source: From "Theology and Verification" by
John Hick in *Theology Today* 17 (April 1960). Used by
permission of *Theology Today* and John Hick.

possible senses of "verify," I wish to argue with regard to one particular concept of deity, namely the Christian concept, that divine existence is in principle verifiable; and as the first stage of this argument I must indicate what I mean by "verifiable."

The central core of the concept of verification, I suggest, is the removal of ignorance or uncertainty concerning the truth of some proposition. That p is verified (whether p embodies a theory, hypothesis, prediction, or straightforward assertion) means that something happens which makes it clear that p is true. A question is settled so that there is no longer room for rational doubt concerning it. The way in which grounds for rational doubt are excluded varies, of course, with the subject matter. But the general feature common to all cases of verification is the ascertaining of truth by the removal of grounds for rational doubt. Where such grounds are removed, we rightly speak of verification having taken place.

To characterize verification in this way is to raise the question whether the notion of verification is purely logical or is both logical and psychological. Is the statement that p is verified simply the statement that a certain state of affairs exists (or has existed), or is it the statement also that someone is aware that this state of affairs exists (or has existed) and notes that its existence establishes the truth of p? A geologist predicts that the earth's surface will be covered with ice in 15 million years time. Suppose that in 15 million years time the earth's surface is covered with ice, but that in the meantime the human race has perished, so that no one is left to observe the event or to draw any conclusion concerning the accuracy of the geologist's prediction. Do we now wish to say that his prediction has been verified, or shall we deny that it has been verified, on the ground that there is no one left to do the verifying?

The range of "verify" and its cognates is sufficiently wide to permit us to speak in either way. But the only sort of verification of theological propositions which is likely to interest us is one in which human beings participate. We may therefore, for our present purpose, treat verification as a logico-psychological rather than as a purely logical concept. I suggest, then, that "verify" be construed as a verb which has its primary uses in the active voice: I verify, you verify, we verify, they verify, or have

511

verified. The impersonal passive, it is verified, now becomes logically secondary. To say that p has been verified is to say that (at least) someone has verified it, often with the implication that his or their report to this effect is generally accepted. But it is impossible, on this usage, for p to have been verified without someone having verified it. "Verification" is thus primarily the name for an event which takes place in human consciousness.[2] It refers to an experience, the experience of ascertaining that a given proposition or set of propositions is true. To this extent verification is a psychological notion. But of course it is also a logical notion. For needless to say, not *any* experience is rightly called an experience of verifying p. Both logical and psychological conditions must be fulfilled in order for verification to have taken place. In this respect, "verify" is like "know." Knowing is an experience which someone has or undergoes, or perhaps a dispositional state in which someone is, and it cannot take place without someone having or undergoing it or being in it; but not by any means every experience which people have, or every dispositional state in which they are, is rightly called knowing.

These features of the concept of verification—that verification consists in the exclusion of grounds for rational doubt concerning the truth of some proposition; that this means its exclusion from particular minds; that the nature of the experience which serves to exclude grounds for rational doubt depends upon the particular subject matter; that verification is often related to predictions and that such predictions are often conditional; that verification and falsification may be asymmetrically related; and finally, that the verification of a factual proposition is not equivalent to logical certification—are all relevant to the verification of the central religious claim, "God exists." I wish now to apply these discriminations to the notion of eschatological verification, which has been briefly employed by Ian Crombie in his contribution to *New Essays in Philosophical Theology*,[3] and by myself in *Faith and Knowledge*.[4] This suggestion has on each occasion been greeted with disapproval by both philosophers and theologians. I am, however, still of the opinion that the notion of eschatological verification is sound; and further, that no viable alternative to it has been offered to establish the factual character of theism.

The strength of the notion of eschatological

verification is that it is not an *ad hoc* invention but is based upon an actually operative religious concept of God. In the language of Christian faith, the word "God" stands at the center of a system of terms, such as Spirit, grace, Logos, incarnation, Kingdom of God, and many more; and the distinctly Christian conception of God can only be fully grasped in its connection with these related terms.[5] It belongs to a complex of notions which together constitute a picture of the universe in which we live, of man's place therein, of a comprehensive divine purpose interacting with human purposes, and of the general nature of the eventual fulfillment of that divine purpose. This Christian picture of the universe, entailing as it does certain distinctive expectations concerning the future, is a very different picture from any that can be accepted by one who does not believe that the God of the New Testament exists. Further, these differences are such as to show themselves in human experience. The possibility of experiential confirmation is thus built into the Christian concept of God; and the notion of eschatological verification seeks to relate this fact to the logical problem of meaning.

Let me first give a general indication of this suggestion, by repeating a parable which I have related elsewhere,[6] and then try to make it more precise and eligible for discussion. Here, first, is the parable.

Two men are travelling together along a road. One of them believes that it leads to a Celestial City, the other that it leads nowhere; but since this is the only road there is, both must travel it. Neither has been this way before, and therefore neither is able to say what they will find around each next corner. During their journey they meet both with moments of refreshment and delight, and with moments of hardship and danger. All the time one of them thinks of his journey as a pilgrimage to the Celestial City and interprets the pleasant parts as encouragements and the obstacles as trials of his purpose and lessons in endurance, prepared by the king of that city and designed to make of him a worthy citizen of the place when at last he arrives there. The other, however, believes none of this and sees their journey as an unavoidable and aimless ramble. Since he has no choice in the matter, he enjoys the good and endures the bad. But for him there is no Celestial City to be reached, no all-encompassing purpose ordaining their journey; only the road itself and the luck of the road

513

in good weather and in bad.

During the course of the journey the issue between them is not an experimental one. They do not entertain different expectations about the coming details of the road, but only about its ultimate destination. And yet when they do turn the last corner it will be apparent that one of them has been right all the time and the other wrong. Thus although the issue between them has not been experimental, it has nevertheless from the start been a real issue. They have not merely felt differently about the road; for one was feeling appropriately and the other inappropriately in relation to the actual state of affairs. Their opposed interpretations of the road constituted genuinely rival assertions, though assertions whose assertion-status has the peculiar characteristic of being guaranteed retrospectively by a future crux.

This parable has of course (like all parables) strict limitations. It is designed to make only one point: that Christian doctrine postulates an ultimate unambiguous state of existence *in patria* as well as our present ambiguous existence *in via*. There is a state of having arrived as well as a state of journeying, an eternal heavenly life as well as an earthly pilgrimage. The alleged future experience of this state cannot, of course, be appealed to as evidence for theism as a present interpretation of our experience; but it does suffice to render the choice between theism and atheism a real and not a merely empty or verbal choice. And although this does not affect the logic of the situation, it should be added that the alternative interpretations are more than theoretical, for they render different practical plans and policies appropriate now.

The universe as envisaged by the theist, then, differs as a totality from the universe as envisaged by the atheist. This difference does not, however, from our present standpoint within the universe, involve a difference in the objective content of each or even any of its passing moments. The theist and the atheist do not (or need not) expect different events to occur in the successive details of the temporal process. They do not (or need not) entertain divergent expectations of the course of history viewed from within. But the theist does and the atheist does not expect that when history is completed it will be seen to have led to a particular end-state and to have fulfilled a specific purpose, namely that of creating

514

"children of God."

The idea of an eschatological verification of theism can make sense, however, only if the logically prior idea of continued personal existence after death is intelligible. A desultory debate on this topic has been going on for several years in some of the philosophical periodicals. C. I. Lewis has contended that the hypothesis of immortality "is an hypothesis about our own future experience. And our understanding of what would verify it has no lack of clarity."[7] And Morris Schlick agreed, adding, "We must conclude that immortality, in the sense defined (i.e., 'survival after death,' rather than 'never-ending life'), should not be regarded as a 'metaphysical problem,' but is an empirical hypothesis, because it possesses logical verifiability. It could be verified by following the prescription: 'Wait until you die!'"[8] However, others have challenged this conclusion, either on the ground that the phrase "surviving death" is self-contradictory on ordinary language or, more substantially, on the ground that the traditional distinction between soul and body cannot be sustained.[9] I should like to address myself to this latter view. The only self of which we know, it is said, is the empirical self, the walking, talking, acting, sleeping individual who lives, it may be, for some sixty to eighty years and then dies. Mental events and mental characteristics are analyzed into the modes of behavior and behavioral dispositions of this empirical self. The human being is described as an organism capable of acting in the "high-level" ways which we characterize as intelligent, thoughtful, humorous, calculating, and the like. The concept of mind or soul is thus not the concept of a "ghost in the machine" (to use Gilbert Ryle's loaded phrase[10]), but of the more flexible and sophisticated ways in which human beings behave and have it in them to behave. On this view there is no room for the notion of soul in distinction from body; and if there is no soul in distinction from body, there can be no question of the soul surviving the death of the body. Against this philosophical background the specifically Christian (and also Jewish) belief in the resurrection of the flesh, or body, in contrast to the Hellenic notion of the survival of a disembodied soul, might be expected to have attracted more attention than it has. For it is consonant with the conception of man as an indissoluble psycho-physical unity, and yet it also offers the possibility of an empirical meaning for the idea of "life after death."

Paul is the chief Biblical expositor of the idea of the resurrection of the body.[11] His view, as I understand it, is this. When someone has died he is, apart from any special divine action, extinct. A human being is by nature mortal and subject to annihilation by death. But in fact God, by an act of sovereign power, either sometimes or always resurrects or (better) reconstitutes or recreates him--not, however, as the identical physical organism that he was before death, but as a *soma pneumatikon*, ("spiritual body") embodying the dispositional characteristics and memory traces of the deceased physical organism, and inhabiting an environment with which the *soma pneumatikon* is continuous as the *ante-mortem* body was continuous with our present world. In discussing this notion we may well abandon the word "spiritual," as lacking today any precise established usage, and speak of "resurrection bodies" and of "the resurrection world." The principal questions to be asked concern the relation between the physical world and the resurrection world, and the criteria of personal identity which are operating when it is alleged that a certain inhabitant of the resurrection world is the same person as an individual who once inhabited this world. The first of these questions turns out on investigation to be the more difficult of the two, and I shall take the easier one first.

Let me sketch a very odd possibility (concerning which, however, I wish to emphasize not so much its oddness as its possibility!), and then see how far it can be stretched in the direction of the notion of the resurrection body. In the process of stretching it will become even more odd than it was before; but my aim will be to show that, however odd, it remains within the bounds of the logically possible. This progression will be presented in three pictures, arranged in a self-explanatory order.

First picture: Suppose that at some learned gathering in this country one of the company were suddenly and inexplicably to disappear, and that at the same moment an exact replica of him were suddenly and inexplicably to appear at some comparable meeting in Australia. The person who appears in Australia is exactly similar, as to both bodily and mental characteristics, with the person who disappears in America. There is continuity of memory, complete similarity of bodily features, including even fingerprints, hair and eye coloration and stomach contents, and also of beliefs, habits, and mental propensities. In fact

there is everything that would lead us to identify
the one who appeared with the one who disappeared,
except continuity of occupancy of space. We may
suppose, for example, that a deputation of the colleagues of the man who disappeared fly to Australia to
interview the replica of him which is reported there,
and find that he is in all respects but one exactly
as though he had travelled from say, Princeton to
Melbourne, by conventional means. The only difference
is that he describes how, as he was sitting listening
to Dr. Z reading a paper, on blinking his eyes he
suddenly found himself sitting in a different room
listening to a different paper by an Australian scholar.
He asks his colleagues how the meeting had gone after
he ceased to be there, and what they had made of his
disappearance, and so on. He clearly thinks of himself as the one who was present with them at their
meeting in the United States. I suggest that faced
with all these circumstances his colleagues would soon,
if not immediately, find themselves thinking of him
and treating him as the individual who had so inexplicably disappeared from their midst. We should be
extending our normal use of "same person" in a way
which the postulated facts would both demand and
justify if we said that the one who appears in Australia is the same person as the one who disappears in
America. The factors inclining us to identify them
would far outweigh the factors disinclining us to do
this. We should have no reasonable alternative but to
extend our usage of "the same person" to cover the
strange new case.

Second picture: Now let us suppose that the event
in America is not a sudden and inexplicable disappearance, and indeed not a disappearance at all, but a
sudden death. Only, at the moment when the individual
dies, a replica of him as he was at the moment before
his death, complete with memory up to that instant,
appears in Australia. Even with the corpse on our
hands, it would still, I suggest, be an extension of
"same person" required and warranted by the postulated
facts, to say that the same person who died has been
miraculously recreated in Australia. The case would
be considerably odder than in the previous picture,
because of the existence of the corpse in America
contemporaneously with the existence of the living
person in Australia. But I submit that, although the
oddness of this circumstance may be stated as strongly
as you please, and can indeed hardly be overstated,
yet it does not exceed the bounds of the logically
possible. Once again we must imagine some of the

deceased's colleagues going to Australia to interview the person who has suddenly appeared there. He would perfectly remember them and their meeting, be interested in what had happened, and be as amazed and dumbfounded about it as anyone else; and he would perhaps be worried about the possible legal complications if he should return to America to claim his property; and so on. Once again, I believe, they would soon find themselves thinking of him and treating him as the same person as the dead Princetonian. Once again the factors inclining us to say that the one who died and the one who appeared are the same person would outweigh the factors inclining us to say that they are different people. Once again we should have to extend our usage of "the same person" to cover this new case.

Third picture: My third supposal is that the replica, complete with memory, etc. appears, not in Australia, but as a resurrection replica in a different world altogether, a resurrection world inhabited by resurrected persons. This world occupies its own space, distinct from the space with which we are now familiar. That is to say, an object in the resurrection world is not situated at any distance or in any direction from an object in our present world, although each object in either world is spatially related to each other object in the same world.

Mr. X, then, dies. A Mr. X replica, complete with the set of memory traces which Mr. X had at the last moment before his death, comes into existence. It is composed of other material than physical matter, and is located in a resurrection world which does not stand in any spatial relationship with the physical world. Let us leave out of consideration St. Paul's hint that the resurrection body may be as unlike the physical body as is a full grain of wheat from the wheat seed, and consider the simpler picture in which the resurrection body has the same shape as the physical body.[12]

In these circumstances, how does Mr. X know that he has been resurrected or recreated? He remembers dying; or rather he remembers being on what he took to be his death-bed, and becoming progressively weaker until, presumably, he lost consciousness. But how does he know that (to put it Irishly) his "dying" proved fatal; and that he did not, after losing consciousness, begin to recover strength, and has now simply waked up?

The picture is readily enough elaborated to answer this question. Mr. X meets and recognizes a number of relatives and friends and historical personages whom he knows to have died; and from the fact of their presence, and also from their testimony that he has only just now appeared in their world, he is convinced that he has died. Evidences of this kind could mount up to the point at which they are quite as strong as the evidence which, in pictures one and two, convince the individual in question that he has been miraculously translated to Australia. Resurrected persons would be individually no more in doubt about their own identity than we are now, and would be able to identify one another in the same kinds of ways, and with a like degree of assurance, as we do now.

If it be granted that resurrected persons might be able to arrive at a rationally founded conviction that their existence is *post-mortem,* how could they know that the world in which they find themselves is in a different space from that in which their physical bodies were? How could such a one know that he is not in a like situation with the person in picture number two, who dies in America and appears as a full-blooded replica in Australia, leaving his corpse in the U.S.A.--except that now the replica is situated, not in Australia, but on a planet of some other star?

It is of course conceivable that the space of the resurrection world should have properties which are manifestly incompatible with its being a region of physical space. But on the other hand, it is not of the essence of the notion of a resurrection world that its space should have properties different from those of physical space. And supposing it not to have different properties, it is not evident that a resurrected individual could learn from any direct observations that he was not on a planet of some sun which is at so great a distance from our own sun that the stellar scenery visible from it is quite unlike that which we can now see. The grounds that a resurrected person would have for believing that he is in a different space from physical space (supposing there to be no discernible difference in spatial properties) would be the same as the grounds that any of us may have now for believing this concerning resurrected individuals. These grounds are indirect and consist in all those considerations (e.g., Luke 16:26) which lead most of those who consider the question to reject as absurd the possibility of, for example, radio communication or rocket travel between earth and heaven.

519

In the present context my only concern is to claim that this doctrine of the divine creation of bodies, composed of a material other than that of physical matter, which bodies are endowed with sufficient correspondence of characteristics with our present bodies, and sufficient continuity of memory with our present consciousness, for us to speak of the same person being raised up again to life in a new environment, is not self-contradictory. If, then, it cannot be ruled out *ab initio* as meaningless, we may go on to consider whether and how it is related to the possible verification of Christian theism.

So far I have argued that a survival prediction such as is contained in the *corpus* of Christian belief is in principle subject to future verification. But this does not take the argument by any means as far as it must go if it is to succeed. For survival, simply as such, would not serve to verify theism. It would not necessarily be a state of affairs which is manifestly incompatible with the non-existence of God. It might be taken just as a surprising natural fact. The atheist, in his resurrection body, and able to remember his life on earth, might say that the universe has turned out to be more complex, and perhaps more to be approved of, than he had realized. But the mere fact of survival, with a new body in a new environment, would not demonstrate to him that there is a God. It is fully compatible with the notion of survival that the life to come be, so far as the theistic problem is concerned, essentially a continuation of the present life, and religiously no less ambiguous. And in this event, survival after bodily death would not in the least constitute a final verification of theistic faith.

I shall not spend time in trying to draw a picture of a resurrection existence which would merely prolong the religious ambiguity of our present life. The important question, for our purpose, is not whether one can conceive of after-life experiences which would *not* verify theism (and in point of fact one can fairly easily conceive them), but whether one can conceive of after-life experiences which *would* serve to verify theism.

I think that we can. In trying to do so I shall not appeal to the traditional doctrine, which figures especially in Catholic and mystical theology, of the Beatific Vision of God. The difficulty presented by this doctrine is not so much that of deciding whether

520

there are grounds for believing it, as of deciding what it means. I shall not, however, elaborate this difficulty, but pass directly to the investigation of a different and, as it seems to me, more intelligible possibility. This is the possibility not of a direct vision of God, whatever that might mean, but of a *situation* which points unambiguously to the existence of a loving God. This would be a situation which, so far as its religious significance is concerned, contrasts in a certain important respect with our present situation. Our present situation is one which in some ways seems to confirm and in other ways to contradict the truth of theism. Some events around us suggest the presence of an unseen benevolent intelligence and others suggest that no such intelligence is at work. Our situation is religiously ambiguous. But in order for us to be aware of this fact we must already have some idea, however vague, of what it would be for our situation to be not ambiguous, but on the contrary wholly evidential of God. I therefore want to try to make clearer this presupposed concept of a religiously unambiguous situation.

There are, I suggest, two possible developments of our experience such that, if they occurred in conjunction with one another (whether in this life or in another life to come), they would assure us beyond rational doubt of the reality of God, as conceived in the Christian faith. These are, *first*, an experience of the fulfillment of God's purpose for ourselves, as this has been disclosed in the Christian revelation; in conjunction, *second*, with an experience of communion with God as he has revealed himself in the person of Christ.

The divine purpose for human life, as this is depicted in the New Testament documents, is the bringing of the human person, in society with his fellows, to enjoy a certain valuable quality of personal life, the content of which is given in the character of Christ--which quality of life (i.e. life in relationship with God, described in the Fourth Gospel as eternal life) is said to be the proper destiny of human nature and the source of man's final self-fulfillment and happiness. The verification situation with regard to such a fulfillment is asymmetrical. On the one hand, so long as the divine purpose remains unfulfilled, we cannot know that it never will be fulfilled in the future; hence no final falsification is possible of the claim that this fulfillment will occur--unless, of course, the prediction contains a specific time clause which, in Christian teaching, it does not. But on the other hand, if and when the divine purpose *is* fulfilled in our own experience, we must be able to recognize and rejoice in that fulfillment. For the fulfillment would not be for us the promised fulfillment without our own conscious participation in it.

It is important to note that one can say this much without being cognizant in advance of the concrete form which such fulfillment will take. The before-and-after situation is analogous to that of a small child looking forward to adult life and then, having grown to adulthood, looking back upon childhood. The child possesses and can use correctly in various contexts the concept of "being grown-up," although he does not know, concretely, what it is like to be grown-up. But when he reaches adulthood he is nevertheless able to know that he has reached it; he is able to recognize the experience of living a grown-up life even though he did not know in advance just what to expect. For his understanding of adult maturity grows as he himself matures. Something similar may be supposed to happen in the case of the fulfillment of the divine purpose for human life. That fulfillment may be as far removed from our present condition as is mature adulthood from the mind of a little child; nevertheless, we possess already a comparatively vague notion of this final fulfillment, and as we move towards it our concept will itself become more adequate; and if and when we finally reach that fulfillment, the problem of recognizing it will have disappeared in the process.

The other feature that must, I suggest, be present in a state of affairs that would verify theism, is that the fulfillment of God's purpose be apprehended *as* the fulfillment of God's purpose and not simply as a natural state of affairs. To this end it must be accompanied by an experience of communion with God as he has made himself known to men in Christ.

The specifically Christian clause, "as he has made himself known to men in Christ," is essential, for it provides a solution to the problem of recognition in the awareness of God. Several writers have pointed out the logical difficulty involved in any claim to have encountered God.[13] How could one know that it was *God* whom one had encountered? God is described in Christian theology in terms of various absolute qualities, such as omnipotence, omnipresence, perfect goodness, infinite love, etc., which cannot as such be observed by us, as can their finite analogues, limited power, local presence, finite goodness, and human love. One can recognize that a being whom one "encounters" has a given finite degree of power, but how does one recognize that he has *unlimited* power? How does one observe that an encountered being is *omni-* present? How does one perceive that his goodness and love, which one can perhaps see to exceed any human goodness and love, are actually infinite? Such qualities cannot be given in human experience. One might claim, then, to have encountered a Being whom one presumes, or trusts, or hopes to be God; but one cannot claim to have encountered a Being whom one recognized to be the infinite, almighty, eternal Creator.

This difficulty is met in Christianity by the doctrine of the Incarnation--although this was not among the considerations which led to the formulation of that doctrine. The idea of incarnation provides answers to the two related questions: "How do we know that God has certain absolute qualities which, by their very nature, transcend human experience?" and "How can there be an eschatological verification of theism which is based upon a recognition of the presence of God in his Kingdom?"

In Christianity God is known as "the God and Father of our Lord Jesus Christ."[14] God is the Being about whom Jesus taught; the Being in relation to whom Jesus lived, and into a relationship with whom he brought his disciples; the Being whose *agape* toward men was seen on earth in the life of Jesus. In short, God is the transcendent Creator who has revealed himself in Christ. Now Jesus' teaching about the Father is a part of that self-disclosure, and it is from this teaching (together with that of the prophets who preceded him) that the Christian knowledge of God's transcendent being is derived. Only God himself knows his own infinite nature; and our human belief about that nature is based upon his self-revelation to men in Christ. As Karl Barth expresses it, "Jesus Christ is the knowability of God."[15] Our beliefs about God's infinite being are not capable of observational verification, being beyond the scope of human experience, but they are susceptible of indirect verification by the removal of rational doubt concerning the authority of Christ. An experience of the reign of the Son in the Kingdom of the Father would confirm that authority, and therewith, indirectly, the validity of Jesus' teaching concerning the character of God in his infinite transcendent nature.

The further question as to how an eschatological experience of the Kingdom of God could be known to be such has already been answered by implication. It is God's union with man in Christ that makes possible man's recognition of the fulfillment of God's purpose for man as being indeed the fulfillment of *God's* purpose for him. The presence of Christ in his Kingdom marks this as being beyond doubt the Kingdom of the God and Father of the Lord Jesus Christ.

It is true that even the experience of the realization of the promised Kingdom of God, with Christ reigning as Lord of the New Aeon, would not constitute a logical certification of his claims nor, accordingly, of the reality of God. But this will not seem remarkable to any philosopher in the empiricist tradition, who knows that it is only a confusion to demand that a factual proposition be an analytic truth. A set of expectations based upon faith in the historic Jesus as the incarnation of God, and in his teaching as being divinely authoritative, could be so fully confirmed in *post-mortem* experience as to leave no grounds for rational doubt as to the validity of that faith.

There remains of course the problem (which falls to the New Testament scholar rather than to the philosopher) whether Christian tradition, and in particular the New Testament, provides a sufficiently authentic "picture" of the mind and character of Christ to make such recognition possible. I cannot here attempt to enter into the vast field of Biblical criticism, and shall confine myself to the logical point, which only emphasizes the importance of the historical question, that a verification of theism made possible by the Incarnation is dependent upon the Christian's having a genuine contact with the person of Christ, even though this is mediated through the life and tradition of the Church.

One further point remains to be considered. When we ask the question, *"To whom* is theism verified?" one is initially inclined to assume that the answer must be, "To everyone." We are inclined to assume that, as in my parable of the journey, the believer must be confirmed in his belief, and the unbeliever converted from his unbelief. But this assumption is neither demanded by the nature of verification nor by any means unequivocably supported by our Christian sources.

524

We have already noted that a verifiable prediction may be conditional. "There is a table in the next room" entails conditional predictions of the form: if someone goes into the next room he will see, etc. But no one is compelled to go into the next room. Now it may be that the predictions concerning human experience which are entailed by the proposition that God exists are conditional predictions and that no one is compelled to fulfill those conditions. Indeed we stress in much of our theology that the manner of the divine self-disclosure to men is such that our human status as free and responsible beings is respected, and an awareness of God never is forced upon us. It may then be a condition of *post-mortem* verification that we be already in some degree conscious of God by an uncompelled response to his modes of revelation in this world. It may be that such a voluntary consciousness of God is an essential element in the fulfillment of the divine purpose for human nature, so that the verification of theism which consists in an experience of the final fulfillment of that purpose can only be experienced by those who have already entered upon an awareness of God by the religious mode of apperception which we call faith.

If this be so, it has the consequence that only the theistic believer can find the vindication of his belief. This circumstance would not of course set any restriction upon who can become a believer, but it would involve that while theistic faith can be verified --found by one who holds it to be beyond rational doubt--yet it cannot be proved to the nonbeliever. Such an asymmetry would connect with that strain of New Testament teaching which speaks of a division of mankind even in the world to come.

Having noted this possibility I will only express my personal opinion that the logic of the New Testament as a whole, though admittedly not always its explicit content, leads to a belief in ultimate universal salvation. However, my concern here is not to seek to establish the religious facts, but rather to establish that there are such things as religious facts, and in particular that the existence or non-existence of the God of the New Testament is a matter of fact, and claims as such eventual experiential verification.

[1]In this paper I assume that an indicative sentence expresses a factual assertion if and only if the state in which the universe would be if the putative assertion could correctly be said to be true differs in some experienceable way from the state in which the universe would be if the putative assertion could correctly be said to be false, all aspects of the universe other than that referred to in the putative assertion being the same in either case. This critetion acknowledges the important core of truth in the logical positivist verification principle. "Experienceable" in the above formulation means, in the case of alleged subjective or private facts (e.g., pains, dreams, after images, etc.), "experienceable by the subject in question" and, in the case of alleged objective or public facts, "capable in principle of being experienced by anyone." My contention is going to be that "God exists" asserts a matter of objective fact.

[2]This suggestion is closely related to Carnap's insistence that, in contrast to "true," "confirmed" is time-dependent. To say that a statement is conformed, or verified, is to say that it has been confirmed at a particular time—and, I would add, by a particular person. See Rudolf Carnap, "Truth and Confirmation," Feigl and Sellars, *Readings in Philosophical Analysis*, 1949, pp. 119 f.

[3]Op.cit., p. 126.

[4]Cornell University Press, 1957, pp. 150-62.

[5]Its clear recognition of this fact, with regard not only to Christianity but to any religion, is one of the valuable features of Ninian Smart's *Reasons and Faith* (1958). He remarks, for example, that "the claim that God exists can only be understood by reference to many, if not all, other propositions in the doctrinal scheme from which it is extrapolated" (p. 12).

[6]*Faith and Knowledge*, pp. 150 f.

[7]"Experience and Meaning," *Philosophical Review*, 1934, reprinted in Feigl and Sellars, *Readings in Philosophical Analysis*, 1949, p. 142.

[8]"Meaning and Verification," *Philosophical Review*, 1936, reprinted in Feigl and Sellars, op.cit., p. 160.

[9]E.g. A.G.N. Flew, "Death," *New Essays in Philosophical Theology*; "Can a Man Witness his own Funeral?" *Hibbert Journal*, 1956.

[10]*The Concept of Mind*, 1949, which contains an important exposition of the interpretation of "mental" qualities as characteristics of behavior.

[11]I Cor. 15.

[12]As would seem to be assumed, for example, by Irenaeus (*Adversus Haereses*, Bk. II, Ch. 34, Sec. 1).

[13]For example, H. W. Hepburn, *Christianity and Paradox*, 1958, pp. 56 f.

[14]II Cor. 11:31.

[15]*Church Dogmatics*, Vol. II, Pt. I, p. 150.

Discussion Questions

1. Why do you think the Christian believer in Hick's parable is not said to have had any special or miraculous experiences?

2. Is it necessary that we retain all our memories in order to be the same person? Before you answer ask yourself if you remember what you were doing on April 23, 1978, at 3:15 p.m.

    a. What memories are necessary?

    b. Can we be the same person we were before death if we have only pleasant memories after death?

    c. Do unpleasant memories contribute something important to your selfhood?

    d. Could a dimension of salvation be the redemption of our memories?

3. Is it necessary that we make room for a doctrine
of soul sleep before the resurrection if our souls
are not immortal? Or, can we suggest an alteration in
our view of time that makes an intermediate state
unnecessary?

4. To what extent is bodily resemblance necessary in
order for us to be the same persons after death as
before?

RETROSPECTIVE

It is not surprising that there should be many issues unresolved in our theologies on a matter of such profound seriousness as the ultimate destiny of creation. But three major issues seem to require some kind of resolution.

The first of these is the Christian attitude toward death. It is a mistake to think that those who do not embrace the Christian faith, or who do not believe in life after death, automatically devalue this life with some "eat and drink" philosophy. On the contrary, many such persons take life very seriously and they cherish each moment's experiences because they know they are finite. Indeed, in some respects those who see this life only as a preparation for an afterlife may actually be the ones who are cheated. Christians take death seriously but not ultimately, and this may also be said of their attitude toward life itself.

A second issue that presses us for resolution is the tension between the presence of the Kingdom and its coming fulfillment. Christians should live as though the Kingdom depended upon their effort for its actualization. They should live free from the fear of death, and liberated from the principalities and powers of this world because Christ has been shown victorious. At the same time, however, no human effort will actualize the Kingdom; in this respect Schwarz is certainly correct. The Kingdom comes by God's act, not our own.

Finally, a third issue that cries for some resolution is whether God's graceful purpose for creation can finally be satisfied with any sort of eternally dual destiny. What can the love of God mean if God punishes with no intention of rehabilitation? What can the power of God mean if God cannot find some way to reach each human? What can hope mean if we do not pray that God will some day be all and all, such that every creature willingly fills the heavens with praises to God and his Son?